Beau James

Also by Gene Fowler

TRUMPET IN THE DUST • SHOE THE WILD MARE

THE GREAT MOUTHPIECE • TIMBER LINE

FATHER GOOSE • SALUTE TO YESTERDAY

THE GREAT MAGOO *(A Play, in collaboration with Ben Hecht)*

ILLUSION IN JAVA • THE JERVIS BAY GOES DOWN *(Poem)*

GOOD NIGHT, SWEET PRINCE • A SOLO IN TOM-TOMS

"Love is no hot-house flower, but a wild plant, born of a wet night, born of an hour of sunshine; sprung from wild seed, blown along the road by a wild wind. A wild plant that, when it blooms by chance within the hedge of our gardens, we call a flower; and when it blooms outside we call a weed; but, flower or weed, whose scent and colour are always wild!"

JOHN GALSWORTHY

THE LIFE & TIMES OF Jimmy Walker

Beau James

BY

GENE FOWLER

The Viking Press · NEW YORK · MCMXLIX

PUBLISHED IN APRIL 1949

PUBLISHED ON THE SAME DAY IN THE DOMINION OF CANADA
BY THE MACMILLAN COMPANY OF CANADA LIMITED

Approximately one-sixth of this book has previously been published as a long article in *Cosmopolitan*.

PRINTED IN U.S.A. BY AMERICAN BOOK–STRATFORD PRESS, INC., NEW YORK

To John J. O'Connor

Contents

PART TWO

PART THREE

List of Illustrations

Beau James

PACH BROS.

James J. Walker

ASSOCIATED PRESS PHOTO

Mayor Walker and Police Commissioner Mulrooney leading the police parade in May 1931

NEW YORK DAILY MIRROR

The sachems of Tammany: Foley, Walker, Voorhis, Smith, and Curry

MOFFETT RUSSELL

Mr. Walker abroad in 1934

The Beau of New York

His hat hangs on the wall. The high silk hat of the one-hundredth mayor of the City of New York hangs in this room where we write of other days. It brings memories, both gay and tragic, of the little man who lies beneath a Celtic cross carved on a memorial stone in a burial place called "Gate of Heaven."

Do you think it a long time since the Honorable James John Walker tipped this shining topper to the assembled metropolitans? It is not as far-off as one might presume, the age of festival before a great hush came over the world. A war makes events that occurred before it seem implausible, distantly unreal, and older men bring swan songs from the past, or speak through the veil of legend.

The period known as the twenties was actual enough to the journalists who reported its fanfare. The man called "Jim" by his nearest friends, and "Jimmy" by the city and the nation and the world, was a twinkling reality; and they would love him in December as they did in May.

This man of rainbow charm appeared forever young in a city three hundred years old. One might easily discern his shortcomings, his thirst for flattery, his random bestowals of friendship and affection, but find in him no intolerance of any kind, no malice, no hypocrisy, no selfishness. As Louis Nizer has said, James J. Walker met success like a gentleman and disaster like a man.

Although he detested silk hats, Jim wore his with a gay deference to the traditions of Tammany Hall. The silk hat was a trademark of success among the sachems and sagamores of that old political order. This formal headdress advertised to citizens outside the Fourteenth Street wigwam that its wearer was a personage, a human skyscraper to be looked up to and admired. Jim liked to be admired.

Here he comes now. Up the street he comes, with the vivacity of a song-and-dance man. Prinked in what he terms his "Court of Appeals" cutaway coat and cuffless trousers with stripes as wide as sticks of chalk, he moves at the head of the police parade. Perplexities of mind and heart beset him this day, but the cheering tens of thousands find no signs of worriment on his face. Jim is never one to advertise his woes. Catastrophe moves like a stormcloud over his personal and his public affairs, but he smiles.

Up from Bowling Green, where the ancient Dutchmen danced on holidays, comes the sprightly Mayor. He is a month on the greener side of fifty but seems a mere thirty-five. There is not so much as a thread of gray among the dark brown hairs of his head as he lifts the high silk hat to the men and women standing on the narrow walks of downtown Manhattan and to the ones flinging ticker tape and bits of paper from the windows of the highest buildings of the world.

Six thousand members of New York's finest, aglitter with polished buttons and shields, march behind the Beau of New York. His Honor's silk hat and thick-soled boots make him appear somewhat taller than his actual five feet eight and one-half inches.

Up lower Broadway he comes, tripping along a thoroughfare of historic reminders. Past the eroded gravestones of Trinity churchyard at the head of Wall Street, where the burrowing subway trains disturb the dust of Alexander Hamilton, Robert Fulton, and Captain James Lawrence, goes the lively James J. Walker. Past the only surviving church structure of pre-Revolutionary times in Manhattan, the reddish gray stone chapel of St. Paul's, in which Washington once sat, white-wigged and immaculate in black velvet coat and knee-breeches with silver buckles, goes the man who is the symbol and expression of the modern city. The one-hundredth mayor moves with the bounce of a stage juvenile in a musical play. His anxious heart cannot be seen.

A dozen bands skirl and tuba-toot in the march-past of blue. The drums boom in contrapuntal cadence to the heavy footfalls of the patrolmen pounding the gray asphalt of the street.

Spring has come to Manhattan. It is the warmest day since Macy's last clearance sale of overcoats. There was a sullen mist early this morning. The slow sea cloud reached in from the Atlantic, and at dawn weighed upon the two Bays and the Narrows, where ships from all the ports of the world lay to like polite and cautious ambassadors. But at noon the sun came out, as though eager to see a mayor whose activities are usually associated with those hours when the moon is in the sky. Winter has gone, and the pall has lifted from ferry slips and skyline. The tugs now are warping the ocean liners into their North River piers. The collision mats of hemp on the bows of the squat escorts give them the aspect of bearded water gnomes. The white gulls wheel, crying out rusty hymns of gratitude to stewards who dispose of garbage illegally from the ports of the berthing ships. The blue-green skirt of the sea shakes white ruffles on the Coney Island shore, and in lower Manhattan the little caliph of Bagdad-on-the-Subway is marching with his men.

Along downtown Broadway, where six-horse sleighs used to carry the citizens in winter, and where stages moved in snowless seasons, and then the horse-cars, and now the dilapidated trolleys, the Mayor leads the police procession.

The vanguard halts at the northern limits of City Hall Plaza. His Honor brings from his upper left-hand pocket a precisely folded handkerchief. As always, he uses his left hand to perform this task, instead of crossing his right hand over his breast. A crossed-over hand separates an actor from his audience. There never is a barrier even momentarily between this man and his admirers.

His Honor dabs his lips and his brow, then restores his kerchief to his pocket with his left hand. He places a denicotinized cigarette in a holder and fires the cigarette with a monogrammed gold lighter. Now he turns a blue eye toward City Hall. Perhaps he is thinking of the first days he spent in that old marble structure, which rests like a Florentine wedding cake on a tablecloth of springtime green.

Mr. Walker cocks his head, as though hearing something beyond the public applause. For a moment the pixy smile leaves his lips. Perhaps he is listening to a skirmish of winds from the political sky, the early voices of a hurricane.

This is to be the last police parade to march in the City of New York. It is the last of many things, perhaps the close of an era. There is more significance to today's pageantry, much more than a display of silk hats and blue uniforms. This is the year 1931. It is May ninth, the day death has come to Dr. Albert A. Michelson, discoverer of the speed of light. Light itself seems to have been retarded everywhere in the land. In Washington, President Herbert Hoover, a beleaguered Ajax, plucks at the starched cuffs of his shirt as public wrath plays upon him. There is panic and hunger and distress in all the world. It is not a tactful thing for high officials to show their persons to the people.

A few days before this police parade, a black cat appeared, as if from nowhere, in the reception room of the mayor of the City of New York. The lean cat padded up and down during Mr. Walker's interview with the press. "Get him some milk," said the Mayor to a superstitious attendant. "He's one of the neighbors' children."

His Honor has just recently returned from California, where he enjoyed one of his frequent holidays. He has come back to Manhattan to defy his assailants, who have petitioned Governor Franklin D. Roosevelt to remove Mr. Walker from City Hall. The Mayor defends his public actions in fifteen thousand words addressed to Albany, then offers to match his private life with that of anyone else in high office. The Governor rejects the political charges against the Mayor, accusations that within a year will have become more challenging. But the gossip about his romantic forays, long muted by everyone except the open-living Mayor himself, has erupted at last in the newspaper columns.

Police Commissioner Edward P. Mulrooney has an abiding affection for the man who is his commanding officer. "Jim," says he, "if you want to test the blood pressure of our citizens, and if you feel up to it, you might lead the police parade."

Against what might seem a more expedient course—to remain out of sight—Mr. Walker decides to go on parade to ascertain at first hand what the people think of him after his five and one-half years as mayor of the six million. "However," he stipulates, "I'll march only from Bowling Green to City Hall. By that time I should know if roses are red and violets are blue."

On the day of the parade, the Mayor surprisingly arrives on time. At 11:55 A.M., at Bowling Green, he pops out from his black Dusenberg town car with its silver trimmings, its liveried chauffeur, and police bodyguard. Commissioner Mulrooney greets him, while the police band plays "When Irish Eyes Are Smiling."

Mr. Mulrooney has on a high silk hat, a morning coat, a gates-ajar stiff collar with a gray- and black-striped scarf of heavy silk. The Mayor's collar is a low, turn-down creation with a thin black tie, and a pearl stickpin. His Honor never wears a four-in-hand with a large knot in it. None of his several hundred pieces of made-to-order neckwear has a lining or stiffening material. A thick knot becomes soiled after contact with one's chin, and James J. Walker is one of the most fastidious dressers ever to occupy public office.

Mayor Walker finds the huzzas of the spectators so stimulating that he decides, during the pause at City Hall, to continue at the head of the blue line, perhaps to Fourteenth Street. When a pessimist at the Chambers Street intersection reminds Jim of the miles that lie ahead he shrugs. To the cry of "How are the dogs, Jimmy?" he replies, "Distempered."

At White Street an old woman flings a spray of apple blossoms in Mr. Walker's path. "At first," says he, "I thought they were lilies."

As the Mayor reaches Prince Street, a bootblack outfitted in a moth-eaten swallow-tail coat runs toward him with a "Hello, Jimmy, how are you?"

"I'm feeling all right, Tony," says the Mayor, and pointing to his own striped cashmere breeches, adds, "I'll give you the pants later."

Still farther along the way a Negro longshoreman leaves the sidewalk to shake hands with His Honor. At Ninth Street there is another parade rest. The Mayor confides to Commissioner Mulrooney, "Ed, I think I'll go the whole distance."

His Honor flings aside his cigarette. Once again the parade moves uptown, northward along Broadway, and eventually past the Flatiron Building and into Fifth Avenue at Twenty-third Street. The bands play. Although his shoulders are slightly hunched forward, as they always are when he walks along, the Mayor steps high, like Chanticleer. He has pleasantries for everyone who shouts familiarly to him from the sidelines. He is Mr. New York.

The parade marches up Fifth Avenue, past the Empire State Building. This high pile, on the site of the first Waldorf-Astoria Hotel, is but one week old officially. Its managing director is Mayor Walker's former colleague in politics, the Honorable Alfred Emanuel Smith. A coolness now exists between the wearer of the high silk hat and the man of the brown derby.

The head of the line reaches the Fiftieth Street intersection, where the spires of St. Patrick's Cathedral rise above the queen of avenues. The parade halts once again. On the broad stone steps of the cathedral His Eminence Patrick Joseph Cardinal Hayes and his entourage are reviewing the procession in which many sons of the Church are participating.

The Mayor and the Police Commissioner find themselves directly in front of the main entrance to the cathedral. "Ed," Mayor Walker says to Commissioner Mulrooney, "would it seem proper for me to leave the formation to pay my respects to the Cardinal?"

"I think it perfectly proper."

Mayor Walker goes up the steps of the cathedral. He kneels and kisses the Cardinal's ring.

Perhaps this gesture, this kissing of the episcopal ring, is an expression of hope that lives deep in a troubled heart; hope for a solution of conflicts of mind and for a true composure of soul, which will come to this man only after many years have elapsed. He will find at last a spiritual refuge, find it after three years of self-exile from the city he loves with great passion, and after other years of doubt and yearning, of loss and heartbreak. Then atonement, and the final victory of redemption.

Part One

1.

Remembrance of Things Once Green

IT WAS of his dead father, William Henry Walker, that Jim always spoke with deepest affection. Only one other man held a like place in Jim's heart and mind—Charles Francis Murphy. Upon the death and burial of that Fourteenth Street sphinx, Walker said, "The brains of Tammany Hall lie in Calvary Cemetery."

As is sometimes the way of imaginative men, Jim wove harmless legends about his father, the stocky carpenter from Castlecomer, Ireland, who, as a penniless youth had spent fourteen days from Southampton to New York aboard the paddle-steamer *City of Paris* with only a coil of rope as a pillow.

To hear Jim tell it—the variations and grace notes accumulating with each recitation—his immigrant father wandered for days over the worst-paved streets of any modern city. His bare toes stubbed against the Belgian stone blocks or pressed upon the littered ground of pre-Civil War Manhattan. Hungry, of course, for he had experienced the potato famine, which in ten years claimed a million lives in Ireland, the forlorn young stranger now had no place to lay his head—not even a coil of rope. It was an awful predicament, youth versus fate, and the recounting of it sometimes made Jim shed a tear.

Jim's father unshipped at Castle Garden in 1857 with few belongings: a bundle of clothing, a carpenter's tool-chest, a prayer book, and his rosary. The voyaging carpenter arrived well clad and well shod, it is said, although he never displayed such Brummelian clothes as his son enjoyed.

A friend, William Brennan the coal dealer, greeted Billy Walker at the pier. Had no friends been available, there always were philanthropists of the Tammany Society to guide the immigrant from the waterfront to a bowl of soup and a place of shelter.

It was during the predatory didoes of Mayor Fernando Wood and of William Marcy Tweed's "Forty Thieves," as the Board of Aldermen came to be known, that Billy Walker began his life in the City of New York. There were but half a million persons in Manhattan. Twenty-third Street was way uptown; squatters had shanties on Murray Hill, and a seedy array of shacks dotted Central Park. Pigs and goats pioneered the lane that one day would become "millionaires' row." The Bronx seemed so far north that it might as well have been in Canada.

Irishmen and Germans populated Greenwich Village, a West-Side community of haphazard streets and narrow dwellings. Washington Square once had been potter's field; now it served as a residential district for important families. Away from the elm-shaded Square, saloons occupied almost every street corner. These were places for political discussion as well as refreshment.

One of the saloonkeepers was the iron-minded James Roon, whom a stranger might easily mistake for a bearded jurist. One found no sawdust on the floor of the Roon establishment at the foot of Little West Twelfth Street. His bartenders were reasonably honest and refrained from profanity and low jests while on duty. Mr. Roon refused to permit women to call with beer buckets under their shawls at the side door, and there was no "family entrance." Fist fights, loud arguments, and card games were forbidden. Oddly enough, this "high-class" place did a good business, and Mr. Roon owned three tenement houses on Washington Street.

Mr. Roon fathered five girls and four boys. He kept his daughters severely aloof from the follies of the world, made them dress plainly, and denied them jewelry. Of social life the girls knew little other than the annual New Year receptions in their home, the St. Joseph's Church affairs, or the chaperoned enjoyment of an occasional symphony concert.

After Sunday morning Mass Mr. Roon saw to it that the window-blinds of his front parlor were tightly drawn. Then he would snooze in the peaceful knowledge that his daughters could not peek out upon the Sunday parade of Village dudes.

Billy Walker had seen the Roon girls at Holy Services, and thought one of them the prettiest creature this side of Erin. He learned that the name of the brown-haired lass was Ellen Ida Roon, and made plans to meet this daughter of the puritanical saloonkeeper.

St. Joseph's Church is more than a hundred years old. It is a low structure of gray stone, with two Romanesque columns at the entrance on Sixth Avenue that are made of wood plastered over to simulate granite. It was behind one of these thick cylinders that Ellen and Billy sometimes contrived to talk briefly after Sunday morning services.

One New Year's Day Tom Conville, the manager of the brewery from which Mr. Roon purchased beer for his saloon, made a formal call with Billy at the Roon house. The vigilant James Roon saw Ellen exchange glances with Billy. That evening he informed her that henceforth she must not look upon this William fellow. She enlisted the secret sympathy of her mother.

Ellen and Billy managed to continue their conversations after church services. It was their desire to be married at St. Joseph's, but one of Mr. Roon's sons, James junior, was an altar boy there, and a bit of a gossip he was. With the assistance of Ellen's mother, they were married in another parish and without Mr. Roon's knowledge or consent.

Mr. Roon became even more watchful than before and kept his remaining daughters as if in a convent. Pretty as they were, they stayed unmarried.

Jim's adulation of his father should not be taken to mean that he loved his mother the less. It was only that he spoke more often of Mr. Walker than of anyone else in his family.

Billy Walker greeted everyone along the Village streets with a baritone brogue and a quick uplift of the hand, as if to bless a constituent. "He never scolded us or caused a storm in our house," Jim said. "But he would raise a brow and pull at his ear when annoyed."

During his public speeches Jim frequently departed from his theme of the moment—a bond-issue campaign or perhaps a funeral eulogy to some theatre-chain proprietor—to tell how his father had come to America at a time when there were but thirty-one stars in the flag and James Buchanan was President. The eventual prosperity of William Walker, Jim asserted, set an example for industrious aliens in a nation where freedom rings.

On one occasion a bedridden friend was listening to a Walker oration over the radio. The man's wife called out from the living-room, "What program is that, honey? The broadcast of a fight?"

"It's Jim," the friend answered resignedly. "He's running his dead father for mayor again!"

Although the elder Walker, while a lad in Ireland, had been

persuaded against strong drink by Father Mathews' temperance movement, Jim's parent acquired the reputation of being able to down great quantities of liquor and yet stay perpendicular.

Former Sheriff Charles W. Culkin, an intimate friend of the Walkers, says, "In those days a great deal of canvassing was done in the saloons. William Walker used to go in and say, 'Give me a milk punch.' In reality this was nothing but milk and seltzer water. Almost everyone except the bartenders wondered how any man could drink so many milk punches without becoming intoxicated."

It was Jim's contention that he resembled his father. "Of course," he would add, "I lack his qualities of self-control and his persevering character."

Survivors of the old days in Greenwich Village say that Billy Walker had the respect of the hard-fisted longshoremen of Hudson Street. Indeed, according to Robert Emmet, the ablest rough-and-tumble performer ever to come from the lower West Side, Billy Walker had the bodily qualifications of a fighter. Notwithstanding this, he was restrained of temper, and in no respect behaved as a bully. Nan Burke says her father was "passive and gentle" at home.

If he resembled his father in appearance, it is agreed that Jim possessed many of his mother's qualities: her lively imagination, her quick wit, and her gay appreciation of the present moment. Among other traits inherited from his mother, Jim had a strong liking for elegant clothes. As a girl his mother had been compelled to go without pretty things, and after her marriage she made up for it. Billy Walker gave her the means and opportunity to dress as she pleased, the right to laugh and to rear her children with a lenient hand. Jim called his mother "Rosie," and his father "the Boss."

2.

The Street of the Third Evangelist

If you were to examine a map of Manhattan you might see St. Luke's Place as a mere raveling on the sleeve of Father Knickerbocker. It occupies but one square between Seventh Avenue and Hudson Street. The quiet byway loses its identity the moment it reaches the Hudson Street intersection. Then, resuming the alias of Leroy Street, it descends three blocks, and with considerable din, to West Street and the North River.

Long-time residents of Greenwich Village accent the fact that Sixth and Seventh Avenues are comparative newcomers to the neighborhood. When these main thoroughfares were extended southward, the crazy-quilt pattern of Greenwich Village became even more confusing than before.

Padraic McVey, a retired bartender and former neighbor of Jimmy Walker's, says that the invasion by the wide avenues was resented by one and all in the Village. Mr. McVey speaks with some prejudice, inasmuch as he surrendered his bathroom and three-fourths of his bedroom when Seventh Avenue sheared off the part of his house on Bleecker Street.

"There I was," McVey laments, "with no place to sleep like a man, and with no place for ablutions, *et cetera*."

During Jim's early boyhood McVey was employed as a bartender in the establishment of James Roon, one of the first lower West Side saloonkeepers to install a cash register. McVey, always a champion of fair dealing, looked upon its advent as an injustice to the common man. He thought and thought about the humiliation of having to ring up each purchase, then decided to do something about it.

One night, when auditing the recording ribbon, Mr. Roon observed that several inches of "No Sales" had been registered during McVey's hours of duty. Since Mr. Roon owned the building which housed his saloon, it was a simple procedure for him to oust a tenant from quarters directly above the place where the cash register stood. Mr. Roon borrowed a brace and bit from the carpenter's box of his son-in-law William Walker and bored a peephole through the floor of the now-vacant room and the ceiling over the bar. He then commenced a lone surveillance. Lying on the floor, resting on his beard, his eye to the peephole, Mr. Roon enacted the role of private detective.

One afternoon, when business was slack, a gentleman ordered a drink of whisky at the Roon bar. He handed over the dime fee for his tonic, hurled the drink against his tonsils, and departed with health improved. The alert proprietor saw his employee approach the cash register and hesitate, fondling the dime. McVey was muttering to himself, "I'll flip the coin. If it comes up heads, I'll ring it up for old Roon. Tails–and it's mine. Why not be fair to everybody?"

He flipped the coin and investigated its position on his palm. He seemed betrayed. "Heads it is." He blinked, grunted, shrugged, then revised the rules of play. "Suppose we make it best two out of three?"

He tossed the coin a second time and caught it in mid-air. "Heads," he sadly conceded.

Paddy barely touched a key, then withdrew his finger as if from a hot rattrap. Next he hoisted his white apron and announced with finality, "To the divil with Mr. Roon and his likes!"

Before Paddy could complete his peculation, however, Mr. Roon's voice boomed out as if from the Judgment Seat of Heaven, "Ring up that dime, Paddy! I won it on the level!"

Small and easygoing St. Luke's Place changes name and character at Hudson. As Leroy, it dips down to the waterfront, where shipping piers usurp the long shoreline. The ferryboats and lighters, tugs with railway-car floats in tow, barges bearing pyramids of brick from Haverstraw, side-wheel excursion steamers, tankers, freighters, fruit ships from the tropics, speed boats, and the official launches of government, all ply ceaselessly. Sometimes a fleet of the United States Navy steams past to anchor in a reassuring line extending from the foot of West Fifty-second Street, below DeWitt Clinton Park, to a point upriver abeam Grant's Tomb and the old Pollock manor house that now is the Claremont Inn.

On the map one may see the piers and slips of the opposite New Jersey shore as a counterpart of those this side of the broad stream. Docking facilities fringe both banks of the historic waterways like a pair of huge combs, with here and there a tooth broken off or missing as though from long usage.

The uproar of traffic testifies to the immensity of the city's needs.

By means of barge, tunnel, and bridge, produce of the nation and of the world crosses riverwise to supply New York. Drays, trucks, and vans load or unload, or come and go in vehicular tunnels or aboard the ferries.

There are police whistles shrilling, foghorns bellowing. Bells, sirens, the backfire of motors, cowbells on junk wagons, the pneumatic guns of riveters, and the sloshing of propeller blades offshore comprise a robust overture. One hears the rasping embrace of ferry-slip pilings, oily green and brown and black with seaweed and barnacles at the tideline, as a ferryboat screws into the slip. There follows a metallic percussion of chains and pawls as a shore guard operates the archaic hoist of the slip platform. The ladies put away their lipsticks and the gentlemen readjust their hats. Bootblacks hurriedly complete their polishings, and all press forward. The pickpockets seize this time of congestion to go to work, then become honest till the next short voyage. Now the iron gates at the bow are folded offside. The passengers charge ashore as if from a racecourse barrier; vehicles roll from the midship area, to fan out and become a part of the city's circulation.

The backsweep of salt sea tides moves against the Hudson's current as far north as Troy, and seems to exercise a sinister influence upon the cargoes arriving for the city's millions. On a warm and humid day the waterfront smells like a convention of all the wet spaniels in the world.

A stranger sees New York as a city of contradictions, among them the peculiar fact that the North River is west of the island of Manhattan. He also wonders at the sustained energy of the pale participants in the seemingly endless marathon. He hears them complain above the subway's thunder of their daily hardships, of the weather, landlords, politics, taxes, and arthritis; but the grumblers would not reside anywhere else in the world.

They behave like persons in love. It is of no use to try to persuade these martyrs that green fields lie to the west, where clean air moves across a less populous land, and that the sky out there may be seen in terms of horizons. The New Yorker prefers to inhale used atmosphere and glimpse mere patches of sunlight, if any at all, as he moves with chronic haste along Broadway or among the towers of Wall Street, a bug lost in a partly opened pocketbook.

To the country lad or the small-town boy coming for the first time to this city of skyline and little sky, New York seems to be a purgatorial menace. Soon or late, however, he contracts the fevers of the metropolis. Then he too grows lover-like in his moods and actions, his dreams of conquest, and regards himself as a true New Yorker. He believes, of course, that everyone else came here just as he himself arrived, to discover New York, and that actually no one ever was born here. He reasons that no woman would have had time for an accouchement in this mad-galloping New York mazurka.

There was one man born here—of that I am sure—and his name was James John Walker. No one loved the city more fervently than he. And perhaps no American city ever loved a son more lastingly than New York did this gay child of the century.

Jim was born on Sunday, June 19, 1881, in a flat at No. 110 Leroy Street, between Hudson and Greenwich Streets. He was christened at the baptismal font of St. Joseph's, and named after one of his maternal uncles, James Roon, Jr. That the child's grandfather also bore that name was ignored by William Walker, who explained, "We are *not* calling our baby after a certain hardheaded party, but in honor of the boy's good-natured Uncle Jim."

James Walker afterward took the confirmation name John, his own personal choice.

New York had a population of 1,200,000 at the time of Jim's birth. William R. Grace was mayor. Boss Tweed had died in Ludlow Jail three years before. After the exposure of the Tweed Ring in the early seventies, and the boss's indictment on one hundred and twenty counts, his two trials, his conviction for one hundred and two offenses, John Kelly had supplanted him as Tammany leader. As one of the earlier "Honest Johns" of machine politics, Kelly levied assessments on all candidates for municipal office, and at the time of Walker's birth had placed Tammany Hall on a "business basis."

The Metropolitan Museum of Art was but one year old when Jim Walker was born. There was no Washington Arch. The Statue of Liberty had not yet arrived at Bedloe's Island; in fact, much difficulty was being experienced in raising funds for the stone pedestal upon which the bronze lady was to stand. Nor had Jumbo, the celebrated elephant, left the London Zoo with his colorful purchaser, Phineas T. Barnum. Caricaturist Thomas Nast, from whose cartoons came the political party symbols of the Democratic donkey, the Republican elephant, and the Tammany tiger, worked for *Harper's Weekly*, "the Journal of Civilization."

Jefferson Davis had published his history, and Northern critics reviewed this work severely in newspaper columns on the Sunday morning of Jim Walker's birth; indeed, they were hanging Mr. Davis's memoir to a sour apple tree.

Brooklyn Bridge, except for two granite piers rising from the East River, remained a blueprint. Henry Ward Beecher of Brooklyn's Plymouth Church, leading pulpit orator of his time, was a hay fever victim the Sunday of Jim's nativity.

It was the age of ladies' bustles, curling irons, and cameos. Horsecars moved along the avenues. Overhead, small steam locomotives hauled the elevated railway trains. The engines burned soft coal and shed live embers from cinder boxes down upon the rumps of horses hitched to wagons or drays, stimulating the beasts and causing much profanity among their drivers. Women patrons of the "El" arrived home with mesh-like patterns on their faces, where soot from the "El" smokestacks had drifted through the veils of fashion.

The city was gas-lit in 1881 although Thomas A. Edison had just completed his Pearl Street electric plant. The first electric sign, modest forerunner of the blazing monsters of the future Great White Way, soon would be strung across lower Broadway, with the illuminated legend: "Manhattan Beach Swept by Ocean Breezes."

It was a time of private houses with high stoops, back-yard lawns, flower gardens, and gingko trees. New York's Chinese still wore queues. This was the year before the Exclusion Act; the Chinese, arriving in large numbers, established a colony of their own and orientalized the residential streets of Pell and Mott.

On this June Sunday of 1881, as on other rest days in summer, downtown families boarded excursion barges to picnic in the groves. The menfolk ran in sack races and strained in tugs-o'-war. The old steamboats that towed the barges frequently exploded, with varying results and casualties. There were clam chowder clubs and bicycling clubs. The mustached German members of rifle clubs, feathers in their hats, trooped with Teutonic objectivity toward the several target grounds, where the smell of powder competed with the yeasty perfume of beer.

Although American baseball, a game derived from the English

pastime of "Rounders," was a generation old, certain prophets predicted that cricket would eventually become the national sport. Walking contests were the vogue. Edward Payson Weston, who had gone afoot from Boston to Washington, D.C., in 1861, to attend Lincoln's inauguration, was striding for long distances all over the land, preaching temperance as he thwacked a small whip against his calves to discourage cramps. Boxing in New York, a brutal and illegal business, was transacted with bare fists in remote suburbs or on barges anchored up the river. At the time the author of the Walker Boxing Law was born, twenty-three-year-old John L. Sullivan was knocking out his opponents with his prodigious right fist.

Overseas Tsar Alexander II of Russia, emancipator of the serfs, had been assassinated the previous March. In Germany, Prince von Bismarck was completing "defensive" alliances to give his Kaiser's empire sway over Central Europe. Charles Stewart Parnell and William Ewart Gladstone were debating the Irish Land Bill. In France the increasingly unpopular premier, Léon Gambetta, had been advised by Georges Clemenceau, doctor, journalist, duelist, politician, and later the defender of Captain Alfred Dreyfus, to visit America, there to study at first hand the customs and institutions of the New World.

Had Monsieur Gambetta taken Clemenceau's advice and arrived in New York on the Sunday in June when James J. Walker was born, the visitor might have come upon much political skulduggery, especially in the Fifth Avenue Hotel. All that day Republican political leaders filed in and out of the headquarters of former Senator Roscoe Conkling. Ex-President Ulysses S. Grant and Vice-President Chester A. Arthur were among these visitors, as also was Conkling's recent colleague in the Senate, the Honorable Thomas Collier ("Me Too") Platt. Both senators just recently had resigned in Washington after a quarrel with President Garfield over matters having to do with federal patronage. Now successors to their seats were to be chosen by the state legislature. Today's hotel conferences were a prelude to the next week's convention.

President Garfield's problems, among them a scandal in the Post Office Department, soon would end. In less than a month a disgruntled office seeker, Charles J. Guiteau, would shoot down the twentieth President of the United States.

James J. Walker was the second son of William and Ellen Ida Walker. Their first boy was William junior. A year after Jim's birth, twin brothers were stillborn. Then George Walker occupied the family cradle. The next few years were unhappy ones. Twin brothers, born prematurely, soon died, and following this a girl, named Anna for Mr. Walker's mother, lived but a few weeks. Then another girl baby was born, and she completed the family. The father asked that she also be christened Anna. "The name's a pretty one," he said, "and it will help us feel that our other little Nan never died."

Of the men destined to influence James J. Walker's public life, all but one had already been born the year Jim began his days on earth. Alfred E. Smith, who became the political paragon of the lower East Side, was eight years old. He had quit school and was selling newspapers to support himself. Charles Francis Murphy, twenty-three, had become ringleader of the burly boys of the Gas House district, an Irish settlement above Fourteenth Street on the East Side. An athletic young man, Murphy served as catcher on the Sylvan Social Club's baseball team, the "Senators." For a livelihood he established a saloon on Nineteenth Street near Avenue A. Charles W. Culkin, who one day would give Jim his first political endorsement, was nine years old. Patrick Joseph Hayes, afterward cardinal of the New York diocese, was fourteen, and resided in the small house of his birth on Duane Street and City Hall Place, site of the present St. Andrew's Church.

About a mile northeast of St. Luke's Place, on Fourteenth Street, stood the somber rectory of the Episcopal Church of the Annunciation. An eight-year-old boy named Samuel Seabury lived there with his father, the Reverend William Jones Seabury, D.D. Samuel sang in the church choir, and on weekdays could be seen bicycling in the vicinity of Union Square. Business buildings with cast-iron façades surrounded this green rectangle where orators of many opinions noised their several gospels. Across Fourteenth Street, on the south side of the Square, Tammany politicians dined at Luchow's Restaurant. East on Fourteenth Street stood Tammany Hall, a post-Civil War building. The bicycling Sammy viewed this political temple with special misgivings, for his father occasionally inveighed against Tammany from the pulpit. As a natural consequence the studious Samuel would enter manhood with a lasting determination to war upon the Fourteenth Street tribe.

Young Samuel sprang from an array of learned, purposeful ancestors. He was the ninth of the American Seaburys and the fifth of their Samuels. The first Samuel, a doctor of medicine, arrived from England with the Puritans in 1639. Samuel the second, a grandson of this physician, became an Episcopalian reverend on horseback, practiced medicine as a sideline, taught school, won five hundred pounds in a lottery, for which in his diary he thanked God instead of Lady Luck, and sired the third Samuel. A portrait of Samuel the third depicts him in his vestments as the first Protestant Episcopal Bishop of America, his hands emerging from sleeves as billowy as the balloons of Monsieur Montgolfier. As a Tory, the Bishop found it expedient to hide from American revolutionists after the Battle of Long Island. The fourth Samuel became a clergyman and rector of the Church of the Annunciation. His son William Jones Seabury succeeded him to that pulpit.

The Seaburys had a family crest, an ibex or wild goat upon it, and on its scroll the Latin motto "*Supera Alta Tenere*"—Hold to the Most High.

Who could have foreseen on this pleasant New York Sunday of June 1881 that fifty years hence the fifth Samuel would move with erudite tenacity to destroy the child who this morning lay in the Walker crib a scant mile from the rectory of the Church of the Annunciation? And who could have foretold the important friendship that would be formed, then broken, and eventually repaired between another eight-year-old, Alfred E. Smith, and the second son of the Walkers? Or that, eight months from now, there would be born at Hyde Park the most important arbiter of James J. Walker's political fortunes?

The Walker children, all but Nan, the youngest, were born in the Leroy Street flat. When Jim was five years old the family moved to a house on the north side of the short street named for St. Luke, biblical physician and third evangelist.

New York had not yet become a city of strangers. It was a city of neighborhoods and familiar neighbors. In one of Jim's last public appearances, in November of 1946, at the clubhouse of the Grand Street Boys, he spoke of the days of his youth:

"I saw the skyline grow, and I saw the city grow, and sometimes

I wonder if it was worth the price we paid. In those days we did not need interracial movements or good-will groups. Then a neighbor meant so much.

"Here in the most cosmopolitan community since the beginning of time, a city composed of sons and daughters of every one of the forty-eight states, and with men and women from every country in the civilized world, we worked together. Here where there were and are more Irishmen than in Dublin, more Italians than in Rome, more Germans than in any city other than Berlin, and more Jews than in Palestine—here we lived together in peace, like one great family, and should so live today and tomorrow.

"We all went to school together, went to work together, and to the theatre and to the fields of sport—with little rancor, no real hatred. We lived like human beings, who asked only the opportunity to work out our earthly existence and worship our God according to the dictates of our conscience.

"This I hold to be humanity. This is democracy. This was New York of the yon days."

3.

The Villagers

SIXTEEN private houses, of which the Walkers' was one, stand like surviving members of the Old Guard on the north side of St. Luke's Place. Wall to wall, these brick houses rise for three stories above English basements and sunken areaways at the street-front. Iron palings, encrusted with long-accumulated coats of black paint, fence off the enclosures. Gates for tradesmen and servants relieve the iron barriers. Stone steps, at one side of each basement entrance, bridge the interval between the sidewalk and the high stoops. Storm vestibules mask the front doorways wrought in the architectural style of Queen Anne's time.

In general, this brick row has remained about the same as it was in the eighties, although Flannery's saloon vanished a generation ago from the northeast corner of St. Luke's Place and Hudson Street.

At this bar a hundred paces west of No. 6 St. Luke's Place, Mr. Flannery served five-cent beer in glasses as large as parlor aquariums.

Billy Walker purchased the house at No. 6 in 1886 while campaigning in the first of his four successful candidacies for alderman of the old Ninth Ward. He resided in this house until the time of his death in May of 1916.

The continuous good will accorded him by fellow Villagers brought the Irish immigrant prosperity as a lumber dealer. The new alderman paid seventeen thousand dollars in cash for his house, but because of an unforeseen event this outlay put him in monetary straits.

There were no mortgages on any of the sixteen residences in St. Luke's Place. The Walker neighbors were well-to-do and regarded a mortgage on one's own dwelling as an omen of bankruptcy. Of all others, a new alderman could least afford to seem insolvent.

Mr. Walker's temporary setback came about in this manner: a building erected alongside the Walker lumber yard in 1885 was regarded by fire underwriters as particularly hazardous because celluloid collars were manufactured on the premises. The fire insurance company increased its rates on this place as much as three hundred per cent, and dealt likewise with the neighboring lumber yard.

The aldermanic candidate declined to pay a premium which he called "highway robbery." Two days after his old policy had lapsed, and almost at the same moment his constituents were drinking Evans Cream Ale to celebrate his triumph at the polls, the celluloid collar factory exploded. The accompanying fire spread to the lumber yard and consumed every shingle and stick in it. "A man knows nothing till he is forty years old," commented Mr. Walker on his failure to renew the insurance, "and then it's too late to do anything about it."

He patiently set about re-establishing his lumber business. The task was underwritten by several close friends, among them the veteran politician John R. Voorhis. Voorhis had sponsored Billy at Tammany Hall, and a Mr. Ryder had backed Walker's first aldermanic campaign. Richard Croker had by now succeeded the late "Honest John" Kelly as boss of Tammany. Mr. Walker paid off his debts and regained his prosperous status.

Voorhis and Walker had worked together on many jobs—Voorhis as an expert stairway builder and Walker as a carpenter. They first became friends while installing a solid black walnut staircase in the mansion of William Waldorf Astor. Now, in 1886, Voorhis was

Commissioner of Police. He was fifty-seven years old, and would live to be a hundred and two, a Tammany patriarch and grand sachem.

A courtly but virile Dutchman of strong voice and strong opinion, Mr. Voorhis attributed his longevity to a glass of good American whisky each day, several cigars, and the frequent shaking up of his liver by means of vigorous exercise. Mr. Voorhis' doctor took away his cigars when the grand sachem reached his one-hundredth birthday, on the ground that tobacco smoke was bad for elderly eyes. This decree amazed everyone, for it was well known that the Tammany sage could read the finest print that lawyers smuggled into documents to conserve paper and/or to hoodwink an astigmatic party of the second part.

Mr. Voorhis' father had been a carter, a lamplighter, and a constable, all at one time. The elder Voorhis had prospered during the pre-Civil War days when medical men had recommended severe bouncing of one's vital organs to encourage long life. Several rich men of the time, among them the Rhinelanders, the Astors, and the Vanderbilts, daily could be seen clinging for their health—for their very lives as it were—to the sides of Mynheer Voorhis' high-wheeled cart as it jolted over the cobblestones of the financial district.

Diagonally across the street from No. 6 lay the graveyard of St. John's, site of the present-day Hudson park and playground. Trinity Parish owned this property until 1898. The first bodies brought there were those of yellow fever victims. There had been a brief recurrence in 1834 of this malady which five times had been epidemic between the years of 1739 and 1822. During pre-Revolutionary days the plague had caused residents of the well-populated Battery neighborhood to move northward to the rural expanse of Greenwich Village.

St. John's Cemetery was a playground for Jim Walker and his brothers. Their favorite loitering place in the graveyard was a tottering brick building, little more than a hovel. A corpulent caretaker, Pierre Ventru, lived there. He was the first philosopher to arouse Jim's curiosity.

This red-haired gentleman spoke in a bass voice that rumbled out from a terrace of chins. His father, or so he asserted, had served in the kitchen of the divorced Empress Josephine at Malmaison from 1810 until her death in 1814. Some fifteen years after that event the royal cook arrived in America, there to wed a French girl, who gave birth to Pierre on a Staten Island farm.

Sexton Ventru possessed two qualities that fascinated young Walker: familiarity with the historic past and a preoccupation with the art of cooking and eating. His graveyard earnings he spent at Washington Market, north of Fulton Street, where he bought the cheaper cuts of meat, ox cheeks and tails, pig's brain, leg bones, the reproductive glands of sheep, kidneys, lungs, and other visceral removes. These bestial organs he transformed into dishes regarded by him as masterpieces. Jim frequently was invited to be his guest at table. Perhaps the boy's polite samplings of this cuisine–which Jim described as "noxious but imaginative"–were responsible for Walker's frequent bilious attacks during his early boyhood, his indifference to banquet fare, and his vehement antipathy to spicy foods.

Mr. Ventru was opposed to the use of profanity, in or out of a graveyard. Perhaps his lectures on this theme persisted in Jim's mind, for Walker seldom swore during all his years, and then only when desperately provoked. Nor did Jim like off-color jokes. He would leave the room if one were told in mixed company.

This puritanical strain in a man who lived in such worldly fashion puzzled some persons who met Jim in the headlong days of unsaintly Broadway. But it should be remarked that Victorian manners ruled the households of middle-class citizens of New York during Jim's boyhood.

It was Mr. Ventru's contention that near-by Leroy Street properly should have been spelled "Le Roi," meaning "the King" in French. He charged that New Yorkers took many gross liberties with the names of streets. As an example of this, he recalled that Grove Street west of Sheridan Square once had been named "Reason Street," in honor of Tom Paine's *Age of Reason*, a work composed in part at the free-thinker's home at No. 59. "But," said Mr. Ventru, "the stupid people soon corrupted the French pronunciation and made it 'Raisin' Street, like it was the fruit of something else than the tree of knowledge." He added solemnly, "Of course, I think Paine was wrong in the head, but even a revolutionist can think at times."

When the weather was unsuited for outdoor play, the three Walker brothers, William, Jim, and George, amused themselves by operating the dumb-waiter at No. 6. This contrivance was used for delivering coal to the seven fireplaces of the three-storied dwelling. The brothers would ride this small elevator, and sometimes leave Nan stranded inside it between floors.

"My brothers were a lively lot," Nan says, "although George was somewhat frail. Jim was mischievous at times, but there never was any real meanness in him."

Jim became a pupil at the Christian Brothers School (afterward the Cathedral School of St. Joseph's) next door to his birthplace in Leroy Street. His teachers were followers of St. Jean Baptiste de la Salle. Jim's favorite friends at this time were the four Higgins boys. Two of them, Peter and Edward, sons of Michael Higgins, resided at No. 104 Leroy Street. The other pair of Higgins boys also were named Peter and Edward, and were nephews of Michael. They lived with their father Patrick at No. 103 Leroy Street.

Michael Higgins had not prospered as well as his brother Patrick had. Jim Walker called the sons of Michael "Poor Ed and Poor Pete," and the sons of Patrick "Rich Ed and Rich Pete."

"Poor Ed" alone survives, and of Jim as a boy Edward Higgins says, "Notwithstanding his love of fun and his fondness for mischief, Jim was very quiet and reserved, and never quarrelsome."

The Higgins and Walker boys collected boxes and barrels for bonfires on election nights and listened to the oratorical cockcrows of the victors. At one of these bonfires, in 1894, when the coals and the speeches had died down, Jim heard his father say to Mrs. Walker, "I've been re-elected, Mother, but it seems I've lost." The elder Walker had spent his last penny upon the campaign. Furthermore, he had bolted from Tammany Hall with the slogan "Croker must go!"

Two years before this the Reverend Dr. Charles H. Parkhurst had exposed Boss Croker from his pulpit at the Madison Avenue Presbyterian Church. Until then Dr. Parkhurst had been regarded as a scholarly sermonizer, a student of dead languages, and, by fellow pedants, as the author of a book, *Forms of the Latin Verb Illustrated by the Sanskrit*. On this February Sunday in 1892 Dr. Parkhurst's parishioners heard their learned pastor describe New York as "Hell with the lid off," and the city's officials as "a damnable pack of administrative bloodhounds."

One of Dr. Parkhurst's communicants was Republican Boss Platt. When the pastor called Platt a conniving politician who openly opposed Croker's machine, yet secretly dealt with it, the ex-Senator hastened to join another, and a less civic-minded, congregation.

Dr. Parkhurst appeared before a grand jury, but at first was unable to support his claims with specific evidence. Then, disguised as a fun-seeking Johnny, Dr. Parkhurst made a tour of the brothels, played leap-frog with scantily clothed ladies of the evening, and returned to his pulpit with affidavits incriminating police officials.

Dr. Parkhurst persisted in his strictures, as had the prophet Jonah against sinful Nineveh. By 1894 his cries no longer could be ignored officially. A legislative committee, with State Senator Clarence Lexow as chairman, began to investigate conditions in the City of New York. A fusion ticket came into being, with the merchant-banker William L. Strong as candidate for mayor. One of the foremost supporters of this reform movement was young Theodore Roosevelt.

The Croker machine was defeated in 1894, and the Tammany Boss announced that he was retiring from his leadership of the Hall. He went to England to race his string of thoroughbred horses overseas, and to wait until the gale died down at home.

When Billy Walker said to his wife, "I've been re-elected, Mother, but it seems I've lost," Mrs. Walker went to their bedroom. She opened the bottom drawer of a chest and brought from it five hundred dollars which she had been saving toward the education of her children. "Now we'll start all over again," she said, handing this money to her husband.

Mr. Walker's defection from his party might have been the political finish of a less hardy man, but he was a notable vote-getter in the Greenwich Village district. He returned to the Tammany fold the next year, and a fourth term as alderman. Subsequently he went to the state legislature as an assemblyman. After that he became Commissioner of Public Buildings in the City of New York.

Years later the aged Dr. Parkhurst fell off a porch while walking in his sleep and died from his injuries. That was in September of 1933, while James J. Walker was a political exile in Europe. "You know," Jim said, "I always had a liking for the Doctor, even though he took a few telling shots at me and my administration. I admired him because he did not seek to bring virtue by coercion, for he once said, 'You cannot legislate the human race into Heaven.' His main blasts were against the hypocrisy of politicians who say one thing, and then, upon their election, and after taking the taxpayers' money, do exactly the opposite thing to that which they lately promised."

Jim left the Christian Brothers School to enroll as a pupil at the St. Francis Xavier Preparatory School. He played the piccolo in the school fife and drum corps, but resigned from that organization after his fingers suffered frostbite during a Washington's Birthday parade.

Jim's mother prevailed upon the organist of St. Joseph's Church to instruct her son on the piano. The teacher was a classicist and permitted his pupils to study only the works of the masters.

When Jim was about fifteen years old he arrived one spring day at his music teacher's home. When no one answered the bell, Jim stepped inside the house. There, in the parlor, he saw his teacher sitting strangely still in a rocking chair. A book of musical exercises had fallen from the musician's hand. He had died from a heart attack.

This was the first dead person Jim had seen. He said afterward, "It was a shock and a grim revelation as well. I had met my teacher in Waverly Place only the day before this. He had been smiling and enjoying life in his own gentle, confident way, and scattering bread crumbs to the sparrows. To an adolescent's eye, the man seated in death seemed a stranger, another person entirely from the man I had familiarly known. Nothing loses its identity as rapidly as a corpse. We speak of a dead man as, 'the body,' or 'the remains,' or 'it,' and give the shell of the man no name, as though he suddenly has become a neutral object. And I wondered then, as I do now, where lives the spirit of man?" Then Jim added, "Somehow I never wanted to play classical music again, ever, or listen to it as played by others. It always brought a surge of tragic feelings to my breast."

William Walker was elected five times to public office without benefit of "repeaters" at the polls or of brass knuckles. To show his appreciation, he persuaded the city to set aside several waterfront piers as recreation centers. Tenement-house families of lower Manhattan enjoyed free concerts and dancing on these piers, and kept comparatively cool there during the summer nights that made of every fire escape a bedroom and of every rooftop a dormitory.

Another of his favorite projects was to change St. John's Cemetery into a public park and playground. In 1898, upon his recommendation as Commissioner of Public Buildings, the city purchased the graveyard from the Trinity Church Corporation. It was decided to call it Hudson Park. Mr. Walker prevailed upon the celebrated architect Stanford White, designer of the Washington Arch and

Madison Square Garden, to submit a master plan for the park. Mr. White also made sketches for a bandstand, where free public concerts would be given in summertime.

Workmen came to St. John's. It had been stipulated that the long-buried bones be treated reverently. The relics were disinterred, re-assembled in boxes, and carted off for reburial in Trinity's newer cemetery, far uptown. Occasionally thereafter, during the operations of the park-makers, a skull popped out, as though to remind the workmen to mend their ways.

New Year's "calls" were a pleasant tradition in a city that enjoyed warm neighborly relationships. Young men accoutered in showy cravats, hard hats, and Sunday clothes called all day long in merry relays at the homes of the young women. The swains left cards with their names written flamboyantly upon them by penmen who made a specialty of this craft. A girl whose silver hall-tray held the most cards after a New Year's Day of chit-chat, tea, and small cakes was accounted the belle of the neighborhood.

The elders also made calls upon one another. If snow or ice lay upon the streets, the great gentlemen of the town drove pairs of matched horses hitched to sleighs. The tiny bells of silver on the harness hames and breechings gladdened the frosty afternoon.

Among those who came to the Walker home was General Daniel Edgar Sickles. The General had but one leg, having left the other in a peach orchard near Gettysburg. Despite his advanced years, the General's eye remained as all-seeing as a cormorant's, and he was a perennial favorite with the ladies. In pre-Civil War days he had shot and killed a careless gentleman who had addressed himself romantically to young Mrs. Sickles. The slain man, Philip Barton Key, was the son of the author of "The Star-Spangled Banner." The resolution of this love problem by means of a pistol ball, as well as the fact that General Sickles years afterward had roused the affections of the Queen of Spain, may have persuaded many ladies to regard him as the commander-in-chief of their hearts. Mrs. Walker, however, looked upon the General as a pest, and said as much to her family.

One New Year's General Sickles brought a large package to the Walker house. This gift, unveiled with much ceremony, was an equestrian portrait in oil of the General. The artist had depicted the officer in the uniform of his rank, his saber upraised, his blue elegance astride a battle steed, against a pyrotechnical background of shot and shell. The General also supplied a large easel so that the portrait could be advantageously displayed in the Walker parlor.

"My mother detested this picture," Nan Burke says. "After the General left it on her hands that day, Mama said, 'Children, take that thing and the confounded easel to the darkest corner of the basement!' "

The very next New Year's, Nan recalls, while guests were coming in or going out of the hospitable Walker home, her mother suddenly became agitated. "Quick!" she said. "The General's carriage is at the door! Get the picture and the easel from the basement right away and bring it upstairs!"

Mrs. Walker tried to detain the martial caller in the hallway, but her sons barely had time to set up the portrait in the parlor before the General stomped into the presence of his gift of last season. The cormorant's eye lighted with appreciation. "Ah!" said he, "I see that you do not forget me."

Mrs. Walker nervously observed the dust which had accumulated on the picture frame. The canvas was dimmed and the easel dirty. She said nothing about this, however, and the General apparently mistook the grime for the smoke of battle.

"It's authentic!" he cried out. "Every brush stroke is fraught with truth!"

After General Sickles' departure, Mrs. Walker again consigned the portrait to the basement.

4.

Father Knows Best

THE YEAR 1901 found Jim's elder brother in medical school. William Walker, Jr., was a methodical young man, and a sound fellow in the classroom. The father had not quarreled with his namesake's choice of profession. Jim had hinted from time to time that he too would like to be a physician, but the Boss decided that his second son should prepare for the bar as a means to political objectives.

Jim's faculty for public speaking, his sparkling aptitude for making friends, his wit, were sure indications—in Billy Walker's opinion—that Jim should book passage on the Ship of State.

It was Jim's desire always to please everyone. Even the foremost saints have been unable to perform this miracle, and instead sought to please God rather than the multitude. Jim's efforts to please all men, and certain women as well, often brought him trouble, especially since he also endeavored to please himself.

They were sitting one autumn afternoon in the music room of the St. Luke's Place house, Jim and his father. Jim was at the piano, playing "Sweet Genevieve," a favorite song of Billy Walker's. The older man occupied a rocking chair, his shoes off, his eyes half-closed, and a handkerchief in readiness if and when the familiar ballad brought his Irish heart to the melting point.

After the song and a bit of nose-blowing on Mr. Walker's part, Jim turned on the piano stool. "If I could only write a song like *that*," he said.

Jim's father went to the front window and looked out at the park which he had created. The shouts of boys playing crack-the-whip came from across the street. "It's a magic city," he said, turning from the window. "Every Irishman wants his sons to be better off than he was. It's law school for you, me boy."

"Could I go to business school first?"

"I never thought you bothered much about numbers," Mr. Walker grunted.

"It's high time I did."

Mr. Walker pulled at his ear. "Maybe you're tricking me?"

"Oh, no," Jim said, "I wouldn't do *that*."

"Well then," Mr. Walker said, "try business school for a while. But I want you to study law eventually."

Jim entered the La Salle Academy, a business school on Second Avenue. He did not let his studies interfere with his love of sports, which he indulged by serving as an usher at the old Avonia Athletic Club on Barrow Street. Jim became an aide to the chief usher, Spider Rafferty. The Spider was a hard-eyed crony of Chuck Connors, boss of Chinatown, a flashy barfly who could recite the alphabet backward.

The Spider's task was to stand guard inside the clubhouse at a gateway where a partition ran the width of the hall. This fence separated the fifty-cent ringside seats from the twenty-five-cent benches at the rear. The Spider tutored Jim on his first night. "Now look here, kid," he said, "I want no monkey business. See? If anybody comes up to youse with a nickel or a dime to let 'em sneak acrost from the twenty-five-cent seats to the fifties, don't take no money. That's a bribe. And me and youse is on the dead level. See?"

Soon after the clubhouse doors opened, Jim saw the Spider passing holders of cheaper seats to the ringside section and receiving bribes from them.

"Remember what I said, kid," the Spider boomed self-righteously. "I got my eye on youse! See?"

After his apprenticeship as an usher Jim became an occasional referee at the weekly bouts at Brotty's liquor house opposite Flannery's saloon on Hudson Street.

Certain of Jim's biographers have labored to make of him a superior athlete during his youth. It simply is not the fact. He had pipe-stem legs, no matter how smart they appeared when draped in custom-built trousers that hung just so. His arms had about as much flesh as an astronomy professor's, and his neck would have folded at the first blow dealt by a pugilist. To be sure, he played baseball and football on the vacant lots, as did almost every other boy of the period. He was agile on the baseball field, yet too slight to bat effectively or throw with needed power.

Jim's enthusiasm for sports, especially for professional boxing and baseball, and in after years football, may be easily understood. If an aspirant cannot shine as an athlete, the next best thing for him to do is to sit as close as possible to those who excel at the games. At a boxing match Jim would be so carried away that it was positively uncomfortable to sit beside him. He would rock about in his chair, punch neighboring spectators, place an elbow in the ribs of anyone near him, and at the close of a bout seem more exhausted than the loser.

La Salle Academy had the distinction of being the first of several institutions to fail to make of Jim a businessman and an arithmetician.

In speaking of his weakness as an accountant, Jim once said, "When I was a prizefight referee, I *had* to learn to count up to ten. But three months at business school couldn't improve me beyond that point."

In 1902, after considerable prodding by his father, Jim enrolled at New York Law School off Union Square. In the classroom

Walker sat across the aisle from Harry Carey, a former student at New York University. Midway in his junior year at the university Carey and another student had offended the faculty of that institution. They had acquired—somehow—the starched and ruffled panties (then known as "picnic drawers") of Madam Eunice Belden, keeper of a Bronx bagnio. One morning the pranksters hoisted this intimate wear to the peak of the campus flagstaff. A horrified dean gave the command to strike this international ensign. Just how the dean and his colleagues managed to identify the garment as Madam Belden's property remained a secret among themselves.

Madam Belden generously offered to appear before the university deans—sitting *en banc*—as a character witness for "these darling boys"; but Harry's father, Judge Henry DeWitt Carey, strongly advised against her presence at the trial. The Judge, an eloquent Tammany man, spoke in behalf of his son and the co-defendant, who subsequently became a general and a hero of World War I. The deans sternly recommended that the two young men resign forthwith from the university.

At New York Law School, Harry Carey observed that Jim Walker had a peculiar way of studying. Instead of reading the textbooks himself, Jim would ask Harry to read aloud to him. Walker's ability to memorize Carey's readings, and to recall classroom lectures as well, astounded his comrade.

When Jim had become mayor, he happened to say to a group of City Hall reporters, "I've read not more than fifteen books from cover to cover." Asked to explain his knack of storing up information without recourse to books, he replied, "What little I know, I have learned by ear."

Just recently I discussed this with Raymond Moley, a learned and affable gentleman who has as many degrees as a thermometer. "More men than you seem to think," observed Professor Moley, "especially successful politicians and lawyers, rely mainly upon their ears. They are men whose memories are phenomenal. They also can reach quickly into the basic elements of a spoken argument. The late Franklin D. Roosevelt was such a man. As President he did not have time to read many books, yet seemed entirely familiar with all sorts of currently printed works."

It would seem that the "ear" men are experts at meeting all comers in rough-and-tumble politics. According to one of Walker's lifelong friends and neighbors, Joseph McShane, "Jim was never a fellow of preparation. In school, or in court, or at the banquet table, Jim would depend upon inspiration when the bell rang. He always felt that he would have an answer—and he usually did have one."

Walker's former associate in the practice of law, Francis J. MacIntyre, said that all Jim's cases were prepared "by ear." When Jim examined a witness or pleaded a case in court, any communication from his associates was whispered into his ear, never written out and handed to him.

"As a rule," Mr. MacIntyre continued, "when an attorney is on his feet in court, it is unthinkable for an assistant to interrupt him with a spoken word. You give your associate a slip of paper, and when he sees fit to do so, he pauses, glances at it, accepts or rejects the written suggestion. Not so Jim. He said that notes confused him. He would point to his ear and say, 'Give it to me right here.' We would whisper to him even when he was talking in court, and it never bothered him at all. He would go right on talking, and sometimes we thought he had forgotten our oral promptings. Eventually he would incorporate our suggestions as if they were long-studied, carefully selected parts of his argument or cross-examination."

Jim confided to Harry Carey that he wanted, beyond all else, to be a successful songwriter. Whereupon Carey disclosed to his friend that he too had ambitions away from the law. He wanted to write plays, and had enrolled as a law student only to please his father—as a kind of penance for having stolen the underwear of Madam Belden.

Jim proposed that Harry write a skit to which he would contribute the songs. "I've been going to the vaudeville houses every evening except fight nights," Jim confided. "And I know a lovely girl who will say your lines and sing my songs. We can be lawyers to please our fathers and writers to please the public.

"The Lackawanna people," Jim went on to explain, "are advertising a mythical girl named 'Phoebe Snow,' a lass who keeps clean only because she rides on a road where the purest anthracite is consumed by the immaculate locomotives. We could get their advertising department to pay for the scenery."

Harry Carey proceeded to write the skit and Jim the songs for "Phoebe Snow and Her Six Pretty Porters." The authors skipped their law classes to attend rehearsals. They went to Yonkers for the opening, and there saw their act fail.

After two years at law school both Jim and Harry were graduated without honors. Had it not been for a lenient dean, the young men might well have flunked out.

Jim did not try for his bar examinations at this time. He persuaded his father that he "must do some post-graduate work." As for Harry Carey, he fell ill with pneumonia. Upon his recovery, his play *Montana* was accepted by a Broadway manager, and Carey went on tour as a member of the cast.

Harry Carey became a celebrated actor, and later on a motion-picture star in Western roles. Persons unfamiliar with Carey's New York beginnings, his boyhood in the Bronx and on City Island, where boats and sails were made, and his law-school education, believed this raw-boned horseman and rancher to be a true son of the West.

5.

Tin Pan Alley

The first professional songwriter to encourage Jim Walker's musical hopes was Paul Dresser, and not, as some would have it, Ernest R. Ball. Walker met the author of "On the Banks of the Wabash" and "My Gal Sal" in 1901. At that time Dresser possessed a much broader renown than that of his brother, Theodore Dreiser, the novelist.

Dresser was a barrel-bodied man, weighed some three hundred pounds, and, as Gene Buck says, "Big Paul oozed charm." As an actor, playwright, songwriter, and man about town, the tuneful Hoosier hugged life to his bosom, in poles-apart contrast to his brother, whose genius employed itself upon the dark complexions of men's souls, including his own.

"I first met this sunrise of a man," Jim Walker said of Paul Dresser, "at a rehearsal one night backstage in the old Park Theatre. It was the memorable September day Czolgosz shot President William McKinley. Dresser was standing among the chorus girls and telling them how to pronounce the name of the assassin. He treated me as though I were an old friend and invited me to have supper with him and two of the prettiest girls at Rector's. Paul Dresser made me feel important."

Jim Walker and Paul Dresser became chums. They compared experiences and discussed the influence of their fathers upon their respective lives. "Paul Dresser described his father as a religious fanatic," Jim once said. "The old tyrant wore earrings, and behaved like a cruel gypsy toward his two boys. He beat them unreasonably and made of their home a kind of noisy sepulcher. Wouldn't allow them any freedom of thought or movement. Perhaps that's why Theodore Dreiser grew up to be an embittered agnostic, and why Paul changed his name to 'Dresser.' "

What Jim said in this respect corroborated the remarks made by Theodore Dreiser's first wife. The late Mrs. Dreiser used to visit my home at Fire Island. She had been separated although not divorced from the novelist for several years, and it was apparent that she still loved him. She kept his letters in a locked trunk, and when publisher Horace Liveright sought to purchase them, Mrs. Dreiser exclaimed, "Oh, no! They are dreams of our private past, and no one shall ever see them."

"Aunt Jug," as the children called Mrs. Dreiser, had been born Sarah White. As a young Missouri schoolteacher, she had won a popularity contest in 1892, the prize a journey to the Chicago World's Fair. While at the Fair she met "Theo"—her pet name for Dreiser—a newspaper reporter who sought an interview with the prize-winner and stayed on to admire her profusion of red hair. Soon after her marriage to Theo, Mrs. Dreiser became acquainted with the members of his family. Aunt Jug described the father as a self-righteous, stern despot, whose harsh ways had made of Dreiser "a resentful cynic."

Dreiser's brother, according to Aunt Jug, had too much natural gaiety to become a brooding realist. Paul had left home to play a piano in a Terre Haute sporting house (and Aunt Jug shuddered to think of it), his first step toward independence.

During one of Aunt Jug's visits to Fire Island late in the summer of 1925 she spoke of her many "sacrifices" while Theo was writing *Sister Carrie*. She made a prediction which I well remember: "Theo hasn't written anything worth while since our separation—and he never will."

She voiced this prophecy in August. The very next January

Theodore Dreiser published *An American Tragedy*, a novel which revitalized his fame. Aunt Jug, one of the best-natured women of my acquaintance, retired as a literary clairvoyant.

Dresser resided for a while in a Greenwich Village flat. He attended Mass at St. Joseph's Church, and after services sometimes went to the Walker house to play the piano and sing. Jim's father liked Dresser, but pulled an ear whenever Paul spoke of the young man as a songwriter.

Although the elder Walker objected to songwriting, he enjoyed his son's parlor music. When Jim—now in his early twenties—played songs made famous by the variety team of Ned Harrigan and Tony Hart, the Boss would hum along. He especially liked "The Mulligan Guard March," "Paddy Duffy's Cart," and "Mary Ann, Go Fill the Growler." When Jim changed over to ballads that had to do with Irish motherhood, Billy would choke up in true Celtic fashion. The Boss also had a partiality for songs pertaining to romantic constancy. One of them, "Sweet Genevieve," always touched his heart.

"Sing it again, Jim," he would say. "It's a fine song."

Jim's singing was third-rate. His was a baritone voice with a slight "burr" underneath it. Whenever he spoke in public, the words rolled out with robust resonance, notwithstanding Jim's bantamweight physique. But as a singer he failed to captivate anyone other than his father and a succession of girl admirers.

It seems a puzzling circumstance that orators and actors seldom excel as singers; or, conversely, that singers do not, as a rule, speak with the authority of elocutionists. Tenor Caruso had a somewhat thin speaking voice, as I recall it; the mellifluous actor John Barrymore sang like a wearied stallion; and when statesman Al Smith vocalized "The Sidewalks of New York," the bullfrogs had met their master.

Jim's father and mother continued to urge their son to take the bar examinations. But Jim was a procrastinator by nature, and in some respects quite lazy. He could think up excuses and pretexts faster, and give them more validity, than could anyone else of his time. His perverse habit of delaying the performance of larger duties while attending to the smaller ones offended his friends. His "out-of-sight, out-of-mind" tactics soon were forgiven him, however, for almost no one could stay angry with Jim.

Edward J. Flynn, Democratic Leader of the Bronx, says, "Sometimes you wanted to murder Jim, but there never was a gun handy at the particular moment."

Billy Walker decided to "wait Jim out," in the belief that his boy eventually would settle upon politics as a career. "Meanwhile," Billy said to his wife, "he is making friends everywhere, and that will be a big asset to his future."

One of the most notable friendships that Jim Walker entered into during the early years of the century began when he met Gene Buck. Buck's grandparents on his mother's side, the McCarthys, had come to America from Ireland in a sailing vessel. Among their fellow passengers in steerage were the parents of Henry Ford. These voyagers, like thousands of other Irishmen before them, disembarked at Boston instead of New York, because the transatlantic fare was six dollars and a half cheaper that way. The McCarthys and the Fords afterward moved to Detroit's "Corktown" district.

When Gene was but three years old his father died. The widowed mother set out to insure good educations for her three sons. While at college Buck took a part-time job at the Dime Savings Bank, at the wage of two dollars a week. An elderly paying-teller observed Buck drawing pictures day after day. "Banking is a no-good business," the money-counter warned him. "You'll only end up in a cage like mine."

The teller introduced Buck to a bank depositor named Liggett, an artist who drew book covers for the firm of Richmond & Backus, printers of novels and sheet music. Buck, like his fellow townsman Henry Ford, had an inventive cast of mind. At the printing house he observed that title-pages of sheet music bore no decorations other than black borders and black type. Buck sat down at his drawing board and created the first illustrated title-page in color for a popular tune, an instrumental work, "When Knighthood Was in Flower," by Henrietta Blank. Buck submitted this innovation to Jerome H. Remick, son of a wealthy lumberman of Saginaw, who had founded a music publishing house of some importance.

Soon after "Knighthood," Buck drew illustrated covers for "Hiawatha" and "Creole Belle." These depicted lovers paddling canoes or strolling down the country lanes, and stimulated the sale of Remick sheet music.

Gene Buck went temporarily blind from overwork. He lived in darkness for almost a year, but never lost the smile that ever since has given hope to so many dispirited souls.

After Buck's sight had been restored, he left Detroit for New York. He arrived in Manhattan on the day Will Irwin's memorable story of the San Francisco earthquake and fire appeared in the news columns of the *New York Sun.* Irwin had been a reporter and editor out West until 1904. When the Pacific Coast telegraph wires went dead, Irwin searched his memory for intimate recollections of the far-off city. His story read as though it were written on the spot.

Buck's reading of this story prompted him to go downtown to Park Row to see Irwin, whom he had met in Detroit. Park Row was a haven for young strangers. There one might find reporters and editors who had come from almost anywhere. Few of them ever failed to welcome and advise a newcomer to the magic city.

Among other newspaper offices, Buck visited the *World* Building, and beneath its gold dome talked with Irvin S. Cobb. Cobb was but two years out of his native Paducah, Kentucky, but had already become a star reporter and staff humorist on the *Evening World.* Cobb advised Buck to keep on drawing song covers instead of trying to compete with Charles Dana Gibson as a "regular" artist.

There were four million inhabitants in the five boroughs of the City of New York in 1906, the year Gene Buck met Jim Walker. G. B. McClellan, son of the Civil War general, occupied the mayor's office. Charles F. Murphy, McClellan's political sponsor, was leader of Tammany Hall. The subway had been in operation for only two years, and the Flatiron Building was the tallest office structure in the world. William Randolph Hearst had come from California in the nineties to compete with Pulitzer as a crusading publisher, and had raided the *World* offices, taking away from Pulitzer such stalwarts as Arthur Brisbane, Bradford Merrill, S. S. Carvalho, and Morrill Goddard. Now in 1906 Mr. Hearst was attacking Mr. Murphy, and was throwing his weight—and his money—around. Richard F. Outcault, originator of the *World's* first comic page, "The Yellow Kid," was drawing "Buster Brown" for the *New York Herald* at the amazing salary of a hundred and fifty a week.

A tailor-made suit cost twenty-five dollars, and there were reasonably good five-cent cigars. The Considines of Detroit had established their Metropole Hotel in the lower Forties. This rendezvous of theatrical and sports figures provided an impetus for the uptown movement of hotels and theatres. George M. Cohan wrote "Give My Regards to Broadway" at the Metropole, and Gambler Herman

"Beany" Rosenthal was slain by gunmen on the sidewalk in front of that hotel.

An ex-prizefighter, Kid Broad, used to shuffle about the lobby of the Metropole to solicit alms from celebrated guests. The Kid followed William A. Brady to the washroom one night. When the Kid saw the famous theatrical producer use one of the several combs which, like the hairbrushes, had been chained to the wall over the washbasins, he asked, "What they chained up for, Mr. Brady?"

"To keep bums like you from stealing 'em."

The Kid tested the chains of a neighboring set of hair implements, found them burglar-proof, then said, "Yeah, but where's the toothbrushes?"

At the music-publishing house of Joseph Stern, Buck met Walker. The music publishers then had offices on both sides of West Twenty-eighth Street, between Broadway and Sixth Avenue. This relatively short street not long ago had been a residential district of four-story brownstone houses. The song publishers altered the old buildings without much regard for appearance.

As many cubbyholes as might be jammed together inside each house became "cells" for the demonstrators of songs. Flimsy partitions separated the cells. An upright piano stood in each small compartment. A publishing house might have as many as fifteen or sixteen pianos, all of which seemed to have survived heavy fire at the battle of San Juan Hill. Cigarette and cigar burns disfigured the music racks and marred the once-white keys, literally making ash trays of these instruments. The publishers did not own the pianos, but rented them.

The larger music firms boasted a grand piano in each publisher's private office, where theatrical stars shopped for new songs. The lesser vocalists of vaudeville and burlesque had to be content with entertainment in the "cells." Here the music of America was born.

The song-pluggers and their accompanists belabored the pianos, both the uprights and the grands, between the hours of noon and seven o'clock each weekday. At seven in the evening the June-moon hucksters scurried from their noisy warrens to the theatres or cafés in quest of business among the stage folk.

A passer-by in Twenty-eighth Street might hear as many as twenty tunes being played and sung at the same time. It was a musical

Donnybrook, and New Yorkers came to know the place as "Tin Pan Alley." It has been said that Harry von Tilzer coined this name, but Gene Buck believes that a newspaperman originated the term.

Jim Walker's friends moved in this Broadway world of actors, composers, and song-pluggers. At this time there was no radio by means of which new songs might be popularized, and no sound-films. The early-day picture houses were ramshackle structures, where silent actors cavorted like huge ghosts on the screens and tireless pianists played various tunes of their own selection to the tempo of the films.

Broadway's song-pluggers served as liaison officers between the publishers and the professional actors and actresses, who in turn brought the new songs to public attention. The pluggers themselves sang whenever an occasion arose for them to advertise their wares.

These more or less tuneful salesmen had come to New York from all the states; and some had been born abroad. One of the ablest of the business minstrels, Mose Gumble, became a good friend of Jim's. The bald-headed thrush regularly sang in Madison Square Garden when the six-day bicycle races were in progress, or at the Polo Grounds where the New York Giants played baseball under the direction of John J. McGraw, or warbled along the boardwalk at Coney Island. Other song-pluggers of Jim's acquaintance were Jimmy Durante, Wolfe Gilbert, and Irving Berlin.

Durante played the piano and sang with the gusto of a Cape Hatteras foghorn. His first thumping-ground was at Coney Island. Later on he appeared briefly at the raucous Chatham Club. Wolfe Gilbert (who afterward wrote "Waiting for the Robert E. Lee" and many, many other hit songs) also roared long and loud at Coney.

Berlin, son of Cantor Baline, once of a synagogue in Temun, Russia, underwent an apprenticeship as a singing waiter at "Nigger Mike" Salter's resort at No. 12 Pell Street in Chinatown. Berlin left "Nigger Mike's" to sing at the Chatham Club in Doyer Street. There he waited upon the "dese-an'-dose" customers and caroled with a towel over one arm and a beer tray in his hands.

The manager of the Chatham was Jimmy Kelly, né John Di Salvio. Kelly fired Jimmy Durante as a piano player, but retained Berlin at the Chatham. Kelly had begun life as an Italian waif on Hester Street in the Mulberry Bend district. As a boy he sold newspapers under the Brooklyn Bridge, then fought in the prize-ring. He had retired as a boxer at the age of twenty with a cauliflowered left ear.

As manager of the Chatham Club, Kelly put aside enough capital to set up a café of his own on Sullivan Street, a resort which he described as "refined but rough." Kelly became a political boss in Greenwich Village. In 1925, Jimmy Walker's first election, he delivered 242 out of 244 votes in the district.

The day after this Mr. Kelly said to a group of journalists, "You'll notice I didn't make it a clean sweep. Last time I did that for a Tammany candidate, they had me pinched."

When Gene Buck met Walker in 1906 Jim had had but two songs published. The first bore the name "Good-by Eyes of Blue," and the second "I Like Your Way." Walker wrote the lyrics and Harry Armstrong the music. Neither song had created a furor, but Jim, as it is said in boxing circles, had drawn first blood.

"The very first New Yorker I met in Tin Pan Alley," Gene Buck says, "was Jim Walker. We didn't bother to announce our last names, but became 'Jim' and 'Gene' right off, and stayed that way throughout the years to come."

Buck says that Jim Walker looked about the same in 1906 as he did just before he died, dapper and friendly. He stood with his shoulders relaxed in an easy, forward-drooping manner, as did George M. Cohan and other song-and-dance celebrities. Jim wore an ascot tie that day, with a starched choker, and there was not so much as a speck of dust on him.

Jim and Buck got to talking. "You know, a funny thing about New York," said Gene, "is you never meet anyone who was born here."

"Where are you from?" Jim asked.

"Detroit."

Jim listened for a time to the surrounding din of the many pianos. "Sounds like the Charge of the Light Brigade," he said. Then he remarked, "I've never been to Detroit."

"No?" said Gene. "Where are you from?"

"I was born down in Greenwich Village."

"Oh," said Gene, "where's that?"

Jim smiled. "Greenwich Village is a part of the City of New York."

Gene seemed astounded, as though Jim were some kind of freak. "Born here in New York? Well, well!"

"I've never been west of Hoboken," said Jim.

"You'd like the West," said Gene. "It's wonderful."

"Then why did you come here?"

"Because," Gene replied, "I want to be an artist."

"What's your last name?"

"Buck."

Walker embraced his new friend, exclaiming, "Gene Buck! The title-page genius!"

"I'm just a plain guy," Buck replied.

"No," said Walker. "All the world knows you're a genius. Greater than what's-his-name, Raphael."

Buck one day would supply lyrics for some of Victor Herbert's songs; collaborate for seventeen seasons with Florenz Ziegfeld of the *Follies*; discover many great comedians, among them W. C. Fields and Will Rogers; originate the first cabaret floor show, "The Midnight Frolics," atop the roof of the New Amsterdam Theatre; supply such carnival innovations on that gay roof as colored balloons and wooden mallets for the applauding audiences. He became a charter member of the American Society of Composers, Authors, and Publishers (ASCAP), which he served as president.

According to Buck, Walker did not wish merely to write an occasional hit song. "He wanted to go further than this. Jim wanted to be a production-writer of shows, to write *all* the songs for a show—every kind of song, a love song, a comedy song, a beautiful one that would bring a group of pretty girls on stage. But by a twist of fate, *I* was the one who became the songwriter, a thing that Jim wanted to do most, and *he* entered politics. But Jim always had a song in his heart, and its title was 'Humanity.' He found it was easier to make a living in the political field. You and I know there are no short cuts in any profession. You have to do things the hard way, starting from scratch, and then if you've got anything in you, you can make the grade. Then you learn about people. And some of us don't turn cynical or pessimistic, because we know the world is full of guys who are trapped, and most of them can't help being where they are."

Walker and Buck spent many hours together talking over their youthful aspirations. Sometimes they would attend the Weber and Fields shows, or performances by the Four Cohans at the Fifth Avenue Theatre up the street from Tin Pan Alley.

Jim once told Gene, "It's a burning desire, this songwriting. You know, a song about a girl and boy? Just to hear a piano or a band play the tune, or a pretty girl sing the words that came from your own heart. It's a thrill. You could be in prison, serving life, and maybe you'd hear a Salvation Army band putting on a song fest, and the music would cheer you."

"Music," Buck said to his friend, "is the second greatest language."

"What's the first?" Walker asked.

"The first," Buck replied, "is tears. A woman can come into a room full of strangers, but if she weeps everybody there instantly knows what it means."

Together with S. R. Henry, composer of "When The Harvest Moon is Shining on the River," Jim wrote "After They Gather the Hay," "Kiss All the Girls for Me," "There's Music in the Rustle of a Skirt," all three published in 1906. The next year the two men wrote "In the Valley Where My Sally Said Good-by" and "With the Robins I'll Return."

Most of Jim's songs dwelt upon the heartaches of parting lovers and their mutual vows to return to the scene, no matter how old they might become or how expensive the railroad or boat fare.

It was not until 1908, after Jim had met Ernest R. Ball, that Walker struck "pay dirt" in the Tin Pan Alley diggings. Jim nicknamed Ball "the Silent Dutchman."

Ball had come to New York from Ohio. He was a somewhat large man with a turned-up nose. "The vagabond spirit that most songwriters have," Walker said, "caused Ernie to leave Ohio, as well as his wife and their four children. He seemed colorless, but what a songwriter he was! The American Tosti. 'Till the Sands of the Desert Grow Cold,' 'Love Me and The World is Mine,' 'A Little Bit of Heaven,' 'Let the Rest of the World Go By,' 'When Irish Eyes Are Smiling,' 'Mother Machree,' and so many others.

"Ernie Ball," Jim went on to say of his collaborator, "was a mighty fine fellow, but so unemotional on the surface as to give you no clue as to whether he liked either you or your lyrics. He would say 'Uh, huh' with a deadpan expression. He was a contract writer for M. Witmark at the time that firm assigned me to him. He wrote many of Chauncey Olcott's ballads. Ernie didn't look at me at all that first day. He stared only at the keyboard of the piano, like a dejected porpoise."

Jim said to the composer, "I've been told you'd help me out."

Ball gazed at the piano keys as though hypnotized; then, after a long wait, said, "Uh, huh."

Jim went home to St. Luke's Place that wintry afternoon cast down in spirit. "Nan," he said to his sister, "would you get the Boss and Mother out of the house tonight?"

"I'll try," said Nan.

"I don't want the Boss to know I'm writing a song."

When Nan tried to persuade her mother to take Billy Walker to a dance, Mrs. Walker said, "I don't want to go out tonight, dear. It's too stormy. And besides I've been having insomnia. Haven't slept a wink for two whole nights."

The elder Walker did not dance. Whenever he did attend a ball, he would visit with politicians on the sidelines while his wife waltzed with friends.

"Mama says her insomnia is bothering her again," Nan reported back to Jim, "but I've talked Papa into escorting me to the dance."

"Well," Jim said, "I'll try my best to shoo Rosie off to bed. Then I'll write my song."

After the family dinner Nan went out with the Boss. It was an evening of wind and snow. Jim and his mother sat at the kitchen table, drinking tea. The coal range kept the room warm. The tea kettle hummed, and wind and snow flailed the windowpanes.

"Rosie," Jim said, "you may catch cold. Better go to bed and keep warm, don't you think?"

"It's warm enough here," she replied. "Besides I can't sleep."

Jim got up from his chair, went around the table, and kissed his mother's bright cheek. "Rosie," he said, "can you keep a secret?"

"You're not fooling me," she replied. "So go right ahead and get out your paper and pencil."

Jim smiled, then kissed his mother again. "I'll always love you."

"Forget the blarney," said Mrs. Walker, getting up from her chair. "Put it in your song."

After she left the kitchen Jim worked on a lyric about being loved "in the good old-fashioned way, when my hair has turned to gray." He was still at it when his father and sister returned home from the dance. The Boss had mislaid his key. He and Nan stood in the storm vestibule trying to arouse someone. Jim's brothers were asleep in the rear room of the third floor, and Jim himself was so engrossed he didn't hear anything but the midnight wind and the voice of his muse.

Mr. Walker shut his daughter Nan inside the storm vestibule and went to Flannery's for two bottles of sarsaparilla. On his return he tossed pennies against the second-floor window of his wife's bedroom. "Isn't it a wonderful thing?" he said resignedly. "You can never wake a mother that does not sleep."

Eventually Jim heard the rappings at the front door and the ringing of the bell. He put away the evidence of his songwriting and then let his father and sister in.

The next day Jim went to the Witmark offices. Ball was at the piano. Walker called out, "Do you live here?"

The composer turned his head slowly, carefully, as though it were a china globe. "Uh, huh."

Jim gave his lyric to Ball. The musician read it, laid the paper aside, then rose and spun the piano stool with the stoicism of a roulette-wheel manipulator.

"Is it that bad?" inquired Jim.

Ball sat down wordlessly and began to improvise at the keyboard. A light came into the musician's eyes, as if he had just seen Lady Godiva ride past. Ball played for perhaps three minutes, releasing the melodic riches that lay beneath the seeming drabness of his personality.

After a time the composer began to speak as he played. "Writing a song is like writing a letter in care of general delivery. Maybe somebody will call there to pick it up. Maybe not. Sometimes it goes to the dead-letter office." Ball left off playing to ask, "Do you drink?"

"Not much," Jim replied. "A little beer. Why?"

"You can't open the door to the Hall of Fame with a corkscrew," Ball said. "Remember that."

The composer resumed his piano playing and sang an unpublished song. Jim later remembered only a line or two of it: "Laughter lies next door to tears" and "Life's too short to quarrel, and hearts too tender to be broken."

Then, quite abruptly, Ball asked, "Got a girl?"

"If I may borrow your own phrase," Walker replied, "I'd say, 'Uh, huh!' "

"In love?"

"I think so."

Ball grew unexpectedly vehement. "*Think* so! Thinking has nothing to do with love—or there wouldn't be any. Wait till she turns your heart inside out. Throws you on the spears, runs you crazy. No sleep. No appetite. And you squirm and spew like a lobster with plugged claws."

"It's a dismal prospect," Jim said with a smile. "Do you know anybody in that fix?"

"Maybe," Ball replied.

"Forget that I asked," Jim said.

And now, as Jim told of it afterward, Ball played furiously, then once again resumed his usual placidity.

"He seemed to find some great escape when playing the piano," Jim said, "and I remember his face losing its anxieties. He became serene as he played, closed his eyes, and I felt as though I were looking at the death mask of a lovely child."

6.

Earthquakes and Roses

A FINANCIAL panic was lowering when James J. Walker's "Will You Love Me in December as You Do in May" appeared. This was in August 1908, three months before the defeat of Bryan by Taft. It was the year of "The Merry Widow Waltz," and of Rex Beach's muscular novel, *The Spoilers*. It was also the third successive year of mighty earthquakes: San Francisco in 1906; Kingston, Jamaica, in 1907; Sicily and Calabria, Italy, in 1908. Apparently some vengeful monster was making a subterranean tour of the world, shaking men's houses, their fortunes, their souls.

There were lengthening breadlines at the Bowery missions; Wall Street tightened its money-belt; but Broadway's people, as always, wore rose-colored glasses and snapped their fingers at tomorrow.

James J. Walker's father became hard pressed financially, and his political fortunes dwindled. Governor Charles E. Hughes had removed Walker's chief, John F. Ahearn, from office as president of the Borough of Manhattan. As a consequence Walker lost his job as Commissioner of Public Buildings.

Each of the five boroughs of the greater city has its own president. The five presidents sit on the Board of Estimate, a body which controls the city's purse. In some respects a borough president has the authority as well as the responsibility of a mayor in his own domain. Among other things, he has charge of paving the streets and supervising the construction of buildings in his borough.

Mr. Ahearn was elected to office in 1903 and re-elected for a term of four years in 1905. In 1905 a non-partisan association known as the Citizens' Union named a committee to find out how the public money was being spent, and what the city departments were doing. In November of 1906 the committee published a pamphlet charging inefficiency and waste in the office of the president of the Borough of Manhattan.

Mr. Ahearn asked that a "thorough investigation" be made of his office. Assistant Corporation Counsel John Purroy Mitchel undertook the prosecution of this inquiry, and thereby achieved his first public fame. Mitchel soon became Commissioner of Accounts in the department which had immediate charge of the investigation. During the course of these hearings three high subordinates of Mr. Ahearn were asked by their chief to resign, among them Mr. Walker. He complied with Ahearn's demands, but did so under protest and announced that he would fight for reinstatement.

The report of the hearings was sent to Governor Hughes. The City Club of New York now preferred charges against Borough President Ahearn. During the hearings before the Governor, Ahearn testified in his own behalf. Governor Hughes issued an order for Ahearn's removal, the first instance in the history of New York State that an executive officer of its largest city was ousted by a governor.

Governor Hughes took occasion to emphasize that the failure in public duty with which Ahearn had been charged did not involve his personal honesty. This ruling established a precedent for the hearings in 1932 when James J. Walker appeared before Governor Franklin D. Roosevelt to answer charges similar in some respects to those brought against Borough President Ahearn.

William Walker began suit against the city for reinstatement and won the action. He again resigned, explaining that he had brought the suit to clear his name. This turmoil, however, saddened him, and he contemplated giving up politics as soon as his son James would make up his mind to enter that field.

Mr. Walker's other sons had settled upon their own careers. Only

James had not established himself in a business or a profession. William was a practicing physician, George an insurance man.

Jim adored his brother George, who exercised a wholesome influence on Jim, never flattered him or smiled upon his faults. Notwithstanding his frail body, George had a forceful character. He asked no quarter and gave none. He had received little formal education, but possessed a searching and excellent mind. "You must play square," George would admonish Jim, "or you should not play."

Perhaps George inherited some of the rock-bound attributes of James Roon. Grandfather Roon was partial to George, as also were Mrs. Roon and her four spinster daughters. When George was about eleven years old he left St. Luke's Place one day to spend the weekend at his grandparents' house. He stayed there for almost four years. When he returned home his voice had changed and he had on a pair of long trousers.

At the time of Mr. Walker's political crisis his lumber yard burned down again. After George had looked upon the ruins, he informed his father that he was going into the property insurance business.

In 1908, with his place of business in ashes, his political life stymied, and panic threatening everyone, William Walker once again urged Jim to forget Tin Pan Alley. In reply Jim promised that his new song would repair the fortunes of the Walkers and the Roons.

The Boss enlisted the aid of his brother-in-law, James Roon, Jr. "Will you have a talk with the boy?" he asked.

Uncle James persuaded his nephew to take a job as a clerk at the Union Surety and Guarantee Company. Jim lasted several months there, largely because he applauded the dream of Frederic B. Esler, the firm's vice-president, to build a vehicular tunnel connecting City Hall in Manhattan with Borough Hall in Brooklyn. Mr. Esler's worthy project expired on his desk, and Jim quit the job.

When the "December and May" song came out, Walker's excitement downed his sense of modesty. One of his intimate friends, Al McCosker (later the head of the Mutual Broadcasting Company) told me just recently, "I was one of Nan Walker's beaux, and Jim was fond of my sister Ann. The young ladies used to have 'at home evenings' on Tuesday nights. Jim's song hit came out on a Tuesday, as I remember it. On that particular night Jim arrived at our house like a glad breeze, a copy of his new song in his hands.

" 'Here you are, Ann,' Jim cried out as he presented the sheet of music to my sister. He bowed elaborately. 'Ann, I wanted you to be the very *first one* to have a copy.' "

McCosker learned some weeks afterward that Walker had obtained a dozen first copies of his song on the day it was published and had given them, together with a pretty speech apiece, to eleven other girls. One of them was nineteen-year-old Janet Frances Allen. Janet had become acquainted with Walker in 1904.

Janet had plump cheeks and pretty blue eyes. She was a tiny girl, with small feet and hands, of which she seemed quite proud. She owned another kind of pride too, which in the years to come moved her to conceal the torments which beset her heart. When she became the neglected wife of a popular idol, she hid her tears from public scrutiny and in private refrained from quarreling with a man who himself shunned domestic squabbles. She hopefully believed that her loved one always would return home after fancy's fevers had cooled. And she was right, except for one time, the last.

There were many women of varying ages and stations who cared for Walker over the years. It is a curious circumstance that not one of them has ever been heard to speak of him with a trace of bitterness.

Janet Allen was born in Omaha, Nebraska. As a child, she accompanied her parents to Chicago, where her father, J. Frank Allen, became city editor on William Randolph Hearst's newspaper.

During her girlhood Janet spent her summers on the Iowa farm of her mother's parents. When she was about eleven, she joined a Chautauqua chorus at Clinton, Iowa. She had an excellent soprano voice, and sang in Iowa and Illinois towns. At the age of twelve she appeared at the Chicago Auditorium. During her teens she joined the chorus of the George Broadhurst musical show, *The Duke of Duluth*, and was also the soprano understudy for the leading lady of that production.

After a tour of the provinces, it was decided to revise the jokes and rewrite the tunes for a New York presentation. The music firm of Marks & Stern assigned Max S. Witt to compose the new numbers and James J. Walker to write the lyrics. Jim was fond of puns, and referred to Max Witt and himself as "the firm of Wit and Half-Wit."

Janet Allen was ill when the musical company reached New York. On the first day of rehearsal at the Majestic Theatre she rested backstage while the others went to lunch. It was there that Walker first saw her. He noticed that she was not well and insisted that she go with him to Reisenweber's Restaurant across the street to "have something hot."

While the new friends were dining and exchanging youthful confidences, a Broadway acquaintance of Jim's jokingly called Walker's attention to a race-track form chart on which a horse named "Duke of Duluth" was listed as running that afternoon at Sheepshead Bay.

"That's a good hunch," Jim said. "Will you place a bet on the Duke for me?"

"He's going to be a long shot, Jim. Doesn't seem to have been in the money since he was born."

"Well," said Jim, "that horse and I have a lot in common."

Jim borrowed ten dollars from the waiter and gave it to his race-track friend to put on what he called "the hitherto neglected nose of the Duke."

That evening, when the rehearsals were broken for the dinner-hour, Jim learned that he had won almost two hundred dollars. He invited Allie and a party of friends to midnight supper at Reisenweber's. He paid the waiter back the ten dollars and gave him another ten. "Lucky at horses and lucky at love," he said. From that time on, says Allie Walker, and until several years after their marriage, she and Jim were together most of the time.

The Duke of Duluth fared badly in New York, and after its scenery had been carted off to a theatrical warehouse Miss Allen went into vaudeville. One of her partners was Harry Pilcer, the dancer who had appeared on the stage with Gaby Deslys. Another was Joseph McShane, who lived in Barrow Street, just around the corner from the Walker home.

McShane had known Jim since the days when Walker, as a teenage Demosthenes, made political speeches from the tailboards of wagons or on the street at the Greenwich Village polls. At that time it was permissible for a candidate or his partisans to harangue the voters in the vicinity of the ballot-booths—sidewalk stalls which resembled pine-board coffins standing on end.

McShane remembers the Janet Allen of the vaudeville years as an animated girl, five feet tall and weighing less than ninety-five pounds. Harry Weber, agent for Allen and McShane, booked the singing and dancing skit at Proctor's Fifth Avenue Theatre at Twenty-eighth Street and Broadway near Tin Pan Alley.

Together with McShane, Janet went to the Stern offices one day to "shop" for a conversational song—and to see Jim. At the music house the vaudevillians agreed to accept twenty-five dollars a week to sing "After They Gather the Hay," to which Jim had written the ballad.

Jim and Allie celebrated this agreement by having another supper at Reisenweber's. That night, as Jim remembered the occasion, they met O. Henry, whose collection of stories, *The Four Million*, had just been published. From Reisenweber's Jim and Allie went on to Rector's, where Walker's theatrical idol, George M. Cohan, introduced them to Oscar Hammerstein, Fred Stone, and Miss Lillian Russell, all in one evening. When Jim learned that America's most beautiful actress smoked an occasional cigar, he remarked, "She's a better man than I am." He had an aversion to cigars, no matter who smoked them.

Jim obtained a season pass for a stage box at Proctor's. Each time the curtain fell on the Allen and McShane act he turned into a one-man claque, to set the pace for encores. It was a thrilling experience to hear his own words sung: "After the roses of summer, we'll be together again. Wait for me, Jennie, my own . . ."

These were seventh-heaven days for James J. Walker. A pretty girl to sing his song; audiences listening to his lyrics in the theatre; cab drivers and newsboys whistling the tune. "Skies of blue, and me for you, just we two." To see the sheet-music of his hit song, "Will You Love Me in December," displayed side by side with "The Merry Widow" in the shops was an unbelievable triumph.

Allie lost her singing voice in 1912. From 1905 until her retirement from the stage she sang all Jim's songs. She also had been the "Phoebe Snow" of the skit written by Jim and his friend Harry Carey, the enterprise which had failed in Yonkers.

Allie Walker agrees that Jim's father had great influence upon the son in the matter of his studying law. But she says that she also played a part in this by urging Jim to go to the lecture room.

"His ambitions were not well defined when I met him," she wrote to me. "In his youth he wanted to be a doctor, but his brother had taken up that profession. Jim's natural ability to express himself well, together with his charm of person and manner, led him to the legal profession—but study was so hard for him—almost impossible."

Of their early days together Allie Walker says, "I was attracted to him at once; loved the way he wore his clothes, his wit, and even adored his funny nose (about which he was a bit sensitive). In the evenings we went to the movies, took long walks, used to clown about, and were always laughing. We didn't have any money, but we did so enjoy life and each other. Specific dates for all this are lost to my memory. All I know is that I enjoy a warm glow when I recall those wonderful days together."

Jim's friends were confident that he would marry Janet Allen. The marriage forecasters, however, would not risk saying *when* Jim might make Allie his bride. They knew that he was hard to pin down, a foe of the calendar, and, in making decisions of a personal kind, acted as though he had taken a strong sedative.

Walker's quickness of mind, a quality which he ably demonstrated in public office, oddly enough deserted him whenever he faced strictly personal issues. In these circumstances he could be relied upon to do only one thing thoroughly and well, and that was to temporize. It might be said that Time had Jim on its hands.

It was plain that Jim's heart was set upon Allie. However, he was not one to discourage admiring glances cast by other young women. Walker never behaved toward the ladies with the zest of a traveling salesman, but he did greatly enjoy the admiration of the fair. He permitted himself and his smart clothes to be seen to the best advantage on Sunday mornings at St. Joseph's Church.

Jim would be the last one to enter the church, so that he could be the first one out. Then he would stand near the place where his father and mother long ago had furthered their courtship. In summer he would loiter outside, his straw hat tilted and his bamboo cane poised. In winter he would attitudinize in a smart derby hat and pinch-back blue topcoat, with gray gloves and spats to match, while the young ladies passed by, their hearts and skirts fluttering.

The parents of Greenwich Village girls spoke of him as "a little gentleman." The mothers remarked that his language always was "proper," and the fathers observed that he drank but an occasional glass of beer at the Dutchman's in Hudson Street. As for the young ladies, they found in Jim many qualities to arouse their admiration: his good looks, his gay spirit, his agreeable ways.

Both Allie and Jim were baseball fans. They went as often as possible to see the New York Giants play. That baseball club always has been an intimate part of the city's life, even after Colonel Jacob Ruppert and his associates had brought the great Babe Ruth to the Yankee team of the rival league. The young couple also went to the races when they could afford them. Jim never was a gambler in a large sense, but he enjoyed seeing the ponies run, and besides, so many of his Tammany friends frequented the tracks.

When Jim could not afford these recreations he and Allie would go for long walks. "My name is Walker," he would say, "and I want to live up to it." After their strolls Jim and Allie would stop at Mock's on Hudson Street for a glass of beer and a sandwich. Sometimes they would find a piano, and then Jim would sit down to it and Allie would sing.

"He was not too good at the piano," says Allie. "He used to say, 'The left never knows what the right is doing.' He would hum, slightly off-key, while he was playing, and did the same while he danced."

In those days Jim enjoyed dancing and was an excellent dancer. On the ballroom floor he held his shoulders high, in contrast to the slightly hunched drooping of his shoulders when he walked. He had perfect balance, coordination, and moved effortlessly to the music.

Notwithstanding Jim's long association with Allie, and the lasting rumors of their plans to wed, Walker's parents did not seriously consider her as a prospective daughter-in-law. For one thing, Allie had been reared as a Christian Scientist. Furthermore, a man should not ring wedding bells until after he has established himself in a good job.

Jim was twenty-seven years old at the time his "December and May" song appeared. When it became almost certain that the ballad would sell briskly, Jim was able to draw five hundred dollars from the publisher against his probable earnings on the song. With characteristic optimism Jim spent this money with the velocity of a good-time Charlie. He ordered three custom-built suits, directing the tailor to omit the cuffs from the peg-top trousers. He bought four pairs of shoes with sharply pointed toes, a dozen silk shirts, a new walking stick, three fedora hats—blue, tan, and gray, blocked to his own specification of "half Theodore Roosevelt style and the other half Cornell University"—and purchased all manner of trinkets for his mother, his sister, and Allie. He wagered what was left of the money on a horse—and lost.

Jim's monetary philosophy of "There's more where this comes from" did not coincide with the policies of his publisher. Quite apart from the general retrenchments caused by the worsening state of national business, music publishers of that day were not celebrated for their liberality.

Not until 1914, with the founding of ASCAP, did authors and composers begin to enjoy royalties commensurate with their efforts. Before that, many writers of successful songs had received as little as fifty or a hundred dollars for a ballad. The great Stephen Foster was an exception. Although that composer died in poverty, Gene Buck tells me that Foster was a much shrewder bargainer than his biographers have shown him to have been. It seems that much of Foster's money went to the bartender.

Jim's career as a songwriter struck a reef when, with composer Herman Avery Wood, he wrote a number called "Black Jim." Whether or not the panic adversely affected the sales, or the song itself lacked elements of popularity, the song failed.

Uncle James Roon took his nephew aside. "You think a great deal of your father, don't you?" he asked.

Jim protested that no one was dearer to him than the Boss.

"Very well then," said Uncle James. "Prove it."

"How?"

"Let's put it this way," said Uncle James. "That last song of yours was not exactly—"

"Instead of 'Black Jim' I should have called it 'Black Friday,'" Jim broke in.

"And now," the older man went on, "money is not to be had easily; besides, you know that your father's pride was hard hit by the Ahearn matter."

"But the Boss," said Jim, "has been completely exonerated."

"Just the same," said Uncle James, "he's ready to retire. And it's Billy's dream for you to carry on where he's leaving off."

The young man seemed to be reaching a decision at last. "All right. What do you suggest?"

"Come with me," said Uncle James. "We're calling on Charlie Culkin."

Charles W. Culkin was a political power in the old Ninth Ward where he had been born in 1872. He was elected to the Board of Aldermen in 1898 and served for three two-year terms in that capacity. He then became clerk of the Court of Special Sessions, but resigned to take an appointment as Commissioner of Records in the Surrogate's Court. Afterward he served as Deputy Fire Commissioner, as head of the Pension Bureau of the city, and finally in 1925—the same year Walker was elected mayor—became Sheriff of New York County.

At the time Walker called with Uncle James upon the affable but shrewd Mr. Culkin, John T. Eagleton was serving his second one-year term as assemblyman from the Greenwich Village district. On both occasions Culkin had sponsored Eagleton for the Assembly.

Eagleton was a friend of two of Jim's young cronies, Timothy J. Corbett and "Poor" Peter Higgins. Whenever Eagleton returned home from the legislative sessions in Albany, it was his pleasure to meet these young men at the bar of the Dutchman's lager-beer saloon on Hudson Street. One Thursday night Jim's friends waggishly suggested that Mr. Culkin might not renominate Eagleton for the Assembly. Tim and Pete pointed out to the legislator that it was the practice of a district leader to nominate an assemblyman for two terms, and then ask him to step aside to give someone else a chance.

At this Assemblyman Eagleton announced that he not only would oust Culkin, but that he meant to take over the district leadership himself.

When Mr. Culkin heard of his protégé's tirade, he sent for him. "I had every intention of renominating you, John. But after what you have said I wouldn't renominate you if I had to name a total stranger."

We have remarked elsewhere that James Roon, as an altar boy, had been a bit of a gossip. During the years he had not lost his grip in this respect. When he learned of the rift between Culkin and Eagleton, Uncle James pounced upon the idea of presenting his nephew to the leader as a worthy substitute.

At Mr. Culkin's house they found the leader still smarting over the behavior of his assemblyman. Uncle James emphasized the fine record of the elder Walker as a sound reason for naming Jim to the Assembly. Culkin studied the young applicant's face for a time and observed his good clothes. "You might be an ornament among the up-state farmers," he said. Then, after a pause, "Jim, I've heard you speak, and if you really settle down to it I think you'll go places in politics. Let's see what we can do."

Arthur J. W. Hilly (later Corporation Counsel of the City of New York) placed Jim's name before a slate-forming caucus of Tammany members. Jim waited in a near-by saloon while these men deliberated. At length he was summoned before the group and formally advised of his selection. He made a speech of acceptance. Unlike most of his speeches, this one had been prepared, and it lacked sparkle. Whenever he delivered a set speech, which was seldom, or read something, it seemed that another and a somewhat dull fellow had taken Walker's place.

When Candidate Walker confided that he had no campaign funds, Mr. Culkin gave him a thousand dollars. The leader provided a like amount for Joseph W. Hannon, the district's candidate for alderman.

Hannon was about the same age as Jim. The two young men canvassed the ward, and soon the Walker speeches began to shine with the ways and words that always drew people to him. Walker objected to visiting the saloons for the purpose of gaining votes and persuaded Hannon to do most of that. Mr. Culkin had to replenish the funds of the candidates twice, each time to the amount of a thousand dollars.

The thwarted Eagleton now announced that it was his intention to oppose Culkin at the primaries for the district leadership. Culkin, as a matter of course, expected Jim to "stump" in his behalf, but Jim said that he did not feel like speaking against the friend of his two good friends, "Poor" Pete Higgins and Tim Corbett.

Instead of showing his appreciation of Jim's courtesy in not speaking against him, Eagleton sought on several occasions to upbraid Walker for accepting the candidacy for the Assembly. After one of these hecklings Jim said to Eagleton, "You talk like a wooden man."

"That," retorted Eagleton, "is the proper way to talk to a blockhead."

Walker burst out laughing. "You put it over on me that time!"

But this made up Walker's mind, and he went directly to a political meeting where Mr. Culkin was present and made an eloquent speech in behalf of his sponsor. Mr. Culkin retained his leadership that autumn, and Jim was elected to the Assembly, his first public office.

The Walkers and the Roons were happy. And Jim—well, Jim was happy because they were. Allie said that she was glad that such a great honor had come to Jim. They announced their engagement. Allie already had become a convert to the Roman Catholic faith.

Jim's mother and sister Nan were on a holiday in Atlantic City when the engagement was formally proclaimed. Mrs. Walker was less than enthusiastic about her son's decision. Later on she would find Allie a pleasant person to have in the Walker home, but now she said to Nan, "Nothing can be done about it, I suppose. But Jim's too young for marriage; too young to make up his mind for such a serious step."

Jim seemed forever young to his mother. Indeed, he would continue to seem young to almost everyone. But at twenty-nine the pattern of his life and the mold of his nature had been fashioned beyond the reach of change. The qualities that later endeared him to so many thousands of men and women everywhere were already evident. The impulses that one day would foster adverse criticism of him as an official, but never any real hatred of him as a personality, were in plain sight in this young foe of worldly cares.

"Jim never changed much in appearance," says Allie Walker. "He was always thin, had a rather florid complexion, wore his clothes well, and was always immaculate. He made everyone happy wherever he went. I don't know just how he did it, and neither did he."

He seemed young, and he stayed young. And perhaps that is why when Walker had become the John Barrymore of the political stage most people looked with lenient eyes upon the foibles of the city's darling, for Jim was created in New York's own image. The thunders of morality could not down the affectionate regard that the city had for the Beau of New York, nor prevail against the memory of him who brought gaiety to a people wearied of slogans, mottoes, and old saws.

His easy and undisciplined childhood in a happy household may have blinded him to the fact that the world seldom coddles a public man, fawns upon him only if he bestows favors, or broadcasts his material substance, or shares his public fame with the vainglorious ones. Jim persisted in his belief that all men loved one another, gave to one another freely, and behaved both in thought and performance with the generosity of spirit which only the noble characters in fiction possess. Jim's heart was a wishing-well.

7.

There Was a Tavern in the Town

BEFORE we write of James J. Walker's bright young yesterday on Capitol Hill in Albany, would you meet me for an informal briefing at Toots Shor's Restaurant on West Fifty-first Street? I suggest this place since Jim's friends and mine, the newspaper cronies, go there for lunch before the football or baseball games or for supper after the fights at Madison Square Garden.

So many facts of the sports world assail you at Shor's that you begin to feel like a record book. You can almost smell rosin-dust, as one does at Stillman's foggy gymnasium on Eighth Avenue, where the boxers of Gotham work out in the twin rings of that old rehearsal hall of the pugs.

You are bound to see many survivors of the twenties at Shor's, and hear anecdotes of Man o' War, Earl Sande, Babe Ruth, and Jack Dempsey. Occasionally you come upon an odd silence, and Toots does not smile or clown about, and you know that the last shadow has fallen upon Mark, or Jim, or upon someone else of the old guard. And there will be a kind of wake that night, with the doors closed to all but those who remember the good comrades and the golden days that never will return. Graves are the footprints of Father Time.

In other years, when the world was a cream puff, and the reporters lived upon the hourly excitements of the nineteen-twenties, you and I would have met at Billy LaHiff's tavern on West Forty-eighth Street. Quite understandably, you would not have paid attention to me in those days—nor today, for that matter—since I spent much of my time in the basement kitchen, trying to write a novel on a table next to the meat-block. Jack Spooner, the big blond captain of the waiters, and former member of the historic flying wedge at Jack Dunstan's all-night café, saw to it that I had an occasional drink "on the house"—Prohibition laws notwithstanding—for the sake of modern letters.

Nor would you have paid much attention to certain other young newspapermen who since that time have gained renown. You might, of course, have observed one pale, intense, and ever-busy fellow darting from booth to booth like an inspired ferret. His name was Walter Winchell. This ex-member of Gus Edwards' juvenile troupe of vaudevillians was collecting Broadway news for Bernarr Macfadden's *Evening Graphic*. I believe that Walter's boss was paying the lad less than fifty dollars a week.

No one was aware of the fact that the buzzing Walter was establishing a one-man beachhead for the tabloid age, spearheading a movement that would change the geography of modern reader interest. How he managed to keep on hopscotching around and about with never a drop of alcoholic fuel in his tank was a matter for wonder. There were few prophets among us in those days.

So many Broadway celebrities gathered at LaHiff's that you might have overlooked another young man, Mark Hellinger, unless perhaps you were to observe the half-grin that he always wore as a true advertisement of his generous heart. Mark had been graduated from the Ziegfeld beauty parlors, at the New Amsterdam Theatre, of which institution he had been a publicity man, and had commenced to write vignettes of New York.

Other "almost-but-not-quite-known" habitués of LaHiff's included the skinny and eager Westbrook Pegler. It was some years later that Pegler gave to the twenties the name of "Era of Wonderful Nonsense." That label has come to mean an indictment of the age; but it is my recollection that Pegler himself was having a marvelous time as a sports correspondent, and seemed as starry-eyed and as credulous as any of us.

It has been one of my deepest personal sorrows that feuds, rivalries, and dissensions afterward sundered the friendly ties that bound some of these spirited journalists who used to gather at LaHiff's. I remember the Heywood Brouns, the Winchells, the Peglers, the Grantland Rices, the Runyons, as they were: good companions, merry with the circumstances of youth and good will.

I never placed friendship under a microscope, and I think that Jim Walker expressed my view as well as his own when he told me,

"It takes only one or two reasons for me to like a man; but it takes a hundred for me to dislike him."

You would not have seen the now mighty novelist John Steinbeck at LaHiff's in the early days, say in 1924 or 1925. That rangy young man, then an "unknown" genius, was carrying bricks to the masons engaged in the construction of the new Madison Square Garden at Fiftieth Street and Eighth Avenue. He told me not so long ago that he thoroughly detests the Garden and never goes near it because it represents old backaches.

I regard Steinbeck as a heretic, and so informed him, for I like every brick in the Garden. For a time I was publicity man there for Tex Rickard, having succeeded Tad Dorgan's stoical brother Ike in that post in 1928. I am remembered only because of the "jams" for which I always seemed to have a peculiar affinity.

On one occasion I tried to dissuade Tex Rickard from investing in a so-called fire extinguisher chemical, a powder which caked easily after storage. Mr. Rickard was a keen man in most respects, but something of a "sucker" for inventions.

He was sitting with two other gentlemen in his office one day, about to sign a large check for a block of stock in the fire-extinguisher project. He kept a supply of the stuff in the drawer of a huge desk which had belonged to President Harding. Tex also kept a rhinoceros-hide cane on his desk–it had belonged to President Theodore Roosevelt.

While Mr. Rickard was reaching for his pen (which, oddly enough, had not belonged to President Lincoln) and the two extinguisher promoters had their attention fixed upon their customer, I decided to protect the interests of my employer. I surreptitiously set fire to his waste basket.

Mr. Rickard was a man of action, a graduate of the Klondike school of emergencies. He had faced the guns of gamblers in his Great Northern Saloon in Nome, Alaska, and no mere fire in a New York office could thwart his presence of mind. Tex promptly opened a drawer of Mr. Harding's desk and got out a box of the fire-extinguishing chemical. The stuff had caked to the consistency of a Steinbeck brick.

"This is the hottest waste basket I ever seed!" exclaimed Mr. Rickard, hurling the cake of chemical into the smoking basket. It only made the fire a better one. The spirit of another President now was invoked as Tex began to flail the blaze with Theodore

Roosevelt's cane. The big stick subdued the fire. From beneath singed eyebrows Tex looked accusingly at the extinguisher salesmen and tore up the check he had intended to sign.

Some time afterward I advised Tex to take out a million-dollar life insurance policy with the Garden corporation as beneficiary. Jim Walker said of this, "He should do it with *you* around!" Tex declined to accept my advice. "It would be bad luck," he said. "A jinx. I never seed a man with a big policy on his life who didn't die right off."

Less than three months from that time Tex fell ill with appendicitis while in Florida. The appendix ruptured, and Tex died of peritonitis. His body lay in state in the Garden, and Jim Walker and Jim Farley and Jimmy Johnston and thousands of other Jims and Jimmies of the sports world filed past the bier. I wrote a poem about the tall Texan and tried to put into it some of the affection I had for the greatest prizefight promoter of all time.

Had you and I gone to LaHiff's during the twenties, we would have seen the now-famous sports authority William Corum, youngest major in World War I. It was Bill who said to Jim Walker, "I don't want to be a millionaire. I merely want to live like one."

You also would have seen the very tall, then slender Dan Parker —my own journalistic "discovery" when I served as sports editor of the *Daily Mirror*. Dan wrote with a blackjack instead of a pen, but never with a police whistle. Ben Hecht called Parker "the Dean Swift of the sports pages."

Hecht himself had come to New York from Chicago to astound the members of the Hotel Algonquin's *bon mot* club not only by his powers as a conversationalist, but also by the pancake hat and tennis shoes he sometimes wore in the Algonquin lobby while waiting for Alexander Woollcott, Bob Benchley, Dorothy Parker, and other wits of the celebrated "Round Table."

Each survivor of the twenties has his own oasis in memory. LaHiff's is mine, and I think more Broadway careers were nurtured there than at any other place. Among the "unknowns" you might have seen the sprouting Louis Sobol, a happy spectator of the daily scene. Ed Sullivan, then a young sportswriter for the *Graphic*, also loitered at LaHiff's to look upon the great and near-great athletes, actors, managers, Follies girls, artists' models, producers, songwriters, politicos, and millionaire whisky runners.

There were booths and tables in this English-style tavern. Pictures of all the presidents (except Jefferson Davis) were hung upon three of the walls. At the northwest corner of the long dining-room celebrities from time to time occupied a semicircular booth. Among those who drank and dined in this "corner" one might find the young heavyweight champion Jack Dempsey and his highly perfumed manager Jack Kearns, Grantland Rice, actor Thomas Meighan, the whirlwind editors Walter Howey and Herbert Bayard Swope, grocery magnate Billy Seeman, band leaders Paul Whiteman and Vincent Lopez, and Jim Walker, George Jessel, Gene Buck, Sime Silverman of *Variety*, George M. Cohan, Harrison Fisher, James Montgomery Flagg, Tex Rickard, the Barrymore brothers, Joe Laurie, Jr., Jacob Ruppert, owner of the Yankees, John McGraw of the Giants, James J. Corbett, David Belasco, Al Woods, and many others.

Among the already famous newspapermen and cartoonists who frequented LaHiff's were Damon Runyon, Arthur "Bugs" Baer (who lived in an apartment over the restaurant), Rube Goldberg, Harry Hershfield, Jack Lait, Billy De Beck, Tad Dorgan, W. O. McGeehan, Hype Igoe, Heywood Broun, S. Jay Kaufman, Ring Lardner, Sid Mercer, Stanley Walker, Bob Ripley, Bob Davis, Irvin S. Cobb, O. O. McIntyre, and so many, many others, all of them friends of James J. Walker.

At the close of Mr. Pegler's Era of Nonsense the huge-bodied and bellowing Toots Shor became a combination bouncer-head waiter at LaHiff's. When the kindly and quiet-spoken Billy died of a liver ailment, Toots operated the place for a time. He then established his present-day restaurant. Survivors of the Tavern, as well as a group of younger newspapermen, began to meet regularly at Toots Shor's new chop house.

And there, during the closing years of his life, Jim Walker would go each Friday night with his great friend and physician, Dr. S. Sym Newman, to have supper after the bouts at Madison Square Garden. These Friday nights were the only occasions in his twilight years Jim stayed out late. He enjoyed these weekly reunions with his friends, and everyone looked upon Jim as though he still were the mayor—in the same way that so many of us continue to regard Jack Dempsey as the perennial champion of the world.

8.

Capitol Hill

MEN CAN fall in love with buildings. It was so with James J. Walker in respect to the sprawling capitol at Albany, where he spent sixteen years as a legislator. Those years, he often said, were his happiest ones.

Few persons regard the Statehouse at Albany as the most handsome of public buildings. This pile seems to have been designed by some desperate fellow who during a nightmare envisioned haunted châteaus and then proceeded to spend twenty-three million dollars of public money duplicating his dream.

The capitol stands on a hill and in a park, with Washington Street on one side and State Street on another. An incredible array of stone steps, rising for two stories, makes entry to the building a solid threat to anyone suffering from a heart ailment. Walker told me that as an assemblyman Al Smith trudged up this mountain of steps for two weeks before he learned that an elevator was in operation underneath one side of the stairs.

The state legislature has met in Albany since 1797. It first convened in a structure called the "Stadt Huis." Then, in 1806, and at the cost of a hundred and ten thousand dollars, the solons erected a building just east of the present one. Ground was broken for the more modern capitol two years after the Civil War; but the laying of the cornerstone was delayed until 1871, and occupancy began in 1879. In 1911 a fire swept the western section of the capitol. The State spent two million dollars to repair the structure.

Al Smith took Jim Walker by the hand in 1910 to guide him through the labyrinths of state politics. By tradition, a newcomer to any legislature, state or national, sits back and says little or nothing from the floor. Not so Walker. He immediately began to debate legislative issues, revealing an aptitude for parliamentary tactics which caused Smith to say of him, "This boy is a greater strategist than General Sheridan, and he rides twice as fast."

The newspaper correspondents found in Jim's speeches a sparkling departure from the dronings of minor politicians, of whom Arthur Brisbane once said, "These elected men convince me that politics and government are managed by the intellectual dregs of the population."

Startled by Walker's spirited self-assurance, some of the Republican up-staters sought to put him in his place, but they were unable to counteract his readiness of phrase and epithet. The state lawmakers also were unable to understand how the bouncing New Yorker managed to thrive upon late hours of a social nature. Evenings when other legislators were studying political moves or else slumbering like placid squires, he was out having a gay time. Next day the well-groomed James would pop into the Assembly cloakroom as fresh as a morning glory. True, he sometimes arrived late—but never bedraggled. When the chairman of a committee once reprimanded him for tardiness at a conference, Jim replied, "Mr. Chairman, I sometimes sleep, but the clock doesn't."

Guardian Al Smith admonished his "ward" to be less social and more studious. In later years Al's worries about Jim's butterfly antics became an obsession and finally caused a rift in their friendship. But during the Albany days Al conceded that Jim "got results" as a legislator. Walker soon became the most popular member of the Assembly.

Al pointed out to Jim that other purposeful legislators were applying themselves seriously to matters of state. He cited the perseverance of certain members of the upper house, among them Robert F. Wagner. Wagner was a man to watch, said Smith, a man to emulate. Mr. Wagner had come to the Senate in 1909 and served as majority floor leader of the upper house from 1911 until his election as Lieutenant Governor in 1913.

From time to time during the next years Smith called Jim's attention to other "students" in the Senate. Perhaps James A. Foley was the most industrious of them all. Foley, son-in-law of Tammany Leader Charles F. Murphy, went to the State Senate in 1912, became minority floor leader in 1919, and was succeeded by Jim Walker. The frail-bodied, self-effacing Mr. Foley might have become mayor for the asking, or even governor. Instead, he chose to put on the robes of surrogate in Manhattan.

In 1912 Al Smith said to his protégé, "Why can't you be like Jim Foley? His light is burning late, but he is studying. While you—"

"I'm lit up too, Algie, at that hour," Jim retorted.

To prevent a misinterpretation of Jim's witticism, lest it be taken to mean that he consistently drank to excess, let us discuss the matter on the evidence. Several newspaper correspondents of Jim's Albany days, among them the reliable Charles S. Hand, have told me what I believe to be true: that Walker drank but was not a drunkard. During his youth he drank an occasional glass of beer or wine. At Albany he drank mostly wine. He sometimes had a highball, but he liked wine best, champagne.

According to Robert Newman, Jim's devoted friend in later years, "Anyone who says that Jim never took a drink is making a foolish statement. Anyone who says that Jim never got 'high' is mistaken. But anyone who asserts that Jim was a drunkard is a liar and an enemy."

Jim lacked the bulk of body to burn up large quantities of alcohol. Although he often was seen with a drink in his hand at the close of a long evening of successive banquets, few onlookers realized that his forced gaiety was a result of weariness, not drink. Among the circumstances which contributed to Walker's reputation as a heavy drinker were his stubborn indifference to criticism, his manner of living openly, and his expressed antipathy to Prohibition as a bluenose violation of personal liberty.

His cheeks always had a flushed appearance. Certain critics attributed this ultra-rosiness to his supposed devotion to the bottle. Others sought to convince their gossiping friends that Walker used rouge. Upon one occasion, when Jim was having a tooth extracted (he had been given a general anesthetic), a dentist's assistant actually tried to rub off the supposed rouge with a bit of gauze.

Cartoonist Harry Hershfield told me an anecdote which, I believe, exemplifies the vitality of bad reputations.

One rainy day in 1926 Hershfield came out of the Commodore Hotel and stood on the curb trying to signal a taxicab. He saw an empty cab, but a big black car cut in front of it and the cab went on by. Harry was muttering when Jim Walker stepped out of the black car, his Dusenberg, which Harry in his rage and preoccupation had not recognized.

The Mayor observed Harry's annoyance. "What's the matter, sweetheart?"

Harry explained his troubles, and the Mayor suggested, "I'll tell you what, Harry; I'm going to be in the barbershop for an hour or so. Why don't you let my chauffeur drive you home, or wherever else you care to go?"

Harry set off in the official car. He was tired and slumped down on the seat. The police on Park Avenue saluted the car smartly as it passed the intersections. At Fifty-seventh Street the car stopped for a red light. A sedan drew alongside, and its driver craned his neck to look at the relaxed figure in the official limousine and said to a woman companion, "Look, it's Jimmy Walker. Drunk again!"

An assemblyman in those days received fifteen hundred a year, a senator twenty-six hundred. At these salaries it would seem that, even at a time when a dollar meant what it said on the face of it, an honest legislator might have difficulty in keeping solvent, and an intelligent one be tempted to find employment elsewhere.

"It is as big a mistake," Walker once said, "to believe that politicians can exist only upon the sound of their titles, as it is to think that newlyweds can live solely upon love."

Walker's expenditures as a well-dressed, free-handed legislator were greater than his income, and this meant that he incurred debts. The management of the Ten Eyck Hotel extended credit in a most generous fashion, but wanted to be paid eventually. Jim's room-service bills were large, and always would be. Almost everyone who dropped in to see him made long-distance telephone calls, ordered meals and drinks, and Jim would sign the tab and tip the waiters generously.

Walker's financial strictures, and the fact that his father kept pounding away at him to practice law, caused him at last to take his examinations for the bar. As a practicing attorney, a legislator might have an opportunity to earn a living.

In 1912 thirty-one-year-old James J. Walker passed the bar examinations in Albany. He then informed Janet Allen that he was in a position to take a wife. Allie had been waiting for a long time to hear this news—seven years.

"I would have preferred," says Allie Walker, "to have had our wedding as early in the day as possible. But Jim's love for his pals influenced him to want the ceremony in the late afternoon, so that all who were attending the Democratic convention in the city could be there. And anything he wanted became my own desire."

It so happened that Allie and the wedding guests waited and waited for the groom to reach the altar of St. Joseph's Church.

It was a pleasant April afternoon in 1912, Thursday the eleventh. The trees of the Village were in bud, and all the Walkers and the Roons—except Jim—gathered together with hundreds of their Greenwich Village friends inside the old church on Sixth Avenue. The visiting political delegates occupied the downstairs pews. In the horseshoe-shaped balcony sat many Irish longshoremen who often had voted for Jim's father.

Organist Edward McGoldrick was playing valiantly to make the time pass. The officiating priest, Monsignor John Edwards, was growing warm under his Roman collar. Walker's sister and her husband Luke Burke, whom Nan had married just the year before, waited in an anteroom.

"What's happened to Jim?" Mr. Burke asked his wife.

"The chances are," Nan replied, "he's taking Thursday off with the servants."

"This is an impossible situation," said Mr. Burke, himself a punctual man of business.

"It's never impossible for Jim to be late," said Nan. "In fact, it's probable."

The bridegroom had a valid reason for his tardiness on this April afternoon. He was waiting at St. Luke's Place for his best man, Joseph Hannon, who had the wedding ring in his pocket. Alderman Hannon, with whom Jim had campaigned in 1909, had promised to call with a cab at the Walker home to take Jim to the church, but he was an admirer of fire wagons and fire horses, and on the way he saw bright fire wagons and big horses charging along the street to answer an alarm. To his ears fire bells were sweeter than wedding bells. The driver of the cab was delighted to gallop after the wagons.

Jim and his best man arrived at St. Joseph's more than two hours late.

"A remarkable thing happened at Jim's wedding," says one of Walker's friends, "Rubbernose" Kennedy. "As Jim's pretty fiancée came up the aisle, the organist began to play a part of Jim's 'Will You Love Me in December as You Do in May' song, mixed in with 'Here Comes the Bride!' "

Sitting next to Mr. Kennedy in the church balcony was Mike O'Toole, an ex-pugilist. When the organist interpolated the December song, O'Toole turned to Mr. Kennedy to ask, "What's this they're playin'? What's the chune?"

"It's thick in the head ye are," said Mr. Kennedy. "Don't you know it's Jimmy's song?"

"I know Jim's song," replied O'Toole. "But this sounds mighty slow-like."

"It's a church you're in, man," said Mr. Kennedy. "It's Jimmy's own tune, but they're playin' it in Latin."

The Walkers went to Atlantic City for their honeymoon. At that seaside resort they visited the cafés, ate salt-water taffy, and each afternoon trundled along the wind-blown waterfront in a wheel chair that resembled an oversize baby carriage. Arrayed in a beige polo coat of camel's hair, the bride took the April breeze on the boardwalk. Her Milan straw hat was trimmed with uncurled ostrich plumes dyed to match her coat, and she wore doeskin gloves on her tiny hands.

To all appearances the first years of this marriage were happy ones. "As a husband," Mrs. Walker says, "he was kind and most generous. He was not the domestic type, however. He had a most casual way."

Mrs. Walker says Jim was devoted to her mother and was always courteous to her. "My mother had come East to live with me in 1908," Mrs. Walker continues, "and stayed with us until her death in 1928. She simply adored him. No matter how gay and fun-loving he was, he never forgot his good manners either in private or in public. He would not think of sitting at table without his coat on. And by the way, he wore a vest even in the warmest weather."

Aside from the fact that Jim regarded a waistcoat as a proper article of clothing, the wearing of one permitted him to dispense with a belt or suspenders. His tailor of many years, Jeann Friedman, says that belts or braces made Walker nervous, restrained him, and caused his trousers to hang improperly.

"Mr. Walker had no hips," the tailor says, "so he devised a way to hold up his trousers by means of the waistcoats, both for formal and informal wear. He had me sew on two tabs, with buttonholes in them, inside the lower edge of each panel of the waistcoat front. Corresponding buttons on the waistband of the trousers not only held up his lower garment, but permitted him freedom of movement and prevented any unsightly showing of the shirt between the vest and the pants. He designed all his clothes, and he was a tailor's dream. Together we worked out a design for his coats which allowed him to stoop over when speaking and never show a sag or a 'break' in the lapels or coat-front. His clothes seemed to cling to him perfectly, no matter what his posture. He had broad shoulders, although he was slender in other ways, no stomach, and superb carriage. Whenever he wanted a dressing gown or pajamas, I would accompany him to Sulka's and help him supervise the carrying out of his own design of those garments."

Jim took Allie to live at the Walker house on St. Luke's Place. The couple occupied quarters on the third floor. There were three dining-rooms there. Mr. and Mrs. Walker, Sr., dined in the basement, and it was there that Jim and Allie usually had their evening and Sunday meals. Jim's parents made Allie welcome in their home, and she became quite fond of them.

After the Atlantic City honeymoon Walker received word that Charles F. Murphy wished to see him. Jim was invited to the Tammany leader's town house on East Seventeenth Street. Mr. Murphy ordinarily saw party members at Tammany Hall, where he sat each weekday, beginning at nine-thirty in the morning.

"Only the elite," Walker said, "the sachems and commissioners and their like, were given the honor of meeting Mr. Murphy in his home in New York or at his country place at Good Ground on Long Island. I was small fry, and the summons to call upon the great man at his home excited my interest."

Walker always referred to the Tammany leader as "Mr." Murphy, and so did everyone else. Even James A. Foley called his father-in-law "Mr. Murphy." There were two "misters" on the New York public scene, men who seldom were addressed by their first names. Charles F. Murphy was one; the other was John J. McGraw, manager of the Giants. Mr. McGraw's insistence upon the formal term of reference had its roots in the days when he played for the Baltimore Orioles and earned the nickname of "Mugsy." Heaven help the person who revived that term in the presence of Mr. McGraw!

Occasionally some of the Tammany followers called Mr. Murphy "Commissioner," because of his service as Commissioner of Docks during Mayor Van Wyck's administration.

The Tammany leader had been a horsecar driver, a semi-professional baseball player, a saloonkeeper, and an oarsman. In those days he had been "Charlie" to his friends. Now he was "Mister" or "Commissioner." He, in turn, usually addressed his lieutenants by their appropriate titles and their first names.

Walker went to the Murphy home unaware that the call presaged political promotion. It would be a year and a half before Jim would stand for election to the State Senate, but Mr. Murphy already had made up his mind to make Jim his "boy."

Walker waited in the leader's library, which contained books mostly of a religious nature. "I had met Mr. Murphy occasionally," Jim said, "but I hardly could believe my ears when he entered the library with the words, 'Keep your seat, young man. And how would you like a seat in the Albany Senate?' "

"I hadn't thought of that," Walker replied.

"Well," Mr. Murphy said, "suppose you say nothing about it right now, but start thinking about it."

"I am greatly flattered," Walker said.

"I flatter nobody," said Mr. Murphy. "And I advise you to treat flattery as you would treat abuse. Pay no attention to either."

Walker once wrote to Walter Winchell: "Mr. Murphy could remember further back and see further ahead than the wisest. If the promises he got had been as good as those he made, he would have known few disappointments. He promoted and supported scores of young men who otherwise might never have been heard of, and while these, his creatures, were being cheered, the creator was being jeered."

Jim recollected that his first interview at Mr. Murphy's home was a brief one. The leader told him, "You seem to have many friends on Broadway and in the sports world. Tammany Hall long has neglected these interesting people. I believe you are making us popular there." Mr. Murphy then rose from his chair to terminate the interview. "Assemblyman Jim, success is always a target," he said. "If you are too thin-skinned to stand up under attack, quit the job now."

"I'll never quit, Mr. Murphy."

"No," said the Tammany leader, "I have been watching you, and I believe you have your father's courage."

Outside the Murphy house Walker met another young man on his way up the front stairs. This young man was John J. O'Connor, a friend of Jim's and afterward a member of the editorial staff of *Variety*, the foremost theatrical weekly.

"You must be getting important, Johnny, or you wouldn't be calling upon Mr. Murphy."

"I don't know how important I am," Johnny replied. "And I don't know how important you are either."

"Me?" Jim laughed. "I'm only one of the neighbors' children."

Jim always liked this phrase. Sometimes he would say it with a happy intonation, to describe a man who had risen from obscurity but had managed to remain untouched by vanity. Or he would say it with sad emphasis, as if to invite pity and understanding when some unfortunate man fell from a public pedestal.

9.

The Gallery God

SEE HIM as they saw him then. See James J. Walker in the arena of the lawmakers.

On the third floor of the capitol the Senate chamber rises for fifty feet. The young man from Greenwich Village and Broadway plays his scenes against a background of onyx from Mexico, mellow panels of marble from Siena, reddish-gray marble from Tennessee, granite pillars from the quarries of New England. Watch him stride with feline grace along the red-carpeted aisle toward the president's desk, which commands the room from a dais set halfway between the east and west walls. Two massive fireplaces, with chimney breasts half as high as the room, jut from either side of this tribune. Two flags, their staffs crossed, are displayed upon the wall above the president's rostrum. One flag is the national ensign. The other is the flag of New York, its blue field charged with the arms of state. On a scroll below this flag's silver shield is the motto "Excelsior."

Of all the lawmakers of his time James J. Walker was the favorite of the galleries. See him in the cathedral light that comes from the arched windows of the south wall. The disks of stained glass are multicolored, with varying shades of brown and ruby red, of olive green and sea-water green, gold and lapis blue. These opalescent lenses make music of the sun. In this play of light the young Senator stands like a figurine set against the tapestry of a memorable yesterday.

This actor differs from others in that the lines he speaks are his own. No playwright lends him words. No director tells him how to supply the bits of stage business, the facial play, the toying with his handkerchief, the prefatory cocking of his head, the raising of the brow, the slight tugs at his waistcoat, the brief caress of his diaphragm with a flicking lift of the palms, the well-timed pauses, the occasional upturn of his face toward the galleries that so admire him.

Hear him speak now, extemporaneously always, never hesitating except for effect. His softer tones carry distinctly to the balconies situated respectively north and south above the lobbies, where visitors sit upon steeply pitched mahogany benches. His louder tones spring to the oaken beams of the ceiling, beams more than four feet in depth, resting upon great stone corbels sunk into the walls.

From January until the middle of April each year the senators are in session. On the Monday nights of thirty-odd years ago, at about eight o'clock, the cathedral took on the atmosphere of an opera house. The senators arrived in white ties and tail-coats. The men and women of the audience also wore formal dress. They came by train from Park Avenue and Fifth Avenue and Broadway to see and hear James J. Walker, perhaps the greatest actor of all the political men of the century. David Belasco occasionally sent his actors to Albany "to learn something from the little master."

In a year when men were whistling "Alexander's Ragtime Band," and women reading *Pollyanna*, and the adolescents getting ready to become what Gertrude Stein, the high priestess of double-talk, called "the lost generation," James J. Walker was entering upon his career as a gallery god.

Walker remained in the Senate for eleven years. During the last six of those years he served as Democratic floor leader. There were fifty-one senators in Walker's time; now there are fifty-six. During Walker's years of leadership the political lines were narrowly drawn between Republican up-state and Democratic down-state New York. The difference between a majority and a minority in the Senate was one seat. Walker's spectacular efforts to hold the line when the margin of one vote meant success or defeat for his party still are talked about in Albany. As a debater, conciliator, strategist, and political showman, his record in the red-carpeted hall of laws remains unsurpassed. In oratorical action, he fought with a rapier against barrel staves.

Few persons contend that Walker was a statesman in the accepted sense of the word. Nor did he regard himself as a man whose likeness one day would be carved upon stone mountains. It was impossible for him to conform to a tradition that made public officials act with the gravity of casket salesmen.

"It is imperative," Jim once said, "that our great politicians never laugh, at least not in public."

"But how about Abraham Lincoln and Franklin D. Roosevelt?" he was asked.

"You have named two exceptions," Jim replied. "Nevertheless, Lincoln's laughter invited strong criticism by his contemporaries; and Roosevelt's banterings outraged his solemn adversaries."

"What of yourself?"

"My wisecracks rose many times to plague me," he said, "but I couldn't help laughing, even though I well knew that the public does not trust a banker who is gay, a clergyman who smiles out loud, or a politician who forgets to frown at the news camera."

The Albany correspondents occupied chairs which stood directly below the arrays of clerks of the upper house. Most of these men became Jim's fast friends. He never lied to them. One of the first things a reporter learns is that the vows of public men are as perishable as the promises of lovers. The Associated Press found it expedient years ago to send *two* reporters whenever the great Theodore Roosevelt granted an interview—so that one scribe might corroborate his colleague in the event of a denial. When a man like Jim meets a reporter halfway, his attitude tempers the cynicism which has become an occupational disease among journalists. They will forgive a man for lies meant to shield a lady, but for nothing less.

Nor did Jim hold the reporters personally accountable, as so many petulant officeholders do, if their newspapers assailed him. Mr. Hearst's *American* began to lambaste Walker in 1925, when he was seeking the office of mayor. Instructions from Mr. Hearst reached Albany correspondent Robert Watson to "open up on Walker with all you can find."

Watson was an able reporter and an excellent man as well. The day he received orders to attack Walker, the stunned reporter met Jim in the corridor outside the Senate chamber. The Senator was quick to observe that something was wrong. The reporter seemed, as Jim pointed out, "kind of droopy today."

Watson gave the telegram to Walker to read, then waited for the blow to fall upon their friendship. Instead, Walker clapped Watson's broad back and said cheerily, "What's there to worry about, Bob? Look, if it's material against me that you want, permit me to help you."

The Senator and the correspondent had a drink together, perhaps two. Then Jim began to "dig up" matters detrimental to his own candidacy. When Watson sought to dilute some of the stronger statements, Walker said, "Don't pull any punches. Let's do the thing right. Bad news is good news for the newspapers."

Charles F. Murphy perceived the vast political value to his machine of Walker's agile mind and bouncing personality. The Tammany leader considered Jim a brilliant boy, not too well-balanced in some ways, none too discreet; but Murphy himself would supply the balance and temper the indiscretions—or so he thought until Jim's romances got in the way.

In the Senate Jim immediately found his orbit as a legislator. His spontaneous wit, his courtesy to everyone, began almost at once to pay dividends to his backers. He was the kind of Prince Charming who gave you a toothpick and made you want to give him a fountain pen in return.

Walker's personal life invited so much attention that his very real abilities as a lawmaker have been lost to view. A recital of the bills which Walker introduced or supported to benefit his fellow citizens cannot change the fairy-tale form his legend has taken. Of all his measures, Walker is remembered mainly for having fathered two, and for having supported two others, which had to do with man's indulgence in his own amusements. Walker sponsored a bill to legalize boxing in New York, and another one to permit Sunday baseball games. He supported and put through the Senate a bill to allow motion-picture houses to operate on Sunday. As Democratic whip he managed the repeal of the Mullan-Gage Act, a New York version of the national prohibition amendment.

Buried beneath the thousands of papers which were in the basement vault of Walker's last home, I came upon a thick manila envelope containing the bills introduced by Senator Walker. The yellowing sheaves testified to Jim's concern with the lives of little men and little women, the welfare of neglected children, the rights of underpaid and underprivileged human beings. Finding this envelope among the disordered heap of Walker papers was like coming upon the man's real nature and looking into his secret heart.

Walker's father attended the ceremonial seating of his son at desk No. 18 in the fan-shaped array of mahogany desks and leather-backed swivel chairs of the Senate chamber. The desk number corresponded to that of the senatorial district which had elected Walker. Since that time the senatorial lines have been redrawn, and the old number of Walker's desk and of his district has been changed to nineteen.

Distinguished visitors were permitted a place on the Senate floor behind a high brass railing that separated them from the legislators. Billy Walker was given this courtesy whenever he visited the chamber.

It was with great pride that Billy Walker observed the attention paid his son by eminent men who were so much older than Jim. After the morning session of the first day the Senate convened in January of 1914, Jim declined all invitations to have lunch with party leaders. Instead, he went with his father to his suite on the sixth floor of the Hotel Ten Eyck.

Father and son looked out from the windows of the hotel which Jim would make his Albany home during the next eleven years. They saw sleighs upon the streets, and snow falling upon the rooftops of the city of the Dutch patroons and hiding the hills of the upper Hudson River valley.

Jim told me that his father turned at last from the window. "I'm glad I lived to see this day, Senator," he said.

"You may still call me Jim," said the son.

"It's up to you," said the older man, "whether or not the world will call you President one day."

Jim put his arm about his father and escorted him to a chair. "Let's not be too ambitious, Boss."

"All my ambitions," said Mr. Walker, "are for you."

"I know," Jim said. He was so moved by the signs of happiness on his father's face that he could say nothing but "I know, I know," over and over again.

Jim went to the house telephone and asked the desk clerk to connect him with Joe Fejer's room.

Fejer, a Hungarian violinist, was in Albany for a theatrical engagement. Jim had known him at Bustanoby's café in New York.

When the call was put through, he said, "Joe, this is Jim. Would you mind bringing your fiddle to 601 right away? I have an old friend here who likes music."

Walker hung up the receiver. "Joe Fejer is coming up."

"Have we time for that?" asked Mr. Walker.

"Always time for music."

"I know," said the father. "But hadn't you better go back to work and–"

"Boss, work was never meant for the Irish. We have to eat, don't we? Joe will play while we eat."

When the waiter arrived with a menu Walker urged his father to "order the whole works." He himself selected a light lunch. "And bring some tea afterward," he instructed the waiter.

Father and son now talked about many things. They reviewed the days in the happy household on St. Luke's Place. They spoke of Rosie and of the Roons and of Ireland.

"I'd like to go back to Ireland one day," said the Boss.

"All Irishmen would," said Jim. "The ancient Harps probably intermarried with the homing pigeons brought to Ireland by the Romans."

"To go back to Ireland is my last dream," said Walker's father.

"We'll go together," Jim said.

"I'd like you to see the place where I was born," the father said. "It was a room over a small bank. Ninety miles out of Dublin, it was, in the village of Castlecomer."

"Do I have to wear a silk hat when we go there?" Jim asked.

"I think they'd like to see you in one."

"And my Court of Appeals costume?"

"Yes, all that, and maybe a walking stick."

"Then that's the way I'll dress for Castlecomer," Jim said, "even though I dislike silk hats."

"As I said, it's only a dream."

"It's no dream, Boss, and we'll take Rosie along."

"Jim, I wouldn't even want to go to Heaven without your mother."

The food and the Hungarian violinist arrived almost simultaneously. "Hello, Joe," Jim said to Fejer. "Meet my very best friend."

"Oh," said Fejer, "you're Jim's father."

"That I am," replied the older man.

"Yes," Jim said, "and peculiarly enough, he's also my best friend."

Mr. Fejer winked at Jim. "I expected to find a pretty girl here."

This remark did not please the elder Walker. "My son is a married man, Mr. Fejer," he said with quiet emphasis.

"Joe's only kidding," Jim explained, then asked Fejer, "Will you have a bite with us?"

"I just finished breakfast," replied Fejer.

"Then," Walker said, "would you fiddle while we eat?"

"Glad to." Mr. Fejer opened his violin case. "What would you like to hear?"

Jim turned to his father. "Suppose you order the tunes."

"Play anything you wish," said the older Walker.

Mr. Fejer tuned his instrument. "If Mrs. Walker were here, I'd play some of her songs."

"She's occupied with a group of senators' wives," said Jim. "They're probably debating about hats and shoes."

The Walkers sat down to lunch. Fejer played gypsy music. When the waiter entered the room with the tea, Jim whispered an aside in Fejer's ear. The musician then played a medley of old Harrigan and Hart tunes. The senior Walker's face brightened. Fejer ended his performance with Billy Walker's favorite tune, "Sweet Genevieve."

"The Boss," Jim said long afterward, "suddenly excused himself to go to the bathroom. He returned in a minute or so to say, 'Thanks, Mr. Fejer. It was splendid,' and then to me, like a command, 'Now you get back to the Senate chamber, Jim. You're more than an hour late.' "

Billy Walker lived to see his son become a senator and a successful practicing attorney as well. When at home in St. Luke's Place, Jim always sat at the right hand of the Boss at table. Allie Walker sat at the right hand of Jim's mother. Nan and her husband, and sometimes Jim's brothers, William the doctor of medicine, and George the insurance man, and their wives dined at this congenial table. Jim made everyone laugh, and life seemed good to all.

One day in May of 1916, when Senator Walker was defending a client in Mineola, Long Island, he received a telegram from William to hasten home. He took the suburban train to Jamaica, changed there to another train, and arrived at Pennsylvania Station. His younger brother George was waiting at the train gate.

"What's wrong?" Jim asked.

"Dad's none too well."

"No?" Jim said. "Then why didn't Bill say so in his wire? What's the matter?"

"His heart again."

They went up the stairs to the street exit and hailed a cab. As they got in Jim asked, "Is Bill keeping the Boss out of pain?"

"He has no pain now, Jim."

Jim studied his brother's face. "You're keeping something from me."

"Dad doesn't need a doctor, Jim."

"No!" Jim gripped his brother's arm.

"Yes," said George.

"Oh, no!" said Jim. "That couldn't be! When?"

"Half an hour ago."

Walker disliked swift travel in an automobile, but he now urged the driver to hurry, hurry. The brothers were gravely silent for a time. Then Jim asked, "Did he suffer much?"

"Not long. It came suddenly."

"How's Mother?" Walker asked. "Is she all right?"

"She hasn't shed a tear. And she wouldn't let Bill give her a sedative."

"Oh, my God!" and Walker burst into tears.

"Now, Jim!" said George. "Pull yourself together."

"She'll not outlive him long. I know."

"Now," said George as the cab drew up at No. 6, "try to hold up in front of Mother and Nan."

George stayed behind to pay the cab fare. Jim went up the front steps of his home, a labor, he said, that seemed like climbing a mountain. Inside the house he found his mother seated with a rosary in her hands, seated in tearless silence in Billy Walker's favorite chair.

Jim did not see Nan and William standing at the doorway of the adjoining room. Nan touched William's arm and whispered, "Let them alone for a while." Nan then signaled to George as he entered the house, and all three went to another part of the now melancholy home.

Jim knelt beside his mother, his head resting in her lap. She said nothing for a while, just stroked her son's hair. Finally, and in a restrained voice, Jim's mother said, "Go to the piano and play something, Jim."

Walker looked up in bewilderment. "What are you saying, Mother?"

"I'm saying," she replied, "that you've been neglecting your piano these last months."

"But how can I play it today?"

"Jim," she said, "go to your piano. He loved your playing, and somehow he'll be hearing it."

Jim rose obediently. At the piano he sat for a while in silence. Then he played "Sweet Genevieve."

Walker's mother died in August of 1918.

"Her death," Jim said, "really occurred on that day in May of 1916, when she shed no tears."

10.

The Time of Skyrockets

VARIOUS opinions have been expressed by qualified observers as to just when the period known as the twenties began and when it ended. Some experts say from Prohibition to the election of Herbert Hoover. James J. Walker held that the age commenced with the celebration of the "false armistice" in November 1918 and closed with the election of Franklin D. Roosevelt as President in November of 1932.

Perhaps Jim was thinking in terms of his own career, for these were his skyrocket years of rise and fall.

The false armistice now seems to have been the preview of a mighty play. This dress rehearsal of victory loosed a mass hysteria. Freed from their bloody occupation of destroying one another, men resumed the classic mischief of destroying themselves.

One remembers many things about the premature explosion of peace: the paper storm on Wall Street; the roaring congestion in Times Square; the carnivals in the parks; the block parties in the streets of Manhattan. Oddly enough, one remembers comic details, such as the serpentine fall of a roll of toilet paper from a sixth-floor window of the Waldorf, an unreeling descent of bathroom-tissue to the lap of a dowager seated behind her liveried coachman in an open carriage stalled among the howling dancers on Fifth Avenue.

And there was the impromptu parade in City Hall Plaza. Ponderous Mayor John F. Hylan came out of doors in response to the call of sirens and steamboat whistles.

His Honor was a stolid man, socially clumsy, suspicious of almost everyone. He lacked warmth except when shouting to maintain the five-cent fare on the subway. Mr. Hylan's supporters called him "Honest John." His detractors referred to him as "Red Mike." Today he seemed almost affable, as if touched by an hour of glory.

The red-haired, red-mustached Mayor had been a locomotive engineer for the old Brooklyn Rapid Transit Company before the electrification of that system. After his daytime service as a throttleman, he read law books at night. A superintendent named I. D. Barton fired engineer Hylan one day, when, as Mr. Barton averred, the engine driven by the future chief magistrate almost ran him down. Perhaps Superintendent Barton was in a mood to discharge almost anyone that afternoon. Two of his engines had collided only the day before at Fulton Street and Miller Avenue, and a fireman had been killed. Mr. Barton, summoned to appear within the hour as a witness at the coroner's inquest, was refreshing his memory of the previous day's disaster at the very moment Hylan's engine began to pursue him down the right of way. Upon regaining his safety and his breath, the Superintendent gave the red-haired engineer his walking papers.

An abiding hatred for the traction interests was born that day in the Hylan breast. Heaven help any superintendent who might appear before the bar when Honest John became a judge in Brooklyn! Upon his election as mayor Mr. Hylan became more indignant than ever in respect to traction people and their ways. His crusades to preserve the five-cent fare cost the subway barons many millions of dollars. They never should have fired him.

His Honor led an exemplary life as a family man. He was likable too, once you got to know him. But getting to know him was difficult for New Yorkers. He had a special kind of ability to alienate the representatives of the press, men who might have shielded him from public scorn had he not denounced them as conniving scavengers. His execrations of the traction interests, however worthy in intention, put his audiences to sleep. His loud stubbornness at council meetings, his appalling lack of humor, his heavy hand in dealing with problems which required nicety of touch, gradually estranged the citizens.

Nor did visitors from out of town find him an impressive figure. When President Woodrow Wilson returned from the Paris conference, Mayor Hylan read an address of welcome, but while orating he unintentionally kept his back turned to the guest of honor. Mr. Wilson, according to William G. McAdoo, said of Hylan, "How is it possible for the greatest city in the world to place such a man in high office?"

Notwithstanding his customary grimness, Mayor Hylan became comparatively "gracious" on the day of the false armistice. His smile seemed less artificial than on other occasions. As he appeared at the head of the steps of City Hall a police bodyguard quickly surrounded him. He waved to the throng. They cheered him in return. His Honor—accidentally of course—moved to the spot in front of the west wing of the Hall where, in 1776, a courier from the Continental Congress in Philadelphia had delivered the Declaration of Independence to General George Washington. The Mayor posed for photographs, with the bronze wall tablet which memorializes the event of 1776 as a background.

As the police formed a line for the Hylan procession a loud disturbance arose in the vicinity of the Mayor's party. Two officers were restraining a vociferous fellow who obviously had had a drop, or a quart, too much to drink. He was demanding an audience with the Mayor, instantly.

Mr. Hylan lifted a large hand of authority. "Officers, release that citizen!"

The dubious policemen lowered their night sticks to their sides. His Honor said in his best public voice, "The mayor of this city is always available to its citizens, high or low. Your executive is never too busy to meet a taxpayer. Step forward, sir, if you please, and state your grievance in person to your mayor."

The weaving fellow addressed His Honor with thick words. "Red Mike, I knew you when you was fired as an engineer from the B. R. T. You was a so-and-so then, Red Mike. And you're a so-and-so now!"

The Mayor seemed stunned by this reference to his locomotive past. The officers again seized the man, prodded him briskly with their night sticks, and hauled him out of view. Honest John stared across the park at the shed-like approach to Brooklyn Bridge, where the elevated trains and cross-river trolley cars contributed to the great din of the day.

The Mayor said through his teeth, "The vested traction interests hired that man to come here as a part of their systematic, cold-blooded plot to break down my spirit."

Now a new voice rose from another quarter. Its owner stood upon the stone rim of the pool above which rose the fat marble of the MacMonnies statue of Civic Virtue. The seedy orator, long-haired and hatless, his black beard descending to the collar of a ragged overcoat, was shouting, "Fools! Fools, all of you! You think peace has come. It has not. This is but the beginning of war and more war, hunger and more hunger, strife and more strife. Repent! Repent and pray; for doom descends . . ."

Doom descended upon the prophet in the shape of a policeman, who dragged him down from his sculptured perch. The Bowery Jeremiah was taken to Bellevue Hospital for observation. Time has proved that he was perhaps the only sane man in the city, possibly in the whole world.

Six years from now James J. Walker would succeed the bumbling John F. Hylan as mayor of the City of New York. Currently he was occupied as a senator at Albany and by his law practice in New York. As an attorney for an association of meat-packing companies, he received a rather large retaining fee. This and other sources of income might well have sufficed for the needs of almost anyone else in Walker's position. But Jim's quixotic generosity, his improvident ways, made of his purse a mere port of call.

When James A. Foley resigned from the Senate in 1919, Walker became Democratic leader. Charles F. Murphy now had brought two men of his political as well as his personal favor into broad public view—Smith and Walker.

Survivors of Murphy's regime at Tammany Hall say that their chief not only wished to place Governor Smith in the White House, but also planned to send James J. Walker to the United States Senate. Mr. Murphy regarded his two protégés as an ideal combination: Smith the able administrator, and Walker the nimble carrier of the "legislative ball."

When Smith became a gubernatorial candidate for the first time, Mr. Murphy gave a dinner in his honor at Good Ground. Among the fifty or more guests was the late sportsman Dan McKetrick. McKetrick told me that Mr. Murphy excused himself from the group on the veranda to make a last-minute inspection of the dining-room. The arbiter of New York politics examined the placecards at the head of the table. He made sure that Al Smith's card lay at the right hand of the host's station. Then he picked up another card to the left of the Murphy plate. It bore the name of a sachem. The Tammany leader substituted for that card the one upon which the name of James J. Walker was written. The guests interpreted this to mean that their political overlord regarded Jim as second only to Al Smith in state politics.

On the day Jim became floor leader he put in a telephone call to Mr. Murphy. After a few polite phrases Jim asked, "What about patronage, Commissioner?"

"You're the leader, aren't you, Senator Jim?" Mr. Murphy said. "Use your own judgment. If it's good, you'll be an asset to the party. If it isn't—well, the sooner we find it out, the better."

Of that conversation Jim long afterward wrote to Walter Winchell, "It was the greatest vote of confidence I ever received."

Across the aisle from Jim at Albany sat the Republican floor leader, J. Henry Walters. That Syracuse attorney entered the Senate in 1911 and left it in 1920. During the sessions of 1919–20—the period of Walters' Republican leadership—the duels between the party whips were frequent and theatrical. There was a Republican majority of but one vote in the Senate, the narrowest of margins. The illness or the absence of a member at voting time in the Onyx Room became a matter of consequence to the respective leaders.

However fierce the struggles on the floor of the Senate, Jim and J. Henry Walters remained personal friends. There was a warm bond of affection between them. Away from the Onyx Room Walker called his opponent "Hank." After an oratorical row they would meet for dinner, or attend the theatre together, the best of comrades. At about eleven o'clock of an evening Mr. Walters would go on home and to bed, but Jim—well, Jim subscribed to the code of Richard Harding Davis. That glittering reporter once remarked that a civilized man never goes to bed on the same day he has risen from sleep.

Jim's nights of play meant that he frequently appeared late at a meeting next morning. Senator Walters never spared his friend for this tardiness. One morning, following a night when Walters had been out socially with Jim, the casual New Yorker arrived long after the gavel had fallen upon an important committee meeting.

"Listen, young man," Walters barked, "there'll be only one occasion when you'll be on time; and that will be at your funeral—and then you'll think it's too soon!"

There existed many seemingly odd contradictions in Jim's character. It is not widely known, for example, that he actually feared crowds, but almost always was at the center of one. Robert Newman says that Walker became almost ill with dread when his admirers pressed about him in large numbers or laid hearty hands upon him, and Dr. S. Sym Newman, Walker's physician and friend, confirms this observation in respect to the panic which seized Jim when crowds surged about him. Sometimes, at football games, Walker would have to stand with his back to a wall or a pillar until after the crowd had left; or else leave before the crowd started to go. A few of his close friends knew this and arranged for him to come in through side doors whenever possible.

This accounts for the fact that, when he used to attend the prizefights as mayor, he would have several policemen surrounding him. Most observers thought the police were present as a bodyguard, which was not so in the accepted sense. These officers were there to shield him from the crowd seeking autographs or attempting to slap him on the back. Nevertheless, he would respond to salutations and shake the hands of many people, then, like a furtive quarterback, duck behind the police interference.

It would be a mistake, I think, in the light of the evidence, to attribute Walker's uneasiness among crowds to shyness, as the term is commonly accepted. Mrs. Walker has this to say about it:

"Jim was never shy. He always loved people, and said that his greatest relaxation, when weary, was to go where there was life and music. However, he couldn't stand being mauled, and very much disliked being slapped on the back or having anyone grab hold of his lapels. He had the wonderful faculty of being able to remember names and situations, which made everyone feel they were important to him—and they were, for he loved people. I often think he could have accomplished so much more than he did if his desire to mingle had not been so strong, and had he applied himself more to his duties than to people."

Jim was uneasy in elevators. And he would not learn to drive a motorcar. The man who traveled fastest in a fast-moving age rebelled at a driving speed higher than twenty miles an hour. Walker forbade his driver to sound the official siren installed in his car after he had become mayor. He instructed his chauffeur not only to "go slow" at all times, but to obey every traffic regulation. The praise given Mayor Walker for this seeming "modesty" and "thoughtfulness," his setting a good example for motorists, was undeserved. He simply did not "want to risk being hit when on the road," and the noise of a siren not only got on his nerves, but also "contradicted the atmosphere" of a town car's elegance.

Jim's horror of automobile hazards reminds me of the time only three years ago when I drove Walker from his hotel in Beverly Hills to Robert Newman's studio in North Hollywood, California. One of Jim's friends had died of a heart attack a day or two before. Whenever a friend of Jim's fell gravely ill or had died, Walker complained of having similar symptoms, and his imaginary ailments were many and varied. Were a comrade down with influenza, Walker would begin to sniffle and send for the same kind of pills his friend was taking. A rumor once spread that Walker had cancer. The horrified city did not know that one of Jim's dearest friends had just succumbed to that malady.

Walker had his share of real illness, to be sure, mostly having to do with a stomach that probably suffered from great nervous tension. Allie Walker says that Jim had had stomach trouble before she met him. Also, that his hands were constantly cold to the touch and sometimes clammy. He frequently perspired at night, and this, together with other "symptoms," I am told, presents a picture of a man whose vast nervous energies have been sapped.

This day, during our drive along a canyon road among the Southern California hills, Jim had symptoms of a heart attack, or so he believed. He thought that he should at once consult Newman's brother, Dr. Irving Newman, and have a cardiogram made. While listening to a recital of Jim's latest symptoms, I lost the way at a fork of the road. In backing the car up to turn it around, I brought the rear wheels to within a few feet of the brink of a ravine. During the remainder of the journey he said little or nothing.

As he got out at the studio gate Jim said over his shoulder, "I had fully intended to have my heart examined, but now it is absolutely unnecessary. I *know* beyond peradventure that I have the disease in its most wicked form."

Other contradictions in Jim's behavior come to mind. His readiness of words when seeking favors for his friends deserted him when he wanted something for himself. He was so timid in this respect that he would send Newman or some other crony on ordinary missions, such as the procurement of theatre tickets. Perhaps Jim's strange reluctance in this respect came from a sense of pride, an unwillingness to expose himself to the possibility of a refusal.

Still another aspect of Jim's behavior was demonstrated whenever the laggard fellow was suddenly roused to prodigious and sustained efforts as a legislator or as an administrator of public affairs. There was nothing lackadaisical or halting about his manner then.

As a rule his speeches were much more forceful and fluent at the time of utterance than they now emerge from the voiceless page; and his powers of persuasion went beyond the political speeches he made. He seemed to possess the qualities of an evangelist. This was so even when he was away from the larger public. A group of harried baseball men once called upon him to "reform" Babe Ruth. It was at the close of a season when the famous athlete's careless way of living had damaged his work. "The Bambino," as the sports writers called the home-run king, liked to stay up late, drink whatever he pleased, and eat enough to sustain a family of giants.

When Manager Miller Huggins of the New York Yankees threatened to suspend the Babe for his numerous breaches of training rules, Ruth replied, "I didn't have a thing till I was eighteen years old, not a bite, not a pair of shoes. Now it's bustin' out all over."

The baseball writers asked Walker to attend a dinner for Ruth at the Elks Club, and plead with the guest of honor to "see the light." When Jim rose to speak, the Bambino clapped heartily, but soon thereafter sat back like a stunned hippopotamus. Walker opened his speech with the words, "Babe Ruth is not only a great athlete, but also a great fool."

The incredulous Babe seemed deflated as Walker went on, "His employer, Colonel Jacob Ruppert, makes millions of gallons of beer, and Ruth is of the opinion that he can drink it faster than the Colonel and his large corps of brewmasters can make it. Well"—and Jim turned to the amazed Ruth—"you can't! Nobody can."

Senator Walker pointed a finger at Ruth. "You are making a bigger salary than anyone ever received as a ball player. But the bigger the salary, the bigger the fool you have become."

Walker let this remark sink in, then resumed, "Here sit some forty sportswriters and big officials of baseball, our national sport. These men, your friends, know what you have done, even if you don't. They are sad and dejected. Why? I'll tell you. You have let them down!"

Walker again paused, and Ruth began to squirm. "But worst of all"—and Jim moved in for the kill—"worst of all, you have let down the kids of America. Everywhere in America, on every vacant lot where the kids play baseball, and in the hospitals too, where crippled children dream of the movement forever denied their thin and warped little bodies, they think of you, their hero; they look up to you, worship you. And then what happens? You carouse and abuse your great body, and it is exactly as though Santa Claus himself suddenly were to take off his beard to reveal the features of a villain. The kids have seen their idol shattered and their dreams broken."

At first Ruth's face had shown anger and resentment. But now he was sobbing. His sobs shook not only the Babe's massive chest, but seemed also to shake the table and the chairs.

Walker permitted Ruth time to weep, then placed a kindly hand upon the most famous shoulders in baseball. "If we did not love you, Babe, and if I myself did not love you sincerely, I would not tell you these things." More sobs from Ruth. Then came Walker's solemn question, "Will you not, for the kids of America, solemnly promise to mend your ways? Will you not give back to those kids their great idol?"

With a Gargantuan cry Ruth exclaimed, "So help me, Jim, I will! I'll go to my farm at Sudbury and get in shape."

Mr. Ruth, his eyes still moist, shook hands all around, then went to the elevator with his friend and mentor, Christy Walsh, patting his back. Downstairs a process server intruded upon the contrite Bambino to tag him with a summons to appear in a lawsuit. The great athlete roared with anger, gave the process server a piece of his mind, then went sadly home instead of to a pub.

The next year the Babe faithfully kept his promise to Jim, made a new home-run record, and at the close of the season was voted the most valuable player of the year.

Sometimes, in private life, Jim seemed to possess the qualities of a faith-healer. He who complained so often of ills which were largely imaginary could lift the spirits of invalids and instill in them the will to recover.

During Walker's fifth year in the Senate he left Albany during a busy session to be operated on for a hernia. At Broad Street Hospital in New York the hernia was surgically corrected, and the Walker appendix removed at the same time.

Each morning Miss Mildred Day, secretary of the law firm with which Jim was associated, would take Walker's mail to the hospital. The second morning after Jim's operation Miss Day observed a chocolate bonbon on the table beside his bed. Jim seldom ate sweets. Whenever he did, he preferred licorice to any other candy. Miss Day asked if the bonbon had been "prescribed" for him.

"Not for me," Jim replied. "Wait here and you'll see."

After a while a little girl of five or six came into the room. She seemed to be suffering from paralysis, wore braces on her legs, and had great difficulty using her arms and hands. The child did not speak, just looked at Jim, who smiled at her and indicated the piece of candy.

The little visitor had so much trouble that Miss Day moved as if to hand the bonbon to her. Walker shook his head. "Reach for it, Irene," he said.

The child made several attempts to pick up the candy and finally succeeded. Then she left the room without a word.

Miss Day saw this performance repeated each time she delivered the mail to the hospital. Every morning the candy was a little farther back on the table, "Reach, Irene, reach!" Walker would say. On his last day at the hospital Miss Day was amazed to see Irene pick up the little present at the first attempt, and do it with comparative ease.

The doctors at the hospital said, "We can't explain the sudden improvement in the condition of this child. We are unable to predict that she ever will be able to go without the leg braces, but it now seems a possibility. We are almost certain, however, that she will regain the full use of her arms and hands."

Against the advice of his friend and colleague in the Senate, Dr. William L. Love of Brooklyn, Walker left Broad Street Hospital a week too soon, to return to Albany.

Howard A. Shiebler, then a correspondent for the *Brooklyn Daily Eagle*, says that he never saw a better example of courage than the convalescing Senate leader displayed. When the day for adjournment finally was reached on April 10, 1924, some of the senators had been without sleep for forty-eight hours. The clerks had not been to bed for three nights. The session was supposed to end at twelve o'clock, but it was almost ten the next morning before the gavel of adjournment fell.

"At midnight," Shiebler recalls, "the journal clerk had completely lost his voice. It had been getting thicker and less easy to understand since early in the evening. Walker, in full dress clothes, stepped to the desk and took the clerk's place. He read the bills in a clear voice, and I can still see him, seated behind the little cage, smartly clad in his tail-coat and stiff-bosom shirt, really a sick man who just recently had been operated on and who belonged in the hospital, but looking as fresh as a lily to the end. It was the first time within my memory that a Senate leader had taken the place of the clerk."

When Jim played, which was often, he played hard. When he worked, which was more often than his critics would admit, he got things done. This was true at Albany, and it was true when he became mayor of New York.

Mayor William O'Dwyer, whom no one, I think, would accuse of laziness in office, said to me, "After some personal experience with the vast business of City Hall, and after a close study of the records of my distinguished predecessors, I must admit that Jim Walker as mayor got more things done in two hours than any of the rest of us could do in ten."

The greatest contradiction of all in respect to Jim's character, I think, is that he performed so brilliantly in a career undertaken against his own personal desires. His devotion to his father had influenced him to enter politics and the law. His admiration for Charles F. Murphy had kept him in the legislature. A war-tired city's discovery of the gay, well-dressed phrase-maker, and its adulation of him, made of Walker a hero, and finally a victim of the age. He became irrevocably bound to the times, and would rise and fall with the era which created him.

"At heart," says author Ben Hecht in a letter, "Walker was a troubadour headed for Wagnerian dramas. No man could have held life so carelessly without falling down a manhole before he was done."

Among the notes which I took during my last conversation with James J. Walker I find these words: "The excitement of politics got into my veins. I had happy years in the Senate, but always my heart was in the theatre and in songs. I really was moving against my own desires most of the time, and the inner conflicts were great. I knew how to say 'no,' but seldom could bring myself to say it. A woman and a politician must say that word often, and mean it—or else.

"I think I would be ungrateful and a liar were I to make excuses for myself or blame others for anything catastrophic that happened to me. Nor can I honestly say that I remained passively on the sidelines, a mere spectator, when the exigencies of war were past. The minds of men were turned inside out, and women were given simultaneous access to the voting booths and to the speakeasy bars. In those days Samson broke training, and Delilah cut her own hair. There are Pied Pipers playing after every war. Can't you hear them now? All pipers must be paid, and paid in full. I know. I was the piper's favorite customer."

Whether or not Walker was miscast when he became mayor of the City of New York, as some men have asserted, his career as a senator at Albany was a brilliant one. Few men have possessed such genuine abilities as Walker displayed on the Senate floor. My very good friend Charles S. Hand, onetime political correspondent of the *Morning World*, describes him as "a meteor among Roman candles." Other correspondents of Walker's time, among them Mr. Shiebler, say that only two Republican Senate leaders could make Walker extend himself in debate: J. Henry Walters and George Fearon.

"These Syracuse senators," Shiebler writes to me, "were smart and could think when on their feet. They possessed a great deal of Jim's urbanity. Walters was smooth, suave; Fearon, tall, good-looking, aggressive. They kept Jim always on his toes."

Senator Walters tells me, "I have seen Jim appear in the Senate day after day absolutely unprepared, and have seen his secretary, Edward L. Stanton, bring him an analysis of a bill. With an immediate grasp of its meanings, Jim would rise to make a fine speech. He was a fast, masterful debater. He handled all situations with drama and wit, the most difficult things for an opponent to combat."

One of the fiercest battles Jim conducted in the legislature occurred during the ratification of the Eighteenth Amendment. Senator Walker opened his speech of opposition with, "This measure was born in hypocrisy, and there it will die."

Walker correctly predicted that Prohibition would cause widespread disrespect of law and be impossible to enforce. "In fact," he said, "even the Army and Navy of the United States are not large enough to enforce this unenforceable mockery."

It was Majority Leader Walters' desire to keep his own personal opinions on Prohibition off the Senate record. He privately opposed the measure, but for him to speak or act against it from the Senate floor meant that his party would be embarrassed and his leadership doomed. The Volstead Act became as repugnant to Senator Walters as it was to Jim Walker when the dry lobby brought extreme pressure upon the New York legislators to ratify it.

The dictatorial leader of this lobby was William H. Anderson. This middle-aged crusader had been Superintendent of the Anti-Saloon League in New York State since 1914. A large-bodied, glossy-mustached man of belligerent piety, he stalked the legislative halls in a black frock coat, and his manner was that of an Old World executioner.

As champion of the Eleventh Commandment, "Thou shalt not tipple," this grim moralist threatened the ruin of any senator who opposed his will. He pounced upon the circumstance that Senator Walters had managed to keep his own views off the record. Anderson determined that Walters be smoked out, lest the Republican majority of one become snarled in a tie vote.

Anderson seemed especially anxious to remove Walters from the influence of the Senator's good friend James J. Walker, and if possible to destroy Jim as well. Mr. Anderson daily occupied a front-row seat in the steeply banked gallery to hear the up-state senators assail James J. Walker. One of the Republicans, Senator Ross Graves of Buffalo, opened his attack by reading a letter in which two little girls explained that their father had gone to Dannemora Prison for a murder committed during a drunken rage. " 'Help bring papa home,' " the Senator read, " 'for he was a good papa.' "

The speaker restored the letter to his desk, then pointed at Walker. "Would the Senator from New York dare deny that the liquor traffic is murderous? Or that our prisons and madhouses are full of its victims?"

Walker sprang up from his chair. "I would like to go with the Senator from Erie County to Dannemora Prison 'to bring papa home,' if, in return, the Senator will go with me to bring home from Bloomingdale Asylum the host of religious fanatics and cranks who never have tasted liquor in their lives and yet have committed the most atrocious crimes."

Toward the close of the ratification debate the Republican senators called a caucus to decide how they were to cast their votes.

Senator Walters conferred with his friend Jim. "If I go into that caucus chamber," he said, "I'll have to pledge my support of the measure or else resign my leadership."

"Just refuse to attend," Jim counseled him. "You have the respect of everyone except Anderson. Nobody will dare remove you from the leadership if you stay away from the caucus."

"No, Jim," said Walters. "I'll go in and try to convince them how wrong they are."

After the caucus the Republican senators filed into the Onyx Room. Walters seemed dejected. Jim said that his first intention had been to "sail into" Walters, but he changed his mind when he observed Hank's stricken appearance.

Walker later said that as he strode into the center aisle to speak the plight of his friend made him tongue-tied. "Ordinarily we would not hesitate, either of us, to bring out our sharpest swords, battle it out, bleed a little, then sit down to a friendly glass. But when I saw Hank sitting there in defeat I could not add to his sorrow by hitting at him. I finally began to mumble, saying practically nothing, and saying it badly. I groped for an idea. Then something happened."

As Jim stood in a confused state of mind beside Senator Walters' desk, he chanced to look up at the gallery, and there was the triumphant Mr. Anderson. "He was leaning on the gallery railing," Jim said, "and his face seemed like that of a well-fed owl."

With a roll of the tongue inside his cheek, a flick of his handkerchief, and a glance all around, the minority leader began one of his impromptu allegories. He pointed at Senator Walters, then said in a sorrowful voice, "Here sits poor Uncle Tom Walters, my old friend, though my political enemy, forced into doing the thing he hates, crushed and beaten."

The fact that Jim now reshuffled two of Mrs. Stowe's heroines went unnoticed as he went on, "And here is Little Eva, the State of New York, betrayed into shame and humiliation, about to cross the Hudson River on the cakes of ice dropped from the hearts of bigots."

Walker then pointed to Anderson and thundered, "And there, above, sits Simon Legree Anderson, who, though he hasn't a whip in his hand, bears one in his heart."

Anderson removed his elbows from the gallery rail. The usually self-contained lobbyist for once seemed uncomfortable as Walker's voice boomed, "Uncle Tom is saying, 'My body belongs to you, Massa, but my soul belongs to de Lawd!' "

Then, in a hoarse whisper, a theatrical change of pace which Jim always managed with dramatic effect, he slowly turned to Walters, "Your body belongs to the Anti-Saloon League, but I hope your soul still belongs to yourself."

The gallery applauded. Many senators rose to congratulate Jim as he left the aisle. When order had been restored the vote was taken. The drys won. Jim had lost—for the time being.

Some four years after this victory, on a cold March day, Mr. Anderson arrived at the Hall of Records to surrender himself to Sheriff Peter J. Dowling. He had been tried on a forgery charge and sentenced to a term in Sing Sing Prison.

When Walker was told that Anderson had gone inside the prison walls, to have his glossy mustache shorn and to exchange his black frock coat for a uniform with a number on it, Jim said, "No matter what a man has done, there is always a sad something about the closing of prison gates. Instead of gloating over the downfall of one man, we should try to correct the causes of bigotry. War is one cause. Bigotry springs like a crop of weeds from every battlefield. The worst drunkenness is not from wine, nor is it to be found only among the scattered weak ones. The whole world has been on a drunk, and its drink was not wine but the blood of young men."

11.

The Point of View

It was a part of Jim Walker's philosophy never to underrate a courteous antagonist. He once lectured a portly journalist friend, whom we shall call Ernest, on how *not* to pick quarrels. When drinking among chance acquaintances, the ordinarily good-tempered Ernest frequently became involved in fistfights. The journalist always came out second best in these affrays. When Jim Walker admonished him, Ernest was wearing courtplaster on his chin, and a piece of raw beefsteak over one eye.

"If you must fight," Jim advised the battered Ernest, "never 'choose' the quietest person in the saloon—the little fellow sitting in a corner minding his own business. The chances are that he is the ex-welterweight champion of the world."

In the Senate, during Jim's time, there sat a quiet-spoken man, described by Walker as "a slumbering arsenal." Senator John Knight had come from the village of Arcade, a place of less than twenty-five hundred population, in Wyoming County. The up-state Republican Senator was accounted the most polite member of the legislature. A scholar as well as a lawyer, he could muster his facts and then project them with a clarity that made up for his lack of oratorical gusto.

It was Senator Knight's habit to inject recurrently into his remarks the phrase "From my point of view . . ." On one occasion he rose to speak against a measure sponsored by Walker. "From my point of view," he began, and went on to say that Majority Leader Walker was making an honest but ghastly mistake in bringing this particular bill to the Senate floor. Jim soon realized that Senator Knight's speech was a machine gun equipped with a Maxim silencer, and that the "point-of-view" logician was shooting the Walker measure to pieces.

The crafty Mr. Walker rose to ask if the Senator from Wyoming County would "yield for a story." Jim's courteous opponent replied that he would be glad to do so.

"I am greatly impressed," Walker said, "by the Senator's 'point of view.' It reminds me of a story my late father once told me. There was a good man in Greenwich Village some seventy years ago, and he had one obsession—a worthy one to be sure—the welfare of the American Indians. He dedicated his fortune, which was considerable, and his efforts, which were vast, to the correction of abuses practiced upon the Indians by the exploiters of their people and of their lands. This man had a son whom he invited to go with him on an expedition to the wild West to see at first hand how the white men were victimizing their red brothers. He said to his son, 'From my point of view, the Indians are the most noble martyrs in all history.'

"The father and son," Walker continued, "came to a ravine in a western wilderness and were seeking a means to cross it when they saw a human being stretched out, helpless, on the floor of the chasm.

" 'Isn't that an Indian, Papa?' the lad inquired.

" 'From my point of view,' replied his father, 'it not only is an Indian, but an important chieftain. No doubt he is desperately ill from malnutrition brought about by some stingy government agent. Climb down, son, for you are younger than I, and much more nimble. And report to me the extent of this stricken chief's plight.'

"The son obeyed. Soon after he had reached the unconscious redskin, he called up, 'Papa, this person is dead!'

" 'Aha!' exclaimed the father. 'Dead, is he? Well, son, from my point of view, this great chief was murdered by a careless government. From my point of view, this noble chief–'

" 'But, Papa,' the son interrupted, 'from my point of view the chief is a squaw!' "

Walker sat down. The logic of the Senator from Wyoming County was lost in laughter.

I am obliged to Stanley Walker, the last of New York's great city editors, for another of Jim's Indian "parables."

In Stanley Walker's opinion, Al Smith and Jim had begun to drift apart as early as 1923 but kept their differences from public notice. Senator Walker's offstage antics were not the only reason for Smith's growing annoyance with Mr. Murphy's bright protégé. As an "elder" of the Tammany Temple and as governor, Smith believed that whenever he gave a political command Jim should obey it. The Governor also thought it undignified for Jim to call him "Algie." As for Jim, he regarded Mr. Murphy, and not Smith, as the infallible arbiter of party policies.

Smith's splendid record as governor caused him to glance occasionally in the direction of the White House. He sought to avoid needless embroilment in "local" issues, of which the five-cent fare in New York City was one, and tried to keep the traction interests, as well as their loud foe Mayor Hylan, out of his hair. According to Stanley Walker, in 1923 Smith was of a mind to put through legislation permitting the subway proprietors to charge seven cents instead of a nickel and have done with the whole business. He called Jim to the executive office in the capitol and requested the Senate leader to instruct his colleagues to get busy on the seven-cent-fare "solution."

"Before I do that," Jim said, "I want to tell you a story, Algie."

"Never mind the stories," the Governor replied. "Just go in there and tell 'em what to do."

But the Senator was determined to have his say. "There was an old Indian chief out West, and he had six wives. He was very happy with them. But the government agent said, 'Chief, you'll have to get rid of those wives, all but one. Go tell 'em.' A month later the government agent called the chief in again. 'Chief, you haven't paid any attention to what I said. Let me repeat: you must get rid of all those wives of yours but one.' Another month rolled by, and the agent once more reprimanded the chief. 'For the last time, I want you to go tell those extra wives of yours to get out!' The chief looked at the agent, then said, 'You tell 'em!' "

Smith's proposed traction legislation was held in abeyance.

From Smith's "point of view" Walker was a gadfly. The Governor often railed in private at Jim's tricks, and one of those occasions occurred when the Walker bill to legalize and control professional boxing was passed. Jim told me the "inside" story, one which I have never come upon in print. Much to my astonishment, I learned from Jim that Smith had been strongly, almost violently opposed to that bill.

The history of pugilism in America goes back to the year 1816, a time of bare knuckles and spiked shoes, when Jacob Hyer fought and defeated Tom Beasley. The sport was illegal almost everywhere in the United States until the 1880's. In 1896 the New York legislature enacted the Horton Law, which legalized gloved boxing bouts. The hoodlum brotherhood, which stands ready at all times to exploit mankind's physical enjoyments, soon put a stranglehold on the sport. During the last four years of the century the surething gamblers, crooked fight managers, corrupt officials, and sometimes the ox-brained pugilists themselves, made of boxing a grab-bag of fakery and fraud. Governor Theodore Roosevelt brought about the repeal of the Horton Law in 1900.

The New York fighters hung up their gloves for the next ten years. The crooked managers and gamblers transferred their talents to other precious fields, such as the race tracks or the houses of prostitution. Then, in 1910, Senator James J. Frawley of New York City sponsored a bill to re-establish boxing, with "safeguards."

This law permitted clubs to charge admission for the bouts but limited the exhibitions to ten rounds instead of twenty-five. The

Frawley measure also stipulated that a referee give no decision if both contestants in a fight remained on their feet at the final bell.

Sports followers objected to the no-decision rule. The enforced silence of the referee seemed an anticlimax. A public which bet on the outcome of sports events—and gambling is an incurable disease—cried out against the hardship of being unable to give their money to pugilism's harpies, and having to waste it instead on their wives and children.

Professional gamblers, like lovers, always find a "way." Together with certain managers, the bookmakers agreed to abide by, and pay off on, the printed opinions of sportswriters whenever a boxing bout lasted ten rounds. Quite often when a manager knew that his gladiator had been outpointed, he would call a messenger boy and write telegrams to out-of-town sports desks. His wires would reach their various destinations before the poll of ringside experts got there. The telegrams sent by managers contained one or both of two themes: "My boy won by a mile," or, "We was robbed by crooked New York sportswriters."

The gamblers flourished. An incompetent boxing commission failed to control other aspects of the sport, and in 1910 Governor Charles S. Whitman prevailed upon the legislature to repeal the Frawley Law.

In 1918 William A. Gavin, an English sportsman, arrived in America with a plan to organize boxing after the manner in which the National Sporting Club of London conducted it. Gavin's rules modernized the code furnished in the 1860's by the Marquess of Queensberry. Instead of one arbiter there would be three. Two judges, seated on opposite sides of the ring, were to participate equally with the referee in handing down decisions. The theory of this arrangement was that gamblers would find it much more difficult to "fix" three men. Do I hear flutes?

Primarily, Mr. Gavin did not aspire to restore boxing as a public spectacle but to present it to the "fancy," the members of athletic clubs. Gavin was informed that his plan could not be carried out unless a bill was passed to legalize boxing. He thereupon turned over his rules and his plan to James J. Walker.

Senator Walker revised and expanded the Gavin pattern. Among other things, he provided for the appointment by the governor of unsalaried boxing commissioners; the licensing of everyone concerned, from the promoters down to the boxers' seconds; the proper punishment of anyone who violated the rules; and a guarantee that a spectator be given the seat for which he had paid.

In other days a ticket-buyer might arrive at a boxing match only to find a politician or a gangster occupying the seat which the trusting customer had purchased. Have you ever tried to argue with a member of either of these professions? And if so, in which hospital did you regain consciousness?

Walker was minority leader at the time he introduced the bill. It came before the Senate during Al Smith's first term as governor. Jim's good friend, Majority Leader Walters, had no personal objections to the measure. The lobby of moralists, however, did object to it. And Al Smith wished to avoid exposing himself to the barrage of muck hurled by the lobbyists.

When Jim proposed the bill—with Mr. Murphy's blessing, as Walker told me—Governor Smith said to him, "Leave me out of it. I'm sitting on the sidelines, Jim, and there I propose to remain."

One of Jim's well-wishers in respect to boxing legislation was Major Anthony J. Drexel Biddle of Philadelphia. During his young days Biddle had written a collection of whimsical tales, *The Froggy Fairy Book*. Notwithstanding the delicacy of his printed works, and despite his prerogatives as a member of one of America's first families, the millionaire Major was all man. He was an amateur boxer and could lick almost any professional. He also had been an officer in the U. S. Marines. And he was the founder and patron of a Bible society which had a membership of more than two hundred thousand students in many lands. His blood was blue and red at the same time.

Major Biddle thought highly of Jim as a person and of Jim's boxing crusade. Together they decided to place pugilism on a "clean basis." Major Biddle had to attend to business in Philadelphia much of the time, but kept in daily touch with Jim by long-distance telephone. When the Walker bill had cleared the legislature and reached Al Smith's desk, the Governor failed to sign it.

Jim called at the executive office. "How about the boxing bill?"

Smith lighted a cigar, puffed at it, looked out of a window, then replied after a long silence, "Jim, you're not going to get away with this."

"Get away with what?"

"You know what. You'll not put this bill over on me *or* the public."

"The public wants it, Al."

"What public?" Smith said in an angry tone. Without permitting Walker a chance to reply, he went on, "You know as well as I do that the boxing game is nothing but a refuge for crooks, thieves, cheats. A low, rotten business."

"You've been listening to the puritans, Al. I've been listening to thousands of sports-minded people. They want boxing."

Smith, according to Jim, struck the desk with his fist. "Baloney! I'll not sign this bill."

Walker rose to leave. "All right, Algie. If you want to become unpopular, I can't help it." At the doorway Jim turned. "Mr. Murphy seems to think it a good bill."

"Don't quote Mr. Murphy to *me*," Al said. "I think I know him as well as you do, maybe better. He's given me no advice whatsoever about this bill. My hand is free." Then Smith added, "I suppose you'll go whining to him about this? Well, go whine!"

Jim's temper flared. He returned to Smith's desk. "Let me tell you something man to man, Al. You've never heard me tell tales to anyone. And if you're the Al Smith I've known all these years, you'll take that back."

Smith relented. "Jim, I'm sorry about what I said. No, you're not a tale bearer or a whiner."

"Thanks."

"But you've put me on a spot with this bill."

"You're putting yourself on a worse spot, Al, by pampering a few reformers at the expense of thousands upon thousands of sports lovers."

Smith thought for a time, then said, "I'll tell you what, Jim. This is Friday afternoon. I'll keep the bill on my desk till Monday morning. If, between now and nine o'clock Monday morning, you can get one hundred representative clergymen to sign their names to letters or telegrams—legitimate and bona fide communications, my boxing friend—and they approve this bill, then, and then only, will I sign it."

"Al," Jim said, "have I your word?"

"You have."

As Jim turned to go Smith called out, "Just a minute! There must be no misunderstanding."

"About what?" Jim asked. "I have your word; and I've got till Monday evening to get the fifty signatures."

"Monday *morning*," Smith corrected him. "And *one hundred* signatures." He paused, then fired point-blank, "*All of them must be Protestants*!"

"Protestants?" Jim began to worry.

"You heard me. If I didn't make this stipulation you'd get fifty Catholic priests who like boxing and coax fifty rabbis who are nuts about Benny Leonard. I want one hundred Protestant ministers of the gospel to say to me personally and in writing that they are in favor of the boxing bill."

"Some of the greatest sportsmen of my acquaintance," Jim said, "are Protestants."

"But not ministers of the gospel," Al replied as Jim was leaving the room.

In his own office Jim put through a telephone call to Major Biddle. "We're sunk!" Jim said and went on to explain Smith's stand. "How in the world, especially over a weekend, can we get one hundred Protestant ministers to send letters to the Governor?"

Major Biddle's calm words came over the wire, "Don't worry about a thing, Jim."

"Did you say 'Don't worry'?" Jim asked incredulously.

"Just leave everything to me."

"But what do you want me to do, Major? Rather, what *can* I do?"

"Do nothing at all, Jim," replied the Major. "Just relax between rounds."

On Monday morning Jim rose earlier than usual to telephone to Philadelphia. He failed to reach Major Biddle, and he could not find out from other sources whether or not one hundred Protestants had come to the rescue. Jim yawned, contemplated his pillows, and was about to return to bed when the telephone rang. Al Smith's secretary said that the Governor wished to see Senator Walker at once.

Jim dressed in a leisurely manner, as always, then called at Smith's office. The executive growled, "Took your time, eh? Well, I suppose you think you're a great man? Bigger than the Governor?"

"Sorry I'm late. What goes on, Governor?"

Smith rose slowly. "Don't try to be cute! You can't be cute with *me!*" He moved to a table upon which lay a pile of letters and telegrams and glared at them for a while. "I don't know *how* you did it. I simply don't know," he said.

Walker sensed that, in some miraculous fashion, the ministerial letters and telegrams had arrived on time.

"It's all very simple," Jim said with a straight face. "Protestants also like boxing."

"Well," said Smith returning to his desk, "my word is good. That much is certain."

"Never doubted that for an instant, Al."

"I'll never understand it," Smith said as though to himself. "There are over six hundred letters and telegrams. Now I've seen everything!"

"Did you call me over to watch you sign the bill?"

Smith squinted at Walker. "Oh, go back to bed and dream up some other tricks!"

"You do me a great injustice, Algie."

"Baloney!" roared Al. "Get out!"

In his hotel suite Walker telephoned Major Biddle. "How the devil did you do it?" he asked. "There are more than six hundred letters and telegrams on Al Smith's desk!"

"The devil had nothing to do with it, Jim. Just the opposite. You see, I recently gave another half-million dollars to my Bible society. I merely requested our New York office to notify the state membership about the worthiness of the boxing bill. We are a congenial organization."

From the "point of view" of his friendly foes in the Senate, Walker seemed a resourceful dramatist. His methods in this respect were demonstrated during the fight to repeal the Mullan-Gage Act.

This measure had been enacted by the Republican drys of New York State to complement the national Volstead Act. Its enforcement costs burdened the taxpayers, and for other reasons also it became as unpopular as garlic in the bottling parlors of M. Coty's palace of perfume.

When the time came to debate the repeal measure, Majority Leader Walker was nominally in command of twenty-six Democratic votes, as against twenty-five Republican votes. Quite unexpectedly he found himself facing defeat. Two of his party members were "lost," or so it then appeared.

One of them was his crony John Hastings, the twenty-three-year-old Senator from Kings County. Hastings had been elected by a normally Republican district in Brooklyn. Now, with the repeal vote imminent, he lay in a Brooklyn hospital, a thermometer in his mouth and pneumonia in his bronchial tubes.

The other "lost" legislator was Mark W. Allen, a Staten Island schoolmaster. Allen was a teetotaler, although he had been elected by a wet district. On the morning of the roll-call Senator Allen failed to put in an appearance. Walker delayed the call-to-order and started a man hunt.

Peter Higgins, son of Senator Pat Higgins, was the first of Walker's "detectives" to report back to Jim.

"He's right outside the capitol," said Higgins, "cranking his car."

"Help!" Walker cried. "That means he's going home without voting. Thinks he can play both ends against the middle! Salve his conscience by not voting for repeal, and at the same time escape the wrath of his wet constituents by not voting against it!"

Walker called for the sergeant-at-arms of the Senate, Jerry Sheehan. "Jerry, catch Senator Allen and bring him back, preferably alive."

"But, Senator," said Sheehan, "what if—"

"If nothing! Tell him the Senate is still in session, and he can't leave before the vote is taken."

"But what if—"

"Then arrest him!"

Jim motioned to his secretary, Edward L. Stanton. "We'll hide till after the explosion." They left Walker's office and concealed themselves in a near-by room from which they could see and hear anything that might happen.

After a few minutes had gone by the corridor began to resound with pedagogical outcries. The hidden onlookers saw the unwilling Senator being propelled by the sergeant-at-arms into Walker's office. The Staten Island educator broke away from his captor, but Officer Sheehan leaped in front of him. "You'll never get out alive, Senator," said Sheehan with dismaying emphasis.

"*This* is the psychological moment," said Walker to his companion, "for us to rescue our Staten Island friend."

Walker and Stanton sauntered into the office. The outraged Allen was being held down in a chair by the sergeant-at-arms.

Jim was appropriately shocked. "What in the world is going on?"

"That man," and Senator Allen pointed, "arrested me!"

"No!" Jim turned to Sheehan. "Am I to understand that you arrested a senator?"

Sheehan nodded, and Senator Allen blurted out, "Not only that, but he assaulted me!"

Jim recoiled in pretended horror. "Are you crazy, Sheehan?"

When Sheehan sought to explain Walker shook his fist at him. "Don't try to justify your insane actions! Nobody can lay hands upon a member of this august body while I have a breath left in me. Nobody! Is that clear?"

"But you yourself–" began Sheehan.

Jim silenced him with, "Get out! You're fired!"

Secretary Stanton led the unfrocked sergeant-at-arms outside. Walker placed a hand on his colleague's shoulder. "I'll stand by you, Mark. Just as you would stand by me. Comrades in every way, from alpha to omega."

Jim assisted the Senator to his feet and adroitly guided him to the corridor. It occurred to Senator Allen that Jim was piloting him in the direction of the Onyx Room. "Where are we going?" he asked.

"Your name is first on the alphabetical list," Walker said, still holding the gentleman's arm. "You are my alpha. We must not delay the roll-call."

"Now look here," said Senator Allen. "I don't propose to–"

"Of course you don't propose to vote against the wishes of your constituents. That would be dishonest, as well as ungrateful on your part."

"But I don't–"

"Nor do I like the rough and uncalled-for actions of the sergeant-at-arms. If you can show bruises, I shall press charges of mayhem against him."

They were now inside the Senate chamber. Senator Allen, with Jim's assistance, settled back in his chair. Walker shook the school-teacher's hand, then said in an emotional tone, "Remember your oath of office, Mark. Remember that you have to go home to face the voters who trust you, and to face your dear family who respect you. You are an honest man."

The roll-call began. Senator Allen voted "aye" for repeal.

Even with Allen's vote, many observers wondered how Jim could possibly achieve more than a tie. Apparently he had but twenty-five voices on his side today. Then, in a dramatic manner, Senator Hastings was wheeled in on a stretcher.

"I'm dying, Jim," the Senator whispered to his friend.

"But you're doing it on the battlefield, Jack," replied the majority leader. "Try to keep breathing—at least till they call your name."

The Mullan-Gage Act was repealed by a one-vote margin. Jim saw to it that his friend Hastings was returned by ambulance and train to the Brooklyn hospital. Some days after the legislative session had adjourned, Jim procured for the sergeant-at-arms a good job for the summer.

Much has been written of Jim's quick knockout of John S. Sumner, whom Louis Sobol has called "the protector of the virtue of New York." Although Jim was a foe of smut, he believed that the creative artist should be kept free from the muzzles of bigotry.

A group of up-state Republicans spoke in favor of John S. Sumner's offspring, the so-called Clean Books bill. Several New York City Democrats also favored its passage. Pages from the books of D. H. Lawrence were read to the solons, several of whom rose to speak about the protection of womanhood and the home from ruinous prose.

Thereupon Jim got up. "I have heard with great interest the addresses of the gentlemen on the other side," he said, "and I have the utmost respect for what they have said. But I submit, gentlemen, that they are either naïve or confused. Why all this talk about womanhood? I have never yet heard of a girl being ruined by a book."

The Clean Books bill collapsed.

From the "point of view" of some editors of the New York press Walker was a charming wastrel. They admitted, however, that he got things done at Albany, and, as a speaker, had become a brilliant star. Other editors, foremost among them the bouncing Herbert Bayard Swope of the *Morning World*, championed Jim's career.

One of Walker's critics was the Hearst editor Arthur Brisbane. Concerning Jim's growing popularity, Brisbane said, "The first step toward political approval is a step down." Mr. Brisbane had great ability as a writer. He also possessed several vanities, among them the conviction that he was a Daniel Webster.

Another thing that pleased Brisbane mightily was the size and shape of his head. It had bulging contours, and his forehead stood out like that of Socrates. The editor frequently wrote about the wonderful things one might expect of a man whose forehead suggested cranial pregnancy. His subordinates at the newspaper office, among them Tad Dorgan and Damon Runyon, nicknamed him (behind his back, of course) "Double-dome."

I can thank Mr. Brisbane's head for having saved my job on one of the many occasions when I came perilously near to being fired. It seems that more of Mr. Hearst's executives were dying or being forced to resign in 1925, the year I was managing editor of the *American*, than ever before. Weekly office "pools" on sports events, boxing, baseball, and the like were current, and I suggested that we set up a new kind of gambling "pool." The names of ten editors would be entered, and each editor would have a number. Tickets were to be sold at a dollar. The ten editors, it may properly be assumed, did not know of this pool, for the winning number was to be that of the next Hearst hetman either to be fired or to expire at his pastepot.

I had drawn number seven, Mr. Brisbane's number. I regret to say that espionage sometimes threatened our fun at the *American*. Mr. Brisbane called me to his office to inquire about "some macabre game that *someone* has originated" on the premises.

"We shall get to the bottom of this, A. B.," I promised.

The great man fixed me with his Socratic eye. "I understand that *you* have *my* number in this so-called pool?"

"A. B.," I said, "I too am a philosopher in a small way, and a student of Greek history."

"This is *not* Greek history," Mr. Brisbane observed menacingly.

"No, but does it seem logical, quite aside from the fact that I am busy getting out the newspaper, that I would waste my time or money by gambling against historical statistics?"

"Statistics?"

"It is well known that men with prominent foreheads live to an extreme old age."

Mr. Brisbane drummed upon some galley proofs of his editorial on the evils of the narcotic traffic, then said, "How true! I can think of a hundred of them, Benjamin Franklin, for one, who lived on and on. That will be all."

One night James J. Walker was asked to appear on the same banquet program with Brisbane. Jim arrived on time, for a change. Mr. Brisbane, motoring to Manhattan from his Lakewood, New Jersey, estate, had not arrived by the time the after-dinner speeches were begun. The toastmaster reported that Mr. Brisbane had been delayed by a traffic accident in the Holland Tunnel. He added that Senator Walker would speak in the meantime.

Jim rose. "If Brisbane doesn't come, it won't be because he didn't plan to do so. It will be because he got his head stuck in the Tunnel."

From the "point of view" of a coterie of wealthy admirers, Jim Walker seemed a refreshing "discovery." He enlivened the traditionally dull banquets of businessmen, and was an ornament at the private parties of moneyed leaders. Millionaires pursued him as though he were some theatrical star. Had he not been a man, one might have thought him a Follies beauty for whose affections the financiers were competing.

Several of these rich men liked Jim for himself and expected nothing from his friendship. Others rode to glory on his coat-tails. The fact that Jim received valuable gifts from some of these well-meaning friends cannot be denied, nor did Jim ever deny it.

Publisher Paul Block once gave Mayor Jim a fur-lined topcoat. It was a magnificent garment, and when someone suggested that it be insured, Jim sent for his brother George. At City Hall George asked to see the coat.

"Looks like something that belonged to Old King Cole," said Jim, putting on the coat.

"How much do you want it insured for, Jim?"

"I don't know."

"Well, what is its value?"

"The donor," Jim replied, "had the good taste to omit the price tag. But I'm told it's worth at least fifteen thousand dollars. Sable lining, you know."

George started wordlessly for the door.

"Hey!" Jim called out to him. "Nobody walks out on the mayor of the City of New York!"

"I'm walking out on him," George replied.

Jim followed after his brother. "What's there to be so mad about?"

"No coat in the world is worth fifteen thousand dollars," George said. "And just because somebody has made a damned fool out of you is no reason to pass it on to the family."

Many of Jim's troubles arose from the exploitation of his friendship by men who *did not* give him presents or lend him money. Doting friends, on the other hand, whether wisely or not, by means of their liberality, placed him well beyond the temptation to make money at the expense of the taxpayer. Whenever a rich friend volunteered to help Jim materially, he accepted the favor as an innocently intended generosity.

Walker's official mistakes, from a biographer's "point of view," seem to have stemmed from his inability to see the difference between personal and public relationships. Both as a man and as an official, Jim always responded to the needs of a friend. Loyalty to those he loved and loyalty to his political party were of the same nature in his opinion. He sometimes misplaced his loyalty in both respects.

On Friday morning, April 25, 1924, Senate Democratic Leader Walker lay fast asleep in his large bed in the house on St. Luke's Place. It was several minutes past nine o'clock in the morning. The bedroom shades and the drapes were drawn, for Jim could not sleep with so much as a ray of light in his room.

The Senator's sportsman friend, Dan McKetrick, telephoned the Walker home, to be told by Mrs. Walker that Jim was still asleep and could not be disturbed.

"Allie," said McKetrick, "you've got to get him up. I have bad news. It's about Mr. Murphy."

After Jim got on the telephone, McKetrick informed him, "Mr. Murphy had a heart attack while he was shaving. He died just half an hour ago. Mrs. Murphy is in Atlantic City, and she . . . " McKetrick paused, then asked, "Are you listening, Jim?"

There was no response. McKetrick kept on saying, "Hello . . . hello . . . Jim? Are you all right?"

Then Mrs. Walker's voice came over the phone to McKetrick. "Jim can't talk, Dan. Yes, he's all right, I guess. He went back to his room. You understand?"

"Yes," said McKetrick. "I understand."

The death of Mr. Murphy had a far-reaching effect on Walker's private as well as his public life. From then on, brilliant and resourceful though he was, and widely loved, there was no one to restrain him when he behaved indiscreetly. His brother George, to whom Jim was devoted, exercised a good influence upon him, but became powerless to persuade him against emotional plunges.

As to Mr. Murphy's influence over Jim's life, Allie Walker said recently, "I do think that Mr. Murphy, had he continued to live, would have controlled Jim to the extent that he never would have become involved the way he did. I think that all of his friends felt that soon he would come to his senses; but they waited too long to try to influence him, and then it was too late. Mr. Murphy would have nipped things in the bud. Jim's dear friend Al Smith tried."

Mr. Murphy died before he could realize his greatest political dream: the nomination of Governor Smith for the presidency. That nomination was delayed until four years later, but persons close to Mr. Murphy knew he planned to make it come to pass in June 1924.

That Mr. Murphy intended to put Walker in the governor's chair to succeed Smith in 1924, and in the United States Senate afterward, is more than a conjecture. I found among Walker's papers a letter signed by Franklin D. Roosevelt, and in it there is a most significant statement. The letter, written at Hyde Park and bearing the date November 24, 1924, was addressed to Mr. Lloyd George, former Prime Minister of Great Britain.

Mr. Roosevelt at this time had retired from his post as Assistant Secretary of the Navy. He was recuperating from an attack of infantile paralysis, and his political activities were mostly confined to his work as a delegate to the national Democratic conventions. It will be remembered that he placed the name of Al Smith before the convention in 1924, and again in 1928.

In the letter of introduction which Mr. Roosevelt gave Jim to deliver to Mr. Lloyd George, he described Walker as "a very old friend of mine. . . . [He] has now risen to be the leader of the Democratic party in the New York State Senate. . . . And Walker would undoubtedly have been nominated by us for the governorship this year if Governor Alfred E. Smith had not consented to run again. . . ."

12.

Who Has Seen the Wind?

In the middle of the ocean, and in the middle of his life, James J. Walker stood on the boat deck of the *Berengaria*. Looking out upon the wake of the vessel, he thought of his country and of its presidents. Would Al Smith ever reach the White House? Only a few months ago, at the Old Madison Square Garden, Jim had heard Franklin D. Roosevelt nominate Al Smith for the presidency, but Smith had lost to John W. Davis. In November Walker had campaigned for Smith during the gubernatorial race against Theodore Roosevelt, Jr., and had seen "The Happy Warrior" elected to Albany for the fourth time.

The fresh breeze from the ice-wastes of Labrador stayed with the *Berengaria* like a conscience. The ship leaned. The track left astern swirled among the random crests. If this wake seemed the train of some vast wedding gown, and if, by means of association of ideas, Jim's thoughts turned to Allie Walker, we cannot know.

At the time of Walker's first voyage abroad it was not yet publicized that he was finding romantic interests away from St. Luke's Place. During the twenty-five years that followed, Allie Walker declined to be interviewed on the subject of Jim's wandering affections. Just recently, however, at my invitation, she wrote the following statement, which is free from the bitterness usually encountered in these matters:

"We were always happy together. If I felt neglected or left out, I tried never to show it, and always cooperated with Jim in anything or any way that would be for his benefit. We never quarreled, and when I talked to him about situations that made me uncomfortable and unhappy, he always said that it was a passing phase, and no one ever would take my place. And I believed him. In the latter years he became involved more deeply in affairs from which he was unable to free himself. The last time I saw him, he made me feel that he still loved me, and that all would be straightened out soon. I was never jealous of him, for I always felt that deep in his heart he was mine. He talked to me of his failings, and bared his heart to me many times. Flattery was sweet to him—and so fatal."

During the "latter years" Jim would merely say, "Allie and I just drifted apart," or, "I was entirely to blame."

The voyager on the *Berengaria* saw the horizon darkening. Larger waves began to form. The sea heaped up, and Jim went below.

"The ship is pitching," said the steward.

"Yes," Jim said, "and I am catching."

"May I suggest champagne?" asked the steward.

"That," replied Jim, "or hemlock."

The 1920's were not conducive to the repair of marriage relationships once the ties began to fray. As did many other men of personality, position, and the means with which to enjoy the carnival, Walker danced with the throng and shook the bells of self-indulgence. Wine flowed illegally. Women, "freed" from conventions, nosedived from their pedestals. Songs took on primitive overtones; the Congo River usurped, then overflowed, the banks of the Danube.

In Russia, Nikolai Lenin had died of apoplexy. In Germany, author Adolf Hitler was writing *Mein Kampf*. In England, Lady Diana Manners had bobbed her hair. In America, Teapot Dome had boiled over. Young N. J. Leopold and Richard Loeb had killed thirteen-year-old Robert Franks during a degenerate quest for thrills. The bonny Prince of Wales had visited the United States and gone home. Calvin Coolidge, golden with silence, had commenced his first year in the White House. The dirigible *Los Angeles* had crossed the Atlantic from Friedrichshafen. The *Daily Mirror*, Hearst's tabloid paper, had been launched under the editorship of the fabulous Walter Howey. Senator James J. Walker was on his way to Europe; and a pert, brown-haired actress of the musical comedy stage fondly awaited his return.

Her name was Yvonne Shelton. Her friends knew her as "Vonnie." Jim called her "Little Fellow." Five feet tall, and a mere eighty-five pounds in weight, she walked like a pretty pigeon. This girl early had fallen in love with laughter and with life. And she found in the blithe Senator from Greenwich Village and Broadway the embodiment of both life and laughter. When among their friends, Vonnie would sit on the floor at Walker's feet. When they had disagreements, and when the uninhibited Vonnie threw pieces of bric-a-brac at Jim, it was noticed that she always "carefully" missed her target. Her moments of anger or jealousy subsided as quickly as they had arisen.

Vonnie was French-Canadian, an orphan. After her adoption, she lived with her foster parents in Washington, D. C. During her teens she came to New York City, there to inspire the friendship of a multi-millionaire merchant. This benefactor encouraged Vonnie's theatrical aspirations, and is said to have backed a show just to see her in the glow of footlights.

Vonnie Shelton had a moderately good voice and danced well. She danced and sang in the midnight performances at the Century Theatre during the administration of Mayor John Purroy Mitchel. The handsome Mr. Mitchel was another mayor who was fond of the musical stage.

Vonnie was habitually late to work, and the stage manager finally became furious. He threatened to expel the tardy Vonnie from the cast, then decided to give her "one more chance." If she were late again, he promised, she would be "dropped."

The next night Vonnie arrived just before curtain time. She was "fired." As she went past the gentleman who had discharged her, Vonnie said, "When I walk out of here, laddie, the midnight license for the show walks out with me."

The man to whom she said this merely snorted, but shortly thereafter he received word that the theatre's license had been revoked.

The next day Vonnie consented to rejoin the cast if the management agreed to double her salary and if the producer of the show sent his limousine to carry her to the theatre nightly. There was a quick capitulation. The license was renewed.

Miss Shelton's confidante for many years was May Weston. This former Follies beauty told me that Mayor Mitchel introduced Vonnie to Jim at a cocktail party in 1917. The late Sid Solomon, onetime owner of the Casino in Central Park, corroborated this statement and fixed the place of the meeting at Sherry's Restaurant. Thereafter Vonnie and Jim often dined together at Leone's Restaurant in midtown Manhattan. There was an intimate, third-floor dining-room in this establishment where the Senator and his friends might spend the after-theatre hours. The late W. C. Fields was a patron of Leone's, and sometimes joined the Senator's parties.

Fields was the star comedian in the *Follies*, in which Fanny Brice, Ann Pennington, May Weston, and Vonnie Shelton also appeared. He once told me that "Vonnie was an all-right little trouper, and an all-right little kiddie."

May Weston says that when she and Vonnie once reported for

rehearsal W. C. Fields announced to them, "Nippers, I want you to go shopping with your Uncle Willie."

The girls accompanied W. C. to an Eleventh Avenue address where, after much haggling, the comedian purchased a large crate. Next, he guided his young friends to a shop in which he bought a roll of white oilcloth. Then, at a hardware store, he selected a hammer and some tacks.

"What are you going to do with all this junk?" Vonnie asked.

"Wait, my little cassowary," replied Uncle Willie. "When these treasures are delivered at the theatre, you will see."

The girls assumed that Mr. Fields was assembling properties for a new theatrical "routine." They stayed with him in his dressing-room until the packing-case and other purchases were delivered. The comedian thereupon proceeded to cover the packing-case with the oilcloth. He seemed very happy as he hammered away; then, when a furtive stranger came in, laden with bottles of liquor, Fields embraced everyone, including the bootlegger, and cried out, "Eureka! The Marines have landed on the shores of Tripoli!"

"You see, children," said Mr. Fields, storing the bottles inside the packing-case, "I never can work properly until I have a bar!"

W. C. Fields and I were close friends during a long and happy time. I could see that he genuinely liked Jim Walker. Fields' opinions of men and women—whenever he chanced to deliver his verdicts without prejudice—were shrewd and convincing. He seldom conjectured upon the more intimate relationships of his friends, but I think he may have been correct in his surmise that "most men make most women cry. And most women make most men curse. Once in a long, long while, a man and a woman make each other laugh and sing and forget their worries. That's what happened when Walker met Vonnie. Neither one was a critic. And when the pinch came, Vonnie stepped aside, made no demands, and kept her mouth shut." Then, as an afterthought, W. C. said, "Vonnie was a good cook too."

As to this, May Weston recalls the time when the "Little Fellow" started upon that avocation. "Like all her decisions," said May, "Vonnie's urge to be a chef came suddenly. She bought a cookbook, studied it, then announced that her first creation would be hash. Instead of using yesterday's beef for this purpose, she bought a steak for four dollars, boiled it, waited for it to cool; then cut it into pieces, added onions and potatoes, and finally served it to Jim Walker."

Vonnie was a creature of fads and fancies. Among other hobbies, it became her ambition to design jewelry. She studied this matter diligently—and expensively. She liked to be waited on and "pampered," but when with Jim she enjoyed waiting on him. She was impulsive, quick-witted, and forthright. I knew her only slightly, during the 1930's, when she used to come to Fire Island to visit Fanny Brice and May Weston. That was after she had parted from Jim. Vonnie held her head high and never revealed to outsiders that her heart was sad. But whenever she spoke of Jim to the inner circle of old friends, she seemed not to be speaking Walker's name but smiling it. She was the only one I know who had a nickname for Walker other than "Jim" or "Jimmy." She called him "J.J."

The popinjay Senator enchanted almost everyone he met during his brief visit abroad in the winter of 1924. His hosts found it difficult to believe that the sprightly fellow in Broadway livery was a real senator. His pinch-waisted suit, the fedora with the brim aslant over his right ear, the toothpick shoes and slender cravat, belied that title. This Yankee also lacked many other aspects of mildewed eminence. The French concept of American political leaders arose from their somewhat recent observations of envoys at the peace conferences. Their own senators, more often than not, were bearded antiques, whose legislative sessions sounded like quarrels in an old men's home.

Walker now was forty-three, but his Parisian friends saw in him a man of younger years. They began at once to call him "Monsieur Jacques." During his next visit they greeted him as "Jeemy." Perhaps Walker subscribed to John Drew's recipe for holding one's youth, a formula disclosed by that actor to critic Ashton Stevens: "Keep the stomach off and the hair on."

Jim's unaffected friendliness pleased his Parisian hosts, but his remarks sometimes startled them, as when he praised the sidewalk comfort stations. "These busy kiosks," he said, "are the greatest evidence of the civilization of the French." He then proceeded to arouse in his listeners a fear lest they had overlooked an honest franc or two. "In New York," he added, "these places would be controlled by a political concession." He went on to ask with a show of gravity, "Tell me: don't the Parisian women ever do that necessary thing for which you have erected these charming structures?"

Soon after he had got off the boat-train Jim looked up an old newspaper friend, S. Jay Kaufman. Some years before Walker's trip abroad Jim and the New York columnist had met at a theatrical first night and then had had supper together. Both men were deeply interested in the theatre and its people. Subsequently Kaufman made several trips to Paris. Each time he returned to New York he would report to Jim upon theatrical matters and the new styles in men's clothes.

As Kaufman greeted Jim in Paris, he asked where Walker would like to go and what he would like to do.

"How far are we from Charvet's?" Jim inquired.

Kaufman took his friend to Charvet's, the foremost haberdashers of the time. Walker purchased several dozen cravats and a great many other things. Kaufman says that, although Jim's taste was excellent, "he was a shade overdressed. One noticed his clothes, which were attracting, but not always attractive."

Walker puzzled his hosts by refusing to witness a performance by nude actors in a small club off the Place Pigalle. To them this seemed a departure from character on the part of one who otherwise appeared quite worldly. The Senator said that he preferred to see a boxing match and went with Kaufman to the Salle Wagram.

In France no one cheers during the course of the fighting and applauds only when the boxers have retired to their corners at the close of each round. Jim stood up and shouted during the first round.

When the spectators booed him, Jim said, "Sorry, I thought I was back in America."

Jim once again leaped up during the second round, and once again was shouted down. "A politician," he explained, "becomes so accustomed to catcalls and boos that he feels lonesome in the absence of noisy criticism."

While Jim was in England he neglected to present Mr. Roosevelt's letter to Mr. Lloyd George. Perhaps he forgot that he had such a letter; or, more likely, his characteristic reluctance to thrust himself upon others may have made him hold back. Instead of courtesy calls upon political celebrities, Jim introduced himself to various Bond Street tailors. One of them, described by Jim as "looking like the Duke of Wellington in mufti," refused to build a suit in accordance with Walker's specifications of wide shoulders, narrow waist, and one button instead of three on the coat-front.

"I trust you will understand the situation, sir," the tailor explained.

"Our establishment has been in existence for more than one hundred and fifty years. The late Prince Consort once honored us with a royal appointment. You will please understand, sir, that we dare not risk our reputation on such a venture as the one you propose."

"That's an amazing coincidence," Jim replied. "I had set my heart upon wearing the suit at a costume ball to impersonate none other than the very one whom you have just mentioned, Prince Albert."

The tailor fixed the irreverent American with a ducal eye. "May I suggest, sir, that you consult a Mr. Willie Clarkson?"

"Is he a barrister?"

"Decidedly not, sir. Mr. Clarkson provides costumes for the theatrical trade near Soho. May I ask, sir, if you are an actor?"

"Most of the time," Jim replied. He then danced sidewise to the door, saying, "This is called 'Off to Buffalo.' "

13.

Some of Those Days

WALKER returned home for Christmas. In January of the new year a Democratic caucus selected him as party leader of the Senate. His courteous antagonist, "Point-of-View" Senator Knight, became the Republican leader.

This year would bring Walker the man, as well as his personal actions, into fuller public view. Until now he had been accountable for his private conduct only to his friends (all of whom except Al Smith were lenient with the charmer), and his wife, and himself. Soon he would find out—if indeed he did not already know it—that a political bandwagon can easily be converted into a hearse. But, midway in the tumultuous twenties, the trumpets were blowing, the drums sounding, and the stars twinkling over Broadway.

An early rainfall helped the Department of Sanitation clear the city of snow early in January of 1925. During that month and the next the newspapers offered two dramatic stories to their readers: the race against death by an Alaskan dogsled bearing a supply of serum from Anchorage to relieve the diphtheria epidemic at Nome; and the protracted death plight of Floyd Collins, trapped at the mouth of a cave in Kentucky.

In New York, William Randolph Hearst and Al Smith were having a rough-and-tumble feud. The Hearst newspapers charged that Governor Smith was responsible for the delivery of inferior milk to babies in the city's slum areas. The Governor's mother wept when she read this attack upon her son. Her tears sent Smith into a rage. He began more violently than ever before to attack Hearst at public meetings.

On Smith's return to Albany after one of his anti-Hearst speeches in Manhattan, Walker met him with the warning, "Al, you're making a tactical blunder."

"Baloney!" Smith replied. "Six thousand people stood up to cheer me last night when I told Hearst off."

"Six thousand people, eh?" Walker replied. "Well, Al, you can't compare your occasional one-night stands with the huge daily audiences Mr. Hearst addresses in his New York newspapers."

"I suppose *you'd* take it lying down if attacked in this manner?"

"I only know," Jim said, "that it is the most satisfying, yet the most expensive luxury to tell a man exactly what you think of him."

When, a few months later, Jim was a candidate for mayor in the primaries against Hylan, there appeared in the Hearst newspapers a cartoon depicting Walker looking on with approval as a leering opium peddler offered narcotics to a child. The man who drew this cartoon was Billy De Beck, the amiable and talented creator of the "Barney Google" comic strip. Billy was one of Walker's favorite friends.

De Beck apologized privately to Jim. "I did it under pressure," he said. "And I wish that I'd never left the Chicago Loop. I was much happier there."

"Billy," Walker replied, "the only way you could hurt my feelings would be for you to go back to Chicago."

"Then you're not mad?"

"Whenever a man gets mad," Jim replied, "he lets down his guard. The knockout follows."

During the first three months of 1925 Jim worked hard and played hard. Although Governor Smith occasionally reprimanded Walker for keeping late hours and making frequent pleasure trips to New

York, the executive found no fault with the Senator's efficiency on the legislative floor or in committee. Jim industriously scored against a Republican majority by bringing about important legislation. Among the bills he introduced was Smith's proposed constitutional amendment providing for an executive budget, a four-year instead of a two-year term for New York's governors, and the short ballot; a bill providing for a forty-eight-hour week for women and minors in industry; a bill to amend the Corrupt Practices Act; and a resolution for the investigation of rates, service, and business methods of the New York Telephone Company. Walker also urged adoption of a resolution for a constitutional amendment to make a state bond issue available for the elimination of railway grade-crossings.

Notwithstanding his duties at Albany, Jim found time to enjoy weekends in New York. Sometimes he would leave during mid-week to attend a boxing match or to see a play. He would reappear at the capitol late the next day, having gone without sleep. Then Governor Smith would upbraid him.

"Oh, now, Algie," Jim once replied to the Governor, "I don't want to grow stale in a plush-lined rut."

Toward the middle of January of 1925 one of Al Smith's political godfathers, Thomas F. Foley, died. While in New York to attend the funeral of the Tammany leader, Smith had a hard time locating Walker. Smith took the Senator to task for having been at the opening performance of the *Chauve-Souris* at a time all Tammany was in mourning.

"Listen, Al," Jim said. "You're confused. It was Tom Foley who died, not I."

Some weeks later there was a total eclipse of the sun. Walker interrupted an executive meeting in Smith's office to say, "No matter what they tell you, Al, I had nothing to do with this."

During one of Walker's weekends away from Albany, on an especially cold and windy night, Jim had dinner with several friends at the Newspaper Club. In this party were Jimmy Johnston, Walker's comrade and an importer of English pugilists; William A. Orr, now a motion-picture executive; and two of the finest reporters of that or any other time, the late Martin Green and the man we referred to some pages back as Ernest.

At about one o'clock in the morning Bill Orr suggested that the party repair to his office on East Forty-second Street, where two bottles of non-poisonous Scotch whisky might be found. The men sat talking in Orr's headquarters until about four o'clock. When someone suggested that it was time to go home, Jim observed that Ernest had "passed out."

"He'll be all right, Jim," said Martin Green. "Time and again I've seen him like this."

"I know," Jim said, "but if we leave him here, he may fall out of that chair and smash his head against the desk."

"He hasn't done it so far," said Bill Orr.

But Jim was not satisfied to leave Ernest behind. "Call the Biltmore and reserve a room for him."

The group set out upon the short walk along Vanderbilt Avenue from Forty-second Street to the Forty-third Street entrance of the Biltmore. Johnston and Orr, the two smallest men in the party, supported the hulking Ernest between them. Green and Walker strode ahead in the icy wind.

Ernest's escorts managed their burden without incident until they turned the corner into Forty-third. The wind almost blew them down. Ernest was partially revived. "So cold! So cold!" he moaned again and again.

While Ernest was stumbling and groaning his two-word refrain, a young police officer, gaily swinging his club, and apparently enjoying the foul weather, approached them from the direction of the Madison Avenue corner of Forty-third Street. He laughed heartily at the sight, but nevertheless made them halt. "You can't do this," said he. "You'll have to stop it."

Walker, always polite to officers of the law, explained that Ernest was an ailing friend and that his comrades were about to bed him down at the Biltmore.

"This is Senator Walker," Martin Green interposed.

"Oh, sure," the officer said, "but you can't do this."

"So cold! So cold!" Ernest was wailing in the background.

"Do what, Officer?" Jim inquired.

The policeman pointed to Ernest with his nightstick. "Do that!"

Ernest's overcoat had come unbuttoned in the icy wind. Also, his trousers had collapsed. It was quite apparent that Ernest had on no undergarments.

His friends quickly hoisted the wailing man's trousers. "Even a brass monkey would complain if he lost his pants in this weather," said Jim.

I was managing editor of Mr. Hearst's *New York American* in 1925, the year of Walker's rocket-like rise in city affairs. I had charge of the merriest staff ever assembled on Park Row. Several of the finest newspapermen in town were in this group. My night city editor was the quietly brilliant Martin Dunn, who had every qualification, except that of cold-blooded ambition, to be editor-in-chief. My day city editors, successively, were two splendid men, Edward Doherty and Charles S. Hand.

The tall and personable Hand just recently had come to the *American* from the *New York Morning World*, for which newspaper he had been staff correspondent at Albany during the legislative sessions. He had also served brilliantly as the City Hall representative of the *World*.

Hand had become city editor of the *American* against his own inclinations. He had stayed a reporter by choice, for not long before this he had declined to sit at the city desk of the *World*. The friend and confidant of every politician of consequence, this able newspaperman undertook the difficult and sometimes perilous job of city editor of the *American* mainly because of his desire to help me during an era of political turmoil in New York.

It may seem incongruous that so many members of the *American* staff were loyal friends and admirers of Walker at the very time their newspaper trained its guns upon the little gentleman. Albany correspondent Robert Watson had a real affection for Jim. Damon Runyon and others in our sports department liked him immensely.

Walker and Arthur ("Bugs") Baer, the famous humorist, had entered upon their long friendship a year or so before this time. Celebrated though Baer has been during more than thirty years, it occurs to me—as it did to Walker—that the true measure of Baer's capacities never has been taken. Jim once said that two circumstances delayed, but would not eventually prevent, Baer's full recognition as a thinker as well as a laugh-maker. One was the nickname "Bugs." That label, Jim said, was as inappropriate as "Toots" would have been for Harriet Beecher Stowe. The second handicap, Jim said, was that Baer's philosophical overtones too often were lost upon readers geared to slapstick gags and broad comedy. Many other "humorists," however, did not hesitate to borrow Baer's creations, disguise them slightly, and then translate them into vaudeville terms

Baer one day posted on the bulletin board of the *American* the clipped-out newspaper columns of six plagiarists, three on either side of one of his own essays, the obvious source of the pilferings. Above this array he tacked a note which read: "Christ had all the best of it. He was crucified between only two thieves."

Baer, Philadelphia-born of a family of fourteen children, began his career as a lace designer, studied art at night school, became an office boy for the *Ledger*, a cartoonist, and afterward a paragrapher. He worked on the *Washington Times*, then came to New York to write for the *World*. In 1919 he joined the *American* staff.

As a member of the Friars Club, a social organization of actors, vaudevillians, horse players, and newspapermen, Baer became acquainted with Walker. Jim's idol, George M. Cohan, Abbot of the club, persuaded Walker to join the Friars in 1924. Almost everyone except Damon Runyon and the bartender made speeches at the Friars' banquets. Walker, of course, always excelled as a speaker at these dinners, in spite of the fact that it was a time of great toastmasters and his competitors at the club's banquet table included actor Willie Collier, Will Rogers, George Jessel, and Captain Irving O'Hay.

Baer's ability as an after-dinner speaker was discovered at the Friars. His inexperience on the dais at first hindered his delivery, but the things he said aroused immediate attention. He soon qualified for membership in the group of superior speakers.

At a dinner to Walker one of the eulogists monopolized the better, or worse, part of an hour. At the close of this boresome harangue the toastmaster called upon Baer. "That," Baer said, "was the first time I ever heard a battleship launched indoors."

As toastmaster at another dinner given in Walker's honor Baer fell into the trap of sentiment. His affection for Jim caused him to speak of his friend as "a man who would fight by your side, and lay down his life for you." Baer went on in this fashion for a minute or so, then realized that he had smothered the guest of honor with adjectives. He paused, looked about the banquet hall, and asked, "And who is this man? I do not see him here tonight."

Of Walker, Baer said, "Jim wasn't a lot of people. He was just Jimmy. Lots of other men have many facets, borrowed or stolen, but Jim's shine was all his own. He was very smart when he wanted to be. He learned a lot about politics from Al Smith; and whatever anyone thinks of Al, you must admit that he turned out three pretty good jobs: F.D.R., Herbert Lehman, and Jim Walker."

Even the music critic of Mr. Hearst's *American*, Leonard Liebling, was a Walker "fan." Liebling, tenor John McCormack, and Walker were dining together on the January day in 1925 when Carnegie Hall was sold.

McCormack earlier that month had sung for the first time over the radio, and the broadcasting station had received more than twenty thousand letters applauding this event. Such public response, McCormack said, made him feel that radio would become a medium for bringing good music to hitherto inaccessible audiences. Liebling was of an opinion that radio would educate its listeners by making them familiar with operatic and symphonic music. As Liebling told me, Walker said that the public's desire was to be amused and not educated; that the people could best be reached by messages aimed at their hearts instead of their heads. McCormack's success, Jim maintained, rested only in small part upon his musical skill. It was the "heart" in his voice, and his choice of sentimental songs, that mattered most to the people. Opera, Jim went on to say, was dying, and deficits piling up in the houses of classical music, mainly because American audiences did not relish the spectacle of fat and aging lovers singing in tongues that only the professors of European languages understood. Symphonies too, he said in effect, uplifted the initiated ones but puzzled the average man, and more often than not made him afraid of seeming ignorant in the presence of "learned fiddling."

Jim mentioned the sale of Carnegie Hall as a case in point, and amazed his dinner companions, who had pleasantly accused Walker of being a special advocate of Tin Pan Alley, by how much he knew of Carnegie Hall's history. Jim correctly recited the facts of the opening of that musical center in 1891; told of the presence of Tschaikowsky as guest of honor at the event; and fixed the dates of the Russian composer's subsequent appearances there as conductor of four concerts. He also recalled that Saint-Saëns and Richard Strauss had conducted at Carnegie Hall and was able to give the dates of their respective concerts.

"After I returned to my office," Liebling said, "I looked up these dates and found that Jim had made not a single error. The man had a memory like Macaulay's."

What amused Liebling most, he said, was an anecdote Jim told about Andrew Carnegie, founder and patron of the hall on West Fifty-seventh Street. During the eighties Mr. Carnegie had been one of the chief sustaining members of the original Oratorio Society. Concerts then were given in Steinway Hall on Fourteenth Street. After the Philharmonic Society came into existence the Scotch philanthropist met its annual deficits. One day toward the close of his life Mr. Carnegie received the secretary of the Philharmonic at his Fifth Avenue home. The gentleman had come to ask for a donation of sixty thousand dollars.

As Mr. Carnegie prepared to write his signature on a check he paused to announce, "No. I've changed my mind. Year after year I've made up these deficits. Surely there are other people who like music well enough to help with their own money. Now I'll ask you to go out and raise half the amount you are asking. When and if you get it, I'll promptly give you a like amount."

Next day the secretary returned to the steelmaster's mansion to report that he had succeeded in his money-raising mission. "You see?" said Mr. Carnegie. "A thing is quite simple to accomplish if it's right, and if you go after it." He then wrote out a check for his promised half of the needed sum. As the secretary rose, Mr. Carnegie asked, "By the way, do you mind telling me who gave you the other half?"

"Not at all," the secretary replied. "It was Mrs. Carnegie."

Smith and Walker came down from Albany late in February of 1925 to attend the funeral of Job E. Hedges at the Brick Presbyterian Church. Although Mr. Hedges had been a lifelong Republican, Smith and Walker were by no means the only Democratic mourners at the services for the late orator, attorney, and political philosopher. Mr. Hedges had been a witty and beloved public figure for many years.

Walker told me that Smith and he had an "uncomfortable" conversation on the train while en route to New York. Smith, as quoted by Jim, said that Hedges' life proved that a man could have a happy time of it and still abide by the moral conventions. Walker replied that his admiration for Hedges had been unlimited, and then quoted from one of the late orator's speeches:

"It is not necessary," Hedges had said, "to go through life with a perpetual grin, which will result in a permanent appearance of idiocy, any more than it is to assume a frown in the hope that it will grow into a wrinkle indicative of profound thought. It is better to be smiled at than laughed at. A hypocrite can force tears without detection. Honest laughter cannot be feigned."

As accurately as I can remember Jim's report of this conversation, the Governor said, "Personally I think that Hedges' witty remarks were a great handicap to him. Most people will not vote for a man who is funny."

"Maybe Job just didn't give a damn, Al."

"A public man can't afford not to give a damn. The only thing that is worse for a public man than being funny is for him to chase women if he's married."

"Algie," Jim asked, "could you by any rare chance be thinking of one of the neighbors' children?"

"Jim, I have a genuine, deep-down affection for you," the Governor replied. "And it's a shame that you won't listen to reason. If you'd only cut out your tomfoolery on Broadway and watch your step, God only knows how far you'd go in public life."

"Yes," Walker said. "It is a great temptation to be like Mayor Hylan. A solid, substantial man who—"

"Baloney!" Smith interrupted. "Suppose we talk about something else."

As yet there had been no evidence of a movement to make Jim mayor of the City of New York. It was plain to all of us, however, that in January of 1925 an old order was passing. The city wanted someone other than a Mayor Hylan as its chief magistrate. Even the conservative *New York Times* characterized Mr. Hylan editorially as "an imperfect demagogue."

We of the *American* staff were plagued by the circumstance that Mayor Hylan had access to our newspaper columns for the unbridled exercise of his long-winded opinions. In a moment of rebellion one day, I wrote a tongue-in-cheek editorial comparing Hylan to Abraham Lincoln. By giving the Mayor an overdose of damp sugar, I hoped to sidetrack his attention from our crowded news columns. Our compositors framed the editorial with little American flags.

The Mayor soon wore out his clipping of the editorial and sent across City Hall Park for a new supply. Instead of resting upon the glories of his partnership with Lincoln, Mr. Hylan became even more demanding upon our time and space. We were most happy when Mr. Hylan left New York to go to Florida in January of 1925, his fourth vacation in six months.

Before he boarded the grapefruit flyer at Pennsylvania Station, the man of many persecutions announced that someone had been sending poison-pen letters to his home. He recommended that his critics, anonymous or not, study his latest pamphlet, entitled "The ABCs of Hylanism."

When Jim Walker was asked the meaning of Mr. Hylan's "ABCs," he replied instantly, "Why, it means 'At the Bottom of the Class.' "

14.

The World Is Waiting for the Sunrise

The March wind made bull-roars on the sidewalks of New York and bent the budding dogwood trees in Central Park. On St. Patrick's Day the parading Tammany men held onto their silk hats as though holding onto their jobs. Governor Al Smith was the grand marshal. Jim Walker overslept, and the Ancient Order of Hibernians marched up Fifth Avenue without him.

After the state legislature adjourned its regular session in 1925, Jim returned home to spend his nights in the theatrical district and his days in his law office at No. 61 Broadway. Jim had no law partners, as is commonly supposed, but occupied one small room in a suite maintained by intimate friends. Former State Senator George A. Blauvelt of Rockland County, Joseph A. Warren, and Francis J. MacIntyre were the partners in this law firm. As a courtesy to Walker, MacIntyre and Warren protected Jim's interests whenever political duties interfered with his law practice. The firm's secretary, Miss Mildred Day, handled Jim's correspondence and kept him reasonably up to date by reminding him of anniversaries, birthdays of relatives, his daily appointments, and other personal matters which had escaped his otherwise remarkable memory.

At the beginning of a trial in the Bronx, it became necessary for Jim to go to Albany. Walker's client had brought a suit for damages against the city for negligence. The man had slipped and fallen upon an ice-covered sidewalk. Eleven jurors had been seated in the box when Walker requested MacIntyre to pinch hit for him and select the twelfth juror.

"I'll be back," Walker promised, "in time to proceed with the trial. Purposely I have approved eleven of the dumbest jurors I or anyone else could find this side of the Belgian Congo. All I ask you to do in my absence is to select the most ignorant person still available for the remaining vacancy in the jury box."

After the Senator had gone to Grand Central station MacIntyre decided to play a joke on Jim. He accepted for jury duty a man who not only seemed to have the soul of an individualist, but who also wore the Phi Beta Kappa key of scholarship.

Upon his return to court Walker chided MacIntyre for having seated such a scholarly man. "We are beaten at the start," Jim said. "Our case is so weak *per se* that even the eleven half-wits I so carefully selected will be swayed by the literate snob you have let into the box."

When the time came for argument Jim kept his eyes and his words upon the "smart" juror. He tried in every way to persuade and charm this man, but the learned one seemed stoical and indifferent. He played tiddly-winks with his Phi Beta Kappa key and yawned when the jurors retired for deliberation.

They were gone for several hours. "Just as I expected," Jim complained to MacIntyre. "That fellow is turning the dumbbells against us. Why didn't you get an ignoramus? Lord knows they're plentiful!"

To Walker's complete amazement the jury brought in a verdict for his client. As the stunned but happy Jim left court, the Phi Beta Kappa juror touched Walker's sleeve. "Senator, you may be interested to learn that the vote was eleven to one against you almost to the last. But I finally convinced them that your client was entitled to the judgment."

Walker had many opportunities to defend clients in criminal actions, but wisely, I think, avoided this type of law practice. I am not alone in the opinion that his ability to sway juries, as demonstrated in the relatively few criminal cases in which he appeared, might have given Jim's reputation the taint of "mouthpiece."

As early as 1920 Jim won a criminal case with a demonstration of skill such as might have opened wide for him the doors of a lucrative practice among the lawbreakers of the Prohibition era. This action was a peculiar one in several ways, and I am grateful to the members of two law firms for their research in respect to this and other cases in which Walker participated: MacIntyre, Downey & Ryan, and Sylvester & Harris.

In *People* v. *McMullin* the charge was first-degree murder. The court appointed Walker to represent the accused; the defendant did not retain him in the ordinary sense of the word. An indictment was presented to the Court of General Sessions for the County of New York on March 15, 1920, charging Stewart N. McMullin with the shooting and killing of Harry Carlton on March 11 of that same year. Thirty-one-year-old Carlton, a chauffeur, was alleged to have been a violator of the Prohibition enforcement laws at or about the time he was shot. He was the first person killed in New York by a Prohibition enforcement agent, which was the official status of his slayer.

Inasmuch as McMullin was a federal agent, the unusual circumstance was presented of the United States Attorney in the New York district defending a case, and the District Attorney of the county prosecuting it. United States Attorney Francis G. Caffey asked that a lawyer unattached to the national government be appointed to defend McMullin. Walker entered the case in September.

The appointed defender faced several obstacles, among them the prejudicial fact that McMullin was an ex-convict. Early in the 1900's he had served a prison term at Fort Worth, Texas, for forgery. In 1908, under the alias of John H. Murphy, he had been imprisoned in Indiana on a similar charge, and afterward paroled. And in 1913 he had been convicted of robbery in Westchester County, New York, and had served a term of six years in Sing Sing Prison.

At Sing Sing, McMullin met a radical convict who foretold the Black Tom dock explosion of July 30, 1916. McMullin relayed this warning, but it went unnoticed until after the blow-up had claimed two lives and caused a property damage of twenty-two million dollars. When the Prohibition agency began its activities, someone suggested that McMullin be released from prison to seek information against violators of the liquor laws. Sing Sing sang good-by to the "singer."

Walker foresaw that his client's record would tell heavily against him at a trial conducted by a district attorney's office eager to demonstrate its incorruptibility. Furthermore, the prosecution would be in the hands of rotund and serious-minded Assistant District Attorney Alfred J. Talley.

Walker filed a petition to transfer the case from the county court to a United States court, on the ground that his client was an agent in the Internal Revenue Service, and that, in the course of duty, he had been investigating alleged Prohibition violations by Harry Carlton. Walker succeeded in this maneuver, and the case was removed to the District Court of the United States.

The trial began on October 5, 1920, before Judge Julius M. Mayer and a jury. In his opening statement Walker asserted that he would be able to prove beyond a reasonable doubt that his client had acted in self-defense. For several days a parade of witnesses appeared against the ex-convict. If, as Walker claimed, McMullin had acted in self-defense, what weapon had the slain man used? No weapon had been found in the room where the victim had died.

Jim finally placed his only witness, his client, on the stand. McMullin said that Carlton had attacked him with a knife. Under cross-examination by the prosecution McMullin was asked, "What happened to the knife? Did you carry it away from the scene?"

"I don't know what became of it," replied the witness.

"That is all," said the prosecutor and turned to the jury with an expression which may have meant, "There was no knife. The ex-convict is a liar."

Jim rose to re-examine his client. "Now that we have already established that Carlton brandished a knife," Walker began, but was interrupted by objections. No knife, Walker's legal opponent pointed out, had been exhibited in evidence. The objection was overruled, subject to Walker's ability to connect up his questions with an actual knife.

"I shall soon show the gentlemen of the jury that there was a knife," Walker promised. He later admitted that he had not the slightest idea as to how he would be able to get a knife into, then out of, the death scene.

"You already have testified," Walker began again, "that you were attacked by Carlton in a fourth-floor room. How did you defend yourself?"

"I tried to run out of the room."

"Did he follow you to the door?"

The witness astonished his own counsel by his reply. "No, sir. I went out the window."

"I'm sorry," Walker apologized. "I meant to say the window. It is unusual for a man, even though desperately defending himself, to retreat through a fourth-floor window. But this is an unusual case."

"We know *that*, Senator," said the prosecutor wryly.

"But what you don't know," said Walker, sparring for time in which to think, "is what became of the knife."

This remark was stricken from the record. Now an inspiration seized Jim. If his man had gone out the fourth-floor window, there obviously would have been a fire-escape landing there. After objections by the prosecutor Jim elicited testimony that his client had been pursued onto the fire-escape by a man wielding a knife.

"Was there a scuffle on the fire-escape?" Jim asked.

"Yes, sir."

"It was there and then that you drew your pistol and fired?"

"Yes, sir."

Now Jim undertook the task of "returning" the mortally wounded man to the room where his body had been found.

"Was Carlton's back to the open window when you fired at him?"

Jim was called upon to rephrase his leading question. He drew out the testimony that Carlton had stood outside and near the window, and that he had fallen back from the fire-escape platform into the room where his body had been found.

Now Walker led up to the main point he wished to bring before the jury. "It has been testified to that no knife was found in the room. Did Carlton drop the knife before or after you shot him?"

"After."

"Inside the room, or"–Jim emphasized the word–"*outside*?" He added quickly, "I mean, did the knife drop to the fire-escape platform and then fall out of sight between the iron treads?"

Objection. The bench admonished Walker to desist from leading the witness. Jim set out once again to establish that the knife had fallen, that his client had seen it flash as it fell and had heard a metallic clatter, that he had looked down but had seen no knife, then had heard a noise of something dropping to the sidewalk far below.

After a trial which lasted two weeks McMullin was acquitted. He was promptly rearrested and extradited to Indiana, as a parole-violator.

At the start of the case Walker had been promised a fee of five thousand dollars. He received nothing. If Walker ever pressed anyone for money due him, his personal records do not show it, nor can any of his intimate friends remember that he did.

In 1922 Caffey wrote Roy A. Haynes, Federal Prohibition Commissioner in Washington, praising Walker's conduct of the McMullin defense and saying that it was "the moral duty, if not the legal duty, of the government to compensate Senator Walker." It would have required a special act of Congress, Jim said, to have brought about this payment. So he forgot all about it.

Before Prohibition, New York gangs had been halted temporarily when Police Commissioner Arthur Woods sent more than two hundred notorious hoodlums to prison. With the advent of Prohibition some of these malefactors emerged from their iron cocoons and recruited new forces for the sale of bootlegged whisky or to serve as hirelings—for either side—in labor disputes.

Two former members of Paul Kelly's defunct Five Points Gang were graduated from Sing Sing at about the same time in 1917: Johnny Spanish and Kid Dropper. These onetime Kelly henchmen operated separate gangs, and hated each other because of a love dispute of bygone years, in which Mr. Spanish's darling had fallen in love with Kid Dropper. Johnny took the more or less sweet cheat for a "ride" to the swamp land near Maspeth, Long Island, and shot her.

In 1919 this modern Othello was found dead on Second Avenue, with several balls of lead in his system. Kid Dropper was discharged in court for lack of evidence joining him to the crime. The Kid now had but one gangland rival in a new and lucrative business: the slugging of labor disputants during strikes. That man was Jacob Orgen, known to his set and to the police as "Little Augie." A former member of the Dopey Benny gang, Augie had come out of retirement to head a company of East Side thugs.

During a strike of laundry workers in the wet-wash controversy of 1923, the gangs of Little Augie and Kid Dropper fought with guns on Essex Street. The gangsters' bullets killed two bystanders, the only casualties of the fight. The police arrested Dropper and a dozen or more of his executive assistants on August 1, 1923. They went free in Essex Market Magistrates' Court because no one wished to testify against these vengeful hearties.

The authorities prepared to take Kid Dropper to the West Side Court to face a Sullivan Law violation charge for having possessed a revolver. The police received word that Dropper's henchmen might attempt to rescue him. Numerous policemen and detectives stood guard outside the courthouse, where a taxicab awaited the Kid and his custodians.

The police saw Little Augie among the many spectators and arrested him on general principles. One man whom the police did not see was a lesser member of Little Augie's gang, a "punk" named Louis Kushner. He was lurking in a tenement-house doorway across the street from the curb where Dropper's cab and three other vehicles were drawn up. Kushner had a gun in his coat pocket. Dropper, it was said, had just recently attempted to shake him down for several hundred dollars. Kushner not only sought revenge, but also coveted the reputation of a giant-killer.

Police Captain Cornelius Willemse, in plain clothes and a straw hat that warm summer day, and two detectives escorted Dropper to the cab. One detective opened the cab door and got inside. Dropper and the other detective followed. Captain Willemse paused to tell the driver where to go. Louis Kushner meantime had worked his way among the crowd and taken up a position behind one of the other cabs drawn up at the courthouse entrance. Kushner could see Dropper's head framed in the rear window of the conveyance in which the gangster sat between the detectives.

Kushner moved to the rear end of Dropper's cab. He pressed the muzzle of his pistol against the window glass and fired. The Kid slumped over, a bullet in his brain. Kushner fired again, and a bullet grazed the ear of the driver. The killer discharged his weapon two more times. One of the bullets knocked Captain Willemse's straw hat from his head.

The police subsequently captured Kushner. He was arraigned for first-degree murder, and the court appointed Senator Walker to defend him. It seemed quite likely that Kushner would go to the electric chair. Walker, however, managed to convince the jury that ten years to life was sufficient punishment for his client.

While the case was going on the dignified law offices of MacIntyre and Warren were invaded by men who spoke in the "dese-an'-dose" idiom. Upon the conclusion of this case several underworld figures sought Walker's legal services, but he refused, saying that the practice of criminal law was "an interesting but thankless job."

One "thankless" client was a man charged with manslaughter in a dice-game quarrel. Jim persuaded the defendant to plead guilty to a lesser charge in order to escape a term in Sing Sing. The court sentenced Walker's client to six months in the Tombs.

"He roared his head off at this," Jim said. "Claimed I had sold him out. After a few months had gone by I happened to be visiting the Tombs and there chanced upon my client, who now seemed most cordial. I observed that he was wearing a silk shirt, had a roll of bills, and was entirely happy, except for one circumstance. In a day or so, he confided to me, he would be freed ahead of time for good behavior. He begged me to use my influence to keep him in jail for the remainder of the six-month term. He explained that one of the Tombs deputies was his partner in the dice-game concession inside the jail and that business was booming."

In the spring of 1925 Walker was contemplating several business opportunities. Among other things, he had an interest in the Silver King Company, a concern that manufactured soda water. His associate and friend in this venture was Arthur Grashoff, whom Jim called "Grassy." They later drifted apart, but now they were good companions.

Grassy had made a fortune as the New York agent of a Canadian firm of ginger-ale and soda-water dispensers. New Yorkers were not soft-drink addicts; but Prohibition paradoxically had stimulated the sale of carbonated waters. Citizens who never before had served gin or whisky in their homes used the soda water to dilute the liquid fire. At cafés to which patrons brought their own liquor, soda water was served at high prices. In other drinking places the proprietors made a show of obeying the Prohibition law by selling soda water. Upon purchasing a bottle of it at a stiff fee, the customer would be given a surreptitious bonus of harder stuff.

Grassy decided to set up his own bottling firm. He saw in Walker a valuable ambassador for Silver King because of Jim's many contacts along the Great White Way.

Grassy was an Englishman of genteel manners and precise speech. He liked a good time and he liked Jim. They rode about the city in Grassy's Rolls-Royce and enjoyed themselves at parties. Somehow the Silver King water, contrary to popular belief, made little money either for Jim or for Grassy. But Grassy didn't seem to mind.

Jim became so engrossed with his soda-water affairs and a number of "inventions" and "discoveries" that some of his clients complained that he was neglecting them. Mrs. Allie Walker says, "Jim was a sucker for inventions and inventors. He would become enthused over almost any kind of scheme of this nature. I recall one man who claimed to be a prince of some sort from Italy. He had two sticks with which he said he could discover oil, silver, or gold, according to the vibrations set up in his sticks. Jim backed him on several expeditions to various places to discover treasure, but nothing ever came of it, except that Jim and I would spend hours planning whom we would give a whole gold mine to, and who would have to share one. It was great fun, and didn't cost too much."

The Walker files contain numerous letters and documents that testify to Jim's gullibility in respect to inventions, discoveries, and treasure hunts. In one instance he heard that a New Jersey alchemist had discovered the philosopher's stone. With Senator Jack Hastings and publisher Paul Block, Walker visited the seer's laboratory, and while Walker was listening to the abracadabra, Block observed that the scientist made tile as a sideline. Walker persuaded Block to finance the scientist, which the publisher agreed to do, but on the more practical basis of the manufacturing of tile. Mr. Block had good reason to repent of this generosity when, during the Seabury inquiries, the prosecution sought to make it appear that Block had bought into the tile-making business in order to sell the ceramics, through Walker's influence, for the new subway-station walls. The circumstances that multimillionaire Block did not need the money and that Jim was an admirer of alchemists and inventions were not used as evidence. A person capable of self-criticism, as Jim was, knew how ridiculous it would make him seem, in a legal inquiry, to acknowledge that he, a grown man, believed in such things as witching-rods and the transmutation of baser metals into gold. Daydreams have no place on a witness stand.

One of Jim's important clients who felt that he was being neglected by his attorney was Walker's good friend Abe Schwartz, owner of the Century Circuit, a string of motion-picture theatres in Brooklyn and Far Rockaway.

At Walker's law office one day Schwartz explained to Jim that he had brought along some contracts that required immediate attention. Jim kept him waiting while he put in several telephone calls of a social character.

Schwartz finally rose from his chair. "I'll see you some other time, Jim."

"Sit down, Abe," said Jim, and put in another call. "I'll be through pretty soon."

"No," replied Schwartz, "I'm going now."

Jim turned from the instrument. "But I thought you wanted to discuss some contracts with me, Abe?"

"No," replied the theatre owner, "I'm going to take that matter to somebody else."

Jim hung up the receiver. "Just what do you mean by that?"

"I'm going to another attorney, Jim."

"But why?"

"You're too busy." Then Schwartz went on to say, "At one time in my life, Jim, I was always busy. Suddenly I made up my mind that I was too busy to do my job properly. So I went home and did nothing. The next day I did nothing. The third day I decided what I was going to do. I started this circuit of theatres; and, by not being too busy, I made two hundred thousand dollars right away."

On Good Friday the hot-cross buns appeared in the bakery shops. Several of the neighborhoods that gave New York an Old World flavor made ready, each in its traditional fashion, for the Easter day when the sun is said to dance for the risen Lord. The candle makers of Little Italy displayed their masterpieces. The German shop-keepers put gingerbread rabbits in their windows. There were eggs made of sugar crystals, with peep-holes in them which permitted one to view wonderful scenes from the holy past. At the street corners on the Manhattan side of Queensboro Bridge the sidewalk stones blossomed with cut flowers and potted plants brought from nurseries across the East River. The sidewalk merchants presided over pyramids of little crates with white rabbits or yellow chicks inside them. There were bowls in which goldfish moved with monotonous lethargy on this day in the coldest April in many years.

Across the sea the King of Spain was washing the feet of the poor in Madrid. There were services at the Holy Sepulcher in Jerusalem. In Arizona the Yaquis Indians were dancing. President Coolidge was shaking hands with hundreds of political pilgrims in Washington; and on Easter Day children rolled eggs on the White House lawn. Babe Ruth, hospitalized in New York with an injured head, was offered thirty thousand yen to tour Japan. Prohibition Agent "Izzy" Einstein raided drugstores suspected of possessing liquor, and James J. Walker put on his silk hat and joined the promenaders on Fifth Avenue for the Easter parade.

On the Monday after Easter Sunday the first rumor that Walker *might* enter the primaries to oppose "Honest John" Hylan for the mayoralty nomination reached the *American*. We "looked into" this report.

Who was the first person to propose James J. Walker as the man to succeed Hylan, now completing his second term at City Hall? Several persons still vie for this distinction. Inasmuch as some of these men are reputable persons and not given to vainglorious boasting, my belief is that Jim freely allowed each claimant to take credit for having blown the first horn. This would seem a small matter, except that it reveals a crevice in Jim's character.

Almost any man who met Jim face to face went away with the conviction that he was not only Walker's friend, but his best friend. Since most human beings yearn to have their egos fed, when a popular figure singles out a man with a compliment or a favor the lucky fellow is uplifted, becomes a hero to his valet, and sometimes even to his wife.

Jim's "you-are-the-only-one" manner gratified many people. It tempted some of his friends to overreach the mark and exploit Jim's name to enhance their social importance or their bank accounts. His failure to halt these self-seekers led to many official woes. The favors turned into boomerangs. It is possible, and indeed seems probable, that Jim's warm nature would not allow him to deflate the ones whom he himself had carelessly inflated. It is also quite likely that Jim thirsted for affectionate admiration, and that his only driving ambition was to be loved. If this were so, as I believe it was, he succeeded beyond the lot of almost any other man of his time.

The boom for Walker originated on Broadway, not in Tammany Hall. Two of his friends—neither of whom ever exploited his name—were among the first to speak of Jim as candidate for mayor. S. Jay Kaufman was one and George Jessel the other.

Kaufman invited Walker to the opening of a nightplace called "The Ringside," operated by the brother of retired lightweight champion Benny Leonard. The dance floor was arranged to simulate a boxing ring. Benny Leonard got into this ring and introduced celebrities, among them S. Jay Kaufman.

The columnist spoke of Mayor Hylan, who lay dangerously ill at Saratoga. Kaufman asked the night-clubbers to pray for Mr. Hylan's recovery, then went on to say, "And I now have the great honor of introducing to you my friend Jimmy Walker, the next mayor of the City of New York."

Walker rose. "I accept the nomination," he said. "My friend Jay Kaufman has had this idea for a long time. He has talked to a great many people about it—mostly the wrong people. But he has the theory that if enough people keep talking about it, the right people will begin to believe that it is a good idea. Quite honestly, I prefer to remain where I am, but if the call came—from the right people—I might be persuaded to accept it. And I'll tell you why. I love New York. I love New York more than I love anything in the whole wide world!"

Jessel's introduction of Walker occurred at the opening of Lew Leslie's night club, the Rue de la Paix. The featured entertainer was Miss Bee Palmer, demonstrator of the "Shimmy," a dance that not only brought all the muscles into play but put them to work. Miss Palmer was late for her performance, so Master of Ceremonies Jessel introduced various members of the audience as a device to pass the time till the busy Bee buzzed onto the scene. Jessel saw Senator Walker in the audience and introduced him as "the man who soon will be mayor."

My own first knowledge of the Walker movement came from City Editor Hand, and I informed our publisher, Joseph A. Moore, of the incipient boom. This news disturbed Mr. Moore.

Mr. Moore was a handsome gentleman of middle age. He had enjoyed considerable success as a magazine publisher, but his lack of familiarity with the gathering and presentation of daily news events frequently caused him to disregard the reader interest of current happenings. He envisioned the support of Mayor Hylan by our paper as the paramount function of our news columns. To his mind it was important that the Hylan headlines take precedence over all other matters—the transfer, for example, of Nicola Sacco and Bartolomeo Vanzetti from the insane asylum to prison; the Scopes evolution trial in Tennessee; the destruction of the Navy's rigid dirigible *Shenandoah* in a thunderstorm over Ava, Ohio; the didoes of

Edward W. ("Daddy") Browning in adopting teen-age girls; and the Santa Barbara earthquake.

Mr. Moore, like several other Hearst executives, sometimes went far beyond the newspaper owner's intentions in carrying out campaigns. Instead of reading the signs of the times, these anxious fellows spent their hours in trying to read Mr. Hearst's mind. A hint from their chief was a Napoleonic command.

Whatever anyone may say in disparagement of Mr. Hearst, he has been a keen newsman. His political policies may have been vacillating, and his attitude on foreign affairs may or may not have been sound. But his judgment of the news, as well as his enterprise in getting the news, has been second to that of none of his competitors. Not once during all my personal contacts or correspondence with Mr. Hearst did he ever ask me to "color" the news or to suppress it.

When the first bulletins of the Santa Barbara earthquake came over the wires our staff made ready to give the disaster full coverage. Publisher Moore, politely as was his habit, warned me that Mr. Hearst had numerous financial and property interests in California, and that I need not advertise the earthquake in the biggest type I could find. Mr. Moore added that the great Brisbane, in his column "Today," had the right idea. That man of Socratic skull must have got his head stuck in the Holland Tunnel again, for he solemnly wrote that the victims at Santa Barbara had not been killed or injured by the earthquake but "by falling bricks."

While the compositors were setting type for the extra edition, I received a wire from Mr. Hearst's Los Angeles publisher, George Young. The Western executive pooh-poohed the extent of the quake. He also pointed out that Mr. Hearst had vast property interests in California. My return wire to Mr. Young merely stated that our New York readers had "vast interests in the news."

This set off an exchange of telegrams, and Mr. Hearst himself called me from his San Simeon estate. Presumably he had been told that his maniacal New York editor intended to ruin both Mr. Hearst and California with one headline.

"How are you handling the earthquake, young man?" Mr. Hearst asked over the long-distance telephone.

"We are merely mentioning it," I replied, "in an eight-column headline across the front page."

"You may be right," said Mr. Hearst, and I thought that I heard him chuckle. "The other New York papers are apt to refer to it in the same obscure way."

Kindly Joe Moore was beset by handicaps other than those pertaining to his lack of news-perception. Cataracts were forming over his eyes. After the city elections in November he planned to undergo an operation at the Wilmer Institute in Baltimore. He was a courageous man and said little or nothing about his eye trouble.

He lost his temper with me but once, and that was the day I notified him of the Walker boom. "It's perfectly absurd," he said. "Don't you think so?"

"No," I replied. "Even 'One-eyed' Connolly could defeat Hylan."

"That," he said, "is disloyalty!"

Upon leaving Mr. Moore's office, I experienced a feeling of regret for having offended him. The anger of a courteous, high-principled man, such as Joe Moore was, could not be shrugged off as could the spoutings of the aggressive blow-hards of newspaper front offices. In those days I seldom repented of anything I did or said. I was thirty-four years old; and if I knew half as much now as I thought I knew then, I could easily become Secretary of State. But I did feel ashamed of myself for having placed the name of "One-eyed" Connolly, the celebrated gate-crasher, in nomination. I moved back across the city room to tell Joe Moore that I was sorry for my impertinence.

As I stood outside his door I heard the man with the afflicted eyes whistling "The World Is Waiting for the Sunrise."

It should never be said that New York lives in the past. Notwithstanding occasional commemorations, such as the recent one for the fiftieth anniversary of the union of the five boroughs, the Greater City speaks and lives in the present tense. It daily enthrones new gods, who seem to spring from nowhere and, more often than not, as swiftly return to their source. These temporarily exalted deities hasten their own heartbreaks, at the polls or in other places of judgment. They learn too late that a honeymoon with notoriety is not a marriage to fame.

New York in the twenties differed from today's metropolis mainly in respect to size and the names of its demigods. Then as now the diehards moaned and the new favorites pranced upon the stage with spotlights lending short-lived halos to their heads.

The city of the six million paused for a moment, but only for a moment, to remark the passing of once-great men and women or the demolition of once-famed landmarks. The people of the Jazz Age, then being accurately chronicled by F. Scott Fitzgerald, made mental footnotes of the deaths in 1925 of artists John Singer Sargent and George Wesley Bellows, of poetess Amy Lowell, orator William Jennings Bryan, Senator Robert Marion La Follette, and Dowager Queen Alexandra of England. They glanced occasionally at the aging giants of yesterday's publicity: Sir Thomas Lipton, seventy-five years old and babbling of another yachting venture; Chauncey M. Depew, at ninety-one; John D. Rockefeller, Sr., still distributing dimes at eighty-six; and the doughty ex-champion of wrestlers, eighty-year-old William Muldoon of the State Boxing Commission.

In May the old Madison Square Garden closed. Perhaps the dooming of the Garden moved New Yorkers more than did any other event of its kind that year. When the St. Gaudens statue of Diana left the tower of the building designed by Stanford White, and in which he was slain by Harry K. Thaw, it seemed like an abdication. Old boulevardiers and old champions popped out of hiding to attend the last sports spectacle at this hippodrome hall where horse-show society had been born, where political pageants and six-day bicycle races had been held, where Patrick E. Gilmore's band had given concerts, and where the fists of Sullivan, Kilrain, Mitchell, Corbett, Fitzsimmons, and of many lighter pugilists had thwacked the chins of adversaries.

The veteran announcer Joe Humphreys read a valedictory, "The Temple of Fistiana." The ringside bell beat out a requiem. The hall, which since 1890 had been the sports as well as the social center of Manhattan, was given over to prosaic wreckers and to excavators who managed to give New York a battlefield aspect of trenches and breastworks.

The city also prepared to tear down the figure of its Mayor. The people were tired of Mr. Hylan and sought to replace him in City Hall with a New Yorker's New Yorker.

15.

Decision at the Half Moon

THE JAUNTY Senator from Greenwich Village exactly suited the specifications of the electorate. Broadway was the heart of their world, and Broadway launched its own candidate with songs and dances and merry shouts at a meeting at Webster Hall on East Eleventh Street.

This old building, in which chorus lines practiced for musical shows, took on the atmosphere of a political convention. But the events of that summer's day in 1925 were unrehearsed. Irving Berlin sang his song "We'll Walk in with Walker." George M. Cohan led a demonstration. Former Secretary of State Bainbridge Colby made a "nominating" speech. Members of the Friars and the Lambs and the Grand Street Boys sent delegations. John McGraw and the baseball men from Coogan's Bluff, Jimmy Johnston and the boxing men, A. C. Blumenthal and the motion-picture men, Gene Buck, Johnny O'Connor, and the theatrical men, James P. Sinnott and the newspapermen—all talked, sang, and shouted in praise of Walker.

Jim's enthusiastic sponsors paraded from Webster Hall to Tammany headquarters on Fourteenth Street. There they waited for an hour or so before Tammany Leader George W. Olvany deigned to emerge from his private office. The current headkeeper of the Tigers, an ex-judge and a man of impassive countenance, eventually appeared in the reception room at Tammany Hall. "Well, gentlemen?" he asked.

The petitioners demanded Tammany's endorsement of their hero. Judge Olvany listened with the gravity of a suspicious pawnbroker—and this was not the first time he had heard a plea in behalf of Jim's candidacy. An examination of Walker's correspondence reveals that Albany correspondent James P. Sinnott advised Jim in the spring of 1925 that James Eagan had telephoned him from New York City, urging Sinnott to ask Judge Olvany to "run Jim." Walker had replied, "Go ahead, but you're only wasting your time."

When the delegation from Webster Hall concluded their arguments, Judge Olvany said, "Good day, gentlemen," and returned to his private quarters.

Several days later vacationing Tammany chiefs met on a golf course outside Atlantic City. Al Smith, titular head of his party in state and city politics, was among the politicians present on the greens. Al frowned upon Walker's proposed candidacy, then drove his ball down the fairway.

Actor William Halligan and Dan McKetrick, among others, have told me that Smith expressed his views in the locker room after the game. "If Walker could keep out of the Broadway limelight—which he can't—and if he would rid himself of that certain party he has been going around with—which he won't—and go back to Mrs. Walker," said Smith, "then things might be different."

During the next weeks, without explanation, Walker absented himself from the city's night spots. Photographs taken of Senator and Mrs. Walker began to appear in the newspapers. Jim no longer frequented Leone's Restaurant at midnight. Where was he? What had happened to the man about town?

Sportswriter Bill Corum has supplied me with the real story of Jim's temporary disappearance from the white-light haunts. Corum says that the Silver King magnate persuaded Jim to stay out of public view between sundown and sunrise. Grassy knew that Al Smith was opposed to having Tammany endorse Walker largely because of Jim's indifference to public criticism. So Grassy persuaded the Senator to agree to a course designed to offset Governor Smith's censure.

It was agreed upon that Jim show himself, if at all, only when Mrs. Walker was at his side. With or without Mrs. Walker, he was to shun all places where gay men and women gathered at late hours.

"Should I enter a monastery?" Walker inquired.

"I have leased an apartment," Grassy explained to Jim. "It is very comfortable, it is very private, and it is all yours."

Walker and Grassy entertained carefully but joyously in their penthouse on West Fifty-eighth Street. The place was leased from a luxury-loving dowager who was on a holiday abroad. Grassy stocked the apartment with vintage wines, caviar, and partridge. His English butler selected a staff of discreet servants.

For the time being Jim might do as he pleased, on the condition that he make whoopee in the penthouse instead of at Broadway clubs. Grassy placed his Rolls-Royce and chauffeur at Jim's disposal during the day, but they were forbidden him after sundown.

Walker's Broadway pals—except the few who secretly visited the penthouse—finally conceded that Jim had gone home to reform his ways. Only once, Corum asserts, did Walker break out of what Jim called his "Chanel Number Five dungeon."

Grassy was attending some social function when a telephone call from the excited butler reached him. "The Senator has vanished, sir!"

Grassy shrewdly guessed where Jim might be. He hastened to Texas Guinan's club. The Senator and a group of friends were just entering that place when Grassy pounced upon him. Somewhat shamefaced, Jim acknowledged that he had broken his pledge, then meekly went home to the penthouse.

In July Grand Sachem Voorhis, now ninety-six years old, announced that he would be unable to address Tammany Hall's annual rally on the Fourth. Al Smith was to speak in his stead. Two days before the rally the Governor sought to escape the sweltering heat of the city. He went with his sons to Coney Island.

From the Half Moon Hotel on the boardwalk Smith telephoned Walker's home on St. Luke's Place. Jim was not there, but Mrs. Walker made a plausible excuse for her husband's absence and promised to give him the message. Smith said that he wished to see Walker at once on a matter of importance and asked that he come to the Half Moon without delay.

Mrs. Walker forwarded Smith's request. Jim's host roused the Senator from sleep and supervised a program of cold showers and massage.

"Are the British coming?" asked Jim.

"No," replied Grassy. "It's the Irish. General Smith has taken Coney Island."

Within an hour Grassy sent his now shining guest to Coney Island in the Rolls-Royce. "Refuse a drink if the Governor offers you one even if your tongue is hanging out," he admonished Jim. "This is *der Tag*."

When Walker appeared at the Half Moon Hotel Smith studied him for several moments. Then the Governor went to a sideboard to pour himself a drink. Jim afterward told Grassy that the Governor looked up from his glass to say, "I understand that you don't want one of these?"

"I'm not having anything to drink. Thanks."

"How'd you ever do it?" asked Governor Smith.

"Do what?"

"Straighten up? Go home where you belong? Keep away from the speakeasies?"

"We all grow up sometime."

The Governor placed a hand on Jim's shoulder. "You've proved that you can rise to the occasion. I've checked up on you. Jim, I've decided to approve your candidacy. You're the man to beat Red Mike. Sure you don't want a drink?"

"Just a glass of soda water," Jim said. "Glad to see that you are using Silver King."

On leaving the hotel, Jim almost leaped into the Rolls-Royce. Back at the penthouse he told Grassy, "Virtue is its own reward."

"Now," said Grassy, "we shall open a magnum of champagne. We've earned it."

Next day the Walker boom was officially placed in the hands of Tammany Leader Olvany. Boss Ed Flynn of the Bronx concurred in the selection of Walker as the logical opponent of Mayor Hylan in the primaries.

The rage of Mayor Hylan over Walker's candidacy caused Jim to say, "Hell hath no fury like a Hylan scorned."

Among the several circumstances that weighed in Walker's favor during the primary campaign was the fact that he had never held an administrative position in city affairs. Hence he was immune to adverse criticism as to mistakes made in office. Furthermore, his legislative record plainly indicated his desire to preserve the five-cent fare, Hylan's constant battle cry. The Mayor, therefore, elected to attack Walker for the horrible things he was going to do, and not the things he had done. Walker, shouted the incumbent, intended to make New York an open city for gangsters, thieves, prostitutes, and dope salesmen.

Instead of replying to Hylan in the orthodox manner, Jim met these onslaughts with full good humor. For example, on August 9, when Jim was posing for a photograph with Babe Ruth at Yankee Stadium, reporters informed him that Hylan had made a statement that Walker was the bosom friend of the underworld. Jim glanced at Ruth. "Please don't steal any bases today, Babe," he said, "unless you wish to embarrass both of us." Then Jim added, "The papers say that my friend Dr. Raymond Ditmars is going to Brazil to collect snake venom. Is such a long journey necessary?"

At about this time in August Grassy permitted Jim to cancel their gentlemen's agreement to the extent that Walker might go to the theatre, but only with Mrs. Walker or with male companions. Certain Tammany Hall envoys called upon Vonnie Shelton. They asked her if she really had Walker's interests at heart.

She was a bright person. "You mean you want me to get out of sight."

"And out of mind too," said one of her callers.

"Out of sight, yes," replied Vonnie. "Out of mind, no. I'll never put J. J. out of *my* mind for you or anyone else."

"He must put you out of *his* mind."

The spirited young lady replied, "Then let *him* tell me what you're saying."

After Vonnie was persuaded that she stood in Walker's way, she burst out laughing. Then she wept. Then she laughed again. Finally she tossed her bobbed head of hair. "I want him to succeed," she said, "and I want him to be happy. So if you'll get out, I'll begin packing my trunks."

Miss Shelton went to Cuba and did not return until after the primaries in September.

Of the five borough leaders, three supported Hylan's candidacy: John H. McCooey of Brooklyn, Maurice Connolly of Queens, and David Rendt of Richmond. Boss Olvany of Manhattan and Boss Flynn of the Bronx endorsed Walker. Jim's first political patron, Charles W. Culkin, became a candidate for sheriff. Al Smith's good friend General Charles W. Berry was selected to run for comptroller. Flynn designated Joseph V. McKee as his own choice for president of the Board of Aldermen.

As a long-time friend of Walker's, Culkin became concerned about Jim's health. The candidate's stomach was bothering him again. Toward the close of the campaign Walker shrank from about a hundred and thirty to a hundred and eleven pounds. He spoke almost everywhere and at all hours, and had little sleep.

Meantime Hylan was assailing Walker on personal rather than political grounds. During a speech to an organization of women voters Hylan said that he would not utter such a depraved name as Walker's in the presence of ladies. When Jim heard of this he smiled. "Red Mike is loaded down with red herrings."

Governor Smith announced late in August that he personally would take the stump for Walker. It was not customary, as Howard

Shiebler points out in a letter to me, for governors to interfere in nominations for municipal office—particularly not when intra-party strife was bound to follow, and when a governor was an aspirant for the presidency.

One of the factors in swinging the Walker-Hylan primary contest in Jim's direction was an issue that had nothing directly to do with the mayoralty.

"During the legislative session of 1925," Shiebler says, "Al Smith had been pushing hard for his 300-million-dollar bond issue to eliminate grade-crossings. Every Democratic legislator had voted in favor of this bond issue. Following the adjournment of the legislature, and along about June, Mayor Hylan made a speech against it, basing his opposition on the ground that it was up to the railroads to finance the elimination of their grade-crossings and not up to the people.

"He thus put the Democratic legislators in an embarrassing position. Having voted for the bond issue, they could not agree with Hylan, and many of them had to announce their disagreement publicly. By raising an issue that did not have to be raised until the following fall, when the bond proposition was to be voted on, Mayor Hylan placed himself in the position of being at odds with the legislators of his own party on a proposal that was extremely popular with the people."

Hylan was a resident of Brooklyn, the largest of the five boroughs. He had demonstrated his vote-getting ability there, and in the neighboring borough of Queens, through his championship of the five-cent fare. As Boss Flynn of the Bronx has said, "Hylan's strength was always in small organizations, some of them only semi-political . . . of small property-owners."

Boss Flynn also has said that when he made up his mind to support Walker he "was not unaware" of Jim's serious limitations.

"His acute mentality," Flynn wrote in his book, *You're the Boss*, "had enabled him to move effectively into situations without the systematic preparation most men required. His quickness and great personal charm combined to overcome opposition far more often than was justified by the merits of the points at issue. . . . I found that his manner was so boyishly disarming that my resentment usually evaporated. This was a beguiling characteristic, but one which was destined ultimately to give him much trouble. Many of the people who surrounded him were superficial and rapacious. He found it hard to believe that any of his friends were bad—or even wrong."

In describing the 1925 fight for control of the Democratic party in New York City, Flynn said of Walker, "I have never met a man with greater ability to absorb knowledge and express it to the public. In a political campaign such as we were anticipating, this supreme capacity to present political ideas pertinently and attractively was a matter of great importance as against the ponderous verbosity of Mayor Hylan."

On August 30 Mayor Hylan winced, in a huge way, when his former assistant, Grover Augustin Whalen, endorsed Senator Walker for mayor at a garden party given in Jim's honor at Far Rockaway. Hylan reacted to this announcement as though Brutus were again on the loose. Whalen had been, among many other things, Mayor Hylan's secretary and his Commissioner of Plant and Structures. Moreover, he had established a formula for welcoming celebrated guests to New York.

Governor Smith's active participation in the mayoralty campaign gave much prestige to Walker's candidacy. It also drew fire from the editorial guns of Mr. Hearst.

On September 2, 1925, with the primaries but thirteen days in the future, I received—as editor of Mr. Hearst's *American*—an open letter signed by Governor Smith in which he replied to one of Mr. Hearst's anti-Smith editorials.

This five-page letter, written under the State Seal, called Mr. Hearst a "liar" and "a debaser of journalism," and charged that he had made "wicked and insidious appeals to race hatred." Mr. Hearst, the Governor went on to say, had the nerve of a Bengal tiger "to be loafing in the splendor and grandeur of his palatial estate on the Pacific Coast, and attempting to dictate the politics of the greatest city in the world."

Publisher Moore was distressed when we printed this letter in full on the front page. Mr. Hearst, however, saw its presentation as a matter of news. Mr. Moore thereupon announced that he was wagering eighteen thousand dollars on a Hylan victory over Walker. City Editor Hand pleaded with him not to throw his money out the window.

"It's the loyal thing to do," Mr. Moore insisted, and put in a telephone call to his betting commissioner at Jack Doyle's poolroom.

The primary election returns conclusively indicated a Walker victory. Moore lost his election bet with quiet resignation, and censured none of the staff for smiling in the I-told-you-so manner.

"That editorial," Mr. Moore said to me with a twinkle, "in which you compared Hylan to Lincoln, seems to have been slightly exaggerated, now that I think it over more carefully. I am glad that you didn't put us further out on the limb by comparing him to God."

Mr. Hearst called me long distance that night to ask, "How is Mayor Hylan doing?"

To which I replied, "The people have spoken, Mr. Hearst." I added, "But they needn't have been so loud."

"He has lost?"

"Mr. Hylan apparently has lost even his own Borough of Brooklyn by five thousand votes."

Mr. and Mrs. Walker received the primary election results at Jim's headquarters in the Commodore Hotel. They stayed up late celebrating.

When reporters called at St. Luke's Place next day Jim was still out on the town. Mrs. Walker received the journalists in the second-floor drawing-room of the old house. While waiting for her to appear, the reporters took notice of the furnishings, the thick-piled green rugs, the overstuffed chairs covered with flowered chintz, the statue of Mercury, the grand piano in one corner of the room.

The newspapermen rose as the chubby, cheerful woman with brown bobbed hair entered the room. She said that she was happy, and she looked it.

"I'm happy for many reasons," she said, motioning for her visitors to be seated. "One of the reasons is that Jim will be home tonight. He just called up to say that my political widowhood is at an end."

Most of the reporters were aware that Jim and Allie, now in their thirteenth year of married life, had just recently come to a new understanding. They could see her unaffected happiness and refrained from putting questions that might cloud her bright moment. Her reference to "political widowhood," however, was not lost upon the interviewers.

Mrs. Walker said that when her husband became mayor she would continue to stay in the background. When asked if she darned Mr. Walker's socks, she replied, "He never wears out his socks."

It would appear that Jim was sincere about his "new start" as a devoted husband. Vonnie Shelton had kept her promise. She returned briefly to the city in October. There was a meeting between Vonnie and Jim at a hotel apartment. Dan McKetrick accompanied Walker to the hotel. McKetrick informed me that when he volunteered to leave, Vonnie said, "Don't go, Dan. Jim doesn't want to be alone with me."

Dan looked at Jim for confirmation.

Walker said, "Maybe it's better this way." Jim appeared uneasy, and unwilling to voice whatever may have been on his mind.

"If this is to be good-by, I want to hear it from you, Jim, and not from Tammany Hall," said Vonnie.

When McKetrick again suggested that he leave, Vonnie said with some spirit, "I told you he doesn't want to be alone with me. It was an effort for him even to come here."

"That's not fair," Walker at last said. "And you always have been fair."

"Then I'll say it for you," she fumed. "This *is* good-by." As suddenly, she repented her flare-up and turned to a window that looked out on Central Park. "You're in love with a town," she said quietly. "It's the first time I ever had to compete with that. And I'm overmatched."

Several persons have insisted that this was the last meeting between Vonnie and Jim. There is evidence to the contrary, however, and Vonnie Shelton's best friend, May Weston, says there was a transcontinental telephone call from Walker to Miss Shelton as late as 1932. At that time Jim also spoke to Miss Weston. "Take good care of the Little Fellow," he said.

After his victory in the September primaries of 1925 Walker went aboard a houseboat to fish along the Florida coast. He was gone two weeks and gained seven pounds and a tan.

The day after his return from Florida he spoke at the closing ceremonies of Forty-second Street's one-hundredth anniversary celebration, and at five banquets in succession. Obviously he could not appear simultaneously at all five of them, and when he became progressively later his reputation for tardiness took root.

Quite often when Walker rose to speak he would say a few words nobody seemed to understand. He explained this to cartoonist Harry Hershfield. "It's a valuable trick, designed to gain full attention. You know as well as I do that at banquets, especially the social ones, the first words of the speaker are lost. So, if you just give them some double-talk, and really don't say anything but mumble, you will find that the people crane their necks and ask one another, 'What's that? What's he saying?' And they will be so worried over missing something that you suddenly have their complete attention and can then go into your speech."

When asked which had been his best speech, Walker replied, "When I sat down."

After one long evening of banquets, during a heat wave that made of the city the world's largest Turkish bath, Walker invited Harry Hershfield to go with him to City Hall.

"But it's two o'clock in the morning," Harry demurred.

"I know that," said Jim, "but I have some work that simply has to be done."

At City Hall Hershfield removed his coat. Not so Jim, who always stayed coated and waistcoated in the presence of a guest no matter how friendly their relationship might be. A loud voice came through the open windows that face the plaza. Jim and Harry looked out to see a man staggering up the outer steps. He was shouting that he proposed to make a speech.

Jim's police guard announced his intention to "pinch" the fellow, but Walker said, "No, Sergeant, I'd like to hear a really *good* speech tonight for a change."

The citizen chose a place upon the marble platform and began a tirade against the administration. He spent about two minutes denouncing the municipal government in general and then got down to particulars. He shouted that Mayor Walker was a disgrace and a cheat. When Walker applauded, the man turned, caught sight of Harry and Jim at the window, and asked, "Don't you agree with me?"

"I am with you one hundred per cent, Cicero!" Walker called out.

The policeman was unable to countenance the scene any longer. He said that he simply had to "get the man going on his way."

"Sergeant," Jim said, "he is already going, and I predict that he is going on his nose."

At this moment the man collapsed upon the steps. "He really is a good speaker," Walker sighed. "Put him in a cab, Sergeant, and pay the driver to take him safely home."

Jim's Republican opponent in the city-wide campaign was Frank D. Waterman of the fountain pen company. Jim liked Waterman and refrained from attacking him in the muddy manner. In fact Jim always avoided the name-calling technique.

The gentlemanly Mr. Waterman, on his own part, presented himself to the electorate as one who would conduct municipal affairs on a business basis. He made one halfhearted attempt in a newspaper interview to link Walker's name with a Coney Island land grab. His information, he said, had come to him by means of a telephone call. He added that the Senator had been seen at dinner with a group of profit-loving realtors. In reply to this, Walker said that he had had dinner with thousands of businessmen. He pointed out that he had once dined with Mr. Waterman, and wondered if that meal had put him in the fountain-pen business.

When it was suggested that both candidates meet in personal debate, Waterman's representatives inquired if Walker would be apt to ridicule their chief. Jim was in Washington—not on a political mission but to see a World Series baseball game between the Pittsburgh and the Washington clubs. His aides assured the Waterman forces that the Senator would return in time to attend a luncheon given in honor of both candidates by the United Women's Wear League of America and would hurl no epithets.

Mr. Waterman spoke first at that luncheon. "When you have to choose between the Senator and myself," he said, "you will probably choose me because of the money I am going to save you during the next four years."

"Mr. Waterman," retaliated the Senator, "is such an outstanding businessman, such a successful citizen, that I shall insist that he work on my advisory committee after the first of the year."

Mr. Waterman announced that he knew little about the women's wear business, but did know how to press his own trousers. "That knowledge has often helped me," he went on to say, "for when I didn't want to pay the price, I did the pressing myself. I have learned to be economical by necessity."

"Frankly," Walker declared, "I never pressed my own clothes. I couldn't. I'm a politician. If I had pressed them, every tailor in the city would have protested. Mr. Waterman, they won't let you press yours much longer."

Walker amazed his audience by saying that he regarded his opponent as his superior in most respects and that he was tempted to vote for him. "In a way," he continued, "it is regrettable that the voters will insist that Mr. Waterman continue in his very successful business; and, by the same token, they will insist that I give up my commercial associations and devote my entire time to the business of government, in which I have been engaged for sixteen years."

Jim then voiced his theory of popular government. "The least government is the best government. Ninety-eight per cent of the people want only to be let alone to enjoy freedom in safety. I maintain that a great majority of people want freedom to do as they like so long as they do not interfere with others."

This statement, I believe, was also an expression of Walker's views in respect to his own private way of life.

The Walker-Waterman campaign proceeded along gentlemanly lines until the latter part of October. An incident then occurred which put candidate Waterman on his back. It is quite likely that Waterman would have been defeated in any event, but the incident made his losing sure and somewhat unpleasant.

Among Jim's partisans was a reporter for the *Morning Telegraph*. Without Jim's knowing, the reporter wrote a letter asking for reservations to the manager of the Fountain Inn, a hotel in Eustis, Florida, owned by Mr. Waterman. He signed the fictitious name "Miss Esther Robinowitz" to the missive.

By return post a letter signed "William Kimball," the name of Mr. Waterman's hotel manager in Florida, reached "Miss Robinowitz" at a Bronx address "in care of Lauer." This letter contained the explosive sentence: "Our clientele is such that the patronage of persons of Hebrew persuasion is not solicited."

On October 30 the *Telegraph* carried a facsimile of this letter on the first page. The Waterman forces strove to offset the implication that their candidate was prejudiced, but the damage was done.

Perhaps, when Jim learned of this ruse, he should have deplored it. The fact is, however, that he was convulsed with laughter.

J. Dunninger, the mind-reader, read the Senator's mind, found him thinking of party loyalty, and predicted his triumph at the polls. Band leader Vincent Lopez played "Will You Love Me in December," and Irving Berlin's song "We'll Walk in with Walker." The Civil Service employees of the city backed Jim's candidacy. A chrysanthemum was named the "Jimmy Walker." Members of the cast of

Gay Paree gave a block party in Shubert Alley. A Fifth Avenue landmark surrendered to the wreckers when the late Senator Clark's seven-million-dollar palace failed to bring two million dollars on the realty market. Rudolph Valentino arrived from Hollywood for the premiere of his latest picture, *The Eagle*, at the Strand Theatre. A hashish field was discovered in Long Island and its narcotic crop destroyed.

On the coldest October 29 on record Mr. Hearst announced his ninth-inning support of Walker's candidacy. Mayor Hylan rose like a sulking Achilles to say that he would "back the Democratic candidates," but he didn't mention Walker by name. Mr. Waterman announced that he had discharged the manager of his Fountain Inn. Mrs. Franklin D. Roosevelt wrote a letter of praise to Walker, and the Grand Street Boys prepared to celebrate Jim's promised victory.

New Yorkers of five boroughs went to the polls on a November Tuesday that was mild in contrast to gale-swept October. A sprinkle of rain fell at noon, but the weather again became as clement as the temper of the citizens. No arguments and no fights occurred at the historically turbulent polling places. A group of schoolchildren presented Senator and Mrs. Walker with a bouquet of American Beauty roses when the candidate and his wife appeared at Public School 95 on Clarkson Street to cast their ballots.

Late that night it became apparent that James J. Walker had been chosen as the one-hundredth mayor of New York. There had been ninety-six elected mayors before his time. Three had succeeded to office because of vacancies at City Hall.

Walker won by a plurality of 402,123. His running-mates on the city ticket were carried into office with him. It was Tammany's first unequivocal victory since Mayor Van Wyck had lost his title in 1902. Other Tammany mayors had held office since Van Wyck's time, but, among them, McClellan had run out on his organization; Gaynor had had a Board of Estimate that was partly "fusion"; and Hylan had warred with his Fourteenth Street sponsors. During the campaign Walker had made it abundantly evident that his allegiance to the Tammany Hall that had created him, and his reverence for the memory of Charles F. Murphy, would govern his actions as mayor.

The November election solidified Al Smith's leadership in state and city politics. In appreciation of Governor Smith's support of his candidacy, Jim volunteered to do some "missionary work" for the presidential aspirant.

Walker canceled his plans to attend the six-day bicycle races and announced that once again he was going on a fishing and golfing holiday in Florida. Major John S. Cohen, Democratic national committeeman and publisher of the *Atlanta Journal*, invited the Mayor-elect to stop off at the Georgia capital to address a banquet of political and business leaders of the "Cracker State." Jim accepted this speaking engagement as a means to woo the Dixie colonels to Al Smith's presidential plans for 1928. The Southerners had not forgotten the Smith-McAdoo feud at the convention of 1924, during which the Ku Klux Klan issue had been raised.

James P. Sinnott of the *Morning Telegraph* accompanied Jim Walker on this journey, as did Arthur Grashoff (Grassy) and William Seeman, the wholesale grocery magnate. Seeman and Walker were inseparable cronies at this time, and on numerous occasions Jim had been a guest at Seeman's bachelor apartment.

At the Atlanta banquet Walker amazed the colonels by eulogizing Tammany Hall. He described the wigwam as a temple of all social and political virtues. It could not be said that he won his listeners to his point of view in respect to Tammany, but he obviously gained their affection for himself. In pleading Smith's and Tammany's cause, he found himself in the position of a John Alden, and some of his listeners suggested that he speak for himself. He smiled, shook hands all around, then went on his way to Florida.

At Coral Gables Walker received an invitation from President Machado to visit the palace in Havana. Jim and his party sailed thither aboard the gunboat *Cuba*. During the twenty-four-hour voyage members of the crew put on a series of boxing bouts.

At Havana Mayor Cuesta expected Walker at City Hall. A police band of fifty pieces was drawn up in the plaza to welcome the New Yorker. Jim stopped over at the Havana branch of the National City Bank and was an hour late at City Hall. Meanwhile the band had played hymns of welcome to two other visitors, mistaking each in turn for Mr. Walker.

Jim and his party stayed several days in Havana. He enjoyed the jai alai games and the night life, and then returned to Miami, where he played golf for two days. From Miami he went to Palm Beach, and telegraphed to worried Boss John H. McCooey of Brooklyn that there would be no reprisals for McCooey's support of Hylan during the primaries. The rotund and elderly McCooey, a jovial patriarch who resembled Santa Claus minus the beard, beamed when he learned that he had not forfeited his rights to patronage.

When Walker left Florida for New York he sent word to his metropolitan friends to cancel their plans for a welcome-home demonstration. Editorials commended him for his good judgment in vetoing the celebration.

It was below zero weather that December. Wall Street gave large bonuses to its employees. And when Dr. Harvey Cushing announced the discovery that the pituitary gland regulates the body's water supply, Walker said, "I must inform W. C. Fields of this at once."

A year of prosperity was reaching its final days. Although Secretary of Commerce Herbert Hoover warned against speculation, the city, the nation, and the world made ready for bigger and better profits. In Rome Pope Pius closed the Holy Door of St. Peter's at the last ceremony of a twelve-month religious season which is observed every twenty-fifth year.

Then, at City Hall, on January 1, 1926, in the three-hundred-year-old City of New York, the one-hundredth mayor bounced up the stairs to be sworn in as the leader of the six million. When reporters and photographers blocked his path, he called out briskly, "Let me through, fellows!"

Part Two

INTERNATIONAL NEWS PHOTO

Mrs. Walker, Mr. Smith, the Smiths' daughter Emily, Mr. Walker, and Mrs. Smith during the mayoral campaign of 1925

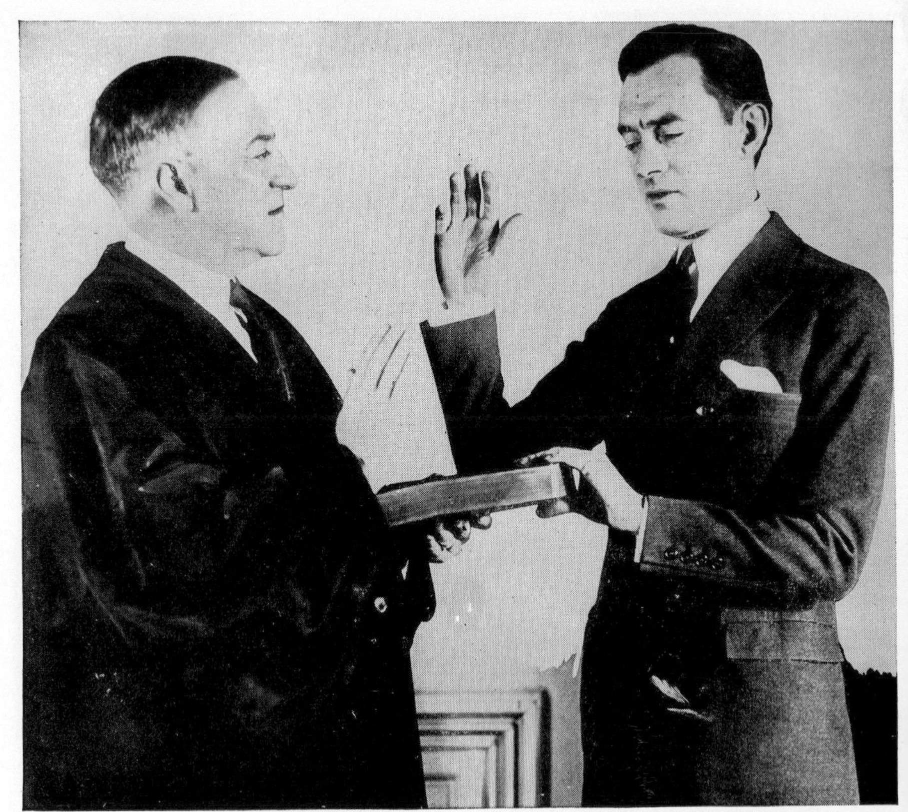

INTERNATIONAL NEWS PHOTO

Judge Robert F. Wagner swearing Walker in as mayor,
January 1, 1926

INTERNATIONAL NEWS PHOTO

Mayor Walker on his return from one of his Southern trips, with Big Bill Egan of the Pennsylvania Railroad and Paul Bloch

INTERNATIONAL NEWS PHOTO

The Lindbergh reception in 1927: Grover A. Whalen, Lindy, and His Honor

16.

Ring in the New

THEY came from every quarter to City Hall Park that forenoon of New Year's Day. They trouped across the triangular common like ants on a piece of pie. Rolls-Royces, trolley cars, taxicabs, and subway trains had carried them here to see their beau ideal.

Many celebrants had stayed up all night. It had been the "wettest" New Year's Eve within the memory of Broadway, and one saw evening gowns draggling beneath the fur wraps of Park Avenue women and glimpsed the disarray of winged collars and formal bow ties beneath the silk mufflers of wine-eyed escorts. The merrymakers brought along noise-making toys. The time of revelry was lasting around the clock. In a larger sense, it would last around the years.

Derelicts from Chatham Square shuffled among the more solvent citizens, soliciting funds with which to purchase raw alcohol or worse. They grinned like demented clowns whenever the police growled, "Move on, you!" The breaths of these seedy intruders made white plumes in the frosty forenoon, as did the exhalations of the rich and important folk. The white vapors ballooned alike from every mouth–smoke signals of democracy.

At ten o'clock this holiday morning the police of Traffic "A" came out of their basement quarters in City Hall's east wing, where the cells for prisoners of the War of 1812 had been. The officers formed a double rank on the marble stairs. Behind them rose a skyline of Tammany silk hats.

At eleven o'clock an automobile drove slowly up to the plaza. Two motorcycle officers escorted this car to a place in the official parking area near the statue of Nathan Hale. This vehicle brought Mr. Hylan to his official funeral. The automobile had been stripped of its Police Department bumper-shield.

There were no cheers when the silk-hatted man got out of his car. There was no applause as he strode up the stone steps of Massachusetts marble worn smooth and grooved by one hundred and fifteen years of political boot-beats. Nor were there any jeers for Mr. Hylan, nor callings out of "Red Mike." He seemed as lonely as a baseball umpire.

Half an hour after Mr. Hylan had disappeared inside the Hall sirens sounded on the Broadway flank of the park and a motorcade of policemen wheeled in from the western street entrance. A smart town car traveled behind the motorcycles. A great cheer arose. The patrolmen guarding the Hall held back the crowd. The gay onlookers tooted tin horns, twirled ratchets, blew whistles, and brandished pocket flasks.

"Jimmy! Jimmy Walker!"

The name bore down from all sides. Again and again it surpassed the clamor of the whistles and the horns. It roared with a sea-sound against the buildings that walled in the historic common which had witnessed many demonstrations, both gala and riotous. Jim's own father had seen police factions embattled here in 1857, the year of his arrival from Ireland.

"Jimmy! Jimmy Walker!"

The man of the hour touched his silk hat three or four times but did not raise it from his head. He walked along, nervously it seemed, his shoulders hunched forward, his eyes fixed ahead. Nor did he smile or offer any word to the bystanders.

Several spectators remarked on the preoccupied deportment of their usually gay laureate. The well-wishers, however, forgave him for this seeming indifference to their overtures. The whims of a hero are interpreted with the utmost lenity—until his hour has struck and he falls from the pendulum.

"He means business," said one.

"Jimmy's going to tackle the job," said another. "You'll see."

What caused his apprehension, if, indeed, Jim had misgivings? We cannot pretend to know. His capacity as an actor, together with his ability to hide his woes, whether fancied or real, ordinarily enabled him to show a glad face to the public. Now, however, in the noonday of his fortunes, it would seem that something resembling stage fright possessed him.

Whether or not Jim heard gypsy whispers instead of the roar of the crowd no one but he could know. Perhaps nothing more than his secret fear of being trapped among demonstrative spectators made him ill at ease. Our friend Ernest, who had been assigned by his newspaper to report the inauguration, had an interpretation of Walker's grave but nervous behavior. "It's a hangover," Ernest said. "And let him who is without gin cast the first bottle."

Ernest was mistaken. Jim and Allie had been up late to be sure, but had drunk only a glass or two as the New Year and Walker's time of glory rode in on the noisy midnight. Jim had postponed his own personal celebration until after his installation. He had been invited by Winfield Sheehan, former reporter and now the "right-hand man" of motion-picture producer William Fox, to attend a private party this night at Sheehan's apartment at the Beaux Arts.

Inside the Hall, Jim and his police guard went up the circular stairway to the second floor. An informal reception in the Governor's Suite was to precede the inaugural rites.

Today's master of ceremonies, State Senator Bernard Downing, greeted Jim. Senator Downing had just recently been designated to succeed Walker as minority leader at Albany. A group of friends quickly filled the rooms where stood the desks of our first three presidents, and where, for more than a century, the Trumbull portraits of Washington, Hamilton, and John Jay had looked down from the high walls.

John Voorhis, grand sachem of Tammany, put out his venerable hand to greet the son of Billy Walker. Jim smiled for the first time that day. "Commissioner," he said to his father's old friend, "I wish the Boss were here."

Toward noon the Mayor-elect and his friends proceeded to the Board of Estimate chamber for the ceremony. The corridors of the old Hall, beautiful in architectural design, were not built to accommodate a press of citizens. Jim and his entourage were delayed several minutes on their way to the room in which, during the next six and one-half years, Walker would perform twice each week. Of course, when he would be out of town on one of his frequent tours this theatre would remain dark. No understudy could successfully act the part of the star, who, this first day of 1926, made his debut in the title role of "Mr. New York."

Such applause as greets a matinee idol welcomed the Mayor-elect as he entered the chamber. Most of the benches had been removed to permit a larger attendance than otherwise would have been possible. The auditorium had a seating capacity of about four hundred.

More than seven hundred persons, dignitaries of the professions and of business and Tammany Hall's elite, now stood as uncomfortably as in a subway station at the rush hour.

The surviving Walkers and the Roons were there. Mrs. Walker sat on one of the few benches near the "well," where the press representatives were taking notes. Allie's happiness at Jim's success had been lessened by a tragic event that morning. Her chauffeur, while driving downtown from his garage in the Bronx to pick up the wife of the Mayor-elect at the Commodore Hotel, had struck the rear end of a taxicab, killing the cab driver and injuring a policeman passenger. Not only did Allie feel sad about this, but Jim also had a Celtic respect for omens.

As he reached the dais to be sworn in, Jim bowed gravely to Allie and to his relatives, and to the sachems and sagamores of Tammany. There was a radio microphone on the dais, the first one ever used for the inauguration ceremonies of a New York mayor. Supreme Court Justice Robert F. Wagner, robed in black, administered the oath of office. Then former Mayor Hylan made a valedictory speech. The red-haired loser declared that he was happy to lay down a heavy burden. He then uttered what seemed a melancholy cry, an indictment of political Hessians: "I want to congratulate you that so many of your friends are present. As I look about me, I remember some of their faces on January 1, 1918, and again on January 1, 1922."

During Mayor Walker's inaugural address a woman fainted near the dais. Jim left off speaking, went to the woman's side, and administered a glass of water. The onlookers admired this gallant action, but the radio audience became alarmed and mystified, for no announcement was made to explain the sudden and prolonged silence. Within half a minute the telephone board at City Hall as well as at the newspaper offices had received inquiries. Had the Mayor been stricken? Assassinated?

After the ceremonies Jim went to the mayor's office in the west wing of City Hall. He looked about at the mellow furnishings, at the Morse portrait of Lafayette, which at that time stood over the mantelpiece.

With a quizzical lift of the brow Walker pretended to be addressing the portrait. "If I may borrow a phrase," he said, "I wish to announce, 'Lafayette, we are here.'"

17.

Merrily He Rolled Along

WALKER promised his wife that they would be able to spend more time together after his inauguration. This was a hollow vow, since New York's City Hall manages a volume of business second only to that which moves through the White House. In addition to his responsibilities as managing director of nearly a hundred and fifty thousand civic employees, Walker exposed himself, as no mayor had before his time or has since, to the personal reach of almost anyone.

The Walkers were guests at the Hotel Commodore during the campaign and for some months thereafter. Jim sometimes did not go home to the hotel. Political business was a pretext rather than a reason for his absence.

With his day-hours depleted, Jim needed the night—or so he seemed to think—to discharge his social commitments. Allie's belief that her husband would find more time for their home was a flirtation with a miracle. She kept in mind the example of devotion set by Governor and Mrs. Al Smith, and patiently assured herself that Jim and she could accomplish what the Smiths had done to avoid the quicksands of fame. What Allie did not seem to know was that these two public men differed, one from the other, in ways sometimes hidden from the eyes of trusting wives.

Smith was a man's man. Jim was not only a man's man, but also a woman's man—or women's. Smith was a Tammany alumnus. Walker had been schooled not only by Tammany, with its rugged, masculine, machine-politics traditions, but also by Tin Pan Alley and by Broadway.

The two popular men whom we have been discussing in broad terms of domestic contrast were alike in some ways, yet miles apart in others. Al Smith drank when he wanted to do so, and without hypocrisy. He would then go on to a political rally or home to his family. The distinguished graduate of Fulton Fish Market declined every request to appear at mixed gatherings unless Mrs. Smith also was invited. Walker drank whenever it suited his whims, and he too had no hypocrisy about doing so. However, he didn't always go home; and, except for the times when Al Smith and other sachems sternly intervened, Jim would appear at social gatherings without his wife.

Joe Laurie, Jr., wrote of Jim: "He loved like a woman; he played like a child; he hoped like a saint."

Allie Walker wanted to return to St. Luke's Place as soon as possible. The old and pleasant environment of the Greenwich Village home, she believed, would remind Jim of his private obligations. Also, she reasoned, he could escape many of the demands made upon him in the exposed areas of a big hotel. Each time he stepped out of his automobile at the hotel entrance he was set upon by persons who asked favors or who applied for "loans."

Jim carried separate rolls of currency in his trouser pockets. In the right-hand pocket was a supply of dollar bills for the "run-of-the-mine moochers"; and in the left-hand pocket bank notes of larger denominations for his "special friends." He never kept count of the money thus distributed by him. "Why should I?" he would say. "Borrowers are short on memory as well as cash; and I'm not an expert accountant."

When Allie pressed Jim to fix a time for their return to St. Luke's Place, he said jestingly, "Oh, what's the hurry? This way I'm always near my barber and my tailor."

Had Jim been as steadfast to his wife as he was to his barber and his tailor, even Al Smith might have praised him for his constancy.

Master Barber Philip Scallato had scissored and razored Jim since 1906, when Walker was but an obscure songwriter. In those days Scallato had a chair downtown in Nassau Street. When Scallato moved successively to various shops uptown, first to the Martinique, then to the Commodore, and lastly to the Lincoln Building on Forty-second Street near Grand Central Station, Jim continued to patronize him. During the forty years in which Scallato shaved Jim six thousand times and cut his hair nine hundred times, the spectacled and somewhat portly barber never addressed Walker by name, but always called him "young man."

Jim had an aversion to face stubble, and he also regarded other men's beards with disapproval. "There are a lot of things in life," he once said, "that we cannot do anything about. But a man's beard is his own fault."

The call, by telephone or telegraph, ordinarily came at seven o'clock in the evening. Scallato stood ready at all hours to minister to His Honor's whiskers. Scallato would put a straight razor, a pair of scissors, two towels, lathering soap and brush, and a bottle of witch hazel in an old brown leather bag and go to Jim's hotel suite, or to City Hall, or to St. Luke's Place, or perhaps to the apartment of one of the Mayor's friends. Occasionally Jim would visit the shop. Wherever the place of appointment, Scallato would shave Jim's somewhat light beard (for Walker was not a hairy person) or trim the dark brown hair that showed not a trace of gray until his last years. When someone had the temerity to suggest that the barber was applying dye to the forty-five-year-old Mayor's hair, Philip replied, "The young man needs none of those things. There's nothing false about him."

"He wanted no frills," the now-retired barber recalls. "I just put on the lather and shaved him, not close, but medium. When this was done, I'd give him a hot towel or two, some witch hazel, and it was over. He could stand the hottest towels. He sat perfectly still when I worked, said little, and paid me well. While out of town he shaved himself. This was unsatisfactory to both of us. He would return to me with cuts and scars on his cheeks and jaw. The young man was not built right to shave himself. I cut his hair every ten days, and trimmed the neck so that no skin would show through. Whenever he came to the shop he treated the manicure girls like they was great ladies. And that's because he was a great gentleman."

Whenever Jim shaved himself he used "Champagne" toilet water, his only perfume, as a lotion. He paid six dollars a bottle for this dressing, which he also used after a bath. One of his servants seemed unable to buy the toilet water for less than ten dollars a bottle. Jim was not the man to quibble about expenses, but somehow he had set his mind upon six dollars as a fair price for his favorite toilet water.

"I wonder," Jim said to the servant one day, "if we might strike a bargain, you and I? I'm going to raise your salary on the condition that you find a place that sells the toilet water for six dollars a bottle."

The servant qualified for the wage increase. "You know," Jim once said to his friend Johnny O'Connor, "if someone stole Brooklyn Bridge I'd be the last person in town to miss it. But when someone gyps me on toilet water, I feel that I am being more used than usual."

As to Jim's tailor, Jeann Friedman's shop was near the Ritz-

Carlton. Walker had patronized Friedman since his election to the Albany Senate. Charles Hand, Jim's intimate friend and onetime secretary, says that Walker always had been "dapper," but that he now became more concerned than before with his "scenery."

Not long ago I consulted Lucius Beebe, an authority on men's dress.

"The late Mayor," Lucius the arbiter told me, "might have been called a snappy, keen, or sharp dresser, and in the Broadway mode at all times. He would not, however, have been considered very *au fait* by the patrons of Dunne, Wetzel, Schantz, or Tony Williams. His clothes were tight and designed on extreme lines. His morning coats and foreign-office jackets were braided; his dinner suits had shiny lapels instead of the grosgrain favored by conservative folk. During his flowery days as mayor, I always felt a slight shudder at Mr. Walker's attire. I think most persons of conservative taste also shuddered, but I am sure that his clothes were a great hit with his more immediate clientele."

The glittering Mr. Beebe by no means intended to thumb his nose at Jim's right to dress as he pleased. "I'll say this for his clothes," Beebe continued, "and I certainly don't have to be patronizing about Walker himself–whom I considered in many ways a pattern of chivalry–they got much better after he was out of office and had lived in England. The last time I saw him alive was at Jack Bleeck's restaurant one day at lunch. His memory was faultless. He identified me with great courtesy and kindness, and he had not set eyes on me in ten years. I felt that in every way, including his suits, he had become a modified and less gaudy fellow. He was immaculately dressed, but the sharp lines and kollege-kut swagger had quite disappeared in favor of a more gentlemanly or Brooks Brothers whole. I can't quite describe it, but both Geoffrey Parsons and Stanley Walker, who were there, commented that, far from dealing harshly with the ex-Mayor, time had made him–to our tastes at least–an even more personable and gracious fellow."

Walker changed clothes three times daily, twice for daytime wear, and once again for evening or formal occasions. He had wardrobes in readiness at several vantage places about town, to permit him to effect his changes conveniently. Sometimes he would dress at Friedman's shop, or at City Hall, or at a friend's apartment, or home.

When Jim took office there was no dressing-room at the Hall. He arranged for one to be installed in a War of 1812 catacomb in the basement directly below his office. A door was let into the northeast wall, and a narrow stairway built with access to the cellar dressing-room and bath. One warm day during the summer of 1928 the Mayor changed clothes five times.

On the occasion of Marshal Pétain's visit to City Hall, Mayor Walker had difficulty in pinning a medal on the Frenchman's breast, failing twice in succession. He thereupon drew back and said gravely, "Marshal, I see that you have been reading our newspapers, but you have been misinformed. It was unnecessary for you to appear before us today in a bullet-proof vest."

In wintertime Walker frequently wore a derby, designed by himself and later copied by a firm of hatters which marketed it as the "James J. Walker model."

I remarked to Mr. Beebe that the derby, or iron hat, is not seen in such large numbers now as in Walker's time. "The hard bowler hat has by no means disappeared from the streets of Manhattan," replied Mr. Beebe, "but I think it is in a state of modified decline. It has, to a certain degree, been supplanted by the black homburg, favored and glamorized by Anthony Eden. The hard bowler, I think, today occupies about the place that the shining top hat had perhaps in 1910: favored by elderly sirs and by very well-dressed or formal-minded young men. I myself wear a derby from October to May almost invariably, for three reasons: it never disturbs your hair, or what hair you have left; it never gets soiled or out of shape and needs absolutely no attention; and a sixteen-dollar Lock derby will outwear five of any other hats ever made. At the moment I happen to have a postwar issue, but the one I bought in 1940 is still ungreened by age, and good in rainy weather."

I spoke of the passing of the derby to another reporter, Alva Johnston. "Why do you think the derby is going out of fashion?"

Alva replied by asking me, "Did you ever try to sleep in one?"

While her flamboyantly dressed husband rolled merrily along, Allie kept pounding at him to go back to live on St. Luke's Place. When Jim countered with a remark that the Greenwich Village residence was "kind of run-down," Allie suggested that the fifty-year-old house be renovated and repaired. Walker yielded to her proposal.

When it was learned that it would cost twenty-five thousand dollars to restore and improve the property, one of Walker's wealthy friends, Jules Mastbaum, said, "Go ahead and fix up the house, Jim, and send me the bill."

One of the front rooms on the first floor of the Walker home was reconstructed at a cost of five thousand dollars. It had cement walls patterned and painted to simulate wood. The latest tenant of the St. Luke's Place property, a most gracious lady, told me that she could not understand why the Walkers had put imitation oak-paneled walls in this part of the house, which she otherwise found so charming. She apparently was unaware that this soundproof chamber had been the scene of political conferences.

Until Fiorello La Guardia's occupancy of Gracie Mansion, New York's mayors had had no publicly owned residential quarters. A mayor's home was his own private responsibility and expense. The city provided but two free things: a police booth at the front door, with an officer on duty at all hours, and a pair of lights at the street entrance. These globes with spiked crowns stood on tall iron standards and burned all night long. When a mayor left office, the police booth was carted away; but the lamps remained—unlighted now, unless the former magistrate or his descendants paid for the electricity.

In 1926 several homes of former mayors still had these iron standards at the doors. A pair of them remained at the entrance to Mr. Hylan's Bushwick residence in Brooklyn, but soon were to be transplanted to his new home in Forest Hills. The lamps of James Harper, a mayor during the gas-lit era, had stayed in front of the wrought-iron balcony of his Gramercy Park address. Just around the corner from that park one might see the lamps of Abram S. Hewitt at the gateway of a large red-brick mansion where his daughter resided. Another pair of mayor's lamps guarded the only house with a stoop which so far had resisted the intrusion of business buildings in the former brownstone residential area of Lexington Avenue mid-town. This had been the home of William H. Wickham, mayor during the seventies.

Two of Walker's recent predecessors had gone without official lights. Mayor Mitchel had dwelt in an apartment house, and it had seemed unfitting to dignify the other tenants with lamps just because they happened to live under the same roof as His Honor. Mayor Robert A. Van Wyck had refused to permit the installation of official lights at his home, saying that they no longer served a useful purpose.

In ancient days, before New York houses were numbered, lighted lanterns marked a mayor's doorway to assist citizens in finding the chief magistrate's home at night. It has been suggested that certain mayors of old themselves found these beacons helpful whenever they had stayed late at the tavern.

In February of 1926, before the Walker house was quite ready for reoccupancy, two official standards were installed at St. Luke's Place. To test them, the electricians turned on the lights and left them burning all one night. Early the next morning two men paused in front of the house after having spent some hours at Barney Gallant's drinking establishment in Greenwich Village.

The two set up a disturbance in front of the temporarily vacant No. 6 St. Luke's Place. The neighbors might have ignored the rattling of the iron gates of the basement areaway, the loud curses, and the occasional bursts of song; but when one of the men demolished the official light globes with his walking stick the police were called.

At the station house it turned out that one of the men was Ernest. The other fellow claimed to be the Archbishop of Canterbury. Ernest effected their release by displaying his reporter's police card and signing an "I.O.U." for the damage. Jim sent for Ernest to inquire just why his house had been singled out for attack.

"We were looking for the Christopher Street subway station," Ernest explained. "We saw the two lights burning, and the Archbishop convinced me that we had arrived at the subway entrance. When we couldn't get in, it made us good and sore."

"Next time," said the Mayor, "call a taxi, and charge it to me."

Jim and Allie moved in in March. Allie and her mother, Mrs. E. T. Allen, had gone there two days before Jim was expected home. Mrs. Walker staffed the house with new servants and arranged for a fine dinner to celebrate the night of Jim's homecoming. She waited until ten o'clock: then, when Jim did not appear, resignedly sat down at table with her mother. At midnight she went to bed.

Belatedly mindful that he had promised to be home, Jim decided at about ten o'clock to telephone Allie. He had mislaid the new number, a private one. Walker endeavored to persuade the operator to connect him with his home, but was informed that it was a "restricted number." An appeal to the supervisor also failed. Jim insisted that he lived at the address where the telephone was and that *he* was the mayor of the city. The telephone people obviously believed that some crank was on the wire and politely but emphatically declined to reveal the number.

Jim might have applied to police headquarters for the number had he been of a mind to do so. Instead, he stayed on at Seeman's apartment, where he had been enjoying himself for several hours. Toward three o'clock in the morning Jim went home in a taxicab. As Walker reached the stone steps of the house entrance a young policeman emerged from the booth.

"Hey," said the officer, "where d'you think you're going?"

"To bed, Officer, where I should have been two hours ago. Good night."

"Not so fast, mister," the officer said as Jim turned to go up the stairs. "You know who lives here, don't you?"

"I have a slight idea."

"Yeah?" The officer began to lose patience. "Well, then, move on. The Mayor wants to sleep."

"And how!" Jim agreed.

The policeman nodded wisely when Jim tried to convince him that he was the mayor. After some argument, and much against the officer's better judgment, the guard roused a servant. The new butler appeared at the door in his dressing gown, sleepily appraised Jim, and said that he had never before seen the fellow.

"I give up," Walker said to the policeman. "Would you be kind enough to call a cab for me?"

"You'll find a cab on Sixth Avenue," said the young sentry. "If you ever try to pull anything like this again I'll call the wagon."

Next day Jim obtained his private telephone number and called Allie. "How in hell does a mayor get into his own home?" he asked.

When Walker again encountered the policeman on night duty in front of the house the officer said, "Mr. Mayor, I hope you're not sore at me. I need my job awful bad, and—"

"Sore?" Jim said. "Why, I've recommended you to the Commissioner for promotion."

Many presents arrived at the Walker home, among them pieces of luggage elaborately fitted out with combs, brushes, and silver holders. Jim did not like these accessories and stripped the various suitcases and stored the toilet articles on clothes-closet shelves.

Clothes closets always made Jim uneasy. For that reason he

kept his hats—and they were many and of various kinds—on tables upstairs and down. At least seven hats lay exposed at all times in the reception hall. When certain unwelcome callers saw these, they assumed the Mayor was in conference. The butler was advised to use the hats as a pretext for getting rid of boresome visitors.

Notwithstanding the saying that no man is a hero to his valet, Walker's successive manservants held him in high regard. Indeed, it is said that two of them voted for him for re-election. His first valet at St. Luke's Place was Sam Greenhaus, a small fellow of French appearance. Greenhaus worried about His Honor's carelessness with money. When Jim threw aside his clothes he seldom bothered to empty the pockets. The conscientious Greenhaus always saw to it that money or other valuables were removed and accounted for before the suits were sent to the cleaner's. Away from St. Luke's Place Walker would entrust his clothing to bellboys. One cleaner found three thousand dollars and a gold cigarette lighter in the pockets.

Greenhaus cautioned the Mayor about this, but Walker believed most persons were honest. "The cleaner always returns what he finds," he said.

"I know that, sir," replied Greenhaus, "but may I suggest that the temptation might worry even an honest person?"

Jim said that Greenhaus was "of immense help" and that he understood the "Walker ways," among them his aversion to a heated bedroom. In winter His Honor slept without benefit of radiators. He said he could breathe better under cool conditions, and smiled when other members of his family called his room "the Klondike."

Greenhaus each day patiently awaited His Honor's waking-up hour. Walker would rise about ten o'clock and glance at the headlines of the newspapers which Greenhaus had placed inside the doorway. After three or four minutes with the big type Walker would throw the newspaper on the foot of the bed, retire again, then get up once more for a cup of tea, for he never ate or drank in bed. Sipping his tea, he would look at the large bed as if it were some irresistible invitation. So he would return to bed, this time sitting up in it with pillows propped behind his back. He would make telephone calls, and at the same time re-examine the newspaper headlines. He seldom read the stories. Greenhaus meanwhile would open the drapes of the two windows, which looked out upon a small courtyard and four gingko trees, and stand waiting for the breakfast order. Now Jim would turn on the radio. Occasionally he would pick up from his bedside one of the many magazines which he had allowed to accumulate on the floor for months and look at the pictures.

Walker used horn-rimmed spectacles for reading but did not wear them in public. Curiously enough for a man so neat in appearance, he was never seen polishing these lenses. They sometimes became so fogged that a friend would relieve Jim of the spectacles and clean them for him. This was always done without comment, and Jim accepted the favor as a matter of course.

After a light breakfast Jim would watch Greenhaus drape the clothes of the Mayor's choice on a tailor's dummy of Jim's exact size. Then Walker would retire to the bathroom for his customary hour or more in that private place. When he had emerged at last—and it would now be nearly noon—the Mayor would throw off his dressing gown—silk in summer, camel's hair in winter—and pace about the room. Greenhaus would follow him patiently, expertly handing him the various garments. During this performance Walker would discuss affairs of a public as well as a private nature.

The valet kept a miniature flatiron on a gas plate just outside the bedroom. After the Mayor had his clothes on, the valet would inspect them; if some slight curl of a lapel or a wrinkle showed, the defect would be pressed out right on the Mayor. Iron in hand, the valet sometimes would follow Walker to the front door to finish the job.

Jim's various housekeepers gave up trying to cope with the paper dunes that accumulated in his bedroom. "Don't disturb a thing," he would say whenever someone endeavored to clean the room. "We'll take care of the chores later." When the piles became so high as to block the way from the bed to the bathroom, say, about once every two months, Jim would permit a secretary to gather up the litter and stow the papers in old trunks and crates. Porters then carried the boxes to the darkness and dust of the cellar.

Once, when Jim suffered an attack of lumbago, his doctor ordered him to sleep on a cot with boards beneath the mattress. The patient was delighted because he now could use his regular double bed as "a filing cabinet."

Jim seldom read any of the thousands of letters sent to him over the years. He so seldom replied to those he did chance to read that he offended important correspondents.

Walker never explained his strong reluctance to answer letters. All he would say about it was, "I use the telephone." When his various secretaries urged him to reply to letters of moment, he would say, "You write them, and I'll sign them."

Whenever an assistant wrote a letter in his name, Jim would leave it on his desk for hours, sometimes for days, unsigned. It became necessary at times for one of his secretaries to copy his signature for the mailing of an important letter.

It may be that Jim merely disliked manual composition. Or perhaps it was a manifestation of his habit of trying to do tomorrow what he had promised to do yesterday. Then again, he may have had the politician's aversion to putting himself on record, even in a letter. There were times, of course, when he finally did write to a friend. These letters were well composed, bright, intimate in tone, and graced with picturesque phrases. His penmanship was irregular but legible. The capital letters, somewhat large, extended below as well as above the lines of draft.

Jim also disliked to autograph pictures. Whenever possible he would keep such photographs of himself in his "do-nothing pile," and then finally have someone else sign in his stead.

The non-replying Jim saved almost every scrap of paper that came to him in the mail as well as newspaper clippings, documents, and memoranda. It would seem that Jim never threw anything away, except his fortune and, in some respects, his public life.

Among the letters I examined, hundreds were unopened. Some contained unused theatre tickets, religious medals, pressed flowers, currency, and uncashed checks. In others I found paper money of the kind in circulation before July of 1929, when the Treasury Department began the distribution of bills of small size. Written upon many of the envelopes, or upon the backs of letters, there appeared in Jim's hand various telephone numbers, notes for speeches, reminders of engagements, and occasionally the fragment of a song lyric.

It required a year of painstaking work on the part of my secretary and myself, and of several volunteers, among them Jim's confidant Robert Newman, to unscramble and put into sequence the papers which Walker's executor, Sidney Harris, permitted me to examine.

I was astonished to discover that he had kept no love letters. It is almost inconceivable that a man of Walker's romantic nature received no letters of this kind. Perhaps Jim made this one exception to his rule of hoarding correspondence. It would have been like him to have done that.

18.

Master of Ceremonies

THE ONE-HUNDREDTH mayor appeared at his office on time, stayed late at his desk, and labored efficiently—during his first six weeks in office. This unexpected diligence on his part made it seem that a Daniel instead of a Beau Brummel had come to judgment.

The *New York Times*, in its lead editorial of February 11, 1926, rebuked citizens who trespassed upon the busy man's time. "Where his predecessor had been churlish," that newspaper said of the new mayor, "he resolved to be courteous. . . . But there are limits to human endurance. . . . Mayor Walker will have to pull up. And his fellow citizens must be ready to help him do it. It is really indefensible, almost incredible, that Americans should incline to overwork their executives so ruthlessly. . . . Mayor Walker has made a fine beginning in office and has most agreeably impressed the city, but that is no reason for killing him with mistaken kindness."

Notwithstanding his first weeks of earnest application, his acknowledged talents in political high-wire walking, his eloquence, parliamentary skill, charm, and quick thinking, the new mayor lacked the temperamental fitness for continuous executive drudgery. Glimpses behind the scenes convince us that Jim would have liked to belong to himself instead of to history.

As early as his fifth day at City Hall Walker announced to the newspapers that he planned to retire from public service at the close of his first term. His sister Nan Burke says that her brother privately expressed his intention to rid himself of official cares once he had completed twenty years of political life. Jim had undertaken the mayoralty because Billy Walker had had such bright expectations for his son. "As you know," she said, "our father suffered political as well as financial reverses, and felt that a cloud had been put upon his name. Jim wanted to clear away that cloud by rounding out his father's dreams."

The indications are that he had an inward reluctance to come to grips with such enduring labors as turn a statesman's hair white. It is significant, I think, that during his campaigns for office Walker neither boasted outrageously nor abused an opponent. Had he been greedy for political fame, it is reasonable to suppose that this well-equipped orator would have shown much less mercy to his opponents.

One day Adolph Zukor, the motion-picture magnate, visited Walker at City Hall. "Jim," said Mr. Zukor, "I want you to come home."

"Home?"

"I want you to come back to the motion-picture industry," said Mr. Zukor, "when your term is ended. We will give you four times what you now are making, and a job for life."

Walker looked out the window at the statue of Nathan Hale. After a pause the motion-picture magnate added, "There's just one little catch to this."

"Tell me about it."

"Shortly before your term ends," Mr. Zukor predicted, "a whisper will start that Jimmy Walker isn't going to run again. The whisper will grow into a chorus, but you will pay no attention to it. Then another whisper will start, 'Jimmy Walker is afraid to run, afraid he will not be re-elected.' This will grow to a roar, and you will hear that too."

"And?" Jim inquired.

"Then," continued Mr. Zukor, "you, being an Irishman, will get mad, and run, and be re-elected."

During a conversation with his younger brother George, Jim once said that he was merely an actor in a play, and that he had to give the kind of performance expected of him.

"Then," said George, "see that you give a good performance."

Jim was devoted to George and was deeply concerned about his health. George was an occasional patient at tuberculosis sanatoriums in Saranac or at Lake Placid. Contrary to the advice of his physicians, he frequently would slip away from the sanatorium at night to visit the village inn; for, like his brother, he was a sociable fellow. Though obviously ill, he managed to persuade the bartenders that a few highballs would do him no harm.

"Uncle George," Rita Burke says, "was a witty man, although he made no attempt to be glamorous in his speech. He liked good clothes too, and had his suits made by Uncle Jim's tailor. The two brothers looked alike, although Uncle George was slightly taller. They wore their hats in the same way."

Neither Jim nor George resembled their eldest brother to any discernible extent. William Walker, Jr., was a stocky man who said but little and seemingly cared not at all for social excitements. Dr. Walker was a total abstainer, a "family man," the father of five sons and two daughters.

Dr. Walker scoffed at Jim's morbid fear of ill health and refused to prescribe for him. But he never criticized Jim for consulting other physicians, among them his successive Health Commissioners, Dr. William Schroeder, Jr., and Dr. Shirley W. Wynne. His Honor's collection of pills, potions, tonics, and capsules was a large one. Once when his niece Rita paid a weekend visit to St. Luke's she was quartered in her Uncle Jim's bedroom. She opened one of the wardrobe closets, thinking to see and admire some of Uncle Jim's newest finery. The closet contained so many medicine bottles that Rita believed she had somehow wandered into a pharmacy. Jim's private drugstore lacked sleeping pills, an oversight on his part. He slept well, but, of course, never would admit it.

When Jim asked Dr. Walker to persuade George to take better care of himself, the quiet-mannered physician replied, "I would gladly help our brother if he'd let me. But no one can do anything with either one of you."

Sometimes George would leave the sanatorium before his course of treatment had been completed and return to his insurance business in New York City. When Jim remonstrated with George, and assured him that he need not worry about money matters, the younger brother looked at the Mayor with a friendly though critical eye. "I'm perfectly self-sustaining, Jim. And so would Nan be, if you'd let her handle things her own way."

Walker refused to permit his sister to work, although she had told him that she wanted to be kept busy. Nan's husband had died a year before Jim became mayor. Although Luke Burke at one time had been quite wealthy, he left his widow with a dollar and a half, three children—one of whom would soon be stricken with infantile paralysis—and the death-bed admonition, "See to it that a Burke never goes without money."

Mr. Burke had become ill with tuberculosis not long after the birth of their first child, and six years of complete invalidism had exhausted the family's resources. After Mr. Burke's death Jim saw to it that his widowed sister wanted for nothing. That kindness ordinarily would have seemed a quite admirable and brotherly one, but Judge Samuel Seabury subsequently pounced upon it as a highly suspicious action.

Jim had much affection for his sister, whose spirit matched his own. The secrets which he confided to her, and which, since his death, she has seen fit to discuss with me for the purpose of keeping the record straight, bear the mark of credibility.

I first met Nan Burke the day after Palm Sunday in 1947. Jim's good friend Richard Buck was taking us in his limousine to the Gate of Heaven Cemetery in Westchester County, where Nan was to select a tombstone for her brother's grave.

The young man who was Buck's chauffeur chanced to be the son of the superintendent of the cemetery. During the thirty-five-mile drive northward on the Saw Mill River Parkway and then along the White Plains Road to Mount Pleasant, he told me something of the history of the cemetery where Jim is buried.

The day was wet and cold. The Westchester countryside could be seen but dimly through the small semicircle made by a windshield wiper, which beat like a metronome. One felt peaceful and remote. That feeling was enhanced as we entered the cemetery, which is as pleasant a place as a graveyard can be. There is a limestone gateway, gentle hills, and an artificial lake.

The Walker grave itself seemed tiny. Storm-wilted pansies bordered the otherwise bare mound of light brown loam. A few palm fronds lay upon the grave, a reminder of the holy yesterday.

Buck's chauffeur kept the motor running while Nan Burke got out to stand by the grave. Below the hill, white swans floated upon the lake. Beyond the lake a long train thundered northward toward Albany, where Jim had once been a bright star.

While Nan and Dick Buck went to the display lot to look at tombstones, I stayed with the chauffeur. He pointed out the monument of actress Anna Held, its four gray pillars flanked by stone benches, then directed my attention to the gravestone of one Arthur Flegenheimer.

I recalled his name as that of a notorious gang leader of the Prohibition years, a numbers-racket chief and "needle-beer" baron. He had been known to the underworld, to the police, and to the public by the alias "Dutch Schultz." The Mr. Flegenheimer of my reportorial recollection had been shot one October midnight in 1935 as he sat counting the day's receipts in the backroom of a Newark saloon. Two of his lieutenants were killed in that bright green room with its silver-trimmed mirrors. The Dutchman died at the hospital, babbling incoherently: "George, don't make no bull moves. What have you done with him? Oh, Mamma, Mamma! Stop it! Oh, sure, Mamma. What happened to the sixteen? Now listen, Phil, fun is fun. Get out! I wished I knew."

"That's the same one all right," the chauffeur said, nodding his head. He then mentioned that the burial of Mr. Flegenheimer had caused a spot of trouble some months back. "Chief of Police Quirk of Yonkers," explained my informant, "for years and years had sworn to catch up with Dutch Schultz and bring him to justice. The Chief tried and tried to get his man. But Schultz always outfoxed him. Finally the Chief died; and, what do you know? He was buried right there beside Schultz."

"But the Chief has no tombstone," I commented.

"It was this way," said the young man. "After Chief Quirk had been buried for a while Mrs. Quirk learned that Mr. Flegenheimer was her husband's old enemy Dutch Schultz. The Chief had had to die to catch up with him. So the widow had her husband's body moved to another place farther up the hill."

The thought of what might happen were the two enemies to rise together on Judgment Day made me laugh. Nan Burke heard me, and I attempted an apology. It was then that I recognized her as Jim's own sister in character as well as by blood relationship.

"I am used to just this kind of performance," she said. "You see, my brother never let environment of any kind stop him from laughing. At the funeral of my husband, with Luke Burke's casket in the aisle, one of the soprano singers missed a high note. Jim solemnly leaned over and whispered in my ear, 'O Death! Where is thy sting?' Grieved though I was, I was almost convulsed with laughter. Jim pretended to be innocently concerned. My friends luckily attributed my behavior to hysteria."

Nan Burke could not immediately decide on what kind of stone to select for her brother's grave. The salesman suggested that a red-brown stone might be the most easily distinguished among the gray granite markers of plots adjoining the Walker grave, where several members of the clergy and sisters of mercy lie buried.

"Also," he went on to say, "the gray ones become tarnished and streaked from the falling leaves. This red one weighs three and a half tons."

She sensed that the salesman was devoted to Jim's memory, and that his heart was set upon her ordering the red-brown stone. So she chose that one, which bears upon its polished face a Celtic cross adorned with shamrocks.

On our way back from the Gate of Heaven burial ground Nan Burke explained that all other departed members of the Walker-Roon clan rest in Calvary Cemetery across Fifty-ninth Street Bridge in Queens. For some years before Jim's death, there remained but a single grave available in the family plot. With unfailing courtesy Jim insisted that this properly belonged to the one surviving Roon, his Aunt Katherine. Jim would have liked to lie beside his father and his mother in death, but the last grave, he said, belonged to Aunt Kate.

Nan Burke told me that her mother had years ago selected the family burial site at Calvary. When asked why she had chosen a plot near the busy boulevard side of the cemetery, Mrs. Walker replied, "It's such a nice healthy spot."

In Nan Burke's opinion, Jim would have found lasting happiness had he followed his first desire to identify himself with the musical stage. "Sometimes," Nan went on to say, "I thought that Jim might have been an actor."

The fact is he *was* an actor.

Among several stage impresarios who remarked on Jim's qualifications in this respect, the late David Belasco observed, "He could have become another George M. Cohan."

Mr. Belasco's comparison of Walker to Cohan is strengthened by an anecdote told me by actor Billy Gaxton. Billy was the leading man in the Pulitzer Prize musical play by George S. Kaufman and Morris Ryskind, *Of Thee I Sing*. In that production Gaxton was assigned to give an impersonation of George M. Cohan, something he had done before at private gatherings of theatrical friends. The critics as well as the audience at the opening night in Boston thought Gaxton was imitating Mayor Walker. When the play came to New York, to run for eighty-six weeks, the audiences continued to regard Gaxton's travesty on Cohan as an impersonation of the Mayor.

Gaxton said to Jim, "I think I know Cohan pretty well, and I've tried conscientiously to give a good imitation. But everyone keeps on insisting that I'm imitating you. Can you explain it, Jim?"

"Billy," Jim said, "whom do you think *I've* been imitating all these years?"

David Belasco first saw and immediately admired Walker when Jim was in the Senate. Later the two men enjoyed sitting together at the Madison Square Garden boxing matches, for Belasco was also a prizefight fan.

Walker once remarked to Belasco, "Boxing is a sport in which you meet only one opponent at a time, and he is always in front of you."

Belasco told Jim that he himself was a descendant of Abraham Belasco, an early nineteenth-century pugilist of the London ring. That may have been possible. At any rate the gentle-voiced theatrical manager had amazing muscular "tone" for his sixty years, owned a brave heart, and was of the same size as his supposed ancestor, who had stood five feet six and a half inches and weighed "ten stone and a half."

"Besides," Belasco said to Jim, "Abie had a shrewd eye for business, and, when not fighting, sold oranges at the ringside. Why, one day, when suddenly called upon to substitute as an opponent for Jake the Butcher, Abie peeled himself instead of his oranges and prepared for action. Knocked out the Butcher too."

Perhaps the dean of the American theatre was spoofing Jim about this, or else exercising his ever-ready imagination. He sometimes created "background" for his stories, as when he displayed a china cup to playwright Charles MacArthur.

"This cup," he said, "was presented by Napoleon to General Grant."

Mr. Belasco's secretary politely corrected the master. "Pardon me, Governor, but the cup was given to Thomas Jefferson."

"That's right," said Mr. Belasco, while MacArthur was examining the cup with an air of skepticism. "A very historic object, don't you think?"

MacArthur indicated a splinter of wood imbedded in the glaze of the cup's bottom. "What's this sliver doing here, Governor?"

In a flash Mr. Belasco replied, "It's a piece of the True Cross."

A short time before Jim became mayor he asked Mr. Belasco to do him a favor. Walker wondered if D. B. could find a small part in a forthcoming Belasco production "for a deserving and pretty girl."

"Yes indeed," said Mr. Belasco. "I am confident that you have an eye for talent."

Early in 1926, after an unseasonal period of summer-like heat, accompanied by thunder, a three-day fog locked in the city and the harbor. Then a furious blizzard descended. A ten-and-one-half-inch snowfall delayed all trains. Public schools were closed, and merchants shut their doors. Mayor Walker put twenty thousand men to work cleaning the streets.

The theatres did little business during the siege—that is, all the theatres but one, Mr. Belasco's. To his pleasant amazement, and while his competitors were expensively snowed in, Mr. Belasco saw a large crew of shovelers making a path all the way from his playhouse on West Forty-fourth Street to the nearest subway kiosks.

This gesture on Walker's part came when Mr. Belasco's wife was ill. She died late that February. "In his hour of trouble," Walker said, "a great man like Belasco should get a break."

During his years in Albany Walker had used the legislative halls as his theatre. A few days after his inauguration as mayor, he returned as a visitor to the capitol. As the sergeant-at-arms escorted him to his old chair on the Senate floor, he was given an ovation. Jim's former opponent, the polite Senator Knight, made a speech in which he said that—from his point of view—the members of both parties missed the presence of their most popular figure. In response to this tribute, Jim said that he was very sorry to say good-by to his legislative comrades.

Jim's successor as minority leader, Senator Downing, mischievously interrupted Walker with, "When you come to a period, sit down."

"There have been many question marks in my life, Senator," replied Jim, "but never a period."

Jim now had to find another theatre to keep his talents employed.

He created a playhouse atmosphere twice each week at the Board of Estimate meetings. It became the "smart thing" for New Yorkers to attend these sessions at which the Board reviewed the city's business and taxpayers' representatives appeared to present their problems and complaints. Walker often referred to the Board as his "cabinet."

During Mayor Hylan's two terms Board of Estimate meetings had been ugly-tempered gatherings. Hylan had many times displayed a surly resentment if any citizen offered adverse criticism. So stormy and inconclusive had these meetings been that it became a byword for his opponents to say, "Send for Dr. Gregory!" Alienist Menas Gregory had charge of Bellevue Hospital's Department of Mental Diseases.

One of Jim's earliest endeavors as mayor was to modernize that ancient hospital. The psychiatric work at Bellevue was carried on in a building more than a hundred years old. After inspecting its wards, he called them "an archaic disgrace, unsanitary and inhumane." Not only did he improve conditions in the city's oldest hospital, but he successfully reorganized the various boards which hitherto had administered all the city hospitals in a confusing and overlapping fashion.

Concerning the city hospitals and public schools, and his efforts to modernize and enlarge them, Jim once said in a speech, "In the garden of hearts of schoolchildren and hospital patients, I hope I have planted a few forget-me-nots."

Something that happened to our friend Ernest illustrates the kind of thing that went on in Bellevue's psychiatric observation ward before Walker remedied matters. Ernest went there one night in 1925 to call upon Dr. Gregory. The doctor was of Armenian descent, had a mustache, and wore glasses. He gave advice freely, scientific and otherwise, to newspaper reporters. The night Ernest sought the learned alienist's counsel the journalist had attempted to enjoy a December-and-May romance with a waitress. Instead of replying to his proposal with mere words, the lass had emptied a cup of hot coffee over Ernest's head.

The scalded Cyrano buttered his scalp to allay his physical pain, then went in a cab to Bellevue to consult Dr. Gregory about his spiritual sufferings. The doctor had gone for a weekend to the seashore home of a friend, and a Bellevue attendant mistook Ernest for a violently daft person and promptly had him confined in the observation ward. When Ernest protested that he was a close personal friend of Dr. Gregory's, the attendant recognized an old, old claim advanced by many batty customers. The guardians of the ward absolutely refused to convey any message whatsoever to the doctor, either before or after he had returned from his holiday.

Ernest remained under observation for five days. His profane howls and threats merely confirmed the diagnosis originally pronounced upon him. Finally, when Dr. Gregory was making his official rounds, he discovered Ernest in a strait-jacket.

Ernest never was quite the same after this experience. From then on he absolutely refused to tip waitresses. His spirit had been broken, he maintained, and, in a moment of pique, he even went so far as to threaten the Mayor with the loss of his vote at the next election.

At Board of Estimate meetings Jim would be courteous and tactful to anyone who rose to criticize the administration. If someone popped up to speak against him, Jim would ask that he step closer to the dais, so that the Board members might catch every word. A flattered foe thus permitted himself to be maneuvered into a position with his back to the audience. The effectiveness of his words and of his facial expression thereby would be lessened insofar as the spectators were concerned.

Early in Walker's administration a Department of Parks official appeared before the Board with a request for funds to exterminate insects in the trees of Central Park. Jim asked what kind of insects they might be.

"Red mites," the official replied.

The Mayor lifted his brows and pretended to be serious. "Did you say 'Red Mikes?' "

At another time he told a long-winded lobbyist, "Listening to you is like seeing a six-day bicycle race. The boys ride for six days but are always in the same building."

The man argued, "But my dear Mr. Mayor—"

"Not dear, but expensive!" interrupted Jim.

The man still persisted, and Jim said, "Listen, can't we two boys play after hours?"

"I've almost forgotten what I wanted to say," said the man.

"It doesn't make any difference," Jim answered resignedly. "You don't have to remember anything. Just talk right along."

To another man who had made charges of mismanagement, but

who added that he wasn't actually accusing the Mayor himself of anything, Jim replied, "Well, you've got an awful tricky way of complimenting me."

Walker observed to one of his critics, "If everybody could be mayor of New York just for a day, the mayor would have an easier time."

Another man whom Jim regarded as a tiresome complainant made an overlong speech one day at a busy meeting of the Board. He had no sooner sat down than he was up again, with the purpose of saying, "I want to straighten out one thing–" He got as far as "I want to straighten out" when Walker interrupted with, "Well, why don't you?"

Upon another occasion a member of the audience interrupted the remarks of the Mayor to shout, "Liar!"

Jim replied with mock courtesy, "Now that you have identified yourself, we shall proceed."

It should not be supposed that all the Mayor's actions at Board of Estimate meetings turned upon witticisms. Walker's frankness and his true modesty impressed his hearers. Jim admitted that he knew nothing about many of the problems of city government, and he never pretended to a knowledge that he did not possess.

Many of his actions and decisions showed his warmth of heart and his understanding of human sorrows, as in the death-benefit of a widow of a city employee. This man had fallen overboard and been drowned while working as a deckhand on a Staten Island ferry. The drowned man's immediate superior appeared before the Board to oppose an award to the widow. He contended that the man had been drunk and negligent of duty at the time of the accident.

To this Walker replied, "There is no greater accident that I know of than that of getting drunk. Very few men set out with that deliberate intention. It sort of creeps up on a fellow, especially with the kind of liquor that is being served these days. In my opinion, this man had two accidents on the same day. The first one occurred at a speakeasy. The next one claimed his life. This widow really should get double indemnity instead of the pension she asks of us. I vote that this benefit payment be made at once."

One of Walker's early actions was to remove the numerous signs bearing the name of his predecessor on the sites of public improvements. He declined to have his own name placarded upon the buildings and playgrounds, bridges and hospitals, he had undertaken to create or improve.

"The Mayor of New York," he said, "still believes himself to be a public servant and not a potentate. My own father refused to have his name posted in the playground which he established across the street from our home, or upon the recreation piers which he opened to the people of our crowded neighborhoods. I think that these advertising politicians lack good taste, and that their signboard boasts should be forbidden by law."

A member of the Citizens' Union usually was present at the meetings to keep an eye upon the city's business and to offer objections. Upon one occasion, when a heckling representative of the Citizens' Union rose to speak, Mayor Walker innocently asked whom he represented.

The man replied, "The Citizens' Union."

Walker pretended that he never had heard of that large committee. "Did you say the Citizen Union?"

The man acidly replied, "The *Citizens'* Union."

"Aha," the Mayor exclaimed, "then there are *two* of you!"

Walker entered into numerous arguments with Stewart Browne, president of the United Real Estate Owners' Association. The Mayor usually had a playful greeting for Browne, such as "Why, here's Little Bo-Peep again!" Mr. Browne's manner of speaking was that of a Londoner. At one meeting he suggested that a certain matter be postponed for a fortnight.

Jim rapped with his gavel. "No, we will adjourn it for two weeks. You're not going to trick me with that fortnight stuff."

The Board of Estimate room was not the only theatre for Mayor Walker. He gave almost three hundred open-air performances on the portico platform outside the Hall, awarding the keys of the city, scrolls, and medals to honored guests. His speeches of welcome were extemporaneous, and the crowds greatly enjoyed the ceremonies, especially the Walker asides.

Upon one occasion a five-hundred-pound cheese arrived at City Hall accompanied by a delegation of Swiss admirers. Jim thanked his visitors for bringing the huge cheese, then said, "Will someone please run out and get me a cracker?"

To Guglielmo Marconi, the Italian physicist, Walker said, "It is gratifying to realize that you did not send a wireless, but came in person. Here we do not know much about transmission, but we have some mighty fine receptions."

When Commander Richard E. Byrd appeared for a third time at City Hall, Walker said, "Dick, this has got to stop; it's getting to be a habit."

The Honorable Grover A. Whalen served as Walker's impresario at these public functions. He had succeeded his friend Rodman Wanamaker as the head of a committee of three hundred and ninety citizens to welcome distinguished visitors to New York. Members of this committee had a somewhat tubby vessel, the *Macom* (a contraction of "Mayor's Committee"), at their disposal whenever a prominent person arrived aboard an ocean liner.

So much has been written about Whalen's activities as a "greeter" that his outstanding ability as a business executive and organizer has been lost to public view. In private life he was general manager of Wanamaker's New York department store. During his long career Whalen has discharged his public duties with conspicuous energy and devotion, and is admittedly one of the foremost masters of personnel on the American business scene. Despite this, Whalen has long been fixed in the popular mind principally as a man with a silk hat on his head and a gardenia in his lapel.

Waggish Arthur Baer said of him, "Jimmy Walker appointed Grover official greeter of Manhattan to remove the accumulation of handshakes from the docket. And I want to say that Grover made as handsome a figure as ever nodded from the waist. Up until Grover arrived in Tammany politics, a nod had been epileptic, and a bow had been a duck. He had the perfect teeth of an aluminum comb, and a wire walker would have mistaken the part in Grover's hair for a continuation of his act. His striped trousers made him glassy with fashion, and when he came marching four abreast down City Hall steps to greet the inbound janitors, he had a flower in his off-lapel, seaweed in his hair, and a wild light of genius in his spare spectacles. I once wrote of him, 'Add spats, and stir with a cane.' "

The first large-scale reception for a distinguished guest during the Walker administration was that for Captain George Fried and the crew of the S.S. *President Roosevelt*. These mariners had rescued the master and the men aboard the British steamer *Antinoe*. There was a military parade from the Battery to City Hall. The

Mayor's herald and factotum, Hector Fuller, presented a hand-illuminated scroll to the Captain.

Fuller, an advertising man, had the bearing and voice of an alumnus of the Richard Mansfield, or "smokehouse," school of acting. The Mayor's Committee entrusted him with the designing, the writing, and the presentation of the official scrolls of welcome. Hector conducted rehearsals for these showy affairs at City Hall. As described by columnist Louis Sobol, the officials practiced their parts with the fervor of extras in a forthcoming play or of bridesmaids before a wedding. Hector sometimes made verbal blunders during his introductions, as at the reception of Ramsay MacDonald, whom Fuller announced as "Prime Minister of the United States."

Queen Marie of Romania was the first "crowned head" greeted by Walker. Whether or not Her Majesty was charmed by Walker's speech of welcome or by two incidents which happened more or less off the record, the still beautiful Queen did not say. One of these occurred while Jim was attempting to pin a medal upon her coat. The lady from the Balkans owned a splendid, although somewhat buxom figure, and the place where the medal properly belonged—high up, and a bit to the left—suggested, among other things, a delicate target for a carelessly directed pin.

"Your Majesty," Jim said, "I've never stuck a queen, and I hesitate to do so now."

"Proceed, Your Honor," replied the Queen. "The risk is mine."

"And such a beautiful risk it is, Your Majesty," Jim said in a low voice.

The Queen and her royal party left New York for Washington at the conclusion of the City Hall ceremonies. Although it was a raw October day, Marie was seated in an open-top automobile so that citizens along the way from City Hall to Pennsylvania Station might look upon a reigning monarch.

Jim sat at Her Majesty's left in the touring car. As the royal automobile was passing a newly begun skyscraper on Seventh Avenue, her lap robe slipped from her knees. Walker leaned over to adjust the robe. At this, one of the riveters perched on a girder of the partly completed steel framework of the building cupped his hands and called out, "Hey, Jimmy! Have you made her yet?"

Just how much slang Queen Marie understood I am not prepared to say. She turned an inquiring glance upon her host and said sweetly, "You Americans are quite droll, don't you think?"

"When you travel across our great country," Jim hedged, "you will come upon many interesting evidences of our democracy."

"Everyone seems to know you in this great city," she observed.

"Yes, Madam," Walker replied, "and some of them know me very well indeed."

19.

The Man Who Was Seven Feet Tall

"At various times during my life," Jim once wrote to a friend, "I have felt about seven feet tall. At other times I have felt that I could walk under a dachshund while wearing a high hat. According to Dun & Bradstreet, the *World Almanac*, and Aunt Jemima's cook book, I'm five feet, eight and one-half inches with my boots on; but when things are not going well, and the heels get a little run down, I'm only five feet, eight inches."

Jim was seven feet tall in 1926. Nor did he shrink politically, as measured by the popular mind, until 1932, when he fell with the age which had created him. So many things take on apparent size, only to be forgotten later, if not condemned, when the hour comes for the world to divorce the moods of yesterday. Who among us remembers the earnest crusade to put an illuminated wristwatch upon the forearm of the Statue of Liberty? Or Rabbi Stephen S. Wise's rebuke to a young woman who applied lipstick during a sermon? Or the indignation of a few old-fashioned fellows who protested to the *Times* when that newspaper, among others, gave much more space to the death of film actor Rudolph Valentino and his mob-scene funeral than to the obsequies for Harvard's illustrious and aged president Charles W. Eliot?

During the twenties, as it now seems in retrospect, many things which then were accounted small, or even ignored, brought on panic and war. In an unreckoning decade of vanity and lust for possession, and in a city of revelry, is it to be wondered at that James J. Walker disregarded the signs of his own personal disaster?

These were the years that brought him applause wherever he

went. When the bouncing Mayor vacationed in Florida, and an alligator nipped his trousers, this caused more attention than did the seemingly dry and routine awarding of a bus contract by the Board of Estimate. Yet that contract was one of fifteen circumstances which eventually threw His Honor up for grabs. Again, when an admirer presented the Mayor with a splendid saddle horse, "Cedar King," and Jim was dragged by the animal across the tanbark of a Brooklyn horse-show ring, the event was widely chronicled. There was little or no newspaper comment upon the financing of the Mayor's trips, among them a triumphant holiday abroad in 1927; that is, no comment until 1931–32, and then a roar.

He could do no wrong during the Peter Pan years of his first term. He was the life of the party, the chieftain of the Broadway Bedouins, and, as George M. Cohan said of him, "a great little guy." A self-appointed palace guard of Walker's cronies usurped the benches and chairs of the reception rooms at City Hall. The faces of some of Jim's sportsmen friends presented a Hogarthian contrast to the calm visages of the austere old portraits on the corridor walls.

Two of Jim's boxing-world pals virtually maintained offices at City Hall: managers Jimmy Johnston and Dan McKetrick. I would be among the first to concede that neither gentleman deliberately sought to compromise the Mayor. They were fiercely devoted to Walker and continued to be loyal in the lean after-years. But both Johnston and McKetrick liked being known as "the Mayor's right-hand men." They received telephone calls on an extension of the City Hall switchboard. This meant to their tin-eared colleagues uptown that they were sitting in Jim's private office instead of, as they were, at the desk of the police lieutenant in the outermost reception room. Damon Runyon nicknamed Johnston "the Boy Bandit" and McKetrick "Dapper Dan." Jim called them "the Altar Boys."

It was an exciting spectacle whenever Mayor Walker went down the aisle of crowded Madison Square Garden on fight nights. He usually appeared a little before ten o'clock, when the far-carrying tenor voice of Joe Humphreys (who munched Breath Hearts between solos) announced the main event.

"The Altar Boys," a millionaire or two, a commissioner of something or other, and a squad of policemen ran interference as the Mayor one-stepped to his ringside seat. The arena bubbled over with sounds of greeting. The fighters, bathrobes flung loosely over their bare torsos and towels draped around their heads, turned in their corners like happy Arabs to see the man who had made it possible for them legally to thwack each other for a living. Oh, that Jimmy! He was seven feet tall, all right.

Journalist Douglas Gilbert wrote in the *World-Telegram*, "New York wore James J. Walker in its lapel, and he returned the compliment."

When the benevolent Jules Mastbaum died in December 1926, publisher Paul Block succeeded him as the foremost millionaire in Walker's coterie of wealthy admirers. An exploration of confidential letters and telegrams sent by Block to Walker fails to disclose that this idolator of the Mayor asked for or expected any material advantage. Block obviously enjoyed reflected glamour. That Jim's wealthy patron profited by this connection, either politically or financially, or even sought to do so, never has been established by any investigator.

Block's munificence, his readiness to supply Jim with a private railway car and other luxuries of travel during the Mayor's many junkets, his defrayment of Walker's hotel bills, tailor bills, and other personal expenses, meant to skeptical minds that the publisher had some cunning reason for his generosity. This seemed especially so when, during the Seabury probe in 1932, Walker freely admitted that he had received nearly a quarter of a million in cash from a joint-brokerage account opened by Block and himself in 1927, to which Jim had contributed nothing. This was one of the principal "tin-box" matters scrutinized by Judge Seabury and submitted among the fifteen charges of malfeasance, misfeasance, and nonfeasance at hearings before Governor Roosevelt.

"I don't know," Arthur Baer once said to me, "whether or not Jim ever had a tin box. But I am sure that everyone else did."

Aside from the joint-brokerage account, the awarding of a bus contract which one day would be investigated, the alleged "tin box," and other matters pertaining to Walker's first term, an event occurred that affected Jim's life more than anything else had done or ever would do. Both his public and private fate turned upon this. He met and fell in love with an actress of the musical stage, Miss Betty Compton.

Walker first saw the dimpled brunette in the musical show *Okay* at the Imperial Theatre. *Okay* was an Aarons and Freedley production. The principal actors in it were Gertrude Lawrence, Oscar

Shaw, Harlan Dixon, the Fairbanks Twins, and Victor Moore. A pretty girl named Sascha Beaumont also appeared in this show; she later became the wife of Robert Newman.

On opening night, November 8, 1926, Aarons invited Walker to go backstage to say hello to Gertrude Lawrence. There Jim met Betty Compton.

"I'm giving a supper party," Walker said to the young woman with the bobbed black hair, "Would you like to come along?"

"No, thank you," she replied.

This rebuff made Jim feel less than seven feet tall.

The Mayor subsequently saw Miss Compton at various large parties. At these chance meetings she seemed most gracious, but Jim made no headway. The actress declined his dinner invitations and supper invitations with a polite finality which heightened his interest.

It was not until the summer of 1927 that Jim managed to be alone with Betty, and then only for the duration of a crosstown automobile ride. On that occasion Jim had been the toastmaster, and Betty one of three thousand guests, at a dinner at the Hotel Commodore honoring Mrs. William Randolph Hearst on the tenth anniversary of the founding of her Free Milk Fund for Babies. When Jim learned that Betty might have difficulty in getting through the Times Square traffic in a taxicab, he volunteered to take her in his official town car from the hotel to her theatre.

As we have said earlier in this book, Jim disliked fast travel in an automobile and had never permitted his chauffeur to use the siren. Now, however, he told the chauffeur to step on the gas *and* to sound the siren. After a time Betty turned her large brown eyes on Jim. "I'm impressed. Now you may stop the siren."

At a dinner party given by Paul Block at the Ritz-Carlton some days after the automobile ride Walker spoke his mind about sirens, both mechanical and human. His remarks made Betty laugh. She decided to have dinner with Jim at a restaurant one day the following week.

There was a new light in the Mayor's eye as he went upon his rounds.

Allie Walker was slow, perhaps deliberately, to see that Jim was entering into another "passing fancy." After their return to St. Luke's Place, and five weeks of patient waiting for Walker to find time to be a husband, Mrs. Walker and her mother went abroad.

The Mayor's wife toured Europe as a guest of the Hotel Owners' Association, met President Doumergue in Paris, the King and Queen of Belgium in Brussels, and was received in private audience by His Holiness Pope Pius XI.

When Allie and her mother returned that April, Jim went down the Bay to greet them. They were photographed together, smiling. In October Allie again sailed for Europe, with the announced purpose of christening the German liner *New York*, which stood on the ways in a Hamburg shipyard.

Allie Walker had no knowledge of the new menace to her happiness until some time in 1927. Even then she had little more than an intuitive feeling about it. Jim was as courteous as ever, even more so if possible, although Allie saw less and less of him. Still, it was a year of hurdy-gurdy excitements, and many activities diverted Allie's attention from the misgivings that had begun to plague her thoughts.

One of the major events of 1927 was the transatlantic flight of Charles A. Lindbergh. It might be of interest to set down one or two episodes which hitherto have not been revealed in connection with that adventure. These sidelights have been supplied by Grover A. Whalen and Gene Buck.

Whalen, at the time of which I speak, the spring and early summer of 1927, was vice-president of the Trans-Oceanic Company. Merchant Rodman Wanamaker had financed this organization for the purpose of studying long-range flights across the big water. As president of the company, Mr. Wanamaker gave a million dollars to the project, and allowed Whalen a free hand to consummate its scientific aims. Whalen selected Commander Richard E. Byrd to attempt the transatlantic flight in a three-motored plane. Floyd Bennett designed the plane for Mr. Wanamaker's company and was to have been the pilot. Bennett was injured, however, and Bert Acosta took his place in the expedition. Acosta was something of a problem child, but one of the greatest natural aviators that ever lived. His chief, the suave, cool, polite Commander Byrd, had faith in him, and also knew how to handle him. The expert and dependable Bernt Balchen and Lieutenant Noville were the other members of the plane's crew.

Whalen and his group established headquarters at the Garden City Hotel, at Garden City, Long Island. Whalen's workmen built a two-mile-long runway—the longest in the world at that time—at near-by Roosevelt Field. There was an atmosphere of high efficiency here, as with any project ever undertaken by Whalen. There also was a feeling of cordiality between his large staff of assistants and members of the press. The refreshments were plentiful and excellent.

Early in May, on a particularly busy morning, our old friend Ernest broke in upon Whalen. "The Flying Fool is here!" he called out.

Somewhat annoyed at this intrusion, Whalen looked up from his papers. "Now look, Ernest, I never criticize another man's drinking, but if you'll please excuse—"

"Don't give me that, Grover," said Ernest, pounding on Whalen's table. "I bring a request from the Flying Fool himself."

Whalen smoothed his mustache. "And *who* may the Flying Fool be? And *what* is the request? And please make it snappy."

"Didn't catch his name," Ernest said. "He's skinny and tall and tousled, and he wants to borrow your runway and your hangar."

"Good Lord!" said Whalen. "Haven't you anything better to do than bring me a request like that?"

"Grover," said Ernest, "I want you to meet this young man. You're always meeting people. One more won't hurt you."

Whalen reluctantly accompanied Ernest. Sitting on the field was a little ship so designed that the pilot couldn't see very well out of it because a large fuel tank was placed in front of the pilot's seat. The Flying Fool introduced himself as Charles A. Lindbergh. The young man, it seemed, did not like to be called by that nickname, but did not mind when his partner, a man from Wright Motors, addressed him as Slim.

"Where do you intend to go?" Whalen asked Lindbergh.

"I'd like to take off for Paris," he said.

Whalen looked at the small ship again. "That would mean suicide."

Lindbergh ignored this opinion and asked if he could use the hangar.

"I can't allow that," said Whalen, "because we have four hundred thousand dollars' worth of equipment, including the big ship, in there. And your plane, in my judgment, is a fire hazard." Then Whalen asked, "Look here, what do you think your chances are on such a foolhardy venture?"

The young man replied in a matter-of-fact tone, "Ninety-nine to one against me."

"Well, there you are," Whalen said. "Wouldn't it be like signing your own death warrant?"

"No," said Lindbergh. "I have one chance."

Whalen now spoke of Lindbergh's duty to his family and friends. The young man said that he was going to fly the ocean "regardless," and from some other place if necessary.

"I'm against it," Whalen said, "but this is the best runway. I'll agree to let you use it, provided you give me twelve hours' notice in advance of your take-off, which must be kept strictly secret. We don't want any hysterical crowds running over the field and ruining our own plans."

They shook hands. Lindbergh and the man from Wright Motors stayed at the field for ten days. They were out each day tuning up the motor of the little plane which had been flown by Lindbergh from St. Louis. By this time Lindbergh had acquired two volunteer press agents. They had asked the New York Newspaper Club to give a reception for Lindbergh, and the club consented "because the Flying Fool was so nuts." That same evening Whalen was giving a supper for press correspondents at the Garden City Hotel. They were halfway through the meal when Lindbergh showed up and called Whalen outside the dining-room.

"I am going to fly at dawn, Mr. Whalen," he confided.

"Have you had any weather reports?"

"No, but when I was on my way from the Newspaper Club, in the middle of Queensboro Bridge, I looked out the taxicab window and up, and it seemed fine to me."

"All right," Whalen sighed. "But remember, we must have complete secrecy about this. If we don't, all New York will be out here whooping it up and gumming up everything."

Lindbergh's press agents got together their few remaining dollars and hired a night watchman. He sat in a chair outside the door of the young man's room to safeguard the aviator's sleep in the event that the plan to fly at sun-up became publicly known.

Lindbergh was unable to sleep, but the night watchman snored peacefully away. As a prank, Lindbergh removed the sheets from his own bed, twisted them and tied up the watchman, and went to the flying field.

Whalen had left a four o'clock call with the hotel switchboard.

While he was drying himself after a cold shower, he heard sounds which suggested a mob scene. From his window he could see automobile headlights cutting through the pre-dawn darkness. He heard shouts and the clamor of horns.

When he arrived at the flying field he found thousands of spectators. Cars were jammed together on Queens Boulevard, which in those days was not the wide thoroughfare it is today. Women from night clubs and men in tuxedos were sitting on the tops of parked taxicabs.

What Whalen did not know was that Phil Payne, editor of the *Daily Mirror*, a tabloid newspaper, some weeks before this time had arranged with a hotel telephone operator to keep the editor up to date on Whalen's conversations concerning the Byrd flight. Payne had promised a "complete wardrobe, from the skin out," to the young woman if she did her duty by the *Mirror*. Instead of a Byrd scoop, Payne now had a Lindbergh "beat." The *Mirror* headline, "Flying Fool Off to Europe," inspired a migration of Broadwayites to Garden City.

Payne was triumphantly present at the scene of the flight. He rode in Whalen's automobile to the place where the *Spirit of St. Louis* stood like an ugly duckling. The runway had been built on a downgrade, to take advantage of a prevailing wind. This morning, however, the wind had veered, so Lindbergh had to take off from the other end of the long lane and make his take-off run uphill.

While the Wright man was tuning up the motor, Whalen offered Lindbergh several charts and meteorological reports compiled by Byrd.

"I don't need them," said Lindbergh. "I have my own chart."

He brought from his side pants pocket a weather-beaten map of the Great Circle Course. He showed Whalen some marks he had made upon it "to avoid landing in Cairo, Egypt."

Whalen belittled the Lindbergh chart and then made a final speech on the subject of suicide. There was a minute of hesitation on Lindbergh's part, Whalen says, but it was not caused by his entreaty. The moment of indecision occurred as the last of many five-gallon gasoline containers was being emptied into the fuel tank. Lindbergh asked the Wright representative, who was toying with the motor, if he thought he should go.

"Go ahead, Slim," said the Wright man.

Lindbergh climbed into the cockpit. He seemed somewhat surly when a mechanic's wife brought him a gift of milk and sandwiches. He tossed the milk overboard. Then he was off and up into the dawn of May 20, 1927, and soon was winging out above the blue water and into the thunderheads of fame.

The Byrd expedition, with its four men aboard, did not depart on their journey until five weeks after the Lindbergh flight. In a manner of speaking, the wind had been taken out of the sails of the million-dollar scientific project. But on Lindbergh's return the silk-hatted Whalen greeted the hero to whom he had denied a hangar and to whom he had spoken of "sure suicide."

That day has been written of so extensively that only one other hitherto unpublicized matter shall be presented here. When Lindbergh arrived in New York from Washington—where the authorities had decreed he must first be greeted officially—the young man had few moments to himself. Hero-worshiping New Yorkers recognized him and followed him everywhere, cheering and adoring him as though he were a young god. Whalen and a police escort accompanied Lindbergh wherever he went.

On the night before Lindbergh was to return to St. Louis there was a private party at the Warwick Hotel given by William Randolph Hearst. The guests of the publisher included, among others, Mayor Walker, Mr. and Mrs. Gene Buck, actor Holbrook Blinn, and actress Jeanne Eagels.

Late that evening Walker was called to the telephone. He talked there for a short while, then returned to the party. "We're going to get a break," he announced. "Whalen has been with Lindbergh to the Brevoort to collect his twenty-five-thousand-dollar prize from Raymond Orteig for flying the Atlantic. Grover wants to know if you'd like him to bring Lindy here?"

"By all means," said Mr. Hearst.

"That's what I told Grover," said Jim, adding, "Mr. Hearst, I've got an idea. It's a good one, I know. And I wish you would join with me in carrying it through."

"What is it?" Mr. Hearst inquired.

"Ever since that young man returned to America," Walker said, "he has had nothing but acclaim. He's the greatest of modern heroes. But," and he turned to the other members of the group, "as much as I love the people of our glorious nation, I must say that it is a dangerous place in which to be a hero. A hero always runs into a time, if he but live long enough, when there are no cheers. Let a man, however popular, make one little mistake—let alone a big one—one misstep that is contrary to the style of the moment, and he is criticized, then vilified, ignored, and forgotten."

"It's a nice speech, Mr. Mayor," said Mr. Hearst, "and contains much truth, but *what* is your present idea?"

"Simply this," Jim said. "When he comes up here, let everyone of us sit quietly—politely of course—but not cheer him or make a fuss over him. Then we'll be the first people in the world to give him a chill."

The ladies of the Hearst party offered their objections. "Oh, no, Jim," they said, "we don't want to play a joke on *him!*"

"It's no joke," Jim said gravely. "It would be a valuable dress rehearsal for his future."

Mr. Hearst and his guests at length agreed to do as Jim proposed. Soon after the noise of sirens came from the street the door to the Hearst suite opened, and Whalen showed in the tall young man wearing a white sailor hat. He seemed tired and shy. In a few moments the ladies had forgotten all about their promises to Jim and had formed an admiring circle about the hero.

Lindbergh stayed for two hours and sat on the floor while the Mayor played the piano.

The Mayor's stature, in his own eyes, had dwindled to less than six feet when toward the close of 1927 Betty Compton still gave little encouragement to his romantic addresses. The pretty actress had a stubborn intention to enter no liaison without a wedding ring.

She had been married once before, in her teens, and that marriage had been dissolved. Betty now was twenty-three years old and Jim forty-six. The Mayor who was the city's darling fretted much over the fact that an obstinate young dancer had offered him the kind of resistance to which he was unaccustomed. He seemed bewildered, like a boxer knocked down for the first time. He grew thinner, weighing less than one hundred and twenty-five pounds. He decided to go to Europe. Allie would go with him.

Jim kept up an appearance of gaiety, and his jests were many. Few persons discerned that a fevered restlessness had come upon him. Perhaps the public was too busy to analyze the Mayor's moods during a year in which corset-salesman Henry Judd Gray and Ruth Snyder murdered Mrs. Snyder's husband, and Nicola Sacco and Bartolomeo Vanzetti died in the electric chair in Massachusetts. Besides, Jim's daily actions were construed as those of a merry-hearted fellow, and a good-hearted one as well, as when in 1929 he appointed former Mayor Hylan to the Children's Court in Queens.

"How come," reporter Alva Johnston asked Jim, "you gave Hylan this job after all the terrible things he has said against your personal character?"

"Alva," Jim replied, "the appointment of Judge Hylan means that the children now can be tried by their peer."

From several remarks which Jim later made in respect to his love for Betty Compton, it would seem that she was much on his mind when he set sail for Europe in August of 1927. Whatever the time of their first concord, theirs was to be a life of anxious battle against the conventions—but not, as Plutarch once observed in an ancient day, against nature.

Now Jim would be lifted up, then cast down; he would be harried and torn apart, and would know the passionate struggle which besets a man whenever autumnal love moves like a belated cyclone across the prairies of masculine peace.

20.

To Castlecomer and Beyond

GREENHAUS was a very busy valet early in August of 1927. He packed forty-four suits of clothes, twenty white piqué vests, twelve pairs of fancy striped white trousers, six topcoats, one hundred cravats, shirts by the dozens, and a basketful of shoes for the master's European tour.

"Be careful of my silk hat, Greenhaus, if you please," the Mayor said to his man. "I promised my father I'd wear it to Castlecomer."

The Grand Street Boys gave a farewell dinner for Jim the night before he went aboard the *Berengaria*. Al Smith was there, as were also His Eminence Patrick Cardinal Hayes, Senators Robert F. Wagner and Royal S. Copeland, Congressmen F. H. La Guardia and Sol Bloom, and Al Jolson, Max D. Steuer, Paul Block, and many hundreds of other men of moment. They gave Jim a golden scroll of the Ten Commandments written in Hebrew.

"I never knew," the Mayor said, "that so many people were glad to see me leave town."

The next evening Walker and his party, escorted by Grover Whalen and a cavalcade of policemen and Tammany sachems, went aboard ship. Sir Arthur Rostron, onetime master of the *Carpathia*, the ship which had gone to the rescue of the survivors of the *Titanic*, shook hands with the Mayor at the head of the gangplank. Sailing with Walker were Mrs. Walker, his corresponding secretary, Miss Evelyn Wagner (niece of Senator Wagner), State Senator Downing, Hector Fuller, and Commissioners Walter H. Herrick and William McCormack. The Fire Department Band played and the Police Glee Club sang the Irving Berlin ditty "Gimme Jimmy for Mine." The Mayor waved his straw hat and his malacca walking stick, made several farewell speeches, then went to the imperial suite to preside over the champagne buckets.

Although the Atlantic crossing was made on a calm sea, Walker took his meals in his suite. During the late afternoons, arrayed in white trousers and a floppy Panama hat, he strolled the promenade deck. After dinner each night he served as auctioneer of the ship's pool.

Sunday night out from New York was Senator Downing's birthday. The Walker party celebrated it in the imperial suite. Jim became so preoccupied with reminiscences about his father and the "coil-of-rope" that he forgot his duties as auctioneer. It was almost eleven o'clock when Fuller reminded him that he had neglected to send word that he would not be present at the auction. Walker went to the smoking saloon, where the passengers were patiently waiting for him.

As the apologetic Walker prepared for bids an Englishman claimed the floor. "Well, look here, I say! I don't care whether it's the Lord Mayor of New York, or any other lord mayor. I don't quite see why we should all be left waiting here until eleven o'clock at night to have this auction. I for one am not in the habit of waiting on the pleasure of lord mayors."

Jim assured the heckler that he had not meant to be rude and explained that the birthday party for Senator Downing had delayed his coming. "Of course," he went on, "I had no idea that this auction was conducted on stock-exchange principles. I thought it was merely a recreation among gentlemen."

The next afternoon, while Jim was standing at the rail and looking out at the smooth sea, the Englishman who had rebuked Walker at the auction approached him.

"Do you like flowers?" asked the gentleman.

"Yes," Jim said, "except at funerals."

The Englishman thought this over. "The rose gardens of England are unexcelled," he finally said. "And I have the finest roses in England."

"I'm sure of that," replied Jim. "You tossed a bouquet of them at me last night."

"I'm very sorry," said the man, holding out his hand. "I was in the wrong, and I wish to show you the perfect rose garden. I have sent a wireless for two motorcars to meet us at Southampton. This will spare you and your party the journey by boat-train, and I am sure you will enjoy the countryside on the way to London."

The *Berengaria's* first port of call was Cherbourg, where the liner put in at five o'clock in the morning. The Mayor of that town came aboard, and Jim received him in his dressing gown and bedroom slippers. Next, at Southampton, the Mayor of that city and his wife, with a mace-bearer and Dudley Field Malone in attendance, welcomed Walker.

Instead of proceeding from Southampton to London by train, Jim and his party went there in the automobiles provided by the lover of rose gardens. The large reception committee and the many journalists who met the boat-train at Waterloo Station were mystified when no distinguished guests alighted from the railway carriages.

Desirous of going on to Ireland as soon as possible, Jim stayed but one day in London. That night he attended a performance at the Carlton Theatre, where his comedian friend Laddie Cliff was playing in the musical *Lady Luck*. After the show Jim and his friends had supper at the Café de Paris near Leicester Square. The orchestra played "Will You Love Me in December," but did it so uncertainly that Walker himself went to the piano, and an American girl, Aileen Stanley, sang the song. The diners joined in the chorus.

Jim's party went on to Dublin the next day, where President William T. Cosgrove received them. Allie Walker sent a complete set of her husband's evening clothes to tenor John McCormack's country estate, Moore Abbey, where the Walkers were to be guests that night. And now the party undertook the ninety-mile journey by motorcar to the village of Castlecomer, where Jim's father had been born. They passed many thatched-roof cottages on the way. Smiling householders stood in their doorways, and here and there a child waved an American flag.

At about four o'clock that August afternoon the limousines entered the public square of the little village. Perhaps a thousand persons were there. A boys' brass band was playing "Come Back to Erin." Mayor Walker and his companions got out of their cars at the small City Bank Building. The silk-hatted Walker gazed a while at the upper story of the building in which his father had spent his boyhood. Jim afterward said that for a time all the hurrahs of this little world were shut out, and all the acknowledgment of his popular fame went unnoticed by him. He removed his high silk hat and stood wordlessly. Nor did he return to the realities of the living present until an old villager, in homespun clothes and waving a shillelagh, began to do a jig. "Three cheers for William Henry Walker's darlin' boy!" he shouted.

The parish priest requested the crowd to stand back while the Mayor of New York went upstairs to see the very rooms in which his father had lived long ago.

"Be quiet, everyone," said the Reverend Father McNamara. "If you behave well, His Excellency will make a fine speech when he comes down."

Jim went into the bedroom where Billy Walker had once slept. He knelt there.

"I had to wait a while before coming down," Jim said later, "for they wanted a speech, and I had a lump in my throat."

As Jim left the quarters which had housed the Walker forebears, the priest held out a small album. "Would you sign your name here? It's not for me. It's for my colleague, the rector of the Church of England parish. His duties this afternoon called him elsewhere. Do you mind?" Jim signed the book.

Outside the bank Hector Fuller had placed a kitchen chair. Jim got up on it and, with his hair blowing in the wind, made a speech about his father and about Ireland. Then he said, "There are some people who would tell you that Ireland is intolerant. I wonder if there could be found any fairer example of real tolerance and broadness of spirit than this: a Roman Catholic priest of the village burdening himself to ask a favor of me, not for himself, but for a pastor of the Church of England?"

And now Mayor Walker and his party left Castlecomer to go to Kilkenny Castle, and then on to dinner at John McCormack's. They arrived at Moore Abbey two hours late. The great tenor sang far into the night. At Jim's request McCormack sang "Sweet Genevieve."

On their return to London Jim and Allie rode to their hotel in the Lord Mayor's coach of state. Then they went on a grand tour of Europe which lasted six weeks.

When they arrived in Berlin large groups of Communists were demonstrating, and the authorities feared for the American mayor's safety. A detective reported to Jim at the station, saying he was his bodyguard. "I need no police protection," Walker assured the detective. "I'm so skinny that no one could hit me with a bullet or a bomb."

In front of the Hotel Adlon a crowd began to hiss Walker. He smiled, waved his hat, and somehow his personality, his unaffected courage, stilled the jeers, and even prompted some applause.

Walker's press interviews in Berlin, as well as elsewhere in Europe, were felicitous. During his first meeting with the Berlin newspapermen he responded to the salutation of "Lord Mayor" with, "Now, fellows, I'm not the Lord Mayor of New York or of any other city. I'm just an ordinary human being. Let's all have a beer, openly arrived at and openly consumed."

"What do you think about Prohibition?" he was asked.

"What do *you* think about it?" the Mayor countered.

"We Germans are against it."

"Well," said Walker, "I'm normal and human too."

He received all acclaim gracefully. "I do not regard it as a tribute to myself," he would say, "but as a compliment to the City of New York."

After stops in Berlin, Baden-Baden, and Munich, Mayor Walker and his troupe went to Italy. Early in September Allie and Jim drifted in the state gondola on the Grand Canal in Venice. Count Orsi, the Podesta of Venice, gave the Walker party a luncheon at which many vintage wines were served. "This is the best meal I've ever drunk," Jim quipped.

From Venice Jim and Allie went on to Rome, where they were

received in private audience by the Pope. His Holiness remarked to Walker, "But you seem so young a man to be the governor of so great a city." The Mayor respectfully replied that he was much older than he seemed.

While in Rome Walker learned of the loss at sea of editor Phil Payne of the *Mirror*, who had gone along as a passenger on the Hearst plane "Old Glory," on its attempt to fly the Atlantic. This disaster was in Walker's mind as he went to the Chigi Palace to see Benito Mussolini.

The interview with the Fascist dictator was held in the second-floor "throne room," a chamber which Jim said was large enough for football practice. The Mussolini balcony, upon which the Duce periodically displayed himself to his slaves, was situated just outside the huge room.

Jim observed that the Duce had a motion-picture crew at hand, with bright lights and a camera ready to photograph the meeting. "Thought I was in Hollywood," Walker later said. "The Duce behaved like a director."

After Mussolini had met the members of the Walker party he placed a hand upon Jim's shoulder—an act Walker never liked any man other than his father, Mr. Murphy, or Sachem Voorhis to do—and said, "Come, let us talk together."

According to Jim's version of the subsequent interview, Mussolini asked Walker, "What do you think of me?"

"I think you have an amazing political approach," Jim replied. "So different from our own."

"What is the difference?"

"Just this," Walker replied. "In our country the politicians promise the people everything, including the moon. After the politicians are in, they have a severe attack of amnesia—forget almost everything they promised. Now, in your system—and I must say you are original—you start off by promising *not* to give the people anything. In fact you tell them what you are going to take away from them. Then, when you get in, you not only keep your promise, but even go further and take away even more from the people than you promised. Your success so far convinces me that you are a master of mob psychology."

Mussolini studied Walker for a time, as though trying to decide whether or not he was being kidded. Then he said, "But I have enemies."

Jim kept a straight face. "Are you sure?"

"Positive," said Mussolini. Then he pointed to a bronze lion on his desk and, with something less than true modesty, added, "But I am no more afraid of my enemies than I am of that lion."

The Mussolini interview continued for more than half an hour, the longest time, it was said, that the Duce ever had given to an alien guest. When Mussolini spoke of his constant danger from bombs, Walker replied, "If you lived in New York, Your Excellency, you would find, as I have, that banquets are much more dangerous than bombs."

"Is that so?" said the puzzled Benito.

"Our banquets," Walker continued, "are a godsend to the medical profession and to the undertakers."

"You mean," said the Duce, "that there actually are persons who seek to poison you?"

"Me or anyone else who sits down to one of those banquets."

As they parted Mussolini said to Walker, "If at any time I can ever do you a favor, please feel free to call upon me."

Jim said that "the old boy" made good this promise a year after the interview. "A party of three New York aldermen visited Naples," Walker told Harry Hershfield, "and had their pockets picked clean. I received a cablegram from their stranded spokesman. I cabled Mussolini. The wallets of the aldermen were returned intact within a few hours."

In Paris Jim and his friends were received with much pomp at the Gare de Lyon. Jim entered upon the social round with such fervor as to cause friends to caution him about late hours and much wine.

"A man," Jim said, "is only young twice."

The American Legion was having its convention in Paris at this time. Together with Marshal Foch and General Pershing, Walker reviewed the parade of the veterans. When the New York delegation marched past the grandstand, their band played "Sidewalks of New York." The Legionnaires from Gotham called out, "Hello, Jimmy!" and "You're our pal!"

Walker did all the official things expected of him. He called upon President Doumergue, placed a wreath on the Tomb of the Unknown Soldier, and spoke at many banquets.

At a luncheon meeting to which he had been invited by a group of American businessmen, Jim was late. According to Briton Busch, father of writers Noel and Niven Busch, these men were unaccustomed to waiting for guests of honor to appear. After an hour's delay a delegation went from the American Club dining-room to Jim's suite at the Hotel Crillon to jog his memory.

The committeemen found Jim in bed and learned that he had been there for less than three hours after a "big night" among the cafés. Walker roused himself long enough to say that he would keep the engagement. Then, half asleep, he was dressed by his valet and escorted to the luncheon. He was more than two hours late already, but asked if he might stop at the bar long enough to "get a restorative."

Mr. Busch says that no one on the committee thought that Jim "would make the grade." Notwithstanding their qualms, they guided him to the seat of honor. The applause was none too hearty as he sat down. When he was called upon to speak the hand-clapping was mild.

"To our astonishment," Mr. Busch went on to say, "the Mayor came alive once he got to his feet. With amazing freshness, and complete charm, he made everyone forgive him for his tardiness."

Jim began by saying, "When an American comes to Paris he is expected to paint the town red. Gentlemen, last night I did what was expected of me." There was some good-natured laughter at this.

"It reminds me of a night not long ago when I spent the hours shooting craps with the boys. I kept thinking that I ought to go home. Then, when seven o'clock in the morning came, I decided that it was too late to go home, and too early to go to the Hall—my present, and no doubt temporary, place of employment. So I meandered downtown and found one restaurant open. I looked in to see sawdust on the floor and the chairs piled on the tables. An old colored man was cleaning the place as I stepped inside.

" 'May I have a little breakfast?' I asked.

" 'I dunno,' said the colored man. 'What do you want to eat?'

" 'I'd like some scrambled eggs,' I replied, 'and a few kind words.'

"He cooked my eggs and served them. I said to him, 'But you've forgotten something; the eggs were only a part of my order. Don't you recall that I said I'd also like a few kind words?'

" 'Well, Mayor,' the man said, 'I'll give you the kindest words I know: Don't eat them eggs.' "

The businessmen went away from that luncheon smiling and

laughing and feeling warm toward Jim, toward themselves, and toward the world. If this quarreling earth were inhabited only by men like Walker, it might well be that trains would be late, the affairs of banks unbalanced, and women crying over unintentional hurts to their hearts; but I wonder if we would not be spared the ugliness of class hatred and of war, with cities as well as railroads destroyed, the money-tills of nations depleted, and the women grieving, not over romantic injuries, but over the graves of husbands and sweethearts and sons. The critics who denounced Walker for his headlong carelessness and held him personally responsible for the woes of the city's days of reckoning lost sight of the common guilt of all men of that age of unreason. I once knew a man who blamed his own shoes for having taken him into a saloon.

During one of Jim's first days in Paris he happened to be standing alone, for a change, at the Crillon bar. While he was drinking an "eye-opener," a Rue Scribe journalist, "Sparrow" Robertson, came in. The Sparrow at that time was a sportswriter for the Paris edition of the *New York Herald Tribune*, and boasted that he knew everyone of importance the world over.

To the bartender the Sparrow said, "Well, my fine sir, whom would you guess I was with all last night? Boy, oh, boy!"

"Who?" asked the bartender. "Or, as you put it, 'whom?' Some gay tart?"

"No, sir," said the boastful Sparrow. "I was with my old pal Jimmy Walker. I have another date with him this afternoon. Hope he's still alive."

Having heard this, Jim moved over to the Sparrow. "Well, before you go to join your old pal Jimmy Walker, how about having a drink with me?"

The Sparrow considered this invitation favorably. "Don't mind if I do. My name is Sparrow Robertson. Say, haven't I seen you around someplace before?"

"Might be," Jim said. "You see, I'm your old pal Jimmy Walker."

Two cartoonists, Rube Goldberg and Clare Briggs, and photographer George Peck, arrived at the bar to take Jim to a luncheon. A heavily jeweled lady happened to sit across the table from Jim and his companions.

"Mr. Mayor," the lady called out, "do you speak French?"

"Fluently, madam," Jim replied, "but the ignorance of these natives is deplorable: they can't understand a word of what I say."

The lady had an especially large diamond on one hand. Rube Goldberg whispered to Jim, "Isn't that some rock though?"

"Yes, Rube," Jim said. "But it would look better between a pair of tongs."

The Mayor and his party returned to America aboard the *Ile de France*. Bands played at Le Havre when Jim embarked; and in New York harbor there were bands and tugboat whistles and cheers—although Walker had cabled Whalen forbidding an official welcome.

"I'm not a channel swimmer or a flyer," he said. "I'm just a tired mayor coming home to work and rest."

The next day at City Hall the Mayor received a Japanese admiral. The admiral spoke English haltingly, but Jim said, "That's the best English I've heard during the last six weeks."

At a luncheon that day at the Advertising Club, Walker said to his audience, "Please don't construe my disposition to smile as a desire to take life lightly. Please sometimes think that behind that smile, or even perhaps when you hear that laugh or that wisecrack, as it is called, please think there may be something deeper down. There may be an anxiety that I would not betray; and, sooner than betray it, I would reach out for a laugh to hide the deep anxiety."

While winter was getting autumn out of its system, there was a display of meteors as earth entered the celestial path of the Leonids. Gales delayed the ships at sea; storms blew through the Midwest. Rain, then snow, engloomed the high reef of stone and brick and steel that is Manhattan.

The master barbers of New York announced that they would charge seventy-five cents for a haircut. Tammany decided to build a new clubhouse overlooking Union Square. Bellevue Hospital made ready to raze the "Gate of a Million Sorrows," the admitting ward to which the poor sick ones of the city had come each day or night since 1869. And James J. Walker rehearsed for the Press Club minstrel show.

The rupture of the real-estate balloon in Florida had been followed by what was called a "mild recession" in national business. But few persons saw in this, or in the early beginnings of unemployment, any warning of a dark tomorrow. There were this year more than two hundred and fifty citizens with personal incomes averaging two million each, and almost all of them issued reassuring phrases that the god of prosperity was in his mechanical heaven and that all was well with the industrial world. Unlike the ancient Romans, we remained indifferent to meteors that coursed the sky.

21.

When Knighthood Was in Clover

As Tex Rickard's publicity man at Madison Square Garden during the summer and early fall of 1928, I heard of various matters cooking in the underworld, some of which would soon bring trouble to the big-little fellow whose port of call was the Garden on fight nights.

One day toward autumn I called upon Tex. He was sitting in a chair made of steers' longhorns, a piece of furniture resembling the throne of some Ubangi chieftain, indulging in a prophetic mood. Also, he was sad about two things of unrelated consequence. Someone had reached into his Alaskan past and discovered that his nickname up there originally had been "Dink." The second cause of his worriment, he confided, was a feeling that business and the stock market were bound to collapse.

This was quite a while before economist Roger Babson called the turn. "It's going to be the damnedest panic you ever seed," said Tex. "And I'm a million dollars in wheat on the grain exchange and up to my belly-button in Wall Street too."

"Why don't you get out?"

"Because I'm a gambler, that's why. I play percentages, but I'm not a sure-thing gambler, like Arnold Rothstein. That ain't gambling, and it ain't adventure. I'm the kind of a gambler who gambles, and don't look to a 'fix' to win.

"You know something?" the prophet continued, "Rothstein is going to get hisself killed."

"You have some inside information?"

"Yes and no." He chewed on his soft-rubber cigar holder for a time, looked out the window and across West Fiftieth Street to Polyclinic Hospital. "You don't need inside information down where

I come from. A real gambler like me, a feller who likes it like some fellers love booze or women, and not just because it's a marked-card deal or a fix, well, we got hunches, and we play 'em. I knew all the time up in Alaska I'd never get shot. Me? I play percentages, but no fixing. I been up against the guns. But I always knew I'd die in bed, because I felt it that way. And one day when I was weighing the gold dust I'd took in at my Great Northern saloon, a sorehead sent word for me to come on out, and he'd shoot me. And if I didn't come out I was a coward. And I sent back word to him, 'I'm a gambler and not a clay pigeon by trade; and I ain't a-comin' out, because I play percentages, and the percentage in this here case is against me. But if *you* want to go against percentages, just you come on in here and I'll shoot you, and I'll lay long odds I will. I wish they hadn't dug up that 'Dink' label. Down in Texas it means somethin' private."

"Is your Rothstein opinion more than just a hunch?"

He thought this over for a while, went to President Harding's old desk, opened a drawer, and got out a pair of ancient boxing gloves. They were four-ounce gloves, cracked with dryness and caked with sweat and bloodstains, the palm grips withered, the knuckle-pads broken inside the leather casings, and the tie-strings shriveled and snarled. "Them's the gloves Joe Gans wore when he fought Bat Nelson forty-two rounds in the sun at Goldfield, just twenty-two years ago today," he said. He put away the gloves, closed the drawer, and sighed like a dowager after an inspection of the dance programs of her youth. "You know?" he said, sitting down again on his throne, "I can't understand some of them there sportswriters like Dan Parker and Bill McGeehan. McGeehan was at Goldfield with Rube Goldberg. I put thirty thousand in twenty-dollar gold pieces on show in the bank window, the purse for the fight. Did you ever try to lift thirty grand in gold?"

"I never even saw it," I said, "let alone lifted it."

"Uh, huh!" He nodded. "Well, I passed around some twenty-dollar gold pieces just to advertise myself and the fight. When I tried to give one of 'em to Bill McGeehan, do you know what he told me to do with it?"

"I've a good idea, or a bad one, however you want to look at it."

"And now," Tex said, "McGeehan has dug up that 'Dink' label. Can you ask him to lay off?"

"I'll do my best," I promised. "But what about Rothstein?"

He seized his Theodore Roosevelt walking stick, the one made of rhinoceros hide, and hit at a fly. "It's my guess that Rothstein will be shot before the year is out. He's been askin' for it. They tell me he's been mighty slow lately makin' good on some big losses in the floatin' card games."

Later that day I went to Rickard's office again. "Tex," I said, "my old publisher on the *American*, Joe Moore, and a syndicate has bought the *Morning Telegraph*. He just telephoned that he wants to see me at Sherry's."

"He wants you to run the paper, eh?"

"You'd think," I said, "that he'd have more sense, seeing what happened when I was his editor downtown. What's your hunch about *my* future?"

Tex was an unemotional man, at least on the surface. But he said, "I was gettin' kinda used to havin' you around here, but when one of you fellers is away from a newspaper, you act like you're away from your girl. Anyways, you'll be right across the street. And you can always walk right in on me."

The *Telegraph* was not exactly across the street. The low, old brick building, dingy and rat-ridden and a onetime carbarn, lay cater-corner from the new Garden, on the southeast corner of Eighth Avenue and Fiftieth Street. In that ramshackle newspaper office several of Jim Walker's friends worked, among them Johnny O'Connor, S. Jay Kaufman, and none other than Ernest.

Ernest was beginning to be a pest at City Hall. He appeared there one day with a matrimonial purpose in mind. He petitioned his old friend Charles Hand to intervene on his behalf, to persuade the Mayor to marry him to a gaudy lady whom he introduced to Hand as his fiancée.

Ernest startled Charlie by explaining, in an aside, "I'm rescuing this little lady from a life of sin, Charlie. She's been working at Madam Baily's hookshop, and I met her there and proposed to her early this morning."

Hand reluctantly informed Jim of Ernest's intentions, cautioning him that if he acted as an agent to join journalism to an even older profession, the Mayor might arouse adverse criticism. "Charlie," Jim said, "harlot or no harlot, the lady is getting the worst of it. Give me the book."

Walker once told me that he had tried his best to place good men in key jobs and spoke of Charles S. Hand as one of them. The Mayor had endeavored to make Hand his secretary in 1926, but failed. Toward the end of 1927 Walker telephoned Hand at the *American*, where Charlie then worked as an editor. Hand left the Hearst editorial rooms on South William Street to go across Park Row to the Hall. He was immediately shown into the Mayor's private office.

Walker pointed to a chair behind a desk. "Sit down there, Charlie."

"What did you want, Jim?"

The Mayor solicitously inquired, "How does it feel, Charlie?"

"How does *what* feel?"

"The chair. Comfortable?"

"The chair's all right."

"But," Jim persisted, "doesn't it feel kind of cozy?"

"What the hell are you talking about?"

"That is the chair of the secretary to the mayor."

"So what?"

"Well, it feels good, doesn't it?"

"Like any other chair."

"Well, Charlie," the Mayor purred, "Ed Stanton is leaving me, and that is *your* chair now. You're the new secretary to the mayor."

"The hell I am!" Charlie got to his feet. "I'm making eighteen thousand a year with Hearst, and I can't afford ten thousand."

"You owe it to the city, Charlie, and to me."

"I don't owe you a damned thing."

"Now, Charlie, look at it this way: I need a secretary and a member of my cabinet with a lot of brains."

"I know that," Hand agreed, "but you don't need me."

Mayor Walker asked Hand to step to the window and look out on the plaza. There was a recruiting sign there with the slogan, "Join the Marines and See the World."

"There you are, Charlie. Join Walker and see America first."

"I've traveled enough, Jim," said Hand, closing the interview.

When Hand returned to his office there was a telegram from Hearst on his desk. The message was that it would be a good thing for the *American* to have a man in the mayor's cabinet and that Hand should take the job for six months.

Hand angrily telephoned Walker. "What have you been pulling behind my back?"

"Charlie," said Jim, "would you mind being more explicit?"

"You've tricked me," said Charlie. "I don't want the job. Is that explicit enough? Tom Foley once told me that the mayor's secretary is just a coat-holder. And you've already got a valet."

But Hand at length yielded to the Walker charm. Seven months after he had become Jim's secretary Hand and Walker went to California. They called at Mr. Hearst's huge beach house at Santa Monica. While wandering about the elaborate place, Hand chanced to enter a room where Mr. Hearst and Mayor Walker were chatting. Mr. Hearst, who was rightly supposed to have a most excellent memory, greeted Hand warmly, then said with an appearance of sorrow, "Mr. Hand, how in the world did you ever happen to leave our organization?"

Hand, whose change of jobs had meant a net loss to him of eight thousand a year, replied with polite irony, "For the money, Mr. Hearst."

Against the 1928 background of political as well as economic hurly-burly, with Prohibition furthering the ascendancy of gang leaders in the big cities, with the emergence of Franklin D. Roosevelt from retirement, and with Alfred E. Smith fog-horning for the presidency, James J. Walker made a decision of a private nature, one which too soon would become public. He left St. Luke's Place and his wife.

It was not exactly a secret when Jim moved into the Ritz, where Paul Block resided. The newspapermen knew of the rift between the Walkers. In our office at the *Telegraph*, O'Connor knew about it, as did Kaufman and Winchell. At this time Winchell, although employed by Bernarr Macfadden's *Graphic*, was contributing anonymously to the *Telegraph's* famous old column, "Beau Broadway." We frequently received letters denouncing us for having a Winchell "imitator" on our staff. And sometimes Winchell's anonymous self scooped his regular column in the *Graphic*.

It was Winchell's self-imposed policy, no matter how hot the news, never to mention the indiscretions of any man or woman unless one or both parties were contemplating an appearance in the divorce court. Indeed, that was the general practice among newspapermen of that day. The reporters tried to protect Jim from himself, for he took almost no precaution to conceal his way of living. The Park Row writers did not wish to penalize the man for his lack of hypocrisy, when all around him there were public figures who posed in piety and righteousness but cavorted behind the doors of their secret harems.

Allie Walker made no outcries when Jim departed from St. Luke's with his new valet, Roberts, and his vast wardrobe. During the past sixteen years Allie had always felt that Jim really was her own, notwithstanding his mercurial actions whenever "a passing fancy" occupied his attention. Even now she hoped, against an intuitive feeling that Jim was gone forever, that he would come back. In September, when Allie's mother lay dying, Jim went to Mrs. Allen's bedside, and he saw to it that her body was sent to Clinton, Iowa, for burial. Allie thought for a time that her sorrow and loneliness would serve to bring Jim back to her.

But Jim went away and did not go home again. He had an aversion to going back anywhere, once he had decided to sever any personal tie. He spoke about this to his sister Nan. "Sis, it may take me a long time to make up my mind, but I never go back to anything or anyone once I've left."

The young English-born woman with whom Walker had fallen in love, Betty Compton, revealed at last that she returned his love. She let Jim know, however, that she would not be content to let their romantic lives lie hidden indefinitely. It was to be no mere interlude, she stipulated, pointing out that Walker himself, and not she, had been the aggressor.

The strong-minded actress wanted marriage, no less. She was mindful that several obstacles lay before them: Jim's legal ties with Allie, his religious tenets, his public responsibilities, the opposition of important friends, Al Smith for one, and that of certain members of Jim's family, particularly his brother George.

George called on Nan Burke one day in 1928. "I was in Jim's suite at the Ritz, Nan, and he had pictures of that woman all over the place!"

"Don't try to interfere," his sister said. "What's done is done. And Jim is Jim."

Walker's first positive demonstration to Betty that he was entirely in earnest was to move out of No. 6 St. Luke's Place. Then his old, old quality of procrastination made him hesitant about asking Allie to divorce him; nor was she then in any mood to do so, particularly since she herself had religious scruples against such a course.

If Jim had not been the mayor and a celebrity, perhaps the matter might have been passed over with no consequences other than the usual broken heart, a financial settlement, and a column or so in the newspapers. But when the gayest of public men leaves his wife for love of another, he mortgages his reputation at usurious rates of interest.

When Al Smith heard that Jim and Betty were being seen together in public, the Governor paid a visit to City Hall. Jim was off duty. Smith cross-examined Allie, of whom he was most fond, but she loyally declined to admit that Jim's new romance was more than a "passing fancy."

The Governor was drawing as near to the White House as he ever would be. He objected to Walker's romance not only because of religious views and of friendship for Allie, but also because he feared that a City Hall scandal, domestic or otherwise, might dangerously reflect upon the Smith chances for election as president. His nomination this time seemed probable, but the election itself would be quite another matter.

Nor did Smith want to break with Walker during these months before the national convention and the November election. Walker was a valuable campaigner. His persuasive speeches and lovable personality were of great value to Smith, especially in the South, where Walker was much more popular than the Governor.

Jim had gone to Georgia in April of 1928, at the invitation of the Stone Mountain Memorial sponsors, to make the principal address at the unveiling and to accept the huge monument on behalf of the people of the United States. This, indeed, was an unusual honor to have been bestowed upon a Northerner, particularly a Roman Catholic, a Tammany man, and one who, in 1923, had introduced a bill to outlaw the Ku Klux Klan in New York with these words:

"We see men of the mask attempting to dictate how we shall worship God, regardless of the conviction of our own consciences. We see the immigrant excluded. We see everything and everybody threatened with censorship. We see blue laws resurrected from an intolerant past. We see the so-called one-hundred-per-cent Americanism of the present day standing out in glaring contrast with the one-hundred-per-cent humanity and democracy of the Declaration of Independence. We thank God that these are the characteristics of only a comparatively few fanatics but, few though they be, they are a menace to the Republic, and they must be obliterated."

Walker had gone to Atlanta in the private railway car of A. C. Blumenthal, the theatrical man, who was now vying with Paul Block in doing favors for Jim. Secretary Charlie Hand, reporter Joe Johnson of the *World*, and valet Roberts, a tall and efficient Englishman, traveled south with the Mayor.

While Jim was taking a bath in his Atlanta hotel suite there was a knock on the parlor door—a loud knock. Roberts went to the door, then came back to report to Secretary Hand, "There is the freshest person I ever saw out there. He demands to see the Mayor, and says he won't bother with valets."

Hand himself went to the door.

"Who are you?" a large and somewhat bellicose fellow demanded.

When Hand had identified himself, the stranger announced, "I don't bother with secretaries or valets. I only see the top guy."

"Is that so?" Hand signaled to Roberts, and together they escorted the man to the elevator; when it arrived, they pushed him into it.

When Jim came from his bath, Hand told him of the incident. "Did he give his name?" asked Walker.

"No," Hand replied. "He just kept yelling about seeing you, or else."

"Well," said Jim. "I don't know who it could be. Probably some old pal who escaped from the Atlanta Prison."

"You are jesting again, sir," Roberts said as he helped the Mayor dress for the ceremonies to be held at Stone Mountain fifteen miles north of Atlanta.

"Roberts," said the Mayor, "I am not jesting when I say, if any Georgia peaches arrive here, don't show them in."

It was on a somewhat raw April afternoon that the Mayor of New York appeared among the Southern dignitaries at the partly completed sculpture of General Robert E. Lee and of many other prominent Confederates—a gray granite tableau, two hundred feet high and thirteen hundred feet long. The Mayor lifted a three-year-old boy in his arms, Robert E. Lee IV, the great-grandson and namesake of the General. Master Lee was to give the signal for the unveiling.

Walker's speech, extemporaneous and eloquent, was regarded by many as one of the most effective of his career. Its context toward the close showed him at his daring best, and, in less able hands, might have invited disaster both to the speaker and to the cause of Al Smith. Whatever Walker's all-around reputation as an orator may be in comparison with Websterian figures of the last fifty years, it is agreed that no one within memory could more effectively disarm an audience, soften them up, as it were, than Walker, just before he moved in for the kill.

The Southern colonels glowed when he began by saying, "I feel that New York might very well have a place on this program this afternoon primarily because it is the largest Southern city in the North."

Then he launched boldly into a topic which often unhorses a Northern speaker in a Southern environment: the War between the States. First, he referred to it as a "family fight," and before the listeners could analyze that statement too closely the Walker wit and charm was upon them with the remark, "Of course, no family fight ever attracted so much attention." And after the perfectly timed wait for the laughter to subside, he fired, "Let's be frank, and speak of it as a war."

Southern ears pricked up at this. Walker continued, "It was a war, a real he-war, and it was predicated largely upon the theory that some men held in respect to the sovereign rights of the individual states. The South of the sixties of the last century fought for states' rights; and today, in the twentieth century, I believe you gave up the fight too soon."

He spoke of General Lee, and quoted B. H. Hill's tribute: "He was a Caesar without his ambition, a Frederick without his tyranny, a Napoleon without his selfishness, and a Washington without his reward."

The applause was mighty. Walker boldly advanced with words expressive of all his actions during all his life: his never-wavering efforts in behalf of the tolerance of men for their fellows everywhere, in what could become a glad world.

"I recall," he said, "having read of the critics from afar, back in the colonial days of America one hundred and fifty years ago approximately, and how they at once laughed, then again derided, promised and prophesied failure and destruction for this new form of government adopted on our soil, but it seemed to be all right then. Afterward there came the Civil War. Surely then the prophets from afar, and with additional emphasis, prophesied the absolute failure and destruction, the final and complete destruction, of our form of government, as a result of that internal conflict. It is not hard to understand why they did make such prophecies from afar. No one could understand our Civil War or our family difference.

"In countries where wars were not strange or unknown, they had difficulty understanding *our* war. When they inquired what we were quarreling about, or what we were fighting for, they necessarily inquired, was it for the lust of conquest? Was it for territory? Was it for the right or the privilege of taxation? And the answer in each instance was 'No.' And back there, they could not understand how men could quarrel or fight unless it was for profit; they couldn't understand how the sons of the original thirteen colonies could fight for a principle that the critics never had reason to understand. They didn't seem to be able to conceive of any such reason as was ours, that made brother take sides against brother, and fathers and sons occupy different positions on opposite lines.

"They couldn't understand that both sides were fighting over the interpretation of a document that they both had assisted in writing. And yet, my friends, it remained until the twentieth century, when a call from the cynical yonder lands, now in travail, found the sons of the North and the South, side by side, traveling across the great Atlantic Ocean for the same simple reasons that the Civil War was fought—devotion to principle and the things they believed in. It was then and from afar that the critics and the sons of critics of our form of government commenced to understand. Then they learned, perhaps for the first time, that family fights are not fought to destroy either side, but to compel the other to be loyal and true to the things that they said they believed in. They saw the gray of the South and the blue of the North blended into the khaki of the United States, marching through the fields of a foreign country to vindicate the principles of the Declaration of Independence, asking for nothing but a recognition of that immortal document by all the peoples of the civilized world. Here was revelation. After that great cataclysm and that great world war, and realizing that the principles of that mighty document were all that America was fighting for, then they understood—I think they understood—the Civil War, and why it was fought.

"As I looked around this assemblage, and saw those dressed in khaki, I thought of the day when *he* came home; no one knew *his* name; no one knew where *he* lived; but he was taken to the capitol of our country, and there he lay in state. His name was not written on the coffin, because he was the Unknown Soldier. No one knew whether he was born and bred in Kentucky, or whether he had gone to school in Massachusetts; no one could tell whether he was a son of California or had been born in Maine. There were no distinctions, and there can be no distinction. No one asked or knew or cared if he were a Southerner or a Northerner, or of what race. He was just an American soldier. As he lay in Washington, lay in state, the Gold Star mothers foregathered from all the states of our country, and each had a right to look down upon that coffin and feel that he was her very own. His state made no difference, because he carried a far greater significance, a more sublime importance. He was the symbol of Americanism—not merely an American, not a sectional American, but a symbol of a reunited America, a unified America, which brings the sons and daughters of the South here today to foregather with the representatives of every state of the Union."

Did this speech, with its very strong implications, offend anyone present that cold April day in the deep South? It did not. It brought Walker an ovation.

That evening Walker spoke again at a banquet at the Capital City Club. This time he managed to get his beloved father into his address, as he so often did, and somehow saw a resemblance between Billy Walker and Robert E. Lee.

Late that night in the depot at Atlanta he shook hands with numerous dignitaries on the station platform, then disappeared with Secretary Hand into his private railway coach. Roberts helped the Mayor divest himself of his formal evening clothes and got him into his dressing gown. Secretary Hand went to his own quarters in the car. When it was almost time for the train to leave he decided to have a sandwich before retiring for the night.

No porter answered Hand's ring, so he went out to get his own sandwich. As Charlie entered the sitting-room of the private car, he observed Walker in conversation with a large, burly visitor. Upon a second glance, and with an "Excuse me, gentlemen," Charlie recognized the visitor as the fellow whom Roberts and he had pushed into the elevator.

Hand was about to go on when the man rose to his feet. "I don't like your looks, and I don't like you!" he called out.

"I regret that," said Hand politely.

"Maybe you'll regret *this!*" said the man, swinging his fist at Charlie.

Although not at all quarrelsome, Hand is a big fellow, and in those days was quite athletic. He countered the blow, and before one could say "Way down South in the land of cotton," Hand's attacker lay senseless on the floor.

Without the least trace of concern, Walker got up, stood over the fallen man, and began to count, "One . . . two . . . three . . . four"–bringing his right hand up and down in the regulation manner prescribed for prizefight referees.

There were cries of "All aboard!" outside the car. Roberts and a Pullman conductor carried the still dazed visitor to the platform and delivered him to two amazed officers of the Atlanta police force.

As the train got under way Jim said to Hand, "Charlie, I'm going to match you at the Garden. You have a beautiful left hook."

"Who was that guy anyway?" Hand asked.

"Oh"–Jim shrugged–"merely a member of my own set. He's the mayor of ——" said Walker, naming a Southern city. "You only knocked down a mayor, my lad."

Back in New York, Jim remembered the little boy who had assisted him at the unveiling of the monument. He commissioned Bobby Lee a major general, attached to the Mayor's staff, and ordered his tailor to make a uniform for the boy, a replica in miniature of the broadcloth dress uniform once worn by the child's illustrious great-grandfather.

Walker's absences from City Hall were being commented upon by some of the newspapers. The *Herald Tribune* pointed out that Mayor Walker had taken seven vacations during his first two years in office, for a total of one hundred and forty-three days, and had visited London, Paris, Berlin, Rome, Houston, Hollywood, San Francisco, Atlanta, Bermuda, Florida, Canada, Havana, and Louisville for the Kentucky Derby. The city as a whole, however, looked upon Walker as an ambassador of good will. Besides, the stock market kept riding high–with here and there a day of recession and then a swift recovery–and the voices of critics were lost in the roar of speculative trade.

Al Smith had several times endeavored to confer with Jim, but Walker, disliking lectures, had played the duck. The Governor, however, did not have any moral preachments in mind. Rather, he sought to enlist Jim's aid in quieting the transit problems of the city, so that he could devote himself wholly to the larger issues of the presidential campaign.

When Al Smith called again at City Hall and found that Jim was out, he said, "If you make a date with Jim in December, he will keep it next May."

The traction interests were pounding away at Smith for legislation to authorize an increase in subway fares. The Governor set the day for a hearing in Albany on this matter. The noted attorney De Lancey Nicoll was to argue the case for the companies. Al Smith notified Walker to be present at the executive chamber on the appointed morning to argue in behalf of the City of New York.

Mr. Nicoll and his brief-bag bearers arrived at Albany at ten o'clock on the morning of the hearing. When Walker did not appear, Governor Smith's secretary did some telephoning. Walker had missed his train for Albany and would be an hour late.

The hearing was postponed until eleven o'clock. When the eminent Mr. Nicoll and his assistants, and as large a group of citizens as could be accommodated in the executive chamber, reappeared, Walker was still missing. Smith restrained his anger with some difficulty. A second telephone call to New York disclosed that Jim had missed another train but was surely on his way to the capitol in his town car.

It was almost four o'clock in the afternoon when Jim, looking somewhat sleepy-eyed and off the beam, reported to the Governor in the anteroom of the executive chamber. Smith upbraided him privately. He inquired of Jim if he thought he was a "fit representative of a great city to be wasting the time of the Governor?" He gruffly ordered Walker to "go in there and listen, and then speak, if you *can*."

It did not improve Al Smith's disposition any when the crowd applauded the tardy Jim. The dignified Mr. Nicoll pretended to be unruffled, and, at a word from the Governor, delivered his speech. The great lawyer spoke for an hour or so in behalf of a fare of more than five cents. When Mr. Nicoll had finished, Al Smith turned to Walker. "The Mayor of the City of New York will now reply."

Jim rose, as jaunty as you please, did his usual handkerchief trick, then said in reference to the lawyer's lengthy speech, "Gentlemen, that was the longest ride I ever had on a Nicoll."

This remark set off such hilarity among the spectators that Smith had to bellow for order.

From this moment on Jim held the stage. He said that he didn't mind if the traction people charged as much as a dollar for a subway ride, provided they could and would guarantee every passenger a seat, and not crowd the citizens of New York like cattle into the filthy cars. He said that the transit officials themselves had admitted to him that they could not possibly put more cars or equipment into the existing subways, and that until they remedied this condition it was useless and illogical for the subway owners to ask for a higher fare for inferior service.

Mr. Nicoll left Albany a defeated man.

Jim announced that he was going on the "water wagon," and his friend the Reverend Christian F. Reisner, a Methodist minister, applauded his resolution.

There were many reasons why Walker needed his clearest head these days. For one thing, an economic paradox presented a puzzling increase of unemployment at the same time that American business leaders felt sure of continued riches. General Motors shares, for example, rose eighty million dollars in value during one day's trading on March 9, 1928, but a long line of hungry men stood in front of a place called "The Tub," operated by Urban J. Ledoux. This somewhat eccentric but goodhearted man was known to the thousands of destitute persons he fed as "Mr. Zero." There was a record turnover of shares on the Stock Exchange on March 27, but the municipal lodging houses were full of otherwise homeless men.

On March 29 C. W. Hutton paid three hundred and seventy-five thousand dollars for a seat on the New York Stock Exchange. "When I visited the Stock Exchange," Jim said to S. Jay Kaufman, "I heard of the big price paid for seats. But I did not see any seats. Everyone was either standing or running around on the floor of the Exchange. The difference between the ordinary citizen and a stockbroker is that the broker rides to work and stands all day, while the citizen sits all day in an office and stands all the way to and from work."

There was to be a market drop in prices in June, but few persons heeded this break as a warning of financial chaos. A great surge of buying and building was in progress, and, while the breadlines lengthened at the Bowery soup kitchens, Harvard polled fifteen thousand Americans for the secrets of their success, a Madison Avenue corner was leased for twenty-two million, the speakeasies and night clubs were filled, bootleggers were social necessities, retiring and undefeated heavyweight champion Gene Tunney lectured on

Shakespeare at Yale, and great flocks of gulls ate clams cast up by sea storms on the Rockaway and Jamaica Bay shores.

Franklin D. Roosevelt placed the name of the "Happy Warrior," Alfred E. Smith, in nomination at the national Democratic convention, and Smith was designated as the party's standard bearer. Jim Walker placed the name of Franklin D. Roosevelt in nomination for governor of New York State at the state convention. How strange it all seems now, in the changeless light of the accomplished past, that the days ahead would bring feuds and bitterness to these men who in 1928 seemed to be the Three Musketeers of the political scene, with big James A. Farley as their D'Artagnan.

One Sunday morning in late October I went to the *Telegraph* editorial office. The sonorous bell-hymns of the churches smashed against the cold morning sky, crashing, then dying with great swooning reluctance.

Inside the dowdy carbarn that housed the *Telegraph* office I found Johnny O'Connor sitting in my chair. As usual, he had not been to bed all Saturday night.

"I've got a tip," Johnny said as I took off my overcoat.

"What's up, Johnny?"

"The boys are going to rub out Mr. Arnold Rothstein, our foremost gambler and fixer."

The recollection of Tex Rickard's prediction of several weeks back sprang up in my mind. "What boys, Johnny?"

"The ones he owes plenty of grands to for that big card game some time ago."

"When is the main event supposed to take place?"

"Tonight. Along about eight o'clock."

"Where, or do you know?"

"In front of Lindy's, when he comes out picking his teeth."

O'Connor was, and still is, one of the best-informed men on Broadway.

"Will you handle the assignment, Johnny?"

"You and I will both go see the shooting."

"Have you reported this to the police?"

"The police know it," said John, "but Commissioner Warren is a sick man. Nervously sick. Only Jim Walker and a few on the inside like Billy Walsh know how dangerously near Joe Warren is to a nervous breakdown. Jim's been urged to ask for his resignation before it's too late; but you know Jim. He won't fire him because of their old friendship."

Warren had been a partner in the law firm in whose office Jim had occupied a room during his time as a legislator. He was a man of excellent character and honest beyond doubt. Warren had succeeded George V. McLaughlin, former State Superintendent of Banks, as Police Commissioner. McLaughlin, himself able, courageous, and honest, had resigned in March of 1927 when thwarted by Tammany political club operators because of police raids on various clubhouse gambling games. Jim then prevailed upon his old friend Warren to accept the post.

At about seven-thirty that Sunday night, thirty minutes before the time O'Connor had specified as the hour for the Rothstein demise, Johnny and I and my assistant editor, Ed Sullivan (not the columnist), walked east to Broadway and to Lindy's. We passed several of our detective acquaintances standing or moving around in the vicinity of the restaurant in which Rothstein frequently dined. The Broadway stream sluiced past the movie houses, the restaurants, the juice stands. The lights of the street set up their garish borealis and turned the pavement to fool's gold. Automobile brakes and horns, endless voices, streetcar gongs, traffic-cop whistles, scruffings of heels—this stomach growl of mid-Manhattan symbolized a massive peristalsis, uneasy, ominous. A bus backfired with impertinent flatulence. An ambulance siren somewhere east of the Great White Way shrilled like an off-key soprano soloist.

The supposedly marked man came out of Lindy's. He moved with casual wooden strides to a near-by doorway, as was his custom, to look at the pedestrian throng.

This tall, pale, and seemingly bloodless man, aggrandized by the press, this suet-skinned Rothstein, was the emperor of the underworld. His biographer, Donald Henderson Clarke, has told of his enormous deals in race-track fixing, smuggling, baseball tampering, and all the rest. He was Broadway's pawnbroker and fence, and he stood at night in doorways, where the shadows turned his face into a slate-gray, spider-gray blob, with a web of intruding light spun about him.

"Rothstein," his attorney William J. Fallon once told me, "is a man who dwells in doorways. A gray rat, waiting for his cheese."

We watched him as he stood there, O'Connor, Sullivan, and myself, and the detectives were watching also, ready to close in on gunners—but there were no shots. Rothstein, his right hand in his overcoat pocket, as if clasping a hidden pistol, moved off with golem-like strides. We three members of the press returned to our office to lay out the next edition.

"Johnny," I said to O'Connor, "I'm afraid the ball game has been called off on account of rain or something."

"It's only a matter of days," O'Connor said. "Rothstein's number is up."

I reported the supposed murder plan of Rothstein's debtors to publisher Joe Moore. He astounded me by saying, "Even if Rothstein gets killed, we won't print a line of it."

"But Joe," I said, "ours is a Broadway newspaper. And Rothstein, in his own sinister but remarkable fashion, is Broadway's banker."

"We are not interested in the troubles of a gambler," he replied.

I forthwith called up one of my closest friends, whooping Walter Howey, editor of Hearst's *Mirror*, explained my predicament, and turned over to him the tip on Rothstein. Walter called me back to say, "Looks like you're barking up a wrong shotgun."

"What do you mean?"

"Well, I decided to call Damon Runyon about it, and Damon said that you and O'Connor should change your bootleggers, or, better still, quit drinking."

"Both O'Connor and I," I told Howey, "haven't had a drink in a long time."

"In that case," Howey said good-naturedly, "you'd better take a drink."

Several nights later, on November 4, Arnold Rothstein sat in on a floating card game. While the cards were being dealt, a half-drunken man upbraided Rothstein for welching on his gambling debts. Rothstein, whatever his demerits, possessed enormous physical courage. "You're drunk," he said to his critic. "When you sober up we'll see how big you can talk to me."

Goaded and befuddled, the man drew a pistol (not his own property, but one which had been stolen from a bodyguard during a recently attempted kidnaping) and fired. His intention, it is believed, was not to kill Rothstein but to scare him, a thing not easily accomplished. At such close range even a drunken man might easily have shot Rothstein in the head and fired more than once. But the man aimed the pistol low, as if to discharge it at the side of Rothstein's chair. The bullet struck Rothstein in the groin.

Although wounded, the gambler said with great coolness, "Is that all?" and added a vile epithet to the question.

The man with the pistol became hysterical. The others endeavored to restrain him, it is said, while Rothstein staggered out of the room. Although bleeding internally, the wounded gambler walked down three flights of stairs. His attacker meantime had raced downstairs to a telephone booth. When he tried to call police headquarters, to offer to surrender, someone snatched the receiver from his hands and two other men forcibly pulled him from the booth.

Rothstein, now at the servants' entrance of the hotel, pressed his long, pale fingers to his groin and asked a passing cab driver to call an ambulance. The pistol with which he had been shot lay in the street. It had been hurled out of the window of the hotel room.

While Rothstein was dying in the hospital across the street from Tex Rickard's office in the Garden, Walter Howey telephoned me. "I apologize for doubting an O'Connor tip. So long as your paper isn't carrying anything about it, how about trying to get someone into Rothstein's hospital room for an interview for the *Mirror?*"

O'Connor had an idea about this. "Rothstein won't talk, of course, but we'll get someone into the room to see at first-hand how he looks."

"Take over, Johnny," I said. "It's for our pal Walter Howey."

"Ernest is the man for this job," said O'Connor.

"Ernest?"

"Yes, he looks so innocent and holy. Bloated, but holy."

Johnny sent Ernest to the Eaves Costume Company, wardrobers of actors, where he was outfitted in priestly garb. The ecclesiastical Ernest went to a speakeasy, several of them in succession, got well boiled, and finally showed up at the Polyclinic. He announced himself as the Reverend Father Considine of Long Island City, and said that Mrs. Rothstein had requested him to visit Mr. Rothstein to give him spiritual consolation.

The hospital officials saw that Ernest was potted, that a *Racing Form* protruded from a coat-pocket of his black garb, and that a smear of lipstick was on his cheek. Ernest was promptly ejected from the building, and we were unable to do a favor for our friend and competitor Mr. Howey.

Arnold Rothstein died the morning of November 6, election day, the day Al Smith was defeated. Had he lived, he would have collected more than a million dollars in election bets. His murder, and the failure of the city administration to find and convict his slayer, brought crime and vice and the underworld of New York into fierce public scrutiny.

The fields of clover were growing sere in the winds of reckoning.

22.

Hold Everything

IT WAS the warmest Indian summer since the invention of the parasol. That autumn of 1928 seemed especially warm to a mayor upon whom the vagaries of politics, gangland forays, and personal love problems descended. Walker had to be not only an actor but a juggler as well.

W. C. Fields, a master of that art, said to Walker, "A juggler fears the day when he will miss, not only one trick, but *all* of them."

Whatever Jim's fears may have been, he concealed them well. During his speaking tour of several large cities in behalf of Al Smith's presidential campaign, Walker charmed almost everyone he met, including Republican Calvin Coolidge. The Mayor was forty minutes late for an appointment at the White House. He explained to the man of Arctic silence that photographers had detained him. Jim then displayed a watch given him by the Grand Street Boys. The timepiece not only told the hours and minutes, but also indicated what day, month, and year it was.

"Mr. President," Jim said, "I didn't know whether to be pleased or insulted. I have often been late, but very seldom as much as a year."

Mr. Coolidge thawed, and the two men spent half an hour in private conversation.

At a dinner sometime after the Washington trip, toastmaster Walker called upon Herbert Bayard Swope to speak. The former executive editor of the *New York Morning World* has an Olympian personality which has brought him international fame as a journalist. Indeed, when Swope was a foreign correspondent during the Paris

Peace Conference he monopolized so many important stories and interviews that a disgruntled English writer sought to stymie the brilliantly aggressive American. Swope's competitor drew up a petition to expel him from the foreign press association. The gentleman signed the paper, then confidently posted it upon the bulletin board at press headquarters. Swope was the first man to appear in the correspondents' room that evening. He read the petition, nodded as though to approve it, and signed it. Swope's name and that of his critic were the only ones ever to decorate the paper.

When Swope spoke at the dinner at which Walker was toastmaster, he made a point of saying that he had just recently spent twenty-eight minutes in conference with President Coolidge, and enlarged the point into a theme. Walker interrupted mischievously to say that he himself had spent thirty minutes with Mr. Coolidge.

Not to be outclassed, Swope said, "I really spent thirty-one minutes with the President."

To which Jim retorted, "Yes, Herbie, but you are including the three minutes you permitted Mr. Coolidge to get in a word."

About a month before the killing of gambler Rothstein, Jim decided to visit Boston to address an Al Smith rally. Betty Compton happened to be there rehearsing at the Plaza Theatre for a tryout of the musical play *Hold Everything*.

Betty had not been advised of Jim's arrival in Boston. She attended a tea given by producer Alex Aarons in his hotel suite, and, on seeing Walker there, seemed unpleasantly astonished. "I felt that I was being thrown at Jim," she later explained, "and I resented it and was cool toward him. Jim became uneasy and overpolite."

Walker did not seem to be feeling well. He complained of having throat trouble, which would prevent his speaking next day at the rally. Whether his ailment was real or imagined, he roused the sympathy of Miss Compton. She consulted the telephone directory for the number of a throat specialist.

While telephoning, she apparently discerned some telltale flaw in the performance of her admirer. Possibly he overdid his thanks. She announced that she was leaving the tea party at once.

Walker protested, and his voice suddenly seemed less hoarse. He told Betty he was returning to New York the following Sunday afternoon. Would Miss Compton please join him and his party for the journey in a private railway car?

"I already have an engagement for Sunday," said she curtly and flounced out of Aarons' suite.

When *Hold Everything* moved to New York, Jim attended rehearsals at the Broadhurst Theatre. It was not mentioned outside the intimate circle of actors that Miss Compton frequently appeared late for her practice rounds. Jim's habit of tardiness seemed to be infectious.

During this autumn Jim suffered from jealousy, something that never had occurred before during his romantic moments. He was tormented (and he himself said it was for the first time in his forty-seven years) over "where she was" and "who might be with her."

One night Jim arrived at a roof-garden ball. Betty was dancing the Charleston with one of Walker's good friends. The Mayor glowered, then rebuked his mystified friend in an aside. With a lack of courtesy unusual for him, Jim did not speak to Betty or apologize for his intrusion. She overhead the Mayor say to her dancing partner, "Of all the girls in New York, why *that* one?" The quick-tempered beauty misconstrued this remark to mean that Jim's friend might have chosen a more winsome partner than herself for his attentions. She held out her arms to Walker's confused friend, and they danced the encore.

Jim pouted. During the next dance number he went in and out of an archway that gave upon the promenade of the roof garden. Betty pretended not to see him whenever he returned inside the room to stand watching her. She did not pursue him, as many other women had done.

The Mayor had danced seldom since his Albany days, for reasons he never discussed with anyone. He asked Betty if she would sit one out with him, he had something to tell her. Jim seemed ill at ease as Betty and he sat near the archway.

"What's the matter with you?" Jim asked.

"Not a thing," she replied. "Could it be that something's the matter with *you?*"

"Your attitude," said Jim, rising, "may give me a cold in the head."

"Last time it was your throat." She too got to her feet. "Suppose you stop worrying about my attitude, Mr. Mayor."

He offered her his arm. "Let's go out on the roof."

There, on the high roof-garden of the hotel, in the cool late evening, with the heart of the city of which he was mayor defined by the lights shining around and below them, Betty heard a speech that meant more to Jim than all the other orations he had ever delivered.

"Let's go inside now," Betty said. "It's chilly out here without a wrap."

They returned to the dance floor. Vincent Lopez' orchestra was playing one of the numbers from Miss Compton's show, a sentimental song, "To Know You Is to Love You." The man who now so seldom danced placed an arm about Betty and astonished her both because he had suddenly decided to dance and because he moved with effortless grace.

It was then, Betty later said, that her love for Jim was fully revealed to her. "There was nothing sophisticated or urbane about him. He seemed as wistful as a college boy at a junior prom."

Jim called Betty "Monk," for what reason no one seems to know. Perhaps the nickname was merely a part of the small language lovers devise; terms that sometimes seem quite silly to others but are beautifully sacred—or something—to the enamored ones.

Whatever the unconventional aspects of Walker's love for Betty, his spirits were uplifted, his health improved. He shrugged off attacks by the Citizens' Union and other hecklers. His wit flashed more brightly than ever at meetings of the Board of Estimate. At a convention of mayors at Niagara Falls he made a mistake of several millions of dollars in discussing his widely assailed budget and turned the error into laughter by saying, "I've short-changed myself; but I promise you it's the last time I'll ever do it."

Allie Walker was vacationing at Hot Springs, Arkansas, that fall, and then went on to New Orleans. At various times she stayed in Florida, where she had a small yacht at her disposal. If, as some persons have charged, Allie was spending large sums of money, it should also be kept in mind that Jim had set a prodigal's example in that respect. At no time did he deny his estranged wife access to his bank account. In fact he never knew how much he had on deposit, except when he was warned that he soon might become overdrawn. The city mailed Jim's salary check to his old law office on lower Broadway. Russell T. Sherwood, an accountant, acted as Jim's business manager and handled the pay check and other financial matters for both Mr. and Mrs. Walker.

Walker's salary as mayor was twenty-five thousand a year. He was preparing to increase this and the salaries of other officials.

Eventually he would receive forty thousand. When he was attacked by La Guardia for doing this, he said, "That's cheap! Think what it would cost if I worked full time."

The evening of November 4 Betty and Jim motored northward toward Westchester. It was a Sunday, which meant that Betty had no theatrical duties that night. Jim suggested that they "go hear some tunes." They decided to visit Joe Pani's Woodmansten Inn, a suburban night club near the Williamsbridge Road.

Vincent Lopez and his orchestra were at the Inn. As one of Jim's intimate friends, Lopez not only played Walker's favorite musical numbers whenever the Mayor visited the band's various places of engagement, but also discussed the meanings of another kind of numbers. Lopez was a student of numerology.

The Woodmansten Inn was one of several suburban retreats for Broadway's fugitives from boredom. "Out in the country," Lopez says, "among the singing locusts and the weeping willows, they danced to the muffled strains of name bands, which had begun to blossom in the mid-twenties, but of which there still were comparatively few. You bought set-ups, although you were theoretically supposed to have brought along your own neutral spirits. But of course you bought the charged apple cider which the places pushed upon you as champagne; or slugged yourself with rye fresh from the fusel farms; or Scotch that tasted like reformed carbolic acid. Tuxedoed gorillas and their molls fronted the ringside tables along with Broadway celebrities. And here and there some visiting butter-and-egg man boasted, boozed, and basked."

As Lopez remembers the incident, the Mayor and his pretty companion had threaded their way among the crowded tables to reach the table reserved for them near the orchestra. The Lopez musicians sat upon a raised platform in the center of the room. While holding a chair for Betty, something he would permit no headwaiter to do for her, the Mayor accidentally jostled a butter-and-egg man seated at the next table.

"I'm sorry," said Jim.

"I guess you don't know just who you're bumping around?" said the man irritably.

"No," Jim replied, "but I'd be only too happy to go out and ask someone to identify you for both our sakes."

Betty was especially gay this night. She was wearing an evening dress that accentuated her shapely figure, and on her feet were white satin slippers. "I feel like Cinderella," she said to Lopez when he came to the Walker table between dance numbers. She turned to Jim. "My slippers may not be glass, but they're new and tight. If only I could lose them and run home barefoot, I'd like it."

"Now don't get any silly ideas," Jim cautioned.

Soon after midnight Betty said to Walker, who had neither danced nor drunk anything other than ginger ale all evening, "Let's dance, Jim."

"I'd rather not, Monk," he said.

"Please," she insisted.

"Well then," Jim said, "just a few steps, and Cinderella must go home."

They moved out on the crowded floor. When they were near the bandstand Betty suddenly kicked off her satin slippers. While several couples nearest her looked on in astonishment, she stooped over, retrieved the slippers, and held them out to Lopez. "Here, Vincent, autograph these to Jim and me."

"Now, Monk," Jim said, "restrain yourself."

"They're my shoes!" Betty retorted as the saxophones and muffled horns played the last bars of a waltz. The dancers paused, not applauding vigorously for an encore but listening and looking at the young lady flourishing her slippers. "Vincent," Betty repeated, "autograph these. I want a souvenir."

Lopez borrowed a fountain pen from one of the dancers, autographed the Compton slippers, and returned them to her. In her stocking feet, she started back to the table. And now there was a rush of women to the bandstand. The ones with light-colored slippers removed them and demanded that Lopez sign them.

The orchestra leader always remembered one of these young women, a mere girl, quite well, because, among other things, she had a beautiful name. She was bright-eyed, slender, and comely. Three years later her body would be found, washed up on the shore at Long Beach. Presumably she was murdered. Her name was Starr Faithfull, and she lived a few doors away from the Walker house on St. Luke's Place. The slipper autographed by Vincent Lopez was found among souvenirs and letters telling of this unfortunate girl's thirst for excitement during the age of "Flaming Youth."

Sometime after midnight there was a noticeable stir at one of the ringside tables, where several men allied with underworld activities were sitting with women companions. A man unknown to Lopez went to the Walker table and whispered something in Jim's ear. The Mayor seemed disturbed. He paid his check. "Come on, Monk," he said to Betty. "We're leaving."

When Lopez stepped down to say good night to them he asked, "Are you all right, Jim?"

"Not exactly," Jim replied.

Lopez handed his baton to a member of the band and went with Jim and Betty to the cloakroom. Betty excused herself to go to the powder room. While Jim was waiting, with her fur wrap in his hands, Lopez said, "Something's happened, Jim. I noticed the 'boys' were acting funny."

"Rothstein has just been shot, Vince. And that means trouble from here in."

Toward the middle of November Walker gave ailing Police Commissioner Warren four days in which to obtain more than hearsay information on the Rothstein murder. The day Walker issued this ultimatum, Whalen was sitting at his desk at Wanamaker's. His secretary entered the private office. "I bet you can't guess who's outside," he said to his boss. The secretary was a middle-aged veteran of the Wanamaker establishment and was permitted familiarities of speech not ordinarily accorded other employees.

"Well," Whalen inquired, "who is it?"

"It's Jimmy Walker," was the reply, "and he's got four hundred girls so excited that they're not waiting on anybody."

The dapper James appeared in Whalen's office. "Grover, do they *pay* you for this?" he said, glancing at the elegant furniture.

"Yes, Jim. And quite a lot too."

Walker sat down to talk about his troubles. "For some time now," he confided, "a few of us have seen Joe Warren's once-steady judgment faltering. Weeks before the Rothstein murder a few of us tried to induce him to take a rest. We even bought him tickets for a trip to Europe. But Joe saw in our friendly action a move to cast him aside. Now he has failed utterly to deal with the Rothstein case."

"You came here for my advice?" Whalen asked.

The Mayor looked Whalen in the eye. "Grover, what kind of a police commissioner would *you* make?"

"Jim," Whalen replied, "I have half a mind to throw you out the window. I've a growing family, and I owe it to them to make a little money, which at last I'm doing."

Walker rose. "Very well. But I wish you'd get out of the rag business and come home."

The following Thursday a Philadelphia member of the Wanamaker firm had lunch with Whalen in the late Rodman Wanamaker's sanctum, where all manner of art objects, priceless violins, and such had been left in place since his death. "Mr. Whalen," the executive said over coffee, "it was my pleasure not many days ago to meet one of the most charming men I have ever encountered."

The unsuspecting Whalen asked, "That so? Who was it?"

"Why," the executive replied, "Mayor Walker."

Whalen began to worry. "*What* was Mayor Walker doing in Philadelphia? And how did he *happen* to visit you?"

"Oh," was the reply, "he was introduced to me at the club by a mutual friend. And, do you know? he confided that he was having difficulty in finding a man to save the city from sin and vice."

"He did, eh?"

"Yes, and I felt flattered on behalf of our organization when he said if only he could have someone like Grover–"

"That damned little schemer!" exploded Whalen, startling the dignified executive.

Whalen called City Hall. Among other things, he reminded Walker that the Gold Dome of Centre Street (as police headquarters was called) had been the tomb of every commissioner's political ambitions after the time of Theodore Roosevelt's occupancy.

One December night the Philadelphia executive of Wanamaker's gave a dinner party for his granddaughter at a New York hotel. When the guests left the hotel to go to the Metropolitan Opera House, they were pleasantly amazed to find several motorcycle policemen waiting to escort them. At the opera house the socialites found still another array of policemen drawn up from curb to door, as if to pipe admirals over the side.

This courtesy so impressed the executive that he again called upon Whalen. "This great mayor needs help, and Wanamaker's feels it a duty to give him all the help it can. If it is a question of compensation," he continued, "your salary with us will go right on during your term as commissioner."

Whalen went to the Hall in person. When the cordial Mayor

showed no resentment at being called "a foxy little so-and-so," Whalen said, "All right, Mr. Mayor, you have been hounding me for weeks. I'm going to take the job."

Walker rose from his desk, put down his long cigarette holder, and extended his hand. "I *knew* you would do it."

"Just a minute," Whalen said. "First I'm going to tell you on what terms I'll take the job."

To which Jim replied, "Terms? They are accepted in advance."

"My terms," Whalen said, "are first that the Hall will not ask, nor will I grant, a single favor, and that means you. Next, that I'll be given a free hand to clean up gambling, no matter whom it touches, and to reorganize the Police Department as I see fit. The minute I'm interfered with, I resign."

"Sold," said the Mayor.

Commissioner Joseph A. Warren resigned on December 13, 1928. He died the following August at the age of forty-seven. Walker's critics said that Jim's old friend died of a broken heart and from the "strain as Commissioner." The cause of death was a paralytic stroke. Mr. Warren had been undergoing treatment for a nervous disorder at a sanatorium in Connecticut.

Whalen's first move as Police Commissioner was to retire some thirty or forty aged officers, thus opening the way for promotions all along the line. He put the department on a military basis and modernized the uniforms. Among the men transferred was Deputy Chief Inspector Lewis J. Valentine. His demotion to a captaincy in Long Island City, and the abolition of the Commissioner's Personal Investigation Bureau, of which Valentine had been the chief, invited criticism. Eventually Valentine became La Guardia's Police Commissioner. Then, at the invitation of General Douglas MacArthur, Valentine reorganized the police in Japan, and died after receiving honors long denied him.

The interior of the old north wing of the police building at 240 Centre Street underwent an aesthetic change when Whalen took over its gloomy chambers. The new Commissioner had an aversion to ancient, varnished woodwork and bare cement floors. On their first call upon the Commissioner the reporters observed that the wainscoting of the anterooms had been painted a bright yellow. A thick blue carpet, with Napoleonic ornaments woven in gold, covered the floors. New mahogany furniture had been installed, including an information desk, and officers on duty had instructions to be polite to visitors instead of glumly indifferent. The woodwork in the Commissioner's oak-paneled office was left untouched, but the room was refurnished. A new lamp with a shade fashioned from an old parchment manuscript shone softly yet with sufficient glow, revealing several elegant pieces of bric-a-brac. On the desk stood a telephone of French design, the kind not yet in common use in America, and an equestrian statuette in bronze of Napoleon. Water colors on the walls, fresh flowers in a vase, and a ship's model gave the well-groomed police chieftain a genteel environment. A pair of antique Chinese columns stood against one wall. Upon their delivery, the janitor had believed them to be junk and had sent them to the basement.

Notwithstanding his fancy surroundings, the new Commissioner performed like an efficient general. Almost his first action was to call up a city clerk and ward leader who was operating a gambling club under the guise of a political headquarters. "You are closing your club this Saturday," he said.

Soon after, the direct private telephone between the Hall and the Commissioner's office rang. The Mayor began to upbraid Whalen. "This man is one of the grandest fellows in the world, Commissioner. And he is conducting a nice little club."

"Then why," Whalen said, "does he have ice-box doors? And why is he there all day long when he is supposed to be in court, acting as a clerk?"

"You can't do this!" Walker shouted. "I'm going to fire you!"

"This club," Whalen replied, "is closing down. If your friend doesn't do it, I have some nice strong boys, a lot of firemen's axes, and enough patrol wagons for him and his pals. And if you're there yourself, we'll take *you* in."

"Will you please repeat that?" Walker said.

Whalen repeated it.

Jim, who had been telephoning in the presence of the complaining politician, turned to the man to say, "You see what I get for taking a ragman and putting him in a position of authority!"

Five minutes later the private line rang again. The Mayor said to Whalen, "Commish, how did I do?"

"Your act was splendid." Whalen chuckled.

"Well," the Mayor replied, "I can't stop a man like you, of course.

But this Tammany bunch has votes. And you needn't treat them like dogs when they call you or come down there."

The Rothstein case went unsolved, but for a while there was a decrease in crimes of violence. Whalen's "strong-arm squad" probably had much to do with this improvement. For example, an informer approached Detective John Broderick at the Paradise Café one evening and confided that Jack ("Legs") Diamond had come to town with two loaded pistols and the intention of shooting Broderick. The stalwart peace officer never carried a gun; his two hard fists were his only weapons.

"Legs" Diamond was known to the underworld as "a clay pigeon" because he had been shot so many times. "Legs" also had been locked up more often than a Follies girl's bracelet. At this time he was operating a distilling plant up-state and had received word from Broderick that Broadway was permanently out of bounds for him.

Broderick nodded to the stoolie who had sung to him, then telephoned headquarters. He was told that Commissioner Whalen had gone with Mayor Walker to the St. Regis Hotel to call upon Vincent Lopez. Whalen, Walker, and reporter Joe Swerling were having their "numbers" analyzed by Lopez when Broderick arrived.

"Your Honor," Broderick said, "and Mr. Commissioner, I want carte blanche on 'Legs' Diamond. He's back in town and says he's going to shoot me."

"Do what you want, Johnny," said Walker, "but you better carry a gun this time."

"I don't need a gun," Broderick replied. "Let's *all* go find this rat."

The Mayor and the Commissioner declined the invitation. Lopez and Swerling, however, decided to go along. Swerling went to a telephone and was back in a few minutes with the information that "Legs" Diamond was at this moment sitting in the third row, left, of a Forty-eighth Street theatre.

"You know something?" Walker said. "I've changed my mind. This ought to be good. Come on, Grover."

At the theatre Broderick left his four companions across the street and went in alone. After a few minutes they saw Broderick emerge from the theatre. In his arms was a slim man in a tuxedo. Broderick was carrying this man by the waist, and the pale fellow's feet were clear of the ground. The athletic detective transported his docile captive for some twenty yards up the street until he found an empty garbage can. He raised "Legs" Diamond high, dumped him head-first, brushed his palms, and rejoined his companions.

"Aren't you going to take him in?" asked Commissioner Whalen.

"He'd only get a mouthpiece to spring him," replied Broderick. "This way, he'll be so embarrassed he won't be able to face the boys. He'll blow town for good."

Not long afterward "Legs" received enough shotgun slugs to slay even a man with his great tolerance for lead.

"Broderick as good as killed Diamond with that garbage-can stunt," Walker said. "It finished the desperado as a leader. Applied psychology."

23.

Who Can Say No?

A NEW YEAR, the last one of the twenties, brought shining promises as well as an influenza epidemic and growing unemployment. Who could cry havoc and expect to be heard in the land which now had fourteen thousand millionaires? Prosperity flitted like a grass-widow from the arms of Coolidge to those of Hoover. Mrs. Alfred E. Smith took Mrs. Franklin D. Roosevelt on a tour of the executive mansion at Albany to show the new first lady of the state where the household things were kept. Defeated Al Smith gave away the several animals in his private zoo and heard the door of his great ambitions slam-bang.

In his new loneliness Smith watched for signs of disloyalty among the sachems with whom he had worked and lived. Jim Walker neglected to telephone or telegraph him the day the less than Happy Warrior stood swordless and unhorsed.

Smith sought to salvage his local prestige and influence at Tammany Hall. The man who had attributed his loss of the presidency to religious bigotry winced when he heard that Walker had said, "There were other reasons for Al's defeat. He exchanged the old blue serge suit for a white tie and tails, the brown derby for a top hat. He took off the square-toe brogans with which he had climbed from the sidewalks of New York to dizzy heights and put on a pair of pumps. It takes a damn good acrobat to do that while at the top of the ladder."

When Walker's Police Commissioner retired several of Al Smith's aging friends, the fallen champion regarded this as evidence that the Mayor had deserted him.

For some weeks reports had persisted of Smith's growing coolness toward Walker. Their respective attitudes were described as "formally polite" as early as January 8, when they stood side by side to see one-hundred-year-old Sachem Voorhis lay the cornerstone of the new Tammany clubhouse. They met again as speakers at a Tammany dinner on January 17, at which the new governor, Franklin D. Roosevelt, was also present. Smith and Walker remained "on polite but restrained terms," it was said. Smith then left town to play golf in the South with John J. Raskob and Bobby Jones. Walker went to Florida on a vacation.

Early in March they were both guests at the annual dinner of the Inner Circle. The members of this society were the press-room regulars of City Hall. Their annual banquets were patterned after those of the Gridiron Club in Washington. Toward the close of the evening, as Jim later admitted, he "brushed Al's silk hat the wrong way" by inquiring about the "health" of Tammany Leader Olvany.

Judge Olvany had been an exceptionally healthy man during his years as Tammany chief, but he was now preparing to resign, offering "ill health" as the reason. A few days after the Inner Circle dinner Smith, Walker, and Olvany met at a social gathering at the home of industrialist William H. Woodin. Both Walker and Smith—as reported by Alva Johnston—overheard Olvany say, "The condition of my health makes it imperative that I resign."

"Did you lose your nerve?" Smith inquired.

Walker, who had had much to do with bringing about Olvany's retirement, said with pretended innocence, "I would have appreciated it, George, if you had given me twenty minutes' notice."

After Olvany's resignation the Tammany policy makers denied Al Smith the privilege of naming a successor to the "sick" judge. Surrogate Foley would have been acceptable to Smith and to many others but refused to consider it. On March 18 Walker summoned the district leaders to a conference at which he let it be known that he desired a Tammany head friendly to the Mayor. When a Tammany committee offered a group of "likely" candidates, among them Senator Wagner, M. G. McCue, and John F. Curry, Walker dictated the selection of Mr. Curry.

Boss Ed Flynn of the Bronx did not agree with Curry's policies and said of Jim's choice, "Walker himself told me that while he was never friendly with Curry, he agreed to endorse him after he had been importuned to do so by some of his close friends."

It was reported that Jim was once again considering withdrawing from public life. He had received several offers from representatives of private enterprises, among them an opportunity to become part owner of a major league baseball club. Overtures were made to him to succeed the late Tex Rickard as head of the Madison Square Garden Corporation. Adolph Zukor's invitation to serve as legal adviser to a motion-picture group had not been withdrawn. While the Mayor was mulling over these prospects, what Adolph Zukor had said would occur did: the inflammatory charge was made that Jim could not be re-elected even though he might seek a second term.

Al Smith made this charge during a visit to City Hall and roused Walker to make a decision. Dudley Field Malone was there when Smith arrived, and just recently he supplied me with the hitherto undisclosed details of that occasion.

Jim was closeted with Malone, and the caller indicated that he wished to speak privately to the Mayor.

"I'll only be a few minutes, Dudley," Jim said.

Malone waited for some forty minutes in the office next to Jim's. When Smith came out, he was obviously angry. Walker now sent for Malone. Walker shut the door, sat down, and looked out the window for a few moments.

"Dudley," Jim said at last, "Al Smith just commanded me not to run again."

The Smith meeting, as described by Jim to Dudley, can be reconstructed as follows:

After overly polite greetings by both men, Smith said in effect, "Jim, do you still regard me as the head of the party in New York State?"

"I'll regard you any way you wish," Walker replied. "What do you want me to do?"

"I want you to promise me not to run for re-election."

"Do you want the job yourself?"

Although there had been reports that Smith might consider the mayoralty, he told Walker that he did not want the job, nor did he seek any other executive post in the political world.

"What's the score then?" Walker asked.

"You'll be defeated if you run."

"That kind of prospect didn't stop *you*," Walker retorted.

Smith listed the things he regarded as handicaps, among them the Rothstein murder and the growing criticism of the city administration by ministers and taxpaying groups. He brought from his pocket a front-page story clipped from the March 14 issue of the *New York Times*.

The first paragraph asked the question: "Who, if anybody, at the present moment is the acting mayor of New York?" The story went on to say that the Mayor was out of town, the President of the Board of Aldermen, Joseph V. McKee, was at Palm Beach, where his wife was recuperating from an illness, and the Vice-Chairman of the Board, Charles A. McManus, was also in the South.

"This," said Smith, tossing the clipping aside, "is only a straw in the wind. The wind is getting stronger and stronger. And you'll be blown sky-high."

After several minutes of argument by Smith, Walker said, "Why don't you tell me the real reason?"

Smith looked at Walker without replying, and Jim blurted, "Then I'll tell you, without all this beating about the bush. It's because I have a girl. Isn't that what's bothering you?"

"It's bothering a great many people," Smith replied.

"As a matter of fact I wasn't going to run," Jim said. "I'm sick of office and tired of living in a glass house that I never asked for. But now I'm going to run!"

"You'd better pray for a miracle," Smith retorted.

In a little more than a week the miracle happened.

It is almost as dull to read or write about the subway's political, financial, or legal aspects as it is to ride like a suffocated gopher on one of the underground trains. Yet the importance of the subway to the city is apparent, and the wars waged over its ownership and operation have been expensively real.

A five-page letter, marked "strictly private," and bearing the date April 11, 1928, which I found among Walker's confidential files, describes the hazardous muddle that, except for the miracle, might well have blocked Walker's way to a second term. The letter addressed to the Mayor was signed by Samuel Untermyer, a man of unselfish zeal who devoted himself to the betterment of his fellows. Attorney Untermyer was also a leading member of the New York bar.

Untermyer had served since 1926, without remuneration, as the city's adviser on the problem of unification of the transit systems. He had envisioned this unification either by means of the purchase of leases and the repayment to stockholders of their investment, or else by recapture through court proceedings. It was his contention that an increase of two cents over the five-cent fare would cost the public an added thirty-six million a year. He further maintained that the total investment of the Interborough amounted to only nineteen million, and that, up to 1918, the stockholders of that company had been paid more than sixty-five million in dividends, or 350 per cent on their investment. Untermyer declared that if the Interborough people had been content with a steady annual return of 7 per cent on their actual investment, and had put aside the balance of their earnings instead of withdrawing 34 per cent, 25 per cent, and other such sums on their investment in single years; and if they had not foolishly bought the antiquated elevated roads, the Interborough might now be paying its stockholders 10 to 20 per cent annually.

Mr. Untermyer's letter discloses that the Mayor and he had had a conference on February 10, 1928, at City Hall. During that meeting the attorney had repeated a warning frequently voiced by him against further delay in beginning suits in the state courts to make the traction interests live up to their contracts with the city. Were this course neglected, he had pointed out, the Interborough would bypass the state courts by bringing an injunctive action in the United States courts.

When the Interborough filed increased schedules with the Transit Commission before the city knew what its next step would be, Mr. Untermyer communicated with the public authorities with a view to checkmating the Interborough's action. He urged close cooperation between the Transit Commission and city officials to avoid divided counsel.

The Interborough brought its ancillary action and procured its injunction. Mr. Untermyer fell ill. The first information that reached his bedside in respect to the city's employment of independent counsel was through newspaper announcements. He read that the Transit

Commission had retained Charles L. Craig, former Comptroller in Mayor Hylan's administration, to represent the city in the United States Statutory Court. Untermyer, in his confidential letter to Walker, characterized this failure to consult him as a humiliating and indefensible action. To avert prejudice to the case, however, by disclosing an open rupture, Untermyer had put aside his personal annoyance and had an interview with Mr. Craig. The Untermyer letter stated that Craig had not then studied the case to a point where he had any plans or suggestions to offer.

The next thing that Untermyer heard, still while he was recovering from his illness, was a public announcement attributed to Mr. Craig that he was quite satisfied to have the case go to a federal court and did not intend to question federal jurisdiction. Then, when Mr. Craig proceeded on behalf of the city to interpose an answer setting up a counterclaim, it meant, in Untermyer's opinion, that the city would definitely be committed to the jurisdiction of the United States court.

A brief and argument were submitted on behalf of the city, and the financial status of the Interborough was described as that of "insolvency." It had been Untermyer's stout contention, supported by more than eighty pages of printed affidavits and tables of official figures taken from the Interborough's own books, that, far from being insolvent, the company was very prosperous, was meeting all its fixed charges, and was earning large sums in addition thereto.

When the Interborough obtained its injunction, the traction gentlemen were understandably jubilant. The city appealed to the United States Supreme Court, but so confident of success were the Interborough's officials that they paid an estimated three hundred thousand dollars for the services of the pioneer public relations genius of big business, Ivy Lee. They also retained the distinguished Charles Evans Hughes as special counsel. Furthermore, the Interborough had the "forethought" to buy six million tokens made of German silver, which, together with tickets and rebate slips, cost nearly a hundred and seventy-five thousand dollars. The prospective fare-raisers placed an additional order for ten million tokens, to be struck at a mint of their own designation.

The day the Supreme Court was to rule upon the transit appeal there was an upward flurry in traction stocks. At Post 18 of the Stock Exchange floor the crowd became so noisy the brokers could not make themselves heard.

It was then the miracle occurred that saved the five-cent fare—and Jim. In an opinion delivered by Associate Justice McReynolds, the Supreme Court reversed the order of the Statutory Court. Among other things, the Court found that the Interborough had brought its federal suit prematurely and that the five-cent-fare rate was not confiscatory when subway and elevated lines were considered separately. The Statutory Court's order, as issued on May 10, 1928, by Judges Martin T. Manton, William Bondy, and John C. Knox, was described by Justice McReynolds as "improvident and beyond the discretion of the court."

"Well," Jim said when the decision was handed down, "subways are built with pickaxes, not thoraxes."

The cost to the Interborough for this suit was about a million dollars. Who do you suppose paid the bill? The taxpayers of New York City had to pick up the check for this effort on the part of the traction gentlemen to charge them an extra fare. The company relieved itself of its obligation to meet legal fees, the minting of tokens, the salary of its press agent, as well as other pertinent outlays, by charging these matters to "operating expenses." Operating expenses were deductible from profits before the city received any payment on its investment in the subways.

The Walker luck had held once again. The editorialists as well as the sachems agreed that his chances for re-election were excellent. Jim called his Police Commissioner to City Hall. "Grover," he said, "it is the custom of reluctant candidates to be drafted. They always hear the call of the people, even if it is but a whisper. Will you see to it that I receive this call? And will you manage it with your usual David Belasco skill, plus a bit of Phineas T. Barnum?"

"You will hear the call," said Whalen, smiling.

Whalen sat down to survey the Walker accomplishments, many of which were, and still are, conceded to be on the side of the angels. He submitted this list to Walker. Jim glanced at the "forty praiseworthy points" and said, "I'm even better than I thought. Haven't we overlooked something?"

"Hardly," said Whalen.

"Now," said Walker, "I must have a large committee of important persons, as many as may conveniently, or inconveniently, be crowded into the Board of Estimate chamber, to bring this call to me in the form of a petition."

"Right," said Whalen.

"We must have someone act as their spokesman, someone venerable, beloved, and *not* a politician."

"August Heckscher," said Grover.

"Yes. He has given millions to improve the health and recreation of children. I love him, and so does everyone else."

"But you'll love him even *better?*" Whalen mischievously suggested.

"Yes," Jim said, "if he calls out to me in a loud tone."

"He's pretty old for calling loudly, Jim."

"But I'll be able to hear him," said the Mayor. "I have sharp ears."

On July 18, 1929, a committee of six hundred and eighty-two well-known persons arrived at City Hall. They crowded into the Board room to hear Chairman Heckscher read the petition. Allie Walker, smiling as though Jim were still her devoted husband, sat on the platform next to the Mayor. Radio microphones picked up the voice of Mr. Heckscher as he read the Mayor's forty qualifications.

Then Jim, as though surprised to hear this eulogy, made a long speech. He closed it with the question, "Who can say no?"

Two days after Walker's acceptance the *New York Times* carried an editorial bearing the caption "The Mayor He Might Be":

"Men are often judged by the wrong qualities. . . . If, for example, the people of this city were asked to sum up the official character of Mayor Walker, nine out of ten of them would dwell upon his great personal charm, his talent for friendship, his broad sympathies embracing all sorts and conditions of men, his ready wit, his brilliance as a speaker at every kind of gathering or function, his skill as a politician, his gift for winning support from the most unlikely quarters. These estimates of the mayor are true enough, but they ignore certain things in him which he usually keeps in the background, but which mark him out as a man naturally fitted for a great executive position.

"Mr. Walker has a singularly alert intelligence. He is quick not only in epigram and repartee, but in grasp of the essentials of a governmental problem laid before him. . . . Probably no man in New York better understands its public business. What has been done, Mr. Walker has at the end of his fingers; what should be done at the end of his tongue. His versatility, his ingenuity in finding ways out of difficulties, his swift dispatch of affairs demanding his attention, his adroitness in dealing with opposition and in composing controversies—all these are high qualities in a public servant and should equip him for a most useful career.

"What has been lacking . . . has been the steady application of uncommon abilities to the uncommonly complicated and arduous work of the office. The city has stood by and seen, as it were, great powers going to waste. Citizens have not so much minded Mr. Walker's frequent absences, or his obvious delight in the social side of life, but they have regretted that he has not devoted himself more exclusively and sternly to the big job placed in his hands. . . .

"Everybody who knows Mr. Walker well is confident that he has in him the makings of a remarkable chief magistrate of this city. The mayor that he has been gives only a hint of the mayor that he might be."

24.

The Last Fling

The Fusion candidate for mayor, Fiorello La Guardia, tossed grenades, and various spokesmen for taxpaying groups passed ammunition to him, but Beau James winked at his opponents and smiled at his friends.

Insofar as I can ascertain, there never existed any deep-down enmity between Walker and La Guardia. The "Little Flower" had a truculent hunger for office and used all the political weapons, but Jim said that he always liked his opponent and admired his ability as a showman.

"His is the keenest political mind that has been operating in many a day," Jim once said, "but he's a great showman too. His rivals talk English, good, bad, or indifferent. But Fiorello is the cosmopolite of this most cosmopolitan city. In the ghetto he talks Yiddish, not because he wants to keep what he says a secret, but because that's the best way to be one of them. In Little Italy he talks Italian, because that makes him one of the boys. When he tells off the Germans, he can do so in their own language. Even when he speaks English he speaks two kinds to suit his audience of the moment—the King's English or just English. This Little Flower is no shrinking violet."

When La Guardia attacked Walker for his manner of dress, Jim replied in a speech, "There is no law to define the kind of clothes the mayor must wear. If I thought that I might serve the taxpayers better by appearing at City Hall clad in overalls, or even a snood, I should do so. But until we have an ordinance to the contrary, I shall bathe frequently, as is my custom; and change my linen often, as is my perhaps eccentric desire; and patronize the tailor of my own choice."

La Guardia assailed Mayor Walker for giving a friend, Sidney Solomon, the lease of the Casino in Central Park and sponsoring its reconstruction as the swankiest restaurant New York City had yet seen. The Fusion candidate was by no means alone in his criticism of the Mayor in respect to the Casino transaction.

Six months before Sidney Solomon died in 1947 I questioned him as to Walker's interest in the Casino, and how the lease came about. Their friendship had cooled in 1936, and it seemed reasonable to assume that anything he might say about Walker would not be freighted with sentimental untruths. From information I subsequently obtained from dependable sources other than Solomon, I can see no reason to challenge any of the statements he made to me.

Solomon had been a partner of Gene Byfield, who had an interest in various Chicago hotels and inns. He also had been in the ready-to-wear industry. He was a gourmet, intimately familiar with the celebrated kitchens of Continental Europe.

Solomon was responsible for introducing Walker to tailor Friedman, and anyone acquainted with Jim's character would agree that this introduction to a remarkable tailor was a favor to be remembered.

While Solomon and Walker were both at Saratoga in 1925 Jim inquired, "Sid, is there anything I can do for you?"

"There is," Solomon replied. "I'd like to take over the old Casino in Central Park and make it an outstanding restaurant instead of the shanty it now is."

"I'll see what can be done," Jim replied. "We have several good restaurants, but of course I'd like the city to have the very finest."

The Casino was a sixty-year-old structure of wood and stone. It stood inside the park about one hundred feet west of Fifth Avenue in the Seventies. Since 1919 it had been operated by Carl F. Zittel, "discoverer" of Eva Tanguay and formerly a solicitor of theatrical advertising for Mr. Hearst's *Journal*. This bustling fellow liked candy-striped silk shirts and diamonds. He was publishing a theatrical trade paper, *Zit's Weekly*. Under his management the Casino served unimaginative food amid clap-trap equipment.

After Walker had taken office Solomon asked the Mayor, "What about the Casino?"

"You may have it," Jim replied, "after I look up the lease and everything is shipshape."

A few days later Walker told Solomon, "I have good news for you. You may have the Casino in two and a half years."

When Solomon demurred, Walker said that he couldn't help it. Zittel's license had been obtained under the Hylan administration and remained in effect. After some litigation in 1928 Solomon obtained the Casino lease.

"Walker's friend Tony Biddle was a principal member of our board," Solomon told me. "I don't think anyone ever doubted his ability to raise money or questioned his honesty. Walker did not put a cent into this enterprise, nor did Paul Block, Blumenthal, or any of Walker's other friends invest in it for him directly or indirectly."

The Casino board decided not to sell liquor, Solomon asserted. A three-dollar cover charge was decided upon, and the price of soda water fixed at three dollars a bottle. If you brought your own liquor and paid six dollars for the privilege of downing it at the Casino, then good evening.

The rebuilding and the decoration of the Casino became an event of much interest to Jim. It would be a place in which Betty Compton and he might dine while listening to the music of name bands. Jim seemed disdainful of the idea that an unwarranted display of romance would make his career quite vulnerable.

"It's Jim Walker's life that I'm living," he said when someone advised him to be discreet. "It's not La Guardia's life, nor Benjamin Franklin's life, nor Carrie Nation's life, but my own. If you have to be a sneak to get votes, then count me out right now. The sooner the better."

Walker now resided at the Mayfair on Park Avenue at East Sixty-fifth Street. Governor Roosevelt's town house stood some forty yards west of this fashionable hotel. Perhaps Jim's preoccupation with plans for the Casino—and with Betty—was the reason that he neglected to pay his respects to the Governor whenever Mr. Roosevelt was in the city. This oversight on Jim's part, as well as his failure to call on Mr. Roosevelt when he visited Albany, caused the Governor to say to Charles Hand, "What's the matter with this fellow? I should like very much to discuss with him several matters having to do with legislation affecting the city. Why doesn't he see me?"

"I don't understand it myself, Governor," Walker's secretary replied. Hand did not wish to admit that architectural and romantic affairs were engrossing the Mayor's attention.

"How would you like to change employers, Charlie?" the Governor asked. "You could be my secretary, and then we would both know what I am doing."

"I'd have to get Jim's consent," replied Hand.

When Charlie informed Walker of this conversation, Jim replied, "Not a chance, Charlie. Let Frank find his own secretaries, and not raid City Hall."

Walker then resumed his extracurricular activities as architectural expert and interior decorator.

Jim and Betty examined the many sketches submitted by Josef Urban, the celebrated Viennese designer whom Solomon had commissioned to do over the Casino. The cost of decorating the place was nearly a hundred and forty thousand dollars, and that of renovating the building one hundred and twenty-five thousand. The kitchen represented an investment of another hundred thousand. A stone terrace surrounded the new Casino, and a fountain on the roof kept the establishment cool during the summer months.

Urban declaimed like a minor poet as he explained his work before the premiere. "The moods of each room are established through rhythmic line and sensuous color, and in the whole composition each room plays up to the next room. In the main dining-room, broad surfaces of silver give a living neutral background to a pulsating rhythm of maroon and green. In the ballroom, the line of the mural composition is like the wave of a conductor's baton beginning the dance music; while dim reflections in the black glass ballroom give space and movement in sympathy to the life of the room. As to the entrance lobby, reliance on proportion serves as a foil to these two formal rooms. In the pavilion, the freshness of spring flowers and joyousness of a wind among young leaves inspires the decoration. In the informal small dayroom of fumed knotty pine, there is a ruddy ceiling and materials of vigorous texture and pattern."

"The Casino will be our place, Monk," Jim said to Betty. Then to Solomon, "How about the music?"

"Two orchestras," Solomon replied. "Leo Reisman's in the pavilion, and Emil Coleman's in the Black and Gold Room."

There were to be two pianos at the Casino. Nat Brandwynne would sit at one, and the then unheard-of Eddie Duchin at the other. Solomon said that young Duchin's mother realized that her son was a good piano player but wanted him to be a druggist. Solomon had persuaded her that the boy prodigy should keep at his music because drugstores now were mostly noted as soda fountains.

"In the Walker days," Solomon told me, "orchestra leader Reisman was growing independent. A man in his position commanded a following of wealthy patrons, who hired him at terrific rates to play at coming-out parties and society balls. I took Duchin in hand and counseled him to watch Reisman's every move as a conductor, and told him I was going to put him in charge of the orchestra if Reisman quit. When Reisman did quit, Duchin succeeded him at the Casino and became what is called a panic. A member of the Grace steamship family once gave a private party and paid Eddie and his orchestra twenty thousand to play from nine o'clock one evening until four the next morning. I shared in the many large fees collected by Duchin and made a great deal of money thereby."

While workmen were completing the new Casino, Walker asked Solomon, "Where are your own quarters?"

Solomon replied that he had forgotten to provide an office for himself. Mr. Urban promptly added an upstairs retreat. The walls were covered with green moiré. There was an inlaid mahogany desk, furniture upholstered in green, a gold-leaf ceiling, and a bath and shower lined with blue tile. Walker sometimes held political conferences in this office, while Betty waited downstairs and listened to the music. Jim drank champagne at the Casino, and Betty sipped beer. The refreshments conveniently appeared in a car parked outside the restaurant. One bottle at a time was delivered inside, and a stiff corkage fee levied for the service.

When the renovation of the Casino seemed at an end, Walker detected a flaw in the arrangement of the lobby. One of the bandstands shut out the headwaiter's view of the main entrance. He would be unable to see incoming guests checking their wraps, and would not have time to make up his mind how important they were and where to seat them. It cost Solomon and his backers another twenty-two thousand to construct a new entrance. A great mass of bedrock had to be blasted away to make room for it.

More than two thousand New Yorkers sought invitations to the preview of the Casino. The seating capacity was but five hundred and fifty-four, and Mr. Biddle restricted the attendance to that figure.

The Casino opened to a select clientele that autumn. Jim did not appear the first night, but the next night came with Betty. Reisman's orchestra played "Will You Love Me in December," and Walker sent a hundred-dollar bill to the conductor.

"Why did you do that?" Solomon asked Jim.

"Because I like to do such things."

"Don't do it again," said Solomon. "I'm paying this orchestra twenty-eight hundred a week, and a tip from the Mayor will not be received."

On his way out with Betty, Walker left a two-hundred-dollar tip with the checkroom girl. When Solomon learned of this, he exacted a promise from Jim never to do it again.

"It is untrue that the Mayor received his meals or anything else free at the Casino," Solomon said. "All I asked of him was not to tip anyone."

During the late autumn, even with the great panic moving in upon the world, business held up at the Casino. "For six years," Solomon told me, "or until La Guardia came in, we never had a losing day, panic or no panic. Nobody connected with Tammany Hall ever demanded or got a quarter from the Casino, a fact that may have had something to do with the place staying solvent. We always closed at two o'clock in the morning—a bit too early to suit Jim Walker—but in that way we needed no protection. It is my belief that money taken in by anyone after legal closing hours becomes a headache."

Only one customer ever failed to pay his bill at the Casino. "He was an insurance man. He was in the habit of coming to the Casino on Sunday nights after the hockey matches at Madison Square Garden, and would cash a ten-thousand-dollar check into thousand-dollar notes and give the orchestra one of them. Sometimes his bill for caviar alone would be as much as three hundred dollars. The

Wall Street people all had accounts with us and paid them promptly by the fifth of each month. This particular man's tab was seven thousand dollars when the crash came. We were unable to collect from him—he committed suicide."

During the summer months before the panic La Guardia's hammerblows apparently were falling unheeded on Jim's jaunty head. Numerous threats were also made on his life, which he disregarded, but Police Commissioner Whalen was much concerned.

On the afternoon of July 31 a report traveled swiftly that the Mayor had been shot in an uptown apartment. The entire police force was sent out to search for him. At about four o'clock Jim arrived at the Hall. Reporters and a crowd of citizens were awaiting him.

"Thank God!" said Whalen.

"For what?" Jim inquired. "Has the Little Flower wilted?"

Informed of the rumor of his assassination, Jim said, "They haven't taken me for a ride yet; but they may take a few shots at me next November."

Walker said that the reason no one had been able to reach him was that he had been taking a walk, unescorted. He neglected to say that his stroll had been along a country lane on Long Island, near the house which Betty Compton and her mother, Mrs. Florence Halling Compton, had taken for the summer. Mrs. Compton and Jim were quite congenial. He called her "the Duchess."

Walker was a frequent weekend guest at the Compton country place. One Sunday night the butler announced that two gentlemen wished to see the Mayor and insisted upon seeing him alone. Walker left the dinner-table and went to the playroom in the half-basement of the dwelling. He was gone for many minutes, but Betty decided to investigate.

The visitors were New York detectives. She learned from the conversation that the butcher in the near-by village had overheard two men plotting to shoot the Mayor through a window as he played ping-pong in the basement room. The butcher had notified the local constable, who in turn had reported the plot to the New York police.

Jim and the detectives sat up all that night, but no assassin appeared. Jim assured Betty that no one would ever shoot him, unless she herself decided to do it. Indeed, there was a report which still persists that Betty did shoot Jim. But his friends, Robert Newman among them, will vouch that Walker bore no marks on his body other than the cleft in his nose and the surgical scar from his hernia operation.

That fall Jim left New York for what the newspapers termed "a much-needed rest in New England." He stayed in Boston most of the time, attending rehearsals of the Herbert Fields-Cole Porter musical, *Fifty Million Frenchmen.*

E. Ray Goetz was the producer of this "musical tour of Paris." The Warner brothers of Hollywood financed it. The director was Monty Woolley, a gentleman who later won renown on the stage and in various motion pictures for his beard and his vinegar remarks. The male lead was William Gaxton.

Soon after Gaxton came to New York from San Francisco he joined the Lambs Club, where he met Walker. In 1928 Gaxton managed to obtain a bit part in the Lambs Gambol planned for that April at the Metropolitan Opera House. Many great stars were to appear on the bill. Gaxton's partner in the fill-in act was vaudevillian Oscar Shaw.

A few weeks before the Gambol, Gaxton received a letter from his mother, a tiny woman whom he called Cecilia, saying she was on her way from San Francisco to the big city. She had never been to New York before.

When Cecilia arrived at Grand Central Station, Gaxton asked, "What would you like to do most of all?"

"Two things, Billy. I want to go up in the Woolworth Building, and I want to meet Jimmy Walker."

Gaxton didn't have much money for night-clubbing, but he spent some at the new Casino in the hope of seeing Walker to make a "date" for Cecilia. At the Casino, to Gaxton's amazement, Jim left a party of "important" friends to go to Gaxton's table to say hello.

"I know that you're busy," Gaxton said to the Mayor, "but my mother has come all the way from California, and she wants to meet you."

"Your mother?" Jim said, wagging his finger. "Four o'clock tomorrow afternoon, Billy, at City Hall."

The next day Gaxton and his mother were immediately ushered into Walker's office. The Mayor was standing beside his desk. After being introduced, Walker put his arms about Billy's mother, spoke to her about her "great son," and kissed her.

Mayor Walker held the door for Mrs. Gaxton as she left.

"Boy, you've just written your name on my heart," Billy said to Jim.

A day or so before the Lambs Gambol, Walker said, "I'll be backstage to see you, Billy."

"If you feel up to a long walk," Gaxton said, "and really want to see me, you'll find my dressing-room way in the back. I'm not very important, Jim."

"No?" Jim said. "Well, don't worry, kid. I'll make you important. I'm going to drop something right in your lap. Will you have anything to drink in your dressing-room?"

"I'll have something. Why?"

"Never mind why. I'm going to make you important."

The night of the Gambol, Gaxton and Shaw sent out for three bottles of Prohibition whisky, then waited in their cubbyhole at the Met to be made important. The big stars of the show were onstage during the first half.

At intermission time Gaxton said to his partner, "I don't think we're going to be very important tonight."

Just then there was a knock on the door. Gaxton opened it. Walker, silk-hatted, was standing there. Almost three hundred persons were jammed around him in the corridor, among them the city's foremost citizens and celebrities. With Walker were the three heroes of the moment, the first aviators to have made the east-to-west crossing of the Atlantic—the Germans Baron Guenther von Huenefeld and Captain Hermann Koehl, and the Irish Free Stater Commandant James Fitzmaurice.

These men had been downed on the southern tip of Labrador, had been given up for lost, then rescued. They reached the city on Sunday, and the Walker-Whalen team of showmen did not permit an official welcome, ever, to be offered on a Sunday, a day the great buildings of lower Manhattan were unpopulated. So the official reception was planned for the following day.

Whalen had kept the men concealed from the lion hunters who sought to stroke the manes of the momentarily mighty guests of the city. When the aviators appeared at the Gambol, however, they were identified at once and cheered. At intermission time the lion hunters planned a hasty safari to capture the heroes. They followed their prey backstage, and were somewhat mystified when Jim and the three guests moved past the dressing-rooms of the theatrical stars and knocked at the door of a privy-like compartment. After

Jim and his guests had gone inside, the lion hunters made inquiries among the stagehands. They heard the unfamiliar name Gaxton, then suddenly decided, as was and is the way of all the fawning opportunists of Broadway, Hollywood, and Peoria, that anyone so prominently endorsed was an old and valued pal. While the Mayor and the heroes were privately closeted with Gaxton and Shaw and the bootlegged bourbon, the men outside the dingy door found themselves speaking familiarly of "good old Billy" and "that wonderful guy Oscar."

When Gaxton and Shaw appeared on the stage, the audience clapped and cheered. The mystified but pleased actors had difficulty in telling their jokes so great was the laughter. Each movement they made became a masterpiece of pantomime, or so it seemed. At the close of the act the performers received an ovation. They were called upon to take numerous bows. Groggy with this sudden fame, the boys started back to their privy, but were detained by newspaper photographers.

A celebrated star put his arm about Billy and said, "Why don't you come to *my* dressing-room for some champagne?"

Walker had made Gaxton important. That was Jim's way of doing things. He might neglect the Governor, or keep the President waiting, or be tardy at a banquet, yet he always seemed to have time to go with a taxicab driver to see the man's sick mother, or to sit at the kitchen table of some person whom he had chanced to meet, or give of himself and of his money to a thousand unfortunate strangers who could not possibly do him any good except in one respect—to remember him always.

William Gaxton has remained a star since that time. His real talent, of course, not merely Walker's endorsement, has given Billy his lasting popularity on the stage. A year and a half after the Gambol he was given the lead in *Fifty Million Frenchmen*. Gaxton kept a friendly eye on Betty, who had a featured part in the musical. It was the least he could do to repay the man who had written his name on Gaxton's heart.

One noonday Gaxton chanced to look out the window of his room at the Ritz Hotel in Boston. A black town car parked at the curb had on its bumper the official shield of the mayor of New York. Gaxton had breakfast in his room, dressed, then went to the Colonial Theatre for rehearsal. He was astonished to see Betty on the stage, alone except for Walker. Jim was telling her what to do and instructing the musicians how to accompany her for her dance. The tune the orchestra was playing was Gaxton's own song in the show. Notwithstanding the fact that Jim's name had been written on his heart, Gaxton was an actor. And actors seldom welcome any threats to their own lines or songs.

"What's going on?" Gaxton asked Betty. "You never dance to a reprise, and can't until it's been sung."

Betty merely lifted a brow. Jim waved Gaxton aside. Gaxton turned from the stage and charged up the aisle to the back of the house. There he found Louis Shurr, Betty's manager.

"Don't you see what's happening?" Gaxton angrily inquired.

"Billy," Shurr replied helplessly, "you know we can't fight City Hall."

Walker appeared on the scene and tried to do some placating. Gaxton repeated the "City Hall" remark. Jim laughed so hard he sank into the orchestra seat nearest him. Then he promised Gaxton that he would retire as a stage director.

Fifty Million Frenchmen opened in Boston on the same October Tuesday that disaster descended on the stock market. Two weeks after that day of doom the musical arrived in New York.

"The piece," says press agent Richard Maney, "damned near never opened. Miss Compton, on inspecting the remote dressing-room assigned her by the stage manager, sped to a pay-station at the stage door and called City Hall. 'Jim! You should see what a lousy dressing-room they've given me!'

"Later that afternoon," Maney continues, "word reached the sensitive ear of Mr. Goetz that city officials were about to slap some fifteen building violations on the Lyric, a strategy that might close it for a week. Goetz caught on and began to refashion Miss Compton's quarters."

While the changes in the dressing-room and other alterations were being made the company rehearsed at the Manhattan Opera House.

The mayoral election campaign was now entering its last days. La Guardia and others had been pounding away at Walker with charges of graft and mismanagement of the city's departments. Petitions demanding that the administration be investigated reached Governor Roosevelt. That Mayor Walker and his Board of Estimate were planning to increase their salaries stirred up much adverse criticism.

Walker's attitude during the last innings of the campaign was almost casual. He told his audiences that the fight was a "dull" one, and not really a fight at all.

"I must apologize," he said in one speech in the Bronx, "for refusing to take the charges of my opponent seriously. If he wants to shout and scream while playing with his toys, let him. Sometimes I think, in speaking of toys, that the Little Flower, when but a child, played with stumbling blocks, and never recovered from the habit."

Ray Schindler, the famous private detective, Johnny O'Connor, and several others tell me that Walker said in one of his speeches, "Before I dignify the accusations of my opponent, I must first obtain an answer to the question: Just why did Congressman La Guardia leave Bridgeport on June the first of this year?"

The story goes that the hotheaded La Guardia denied that he had been in Bridgeport for at least fifteen years. The Mayor then said, "That's very interesting. You will note how carefully he denied having been in Bridgeport last June. And once again I ask, Why did he leave Bridgeport on that peculiarly significant day in his life, June the first of this year?"

Candidate La Guardia, who really had not been in Bridgeport for many years, is said to have asked, "What does he say happened on the June first I am alleged to have been in Bridgeport?"

Walker is described as having said, "Let him tell us. We're not interested in his questions. We're interested only in an answer. And he's afraid to tell us. That much is obvious. He does not dare to tell the voters why he left Bridgeport."

On election Tuesday in November of 1929 the cast of *Fifty Million Frenchmen* worked until midnight at a dress rehearsal. It had been a stormy day and snow lay upon the streets. Late in the evening Betty Compton stood waiting offstage for her number to be rehearsed. She was somewhat lightly clad in her dance routine costume.

The doorman informed her that a policeman wished to see her. Betty went to the alley entrance. The officer was holding a large blanket.

"The Mayor wants to see you," the officer said.

The policeman flung the blanket about the protesting actress, lifted her in his arms, and carried her across the street through the snow. He delivered her to the Mayor's automobile, in which Jim and Grover Whalen were grinning happily.

"What *is* this?" Betty inquired angrily.

"I want you to be the first to congratulate me, Monk," Jim said. "I've been re-elected."

"By a plurality of about five hundred thousand," Whalen supplied.

"Well," Betty replied, "it's no surprise. Or is it?"

Walker seemed hurt by her tone. "You don't seem very enthusiastic, Monk."

"Why should I be?"

"Why *shouldn't* you be?"

"Because," she replied, "I believe you'd be better off and happier if you quit politics."

The men laughed, but none too heartily. "All right," Jim said. "I've got to hurry along to headquarters. See you later."

The policeman again bundled Betty in the blanket and carried her back to the rehearsal.

In view of the financial panic Gaxton asked producer Goetz how much he was going to charge for orchestra seats.

"Six-sixty," was Goetz's calm reply.

"What?" Gaxton howled. "With everybody going broke!"

"People love the theatre," Goetz said, "and they'll find a way of digging up the price."

Gaxton says that despite the continued depression *Fifty Million Frenchmen* ran on Broadway for a year and grossed an average of forty-nine thousand a week.

The re-elected Mayor attended the opening. The first-night audience stood to applaud him as he escorted Miss Compton's mother, a particularly handsome woman with white hair, to their seats near the stage. Walker did not seem to care if the whole world knew of his love for Betty. Nor did a majority of the people of the city who had just re-elected him seem to care—not as yet.

However, Tammany Hall did care. Its sachems regarded Miss Compton as a menace and made plans to induce Walker to put her aside.

After the premiere Betty and the Duchess went with Jim to the Casino. Betty told Jim that she was nervously ill. After three weeks at the Lyric, Betty suffered a collapse. She withdrew from the company for a short period, then returned to the cast early in 1930. She soon fell ill again from nervous exhaustion and left the production for good.

Betty went with her mother to Florida to recuperate. In February of 1930 Jim also took a vacation, joining Betty and the Duchess in the South. They were guests of circusman John Ringling at Sarasota.

"The idea of anyone being happy," Betty said to Dudley Field Malone when discussing the obstacles to her romance with Jim, "drives some people crazy."

No matter how compelling the love of this gay man in public office and this beautiful woman, they soon found themselves adrift on a turbulent sea.

25.

As the Sparks Fly Upward

LONG days of hunger and unemployment followed the ringing of the New Year's carillons. The bourdon bells, it seemed, had invoked a curfew upon an age of ruinous enterprise.

The breadline processions inched with footsore slowness along the frosty cobblestones. Apple sellers crouched at the street corners like half-remembered sins sitting upon the conscience of the town. These and other evidences of broken fortunes were enough in themselves to harass the mind of any mayor. The plight of the "neighbors' children," however, was but one of several challenges to the political peace of James J. Walker at the beginning of his second term. Tammany's waiting foes moved in from all sides with loud cries against the conduct of the municipal courts and of various departments of the city government.

In addition to his administrative woes, the Mayor began at last to feel the stings of adverse criticism directed at his romance with a woman other than his wife. It was said that Cardinal Hayes summoned Mayor Walker to the "Power House"—as the archiepiscopal residence was called by Tammany—rebuked him severely, and demanded that he mend his behavior. The churchly reprimand weighed upon Jim's mind, as did the opposition to his romance expressed by members of his own family. Perhaps the disapproval of his brother George hit him the hardest, for Jim had a deep affection for the younger man who now lay hopelessly ill with tuberculosis. But the fevers of Jim's heart made him hold on to his love for Betty Compton. He would not give her up, because, he said, he could not.

Amid all these worriments, it may be assumed that Mayor Walker was not malingering when absent from City Hall and reported ill. He caught cold frequently. He had heart flutters. He grew quite thin. His stomach bothered him. And there were other minor ailments to annoy him. In March Jim's Chinese dentist extracted one of his wisdom teeth. Then an attack of lumbago gave him many hours of discomfort. That spring he almost had a nervous breakdown, and his Health Commissioner recommended that he rest. Rest? Where was it to be found now that a time of gay hopes had vanished, as though lost in a broken mirror?

Walker vacationed at John Ringling's Florida estate and then spent two weeks bicycling and golfing in the Bermuda sun. He was forty-nine years old. In spite of the surfboard momentum of his troubles and the rip of the political tide, he remained young in appearance.

Although Walker, as columnist Henry McLemore once said, had been created for a time of brass bands, waving flags, parades, and bright lights, he tried as best he could to aid the many thousands of unemployed persons in the City of New York. He worked long hours with committees, helped distribute funds, appeared at benefits. But he exposed himself to adverse criticism by signing the document providing salary increases for members of the Board of Estimate and himself at the moment his adversaries clamored for retrenchment.

Jim gave his increase of fifteen thousand to charitable institutions (he himself never used the word charity as applied to persons in need), but it became a lost fact. He continued to live expensively, as long had been his way. Most of his wealthy benefactors had been or were being mauled by stock-market bears, and Jim's cash position, always an uncertain one, was becoming perilous. He incurred debts.

In his ninth-inning efforts to stave off charges of administrative sins, Walker's personal loyalties plagued his course. His party regularity, together with an almost fierce trust in his friends, prevented the dismissal of self-seeking exploiters.

When the Board of Sanitation was under fire in January of 1930, Walker appointed Charles Hand as a lay member of that bureau. The Mayor hoped that his secretary might find some means of keeping the department free of criticism. Hand succeeded for a time, but eventually found the Mayor's own sentimental obstinacy too great a barrier to be hurdled. When Hand sought to defy one of Jim's friends who had overreached himself in the matter of contractual favors, Walker said, "Charlie, I simply can't believe he'd do that to me. We're pals."

Because Mayor Walker would not, or else could not, see that he was being imposed upon outrageously, Hand resigned in 1932. He did not, however, believe that Walker himself had at any time received graft from those who had abused his trust. It is unlikely that the keen-eyed ex-reporter, a man who had made more than just a casual survey of the Mayor's actions, would have remained ignorant of his chief's graft had there been any. Nor would Hand have condoned such malfeasance.

Charlie himself has told me that Governor Roosevelt asked him in 1932 if he had ever suspected Walker of dishonesty. He replied that, if he had, he would have quit, that very moment. "I am sure of that," Mr. Roosevelt replied.

Among the many ex-reporters who have written to me in respect to Walker's stubborn refusal to see faults in his friends, I shall quote an excerpt from a letter by Ik Shuman, at present the publisher of *Script Magazine*.

"He was so loyal a friend," Shuman writes, "and so completely trusted his friends, that he could not believe any man to whom he had given that friendship would use it to betray him. . . . He put so much faith in friendship that this virtue became a weakness. I've known of men going to him to ask a favor, quite legitimate, such as the expedition of a license to hold an auction at night, for which the Mayor personally had to sign. 'Do you know the man?' Jim would ask. 'Yes, he's okay,' and Jim would sign the permit. The point is that Jim would take a friend's word, and sometimes that friend would impose upon him. . . . He once, as a lawyer, refused a fee of twenty-five thousand dollars to read a brief before the Supreme Court of New York to uphold the legality of slot-machine operation. He turned it down when a friend told him that someone's wife had been upset because her two sons had been losing their school-lunch money in neighborhood slot machines. Jim was convinced thereafter that slot machines contributed to juvenile delinquency. Once, and on my sole say-so, after the police and the politicians had ignored my request when I tried to get slot machines thrown out of Brooklyn candy stores, Jim ordered the police to seize every slot machine in sight. They did it too, hundreds of them, plus many more in warehouses. Walker did this after only the briefest outline of the situation, and without consulting anyone."

Against the mighty cyclorama of Franklin D. Roosevelt's career as president, Jim Walker's figure may seem small, if not entirely lost to view. The massive aspects of war and social revolution quite understandably have claimed the attention of historians and analysts. What happened at Albany with respect to Governor Roosevelt and Mayor Walker from 1930 to 1932 cannot vie with the events of Yalta, Potsdam, Teheran, or the rest. Still, those were the years of Roosevelt's becoming, and the Walker episode had an importance, I should think, which deserves more than an asterisk and a footnote in the Roosevelt chronicle.

It has been a popular misconception that Mr. Roosevelt disliked Walker as a person and gladly threw him onto the political spears. The evidence, both circumstantial and real, contradicts this.

Although we are concerned at this point (the year 1930) with Mr. Roosevelt's executive actions pertaining to Walker and Tammany Hall, it might serve to clarify the impending events were we to present Walker's own summation of his personal feelings toward Mr. Roosevelt. He expressed his opinions quite frankly during an interview I had with him in California in the late summer of 1946. We were to have resumed our talks, for the purposes of this book, in January of the next year. Walker's death in November 1946 intervened. Many questions he had intended to answer were consequently stymied, but I find among my notes the following:

Q.: "Some persons have charged that Mr. Roosevelt was a vindictive man?"

A.: "Anyone who fails to get a favor from a man in high office is apt to think that the refusal comes from spite."

Q.: "Let us put it this way: was the late President ruthless with friends whenever they stood in the way of his political ambitions?"

A.: "Not unless the friends became rambunctious, as in the case of Al Smith. Roosevelt really loved Al, but Al had the presidential bug, played coy, and mistakenly thought that the nomination would be handed to him on a silk cushion in 1932. He failed to say 'yes' or 'no' to Jim Farley's repeated questions as to his intentions, and then went into a sulk when Roosevelt got the nod. As to Roosevelt's loyalty to friends, let us take the case of Henry Morgenthau. Henry is a splendid fellow, but perhaps not the greatest Secretary of the Treasury. When Roosevelt suffered paralysis, and lay in bed or sat in a wheel-chair at Hyde Park, Morgenthau was his neighbor. He spent a lot of time reading at Roosevelt's bedside, and for no ulterior purpose kept the ill man company. When Roosevelt reentered political life he never forgot that kindness, nor as President would he listen to the attacks upon Morgenthau as a cabinet officer."

Q.: "Do you think that Roosevelt disliked you?"

A.: "No, although he had many reasons to dislike me."

Q.: "By that you mean—just what do you mean?"

A.: "I mean that I was most careless and inconsiderate of both Governor and Mrs. Roosevelt. As to Mrs. Roosevelt, I regard her as a very great woman. She always went out of her way to be nice to me, and it is one of the great regrets of my life that I repaid her many courtesies by neglecting to respond to her invitations to be a guest at the [Albany] mansion. The reason—and it is a bad reason but a true one—I neglected the Roosevelts was that, as a former senator, I preferred the company of my old comrades on the Hill to sitting among career-seekers at table at the mansion. But Mrs. Roosevelt never seemed to hold this against me; and Frank Roosevelt certainly proved in the long run that he not only forgave but forgot my rudeness and neglect."

Q.: "Would you say that Mr. Roosevelt and you were close friends, cronies?"

A.: "No. We might have been, had I been more thoughtful. You see, when Roosevelt was a senator [1911–13], I was an assemblyman. At that time Al Smith had a case on Roosevelt and introduced me to the Senator from Dutchess County. Neither Al nor I, of course, foresaw the great place in history which was to be Roosevelt's. Al, however, believed that his friend Frank would go far. I was unable at that time to envision him as a prospective pal. He then seemed, as Frances Perkins has said of him, to be 'looking down his nose,' or engaged in a slumming expedition. I suppose this mannerism suggested an aloof son-and-heir conceit to my sidewalks-of-New-York mind. The man, however, could unbend when with Al

Smith, and, as the world now knows, possessed great charm. However, when he tried to exercise his charm upon me in those days, I mistook it to mean that he was patronizing me. Now I know that he was offering me his friendship."

Q.: "But didn't he become quite angry at you sometimes?"

A.: "You mean when I was mayor?"

Q.: "In 1930, 1931, 1932?"

A.: "Piping hot, but it was largely my own fault in almost every instance. He was patient beyond reason, but finally I stood in his way—as a symbol, but not, I am confident, as a person. And let me tell you something I have learned from experience: there are two things no one can do with impunity: stand in the way of a man and his woman, or a candidate and the presidency."

Q.: "Do you hold Mr. Roosevelt responsible for your political reverses?"

A.: "Only one man is responsible for Jim Walker's troubles in or out of office."

Q.: "Who is he?"

A.: "You are now seated opposite that man at the luncheon table. And by the way, instead of ordering curried shrimps and a chocolate eclair, why don't you order a Mickey Finn? It's quicker."

The Governor had refused in 1929 to entertain charges against the Walker administration. In January 1930 Mr. Roosevelt again stayed Republican State Senator Samuel H. Hofstadter's efforts to launch an investigation of the Magistrates' Courts in New York City.

In the Senate once more there was a narrow majority of one vote, and it was a Republican majority. Senator Hofstadter had been the only Republican solon elected in 1928 from a New York City district. Had a Democratic senator been elected in his stead, the Walker imbroglio might have been forestalled.

In February the Governor privately warned Tammany leaders that an investigation might be unavoidable, but he continued to resist pressure exerted upon him to bring about such an inquiry. In April he demonstrated his unwillingness to bear down upon Walker and the Tiger when he vetoed a bill to prohibit officials from increasing their own salaries.

The critical roars grew loud that spring and summer. In March the New York sachems announced that the Republicans were attempting to force an investigation "to put the Governor in a hole." If he broke with Tammany, he would forfeit its support for his re-election in 1931. If he didn't crack the whip, his national prestige might dwindle because of Republican charges that he condoned the Tiger's forays.

In June of 1930 W. J. Maier attacked the Governor for his failure to order an investigation. During that same month Mr. Roosevelt rejected the Socialist party's plea for an inquiry. In July Senator Knight and Speaker McGinnies urged the Governor to call an extra session of the legislature to authorize an investigation of the New York City government. Mr. Roosevelt promised to confer with these leaders on his return from a governors' conference. Then, on July 20, in a letter to these Republicans, he refused to call the legislature into extra session unless more evidence of misconduct were shown. Amid howls that he was protecting Tammany grafters by means of his inaction, Mr. Roosevelt met with Knight and McGinnies on July 22. Whatever may or may not have been agreed upon at that conference, plans for an immediate inquiry were dropped.

Governor Roosevelt's obvious reluctance to move an investigation would seem to indicate that he had no present desire to break with Tammany. That organization, however, did not act with much foresight in respect to Mr. Roosevelt's presidential ambitions. There was a poorly concealed revival of Tammany hopes, under Curry's leadership, to trundle Al Smith back into the presidential arena, although Smith himself remained mute among the blueprints of his Empire State skyscraper project.

Several events of seemingly minor importance annoyed the Governor. One of them had a somewhat ludicrous twist. A double-barreled anecdote, involving two separate feuds, provides a glimpse of the cross-purposes of politicians. Police Commissioner Whalen was the target in both instances.

Commissioner of Correction Richard C. Patterson, Jr., as custodian of the city's prisons, differed sharply with Whalen on matters of policy. Patterson believed that inmates of jails and penitentiaries could be reformed by treating them gently and giving them numerous privileges. To demonstrate the efficacy of his methods, Patterson invited Whalen to sit among the prisoners of the Tombs and eat a luncheon prepared and served by them.

"I hesitate to do that," Whalen told Patterson. "You see, I have sent at least three hundred of these mugs to this same jail. They might resent my presence at the table."

"I think you're right," said Warden Barr to Whalen.

"Nonsense," Patterson insisted. "These men have been made to see the light."

As a precautionary measure Whalen detailed a number of his own men to accompany him to the luncheon and stand by at strategic points. Observing the unfriendly faces of the inmates, Whalen decided not to eat anything other than hard-boiled eggs, which he shelled himself.

At the conclusion of the meal, during which only Patterson and Whalen had conversed aloud, the prisoners rose. They formed a line and, chanting, did a lock-step. To the tune of a bawdy old song, they chorused over and over:

"Grover Whalen is a good old soul.
Yes, he is, in ——"

The last phrase of this lyric had to do with a little-esteemed portion of a pig. The inmates marched and sang until they were rounded up and locked in their cells. Beating their tin cups upon the bars, they slandered Whalen's ancestors. The tumult continued for almost an hour.

"It's plain to see," Whalen said to his host, "that these are nice fellows."

Another of Whalen's feuds was with Maurice Campbell, National Prohibition Administrator of New York State. One day in 1930 Campbell issued a statement blasting Whalen for not ordering his police to watch the thirty thousand speakeasies in the city to prevent the sale therein of liquor. Whalen called a conference of the district attorneys of the five boroughs. They agreed that Prohibition enforcement was strictly a national problem. Whalen composed an open letter to Campbell, stating that three patrolmen, working in eight-hour shifts, would be required to watch each and every speakeasy of the thirty thousand. This surveillance, he added, would increase the cost of Police Department maintenance by as much as forty-five million a year. The Whalen estimate, together with the supporting opinions of the five district attorneys, caused New York City editorialists to uphold the Commissioner's views.

Whalen soon learned that his open letter to Campbell had perturbed Governor Roosevelt. The Governor already was making a drive for delegates to put his name in presidential nomination. He did not wish needlessly to arouse the opposition of dry delegates, and was said to have felt that Whalen, as a Tammany man, had carelessly exposed him to this danger.

The minority leader of the Assembly telephoned Whalen that the Governor wished to see him next day at the executive mansion.

"Is it social or official?" Whalen asked.

"It's official," he was informed.

"Give me an hour to think it over," said Whalen and hung up. He tried to locate Walker, to seek his advice, but could not find him. Whalen then called the minority leader back.

"The Mayor is my boss," the Commissioner explained. "He should be invited to any conference I attend in Albany. So I'll not come without his consent."

When Whalen eventually got Walker on the private telephone late that afternoon, Jim said, "You're dead right. Don't go."

Whalen had barely hung up when Walker called back. "Big Cop, I think you'd better go."

"But," said Whalen, "you just told me not to."

"Well," Walker replied, "maybe I was doing some horseback thinking and suddenly found myself sitting on an ass. Go ahead."

"I'll not go unless you order me to do it."

"Then," Walker said, "I hereby order you to go up there and get some of that bad food. Thank God you don't drink!"

The next day Whalen went by car to Albany. He wished to avoid the newspapermen, for once. They had been apprised of the conference and would expect him to travel by train.

Whalen says that when he entered the reception room of the Albany mansion he found the Governor's law partner, Basil O'Connor, present, as well as the respective leaders of the majority and minority groups of both the Senate and the Assembly. The Governor was most amiable as they went to the dining-room. After the luncheon, when cigars, cigarettes, but no hard drinks, were being served in the library, the Governor inquired, "Well, Grover, are you concerned about why I asked you to come to Albany?"

"No, Frank. Not concerned. Curious."

"Well, if you wish to split hairs," the Governor said, "we'll call it curiosity."

The Governor then told Whalen that he had done a very foolish thing in writing the Campbell letter. Whalen disagreed. He produced several laudatory editorial clippings from his pocket and placed them before the Governor. Mr. Roosevelt ceased calling his guest "Grover" and addressed him as "Commissioner." So Whalen also changed his own familiar way of speaking to Mr. Roosevelt as "Frank" and called him "Your Excellency."

Whalen pointed out that, in his opinion, the Mayor should have been invited to the conference. Mr. Roosevelt replied, "I think that the Governor should be permitted to run his own business."

"But," Whalen objected, "Mayor Walker is my superior officer, the man who appointed me."

"Has it occurred to you," Mr. Roosevelt inquired, "that the Governor has the power to remove the Police Commissioner?"

Instead of giving a direct answer, Whalen said, "One thing's clear: you can attempt to restore the Mullan-Gage Act; and, if you succeed, on the morning after it's restored every speakeasy in New York City will be closed by the police."

The Governor offered no comment. After a long silence Whalen asked for permission to go back to New York City. Mr. Roosevelt nodded. Whalen advised him that several New York City reporters were waiting outside the mansion and recommended that any statement about the conference should be issued by the Governor. Mr. Roosevelt agreed to see the press. His Excellency shook hands with the Commissioner, who then went out to advise the reporters that he had absolutely nothing to say.

The next day Whalen was amazed to read in the newspapers that "Governor Roosevelt conferred yesterday with Commissioner Whalen concerning the establishment of a new prison, similar to Sing Sing, on Long Island."

While Whalen was pondering the headlines the private telephone in his office rang. Whalen answered the ring, and Walker's voice came over, "Hey, Commish! There's been quite a holler about your conference yesterday with the Governor."

"How do you mean?"

"Just this: Commissioner Patterson stormed in here just a few minutes ago. He was waving the newspapers and yelling, 'What is this buttinsky Whalen doing? Why doesn't he stay in his own stall and not go out of the city to confer with the Governor on prisons, a matter having solely to do with the Department of Correction?' "

Jim disclosed that he had placated the angry Commissioner by denouncing Whalen. "You are so right, Dick. I can't handle the fellow at all. I'm tempted to remove him from office. I never should have lifted him from behind that ribbon counter at Wanamaker's."

At this, Jim said, the Commissioner of Correction beamed. Having heard the Mayor himself criticize Whalen for doing something which actually never had occurred, Patterson left the Hall smiling, and, as Jim reported, "walking on air."

Whalen retired from his post on May 20, 1930. He had been "lent" to the city by Wanamaker's, and now returned to that store. He felt that he had accomplished the dual purpose for which Walker had chosen him: to put the Police Department on an efficient basis and raise the morale of its members. Moreover, he had added four thousand men to the force, won pay increases for the higher ranks, established the Police College, created the Crime Commission for the study and prevention of crime, and formed an aviation unit. With the cooperation of First Deputy Commissioner Philip D. Hoyt, formerly a star reporter on the *Times*, Whalen did much to alleviate New York's traffic problems. Whalen and Hoyt formulated zoning rules, instituted the stagger system of raising theatre curtains, and devised parking restrictions.

The announcement of Whalen's resignation was made in his presence at a newspaper conference in the Mayor's office. When the Mayor laid down a bundle of papers on his desk, the reporters mistook them for copies of letters pertaining to Whalen's successor. There was a scramble, and the Mayor said, "Now, now, this isn't Wanamaker's bargain counter."

"Then," asked one reporter, "who is to be the next Commissioner?"

The Mayor gave a signal, and tall, sandy-complexioned Chief Inspector Edward P. Mulrooney came in from the room next to the private office.

Mulrooney is one of the most honorable men I have ever met. He always stayed out of the regions of personal applause, but steadily won his way upward because of his great force of character, his devotion to duty, and his wise head. At the time of his appointment he was fifty-six years old. He had been on the police force since 1896. He achieved a record for several brave acts in line of duty, and, although he was anything but pugnacious, criminals feared him. What criminals dread the most in a policeman is not his physical strength—which Mulrooney possessed—but honesty. Mulrooney had that too, and that is one of the principal reasons Walker named him. A brotherly affection existed between these two men, and it never waned.

Commissioner Mulrooney's frequent presence at such a gay place as the Casino mystified some observers, for his was anything but a night-club personality. The motive for these visits to the Casino later became apparent. His reserved but friendly way somehow encouraged boastful society ladies to confide in him where they were gambling. Raids followed, and the proprietors of high-class gaming resorts simply could not understand how their secrets had been betrayed.

On July 9, 1930, the *New York Times*, in commenting editorially upon conditions in the city courts, said in part: "Till now nothing has come from the City Hall to indicate that Mr. Walker is aware of the discredit brought by his associates and subordinates upon his own record, or to serve as a sharp warning to all the members of the official family. When so many cracks show in the structure, there is lowered resistance to stress. The hour has come for the mayor to summon both the demolition and reconstruction crews. . . . It is not too late for Mr. Walker, who has in no personal way been even slightly connected with any of these scandals, to voice the indignation of the community which has twice elected him. . . . A Republican investigation is both inevitable and desirable, however the governor may deal with the proposal for an extra session, and however his own chances of re-election are shown to be affected by what is happening here. . . ."

The *New York Telegram* (it soon after became the *World-Telegram*) set out on a crusade against irregularities in the Magistrates' Courts. The *New York Evening Post* was also conducting a similar campaign. Although Roy Howard, head of the Scripps-Howard chain of newspapers, liked Walker, he gave the go-ahead to his *Telegram* editors to get the facts and print them, no matter whom the crusade might destroy.

These New York newspapers demanded a grand jury investigation of the Magistrates' Courts. The city already had been shocked by what might be called chance disclosures that Tammany judges were holding office as directors of financial corporations.

The death of banker Francis M. Ferrari coincided with the failure of Ferrari's City Trust Company, in which five million dollars had been deposited, mainly by small wage-earners and tradesmen. State Superintendent of Banking Frank H. Warder took charge of the company's affairs. General Sessions Judge Francis X. Mancuso had been chairman of the bank's board of directors, and other Tammany members also had served as members of its board. Governor Roosevelt designated Robert Moses to investigate the failure of the Ferrari company.

Commissioner Moses, celebrated mostly for his administration of the state's parkway system, was and is an efficient, independent official. He reported Superintendent Warder's alleged acceptance of bribes from Ferrari to permit the bank to evade certain laws of management. Warder went to Sing Sing.

Judge Mancuso was threatened with an indictment because of alleged misstatements made before the grand jury. He resigned. Under pressure from the *Telegram*, the sixty-nine-year-old district attorney, former Supreme Court Justice Thomas C. T. Crain, obtained an indictment against Judge Mancuso. The indictment was thrown out in General Sessions Court but was reinstated by the Court of Appeals. Judge Mancuso was acquitted of all the charges after a trial in June of 1932.

The next of several disclosures to arouse the public came after a testimonial dinner given for Magistrate Albert H. Vitale. Six hold-up men invaded this party at the Tippecanoe Democratic Club in the Bronx. They not only robbed the politicians of several thousands of dollars, but also relieved a city detective of his service pistol. The loot was recovered and the detective was dismissed from the force; but the Bar Association decided that Judge Vitale needed investigation. Upon the motion of that body, the Appellate Division ordered a trial of the magistrate, during the course of which it was revealed that he had deposited more than a hundred thousand dollars in the bank in five years, on a salary of a thousand a month. It had long been La Guardia's contention that Magistrate Vitale had accepted a "loan" of nearly twenty thousand dollars from Arnold Rothstein—and it was on this count of "associating with a common gambler" that Vitale was removed from the bench.

Now it was charged that another magistrate, George F. Ewald, had paid ten thousand dollars for his judicial post. This money, according to evidence presented by reporters to District Attorney Crain, had been given by Ewald to Tammany District Leader Martin J. Healy, who was also First Deputy Commissioner of Plant and Structures. The grand jury held that the charge was without foundation. The crusading newspapers criticized Crain for being inept and careless in his presentation of the evidence. They demanded of Governor Roosevelt that Crain be superseded by the State Attorney General.

Mr. Roosevelt showed a disposition to yield to these many thunderings. He ordered Republican Attorney General Hamilton Ward to take over the Ewald investigation. At about this time United States Attorney Charles H. Tuttle, who had aspirations of running for governor against Mr. Roosevelt, announced that he possessed important evidence involving Ewald and Healy. Furthermore, Tuttle went on to say, he had come upon evidence that Judge W. Bernard Vause of the Brooklyn County Court had accepted a fee of a hundred and ninety thousand dollars for procuring a lease of two city-owned piers for one of the large steamship lines. Vause was later convicted on another charge, that of using the mails to defraud, and received a sentence of six years in Atlanta Prison.

On August 21 Governor Roosevelt ordered Attorney General Ward to confine his activities to determining if former Magistrate Ewald had obtained his post by means of corrupt acts. The Governor then asked the Appellate Division to investigate the magistrates and the Magistrates' Courts in Manhattan and the Bronx. On this same day Joseph Clark Baldwin III, minority leader of the Board of Aldermen, made public a letter he had written to Governor Roosevelt in which he urged the executive "to go to the root of the whole matter" at once and investigate the office of Mayor Walker. Baldwin, one of the four Republican members of the Board, used such terms in his letter as "scandals," "salary grabs," "dishonest budget," and "misrule."

Mayor Walker on this day was at Camp Smith, Peekskill, reviewing the "Old Sixty-ninth" Regiment and the "Red Devils." He stood on the parade ground, his hat off as the colors passed by. News of the Governor's action and of the charges brought by Alderman Baldwin was whispered into his ear.

After the review of the troops the Mayor said, "No one welcomes such an investigation more than myself. If I didn't, I would have been out long ago. Baldwin is playing politics, and when his party is recognized by the people then we may recognize him. Until then he is nothing but a politician, and a poor one. He is third-rate. That's why he has the Roman numeral III after his name."

In New York, State Assistant Attorney General Robert S. Conklin issued a statement which seemed to indicate that Mr. Ward's inquiry would be all-embracing in respect to the corrupt purchase by magistrates and other city officials of their posts. In Albany, however, Governor Roosevelt was quoted by the *Times* as saying, "I intended that the Attorney General should be limited solely to the Ewald case."

The Associated Press quoted Attorney General Ward as having said of Governor Roosevelt's statement, "I shall be bound by the Governor's wishes regarding the scope of my powers. I am only a fisherman, and it is difficult for a fisherman to be told where to fish."

The day after the ruling on the limited scope of the investigation Jim invited Betty to go with him on a cruise off Montauk Point, Long Island.

"I read in the papers," he said to her, "something about fishing. If the Attorney General fishes, why can't we?"

Jim and Betty and a party of friends boarded the yacht *Florida* and put out to sea. A fourteen-hour rainstorm came up, and a forty-mile wind, blowing out of the north, rocked the yacht. Jim became seasick. The skipper got the party ashore that evening after a rough time, and Betty suggested they go to a casino at Montauk. The weary Mayor assented.

The casino had a gaming-room hidden behind the kitchen. Betty liked to play hazard, so Jim went with her to the room in which a group of ladies and gentlemen in evening clothes were at the roulette table or playing dice.

When Jim and Betty entered, the manager politely refrained from recognizing the Mayor except to use his initial. "Good evening, Mr. W. What is your pleasure?"

"I haven't any pleasure," said the Mayor. "I'm still seasick." He indicated Betty with a gesture. "But Miss C. would be pleased to play hazard."

Jim did not play but stood looking on as Miss C. had a great deal of pleasure. In fact she accumulated almost two thousand dollars' worth of chips. Her pleasure, however, was interrupted shortly before midnight when several purposeful men, not clad in tuxedos, entered the room.

One of them called out, "Stand where you are, everybody. This is a raid!"

It appeared that four separate but simultaneous raids were made that night on Suffolk County gambling places. Betty and Jim were not interested in the three other raids.

When Betty looked for Jim, she saw him disappearing through a door leading to the dining-room. She started to follow, but an officer warned her to stay put. The raiders placed the guests in temporary custody and led them outside the restaurant. Passing through the kitchen, Betty saw Jim in a waiter's apron sitting at a table calmly eating a plate of beans.

"Jim, are you going to let these farmers–"

"Come on, lady. Tell it to the judge," the officer nearest Betty interrupted.

Jim paid not the slightest attention to Betty, just kept on eating beans. She became furious.

She was released a few hours afterward and returned to the yacht. For a long while she did not speak to Jim. Finally she said, "Why did you desert me? You and your beans!"

"Monk," Jim said, "I knew you'd get out all right. But as for me, Governor Roosevelt has decided to keep that investigation within reasonable bounds. It might be a good idea if I didn't tempt fate at this moment by showing up in a rural hoosegow."

There followed a long list of accusations, resignations, and prosecutions of Tammany officials, many of whom had not been appointed by Walker but for whose malfeasances he was blamed by some of the newspapers. During certain of these hearings Tammany leaders refused to waive immunity. Walker, however, issued a demand that everyone concerned waive immunity.

One of the magistrates under fire was a Walker appointment, but had been named by him at the request of none other than Bishop William T. Manning.

"I wish," Walker said to reporter Alva Johnston, "that the Bishop had made *all* my appointments."

One of Governor Roosevelt's appointees, Supreme Court Justice Joseph Force Crater, who had been endorsed by the New York Bar Association, disappeared from his chambers on a hot day in August 1930. He never again was seen by his family or his associates.

Beyond the fact that Crater had withdrawn several thousand dollars from two bank accounts a short time before his disappearance and had sold his stock holdings for sixteen thousand dollars, little has been established since then as to his actions at the time he vanished.

The public, of course, thought that his disappearance somehow was caused by the Ewald investigation.

Socialist Norman Thomas assailed both Governor Roosevelt and Walker in August, saying that "graft is rampant." Walker admitted in a speech to civic and commercial leaders that petty graft by city employees existed, and asked the cooperation of the public to halt it. Congressman La Guardia called Walker's plea a joke. The Socialists termed it a smoke screen.

Governor Roosevelt informed newspapermen that any general investigation of the Magistrates' Courts was a matter for the Appellate Court to demand, and not for the executive branch of the state government to institute. He said also that any broad inquiry into the city government would be within the province of the legislature.

Soon thereafter Mr. Roosevelt sent a letter to the judges of the Appellate Division of the First Judicial Department (the Boroughs of Manhattan and the Bronx), recommending that the justices undertake an investigation of the magistrates. White-haired Samuel Seabury was chosen to conduct the first of three separate though interlocking inquisitions which shook the city as no other investigation—not even the Lexow inquiry—had done.

26.

The Grand Inquisitor

A London messenger boy bearing a cablegram addressed to the Honorable Samuel Seabury set out to deliver it one afternoon in August of 1930. The former judge was not at his hotel, but the messenger was correctly informed that the gentleman might be found at one of several bookstores. It was Seabury's habit, during his annual holidays in Europe, to search for rare volumes pertaining to the British or the early American bar.

At the present moment he was looking for a first edition of *The Just Lawyer*, a work published in 1631. According to author Richard O. Boyer, who wrote a *New Yorker* "Profile" on Seabury, there were but three first-edition copies of this book in existence. Seabury had traveled thousands of miles and spent a large part of three years trying to find a fourth one. The fact that even the British Museum had been unable to procure a first-edition copy of this work was disregarded by the Judge. Whenever he undertook a quest, great or small, he displayed the same iron-minded persistence that had characterized the actions of his distinguished forebears.

Likely enough the messenger boy had been instructed to look among the bookstalls for a fifty-seven-year-old American whose white hair was parted precisely in the middle, who wore rimless glasses, and had the general appearance of a muscular bishop.

The boy eventually delivered the cablegram. It contained the information that the Appellate Division had designated Seabury as referee in an investigation of the Magistrates' Courts of Manhattan and the Bronx. The invitation astonished Judge Seabury, as it astonished the seventy district leaders of Tammany, many of whom had been browsing—but not in bookshops. In the spirit of Cincinnatus, who centuries before had put aside his farming implements and emerged from retirement to save his city, Samuel Seabury left his rare old books, returned to America, and shook the mothballs from his judicial robes, which had been folded away for the past fourteen years.

These somber robes of a justice of the State Court of Appeals had been put aside when Seabury resigned to become the Democratic party's candidate for governor. His political leanings had been varied, ranging from his youthful support of Henry George's single tax through Populist, Anti-Tammany, Democratic, Municipal Ownership, and Independence League movements. A temporary alliance in 1905 with Hearst, who had then advocated a municipal ownership program, found Seabury, the youngest magistrate in the history of the Municipal Court, nominating the publisher for mayor. That election was allegedly lost by Mr. Hearst when numerous ballot boxes were seized by his enemies and given with their contents to the Hudson River. Judge Seabury, as a candidate for the Supreme Court on the Municipal Ownership League ticket, was also defeated, and his regard for Tammany lessened—if possible. Shortly thereafter, running on the Independence League ticket, Seabury was elected a justice of the Supreme Court of New York. He was thirty-three years old.

Despite his tender years, Judge Seabury had the bearing and the manner of an austere sage. The foremost lawyers of the time learned not to take liberties with him. When but a young magistrate he had rebuked the celebrated district attorney William Travers Jerome, and now as a Supreme Court justice he occasionally reprimanded the mighty Samuel Untermyer and other noteworthies of the bar.

He served seven years on this bench and wrote several important opinions, among them the one which denied to the courts the right to censor literary productions. His decrees were held in high regard for their literary as well as their legalistic excellence. He had amazing capabilities for hard work and allowed himself but few recreational hours for rounds of golf or games of chess.

As a nominee of the Progressive party, Judge Seabury was designated in 1913 as a justice of the New York Court of Appeals to serve the remainder of an unexpired term. In 1914 both the Democratic and the Progressive parties returned him to this bench for a full term of fourteen years.

Judge Seabury resigned from the high tribunal in 1916 to run for governor. He anticipated having the political support of his former fellow Progressive, Theodore Roosevelt. But T. R. quite suddenly, and without any warning or explanation, urged the voters to elect Charles S. Whitman. The betrayed Judge thereupon went to Oyster Bay to dress down the lord of Sagamore Hill.

This was the man who now was called from scholarly retirement to bring the Tammany Tiger to heel. He set about the task with the same thoroughness and tenacity that had characterized all his other public actions. There was an ominous courtesy in his manner whenever he examined reluctant witnesses. His lips seemed unable to accomplish more than half a smile, as though he were about to say, "Go right ahead and hang yourself." Facts were his gospel, and he preached it in a strong baritone voice, with an occasional self-interrupting "harrumph," a vocal mannerism that in no way threatened his dignity. In his chambers he overawed even the newspaper reporters, addressing them in glacial stage whispers. It was said that members of his own family spoke of him in the third person even when he was present.

Perhaps he was more admired as a jurist than beloved as a man, for outwardly he was as aloof as the ice-cap of Mount Everest. Although his record showed him to be a strong advocate of worthy reforms and a champion of unfortunate or exploited minorities, he was unable to make allowance for the moral lapses of a black sheep or to forgive a foe such as Jim Walker. Even the death of an antagonist or the passage of time apparently did not soften his recollections of bygone duels. A man's character was either black or white; there were no modifying grays. Perhaps it takes a sinner to understand or forgive another transgressor, and Judge Seabury was a stranger to acts of dissipation, either physical or intellectual.

Possibly, as has been charged, the once-again active reformer gradually saw a way opening for him to become a presidential candidate, because of his publicity as an investigator. But whatever the truth as to Judge Seabury's political motives, and however arbitrary his methods sometimes seemed, no one can successfully impugn his ability as a prosecuting agent or his standing at the bar.

Walker's friends have pointed out, however, and with some justice, that had a Judge Seabury investigated any New York City administration previous to Walker's he would have found similar corruption. And had Seabury been designated in 1930 to investigate corruption in some other city in the United States, Chicago, for example, he might well have turned up an even gorier tale. This does not absolve Walker, but it places him in a more proper perspective.

The adroitly thorough prober asked the justices of the Appellate Division to amend their order designating him as referee to investigate the magistrates and their courts to include "the attorneys practicing therein." Next he invited the Bar Association and certain other law societies of New York City to name counsel to assist him in the inquiry. These societies named Isidor J. Kresel, a former assistant district attorney under Jerome.

Judge Seabury then assembled as his staff a "team" of nine young lawyers, only two of whom were more than thirty-two years old. He also enlisted the unofficial assistance of Professor Raymond Moley, an authority on many subjects of government and a political economist of the first rank. Professor Moley served as a consultant during two of the three Seabury investigations and editorially supervised reports sent by Seabury to Governor Franklin D. Roosevelt.

At the beginning of the investigation Judge Seabury formulated a policy which in certain respects set a pattern for the present-day gathering of evidence by the Federal Bureau of Investigation. First he would scrutinize the respective bank accounts of everyone under suspicion. If the deposits seemed incongruously large, he would trace these moneys to the source. Next, he would hold preliminary hearings in private. On evidence obtained behind closed doors he would proceed to conduct public hearings.

The first public hearing was held in September. The Judge confined himself largely to a statement of purpose, into which one might read a challenge to Tammany. Then came a recess for seven weeks, during which time rumors of what had gone on at private hearings rose above the political clamor of the state election campaign.

The landslide victory of Governor Roosevelt made Tammany feel reasonably safe from exposure. The organization had given Mr. Roosevelt its large vote in the city, and it expected a grateful governor to apply the air-brakes to the Seabury wheels if the investigator gathered too much speed.

The public hearings were resumed in November, and bombs began bursting in air. It was testified that certain members of the police vice squad, patrolmen who operated in plain clothes, had "framed" the arrests of many women by employing stool pigeons. The accusations of these paid informers, whose names had not been disclosed during testimony in the Magistrates' Courts, were used to send hundreds of women, many of them innocent, to jail.

One of the most publicized of these police informers was Chile Mapocha Acuna of Santiago, Chile. He admitted before Referee Seabury that he had often been "the other man" in the framing of women and had received fees for this service from members of the vice squad. He named names. When Commissioner Mulrooney learned of these long-hidden abuses, he abolished the vice squad and shook up the Police Department.

There were resignations by several magistrates and the removal of others from the bench. Toward the end of the year Tammany's hopes were temporarily brightened by an event that for the time discredited Judge Seabury's chief assistant, Isidor Kresel. The Bank of the United States, for which Kresel was counsel, failed, and its fifty-nine branches closed their doors.

Attorney Max D. Steuer now entered the picture. This celebrated lawyer stood high in Tammany councils. It was rumored that Steuer regarded Kresel with considerable animosity. In 1915 Kresel had presented a complaint to the Bar Association seeking Steuer's disbarment. The charges against Steuer were dismissed, but Steuer never forgot the proceedings, or Kresel who conducted them.

Soon after the failure of the Bank of the United States, Steuer was named special assistant district attorney and deputy attorney general as well to prosecute the case. Steuer charged that the bank officers

PRESS ASSOCIATION, INC.

Governor-elect Roosevelt and Mayor Walker conferring at the Roosevelt home

INTERNATIONAL NEWS PHOTO

The re-elected Mayor and Mrs. Walker receiving flowers from a youthful admirer

Betty Compton

INTERNATIONAL NEWS PHOTO

Judge Seabury and Mayor Walker before the Hofstadter Committee

had manipulated figures by pyramiding real-estate values, and that Kresel had given them illegal advice. It was a time of bitterness against banks and bankers, and four hundred thousand depositors had been affected by this failure. Kresel and the principal officers of the defunct bank were indicted. A jury found them all guilty.

"After twenty-five years of rectitude," writes writer-editor Lou Shainmark, "Kresel seemed disgraced, and a prison cell apparently awaited him. He resigned as chief counsel for Seabury, then appealed his own case. After six months the Appellate Court unanimously reversed the verdict of the lower court. Kresel was completely exonerated."

During the Kresel setback Judge Seabury remained calm, as indeed he always had and always would. In January of the next year he filed an intermediate report with the Appellate Division, citing one magistrate who had engaged in huge stock-market activities. He continued to disclose other irregularities in the city courts, and then moved out into the open as a prosecutor to try the city's first woman judge, Mrs. Jean H. Norris. She had been a Hylan appointee to the Women's Court and had been kept on by Walker at the behest of Tammany Leader Olvany.

Judge Seabury acted as prosecutor of Magistrate Norris before the Appellate Division. Martin Conboy defended her. Seabury charged that the lady magistrate had administered affairs with a harsh disregard for justice. Among other things, he introduced evidence purporting to show that she had altered the stenographic transcripts of several hearings held in her court. These alleged changes in the trial records, Judge Seabury sought to prove, had been made by, or upon the instructions of, the magistrate for the unethical purpose of absolving her of any appearance of bias or unfairness. Numerous women, Judge Seabury's witnesses testified, had been sent by Magistrate Norris to jail or prison after having been denied their constitutional rights to present evidence of their innocence of immoral acts.

The Appellate Court removed Mrs. Norris from the municipal bench "for unfitness for judicial service."

While the investigation of the magistrates and their courts moved toward a close and an inquiry into the conduct of District Attorney Crain's office threatened to break soon, a series of misunderstandings occurred in the personal lives of James J. Walker and Betty Compton which brought them distress of mind. The two who had lost their hearts to each other and had stood openly against the world now lost their heads and for a time stood apart and alone.

27.

Where Are You Going, My Pretty Maid?

Betty Compton had an exaggerated fear of being left alone. When she was but a child in her native Isle of Wight, her parents separated; but she continued to think affectionately of her father.

Mrs. Florence Halling Compton and her child went from England to Canada. The lack of a devoted father's attentions during Betty's young years conceivably may have brought about her lifelong fear of loneliness and insecurity. Betty also dreaded growing old. She confided to Robert Newman that she did not wish even to reach the age of forty.

In Canada Mrs. Compton opened a secretarial school. The daughter became extremely nervous whenever her mother was away for any length of time. Mrs. Compton decided to give up her successful business enterprise and stay at home with the girl.

Always chaperoned by her mother, Betty studied dramatics and dancing, won a beauty contest, then appeared as an entertainer at a Toronto cabaret. At eighteen she married a young Canadian, Stanley Reed Riches, an attorney. A divorce followed in 1923, and Betty and Mrs. Compton moved to New York City.

James J. Walker became aware of Betty's childlike anxieties of mind soon after their friendship began. She was afraid to go for a short stroll by herself even on a brightly lit, well-policed street. She felt strangely uneasy when left alone in a room. Jim tried patiently to convince her that loneliness was not of itself a dangerous predicament. His arguments failed. Moreover, she could see that her new counselor possessed enough phobias of his own to disqualify him as a practicing psychologist.

As political matters worsened for Jim, and the Furies moved ever closer during the early part of 1931, Walker's hours with Betty were comparatively fewer and more uncertain than before the time of financial panic. Betty became more and more lonely and apprehensive. She apparently could not be persuaded that the harried and nervously depleted man, careless at best, meant no injury when he failed to call her on the telephone or to meet her at the Casino, or neglected to do the many small things which seem all-important to the romantic ego.

Whenever Jim did come to her, she would break out of the web of her misgivings. They would be gay again, and life once more seemed brightly designed for them and for no one else. But their hours together now had the haphazard quality of enjoyments seized, borrowed, or stolen. There were jealousies and quarrels, promises and partings. Then loneliness would again bring to Betty Compton that heart-devouring sadness known to one who waits for a telephone that does not ring or for a knock that fails to come. And this young lady was not fashioned of passive flesh or ruled by a placid mind.

One day Jim saw in a shop window a china drinking cup decorated with the first bars of "Will You Love Me in December." Jim purchased the cup, and although he had never sent flowers to anyone except dead politicians, went to a florist's and had the cup filled with rosebuds, and sent it to Betty's apartment on East Seventy-sixth Street. She was delighted until she suddenly realized that it was the first time Jim had ever remembered her with flowers. She angrily pushed the gift aside. "It's a fine thing for him to send me flowers at *this* late day!"

During her brooding hours Betty felt certain that Tammany Hall politicians were trying to compel Jim to put her out of his life. She said as much to her closest friends, and let it be known that she did not relish her present status as "the other woman" in Walker's life.

Her nearest friends knew that she had a strong maternal nature, quite at odds with her public reputation as a glamorous daughter of the theatre. She wanted marriage and children. Denied the fulfillment of this natural desire for a husband and a home, the impetuous Betty no longer felt able to endure either the procrastinating ways of the man she loved or the opposition by Tammany politicians to that love.

After her retirement from the stage Betty had occupied herself with stock-market transactions. While trading in the great bull market she frequently received "tips" from important friends of the Mayor. She had made a profit of perhaps two hundred thousand dollars before the market collapsed. Walker informed me that Betty had put forty or fifty thousand dollars in cash or its equivalent well out of reach of the market. Jim said that she was generous in most respects but always guarded her "nest egg" with a firm resolve never to become insolvent.

Now in 1931, with her stage days past and her stock-market activities done, and with politics and unemployment problems frequently keeping Walker away from her, Betty began to look too long into the mirror of her apprehensions. She became even more emotionally frayed than before.

In the hope that a motion-picture career might divert her, she signed a contract with Warner Brothers. Jim was opposed to a three-thousand-mile separation but yielded—as he always would—to her "whim." An hour after she boarded a train for the West, Betty regretted having left New York and Jim. On arriving in Los Angeles, she announced to her adviser Louis Shurr that she meant to return to New York at once. Shurr prevailed upon her to stay in Hollywood long enough to make two "short subjects."

Betty was homesick during her six weeks in the West. She telephoned Jim every night. Finally she tore up her picture contract and packed her bags.

Home again in New York, Betty's feeling of loneliness oppressed her anew. She became unreasonably jealous and resented the time Jim necessarily spent away from her, as though time were a woman seeking to steal him.

Betty's and Jim's close friends also suffered from the Compton temperament. On one occasion Peggy Fears, A. C. Blumenthal's actress-wife, gave Walker a framed photograph of herself. As was plainly evident to everyone who knew her, Miss Fears merely regarded the Mayor as a good friend. Betty threw the photograph to the floor and smashed the glass.

Miss Fears possessed a keen sense of the ridiculous. She had the photograph reframed—under glass reinforced with rabbit wire. When Betty saw this, she burst out laughing, and all was well again, temporarily.

Sometimes Jim would take Betty upon a more or less official mission, such as that in which he sought to end a walkout of millinery workers. The striking union members had asked Jim to mediate for them at the Fifth Avenue shop of a maker of women's hats. He thought it might be a good idea to have Betty, as a gesture of good will, select some hats for herself while he interceded for the strikers. The owner of the establishment was a woman.

While Betty was trying on hats, Jim made considerable progress with the proprietor of the store, for he was especially gifted as a conciliator. It appeared that the lady was about to yield to the Mayor's proposals for a strike settlement when a worried manager of the retail sales department interrupted the negotiations to whisper something to his boss. That lady stiffened. She informed Mayor Walker that their parley was at an end.

While trying on hats, Betty had said that they were "completely unstylish atrocities" and that she would "not be found dead within ten miles of any one of them."

At City Hall, on Friday the thirteenth in February 1931, the Mayor had a long, hard day presiding over the Board of Estimate meeting. He went downstairs to his office, planning to take a shower, change to evening clothes, and keep an engagement—really keep it this time—with Betty. He was quite tired, and he had a headache as well as a toothache.

On the desk in his office he found a subpoena. His presence was requested as a witness on February 18 in connection with the trial of two persons arrested in a Communist riot earlier in the year outside City Hall.

"Friday the thirteenth," he said, "simply isn't my day."

It wasn't his day.

Before he could get to the shower a solemn-faced caller of much political consequence was shown into his private office. The Mayor instructed his secretary not to put through any telephone calls until further notice, and not to permit anyone, not even the Governor, to disturb him. There was some mystery about this conference, for the person closeted with the Mayor had not recently been a visitor to City Hall.

After perhaps twenty minutes the politician emerged from the conference. He said nothing to anyone, but seemed even more grim than when he had first arrived. The few members of Walker's staff who had remained on duty after regular office hours waited for a signal from the Mayor to cancel his previous order for silence. After perhaps fifty or sixty minutes, during which time no one had gone in or come out of the private office, the lieutenant at the reception desk received a call from the Mayor over the extension telephone.

"Get me a cab," the Mayor said.

"Yes, Your Honor," said the lieutenant. "Any instructions for your chauffeur?"

"Tell him I'll not want him tonight. Call a cab right away."

"Yes, sir."

When the Mayor came out of his quarters it was observed that the usual high coloring had gone from his face. His grave manner somehow discouraged everyone from asking if he were ill. Wordlessly he walked out of the almost deserted building, his police bodyguard following after him. He dismissed the policeman with a weary gesture and got into the cab. City Hall did not see him again for five days. Nor did he appear as a witness at the trial of the alleged Communist rioters.

No one among his friends or family knew where the Mayor had gone that evening, or where he stayed during the next days. Even now we do not know. All that Jim ever would say of his disappearance was, "I was sick and tired, and I hid out on Long Island."

He did not tell Betty either, but she correctly guessed the cause of his worriment. She later described the episode in an unpublished memoir written for her by Frank Scully but suppressed by her when she had a change of mind.

According to Betty (and there is some hearsay evidence to support her claim), the telephone at her hotel suite had been tapped soon after she began to rehearse for a forthcoming screen test. It was Betty's contention that certain Tammany politicians, fearful that Jim was heading for a fall, sought to get Betty out of the way for the sake of his official welfare.

At the time Betty agreed to take a screen test for a motion picture to be produced at the Astoria, Long Island, studio of Paramount Pictures, there was an influenza epidemic in New York. She balked at rehearsing in a studio where the temperature reached no higher than forty degrees above zero. It was arranged for Miss Compton to rehearse at her apartment, and dialogue director Edward D. Dowling was assigned to go there to work with her.

On Friday, February 13, she received a telephone call from Dowling. He asked if she were expecting him that day for rehearsal.

As theatrical persons often do, Betty used such words as "darling" during their conversation. Betty said that a typed record of this telephone conversation was shown to Walker that same evening.

No one of the many persons whom I have interviewed has seen such a transcript as the one Betty described. Walker himself frowned upon any discussion of the matter.

We are thus restricted to a somewhat speculative position as to the question of wire-tapping. The immediate, almost weird succession of events, however, can be set down without too much guesswork. It was as though two characters from a nineteenth-century melodrama were responding to long-forgotten cues to re-enact in a modern world their strangely woeful, wrong-headed roles.

Late that same evening, according to Betty, she received word that a politician had called on Jim just after he had come from the Board of Estimate meeting. She was also told that Jim had seemed obviously shaken and had gone away from City Hall—no one could say where—in a cab. She learned all this after waiting several hours for Jim to take her to their promised supper at the Casino. When he neither appeared at her hotel nor telephoned to cancel their engagement, Betty became greatly concerned. Her memoir does not disclose the source of her information.

She decided to take some aspirins to relieve a severe headache. By mistake she swallowed sleeping tablets. According to her own account, she had no suicidal purpose in mind. The following Monday she awakened in a hospital.

On February 18 Jim returned from his Long Island truancy. He learned from a newspaper friend that Betty had married Edward Dowling, a comparative stranger.

Two men in Walker's confidence, Charlie Hand and Robert Newman, have assured me independently that Betty's elopement came as a shocking surprise to the Mayor. In their opinion, Jim had taken no part in the supposed wire-tapping episode; nor would it seem consistent with his character, however jealous he may have been, for Walker to have approved an ungallant enterprise of this kind.

Newman says that Betty was never fully convinced that Jim had not been involved to some extent in the alleged eavesdropping. Whenever, in after years, she implied as much, Jim would frown and shake his head.

It was clearly evident that Walker had received news of a most disquieting nature that Friday evening. His subsequent comments, fragmentary as they were, strongly implied that his visitor had dared to speak of Betty Compton in a critical fashion.

When the Mayor first learned of the elopement he seemed bitterly resentful. Like the lass in the Icelandic saga, Betty "had done the worst to him she liked the most."

On the night of Jim's return to the city he was the principal speaker at a dinner of five hundred men chosen from among the seventy thousand heads of families now unemployed in New York City. It required all his powers as an actor to deliver words of hope to a group of men conceivably less dispirited than himself.

Although the Compton-Dowling marriage occurred on February 16, it was not revealed by the newspapers until the 18th. By that time Betty and her husband were already aboard the Ward steamship *Oriente* en route to Havana. They had booked passage as "Mr. and Mrs. Edwards."

When an official of the steamship company recognized Miss Compton, she admitted her identity and then disclosed the fact that she was newly married. The newspapers made no reference to Mayor Walker in the stories about the elopement.

Jim rode in his car with Charlie Hand to City Hall next day and spoke angrily of Betty.

"Now, Jim," Hand said, "what's the use of saying these things? She will be back in no time."

"This is the finish."

"No," Hand said, "it's not the finish. She'll come back, and very soon too."

"Are you insane? Even if she did I wouldn't see her."

"I think otherwise."

The Mayor now spoke of going to Havana for a rest. Then he seemed suddenly to realize that Betty and her husband were on their way to Havana. By some freak of reasoning, he believed that the newly married couple had somehow foreseen that he would want to go to Cuba and had deliberately sought to thwart his plan. He postponed the holiday.

Meanwhile the incessant pounding by Republican legislators for an investigation of the Mayor's office continued. Senator Jack Hastings and others were trying to fight this off. On February 18 the Senate voted down immediate action on the proposed inquiry.

Republican Boss W. Kingsland Macy thereupon began a crusade to arouse the public to demand an inquiry by the lower house.

A week after Mayor Walker's return to City Hall the body of an important Seabury witness, Vivian Gordon, was found in Van Cortlandt Park in the Bronx. She had been strangled.

Mrs. Gordon had just recently testified as to her allegedly improper arrest by a member of the vice squad in 1923. Judge Seabury was anticipating other and more damaging evidence from her at subsequent hearings when he received word that her body had been found. Mrs. Gordon's daughter, appalled by this tragedy, committed suicide.

The Gordon murder set up an immense new wave of critical cries against the municipal administration. Governor Roosevelt cleared the way for an investigation into the affairs of the office of seventy-year-old District Attorney Crain, for failure to prosecute hundreds of cases involving crimes committed in New York. The Governor publicly commended Judge Seabury for his services as referee in the magistrates' inquiry, which was still continuing, and named him to serve as his commissioner to hear charges of inefficiency brought against Crain. Samuel Untermyer prepared to defend Crain.

In an atmosphere of attacks from without and misgivings from within, Walker's health buckled. He accepted Untermyer's invitation to spend a month at that attorney's estate in Palm Springs, California. Walker left New York by train on March 9, the same day Rabbi Stephen S. Wise urged Governor Roosevelt to remove District Attorney Crain from office.

A delegation of Palm Springs Indians met Mayor Walker on his arrival on March 14 at the California desert resort. These tribesmen reminded Jim of Tammany Hall sachems, in that they owned certain valuable "concessions," which real-estate men had been unable to wrest from them. Among their valuable properties were thermal pits in which tired or ill motion-picture personages "bathed" in the bubbling mud.

When a chief invited the Mayor to have a free mud-bath, he replied, "Thank you, no. I've been in one constantly during the past eighteen months."

At the Untermyer house in Palm Springs, Jim kept up his legendary show of gay spirits. But he felt less than cheerful or well. "I'm like a burlesque theatre—a lot of ballyhoo outside, but not such a good show inside," he told columnist Leonard Lyons.

Jim received as many as twenty long-distance calls a day, met reporters, and entertained numerous visitors. The doctors recommended that he stay in the desert for at least a month, for his blood-pressure was alarmingly low. He weighed only one hundred and fifteen pounds and suffered recurrent headaches.

In the serenity of the desert night, near-by Mount San Jacinto, a peak that rises at the edge of the sandy, cactus-bearing flatland, sometimes stirred with seismic roars. Lights would flash on in the neighboring houses and in the hotel rooms. An earthquake, however slight, reminds men of their unimportance in the arena of measureless time.

One day during Jim's stay in Palm Springs he played baseball and almost had a sunstroke. His temperature rose to 102 degrees. News of the New York investigations did not ease his headaches or lessen his fever. In addition to the formal inquiries, Rabbi Stephen S. Wise and the Reverend John Haynes Holmes were attacking the Walker administration.

"How much longer," the militant Pastor Holmes shouted at an open meeting of the City Affairs Committee, "shall we be amused by this little man?"

Late in the evening of March 17 Wise and Holmes called at the Roosevelt town house. They waited in the library until the Governor returned home from a dinner of the Friendly Sons of St. Patrick at the Hotel Astor. The visitors gave the Governor a four-thousand-word document containing ten specific accusations of general negligence and incompetence on Walker's part. The Governor placed this document in his brief case, said good night to his callers, and boarded the twelve-twenty train for Albany.

The next day Dudley Field Malone called Walker in Palm Springs to tell him that he was "breaking off relations" with his long-time friend, the Reverend Mr. Holmes, and was canceling an engagement to speak at that pastor's Community Church.

Malone wrote an open letter to Holmes, in which he stated: "For years I respected you and enjoyed happy comradeship with you in many liberal movements. But your recent action . . . in filing charges against Mayor Walker, and waiting to file them until the Mayor left town . . . compels me to revise my estimate of you and your motives. . . ."

The Mayor decided to return to New York. The public believed that political considerations persuaded him to curtail his vacation, but there was a private reason for it. He had received a telegram from Dan McKetrick announcing that Betty Compton had obtained a divorce from Edward Dowling. She obtained her decree in Cuernavaca, Mexico, on March 20, but this news did not reach the United States until March 31.

When Walker's train stopped in Albuquerque a porter brought the newspapers to the Mayor's drawing-room. Walker read that Betty had visited Cuernavaca (until now Jim had not known exactly where she had been) to establish legal residence. The dissolution of the marriage was effected four days after Betty filed her petition.

According to an Associated Press dispatch, the divorce failed to astonish Betty's theatrical acquaintances. Jim looked among the newspaper columns for a statement by Betty, but she had refused to see members of the press. Previous to the divorce, the newspaper dispatches said, Miss Compton had declared that she had separated from her husband "almost at once" after their arrival in Havana, and added that they "never could get along together."

When Jim reached New York City a casual throng of but a few hundred persons were at Grand Central Station. There were several rounds of hand-clapping as he came through the gate, but no cheers. Although Tammany had agreed not to stage a demonstration, the Mayor had a feeling that his popularity had lessened.

On Easter Sunday the Mayor attended church, then spent the rest of the day in seclusion at his apartment at the Mayfair. Next day he began work upon a fifteen-thousand-word reply to the Wise-Holmes charges. When he had finished this and sent it to the Governor, his spirits improved.

In formulating his reply Walker declined the aid of counsel. He also said that he could win vindication without the aid of Tammany Hall. Jim felt that a public disclaimer of Tammany assistance would allow Governor Roosevelt, as a presidential aspirant, to pass upon the charges without further exposing himself to critical attacks for leniency to the Tiger.

Allie Walker was now in Miami and was saying for publication that she would be starting home soon "to help Jim." She wanted to arrive in New York, she told newsmen, in time to celebrate the nineteenth anniversary of their marriage on April 11. With Betty Compton apparently out of the way, Allie believed that she might once again resume her proper role. "I know that everything will come out all right," she said to the reporters.

Some time during the first week of April Betty Compton called Jim by telephone. He astonished her by asking, "Why, Monk! Where in the world have you been keeping yourself?"

There was a long silence. Then Betty's ability to laugh asserted itself. "I want to see you, Jim."

Thirty-three days had gone by since they had last met. Her story of the elopement and the short-lived marriage would have given each of the Brontë sisters enough material to write another novel. She said that when Jim had not called her, and when she failed to find any trace of him following the alleged wire-tapping episode, she had almost gone out of her mind.

She had taken sleeping tablets, mistaking them for aspirin, and had "drawn a blank." She had awakened the following Monday, she continued, in the hospital. While she was still in a dazed condition she became vaguely aware of the presence at her bedside of "some men." One of them tried to persuade her that "it was all off" between her and Jim. This she had refused to believe, and the spokesman thereupon had declared that the Mayor's career was hanging in the balance and that he would be ruined unless she did something about it at once. One of the men, Betty went on to tell Jim, suggested that she marry "somebody." Betty described herself as having been dazed, limp, and unable to make a clear-headed decision. The next thing she remembered was a private apartment, where she went through with a marriage ceremony.

Betty further declared to Jim that her mind had not cleared itself of the numbing medicine swallowed on February 13 until she was aboard the steamship bound for Havana. Soon after her arrival there, she left Havana and went to Florida alone. There she chanced to meet Walter Winchell. Betty confided her troubles to the columnist but asked him not to publish anything about her plans to seek a divorce. Winchell kept the secret.

Walker accepted Betty's story without reserve. But when she suggested that Jim quit politics and turn his back on the struggle she believed was endangering his health and destroying their chance of happiness together, he said that he could not.

Walker explained that he wanted to fight on for vindication, partly because of the late Mr. Murphy's belief in him, and partly because he felt that he owed it to the memory of his father never to run away from battle.

Once he had won, Jim promised, he would retire from public life.

Meantime Betty must have faith in his love and await the time when he could, as a private citizen, persuade Allie to divorce him.

Walker and Dowling became good friends. Jim never criticized the well-respected, pleasant-mannered young man for entering on the short-term marriage with Betty. As for Dowling, he maintained a gentlemanly silence concerning the elopement and the divorce.

Betty and Jim agreed to spend a year apart. She sailed with her mother aboard the *Europa*.

Although Betty had intended to find a quiet home for herself and her mother in Surrey, England, she decided to return to the stage in an English version of *Fifty Million Frenchmen*. She played for only two weeks in Glasgow, then fell ill and left the cast. The show went on tour without her and failed in the provinces. Betty retired to Harrogate to recuperate. At that health resort she broke an arm. Three weeks later Betty and her mother went to France.

At Cannes Betty realized that she could not "keep out of touch" with Jim, nor could he with her. She called him by transatlantic telephone, or else he called her, almost every night. Sometimes they would talk for half an hour, occasionally for an hour. The first three minutes of a person-to-person call from Cannes to New York in 1931 cost thirty-three dollars and ninety-five cents and each additional minute eleven and a quarter. Frank Scully, who knew Betty quite well at this time, says that her telephone bill was more than ten thousand dollars that year.

Betty left the Riviera to tour Italy. She kept a diary and sometimes read excerpts to Jim over the telephone. On one occasion she reported that her suite had been burglarized of several thousand dollars' worth of jewelry. It was Betty's habit, when traveling, to hide her valuables inside a hot-water bottle instead of depositing them in the vault of a hotel. The jewelry eventually was recovered.

There were two bright hopes held out to Walker in May of 1931: the Governor refused to act upon the Wise-Holmes charges; and when Jim appeared in public for the annual police parade, many thousands of New Yorkers once again cheered Beau James as he marched along with head held high.

In dismissing the Wise-Holmes charges against the Walker administration, the Governor wrote: "It has ever been a fundamental principle of our government that the people of the state and of our various communities shall be allowed to exercise without restriction their right to select whomever they see fit to fill elective offices. The greatest caution must therefore be used in the exercise either of the impeachment power by the legislature or the removal power by the governor, in order not to annul the deliberate decision of the voters of the state or of any municipality thereof. Otherwise, precedent might be established by which the will of the electorate might be set aside for partisan advantage or for personal advantage."

Tammany and Jim both breathed more easily for the moment. For that matter, so did Judge Seabury. The Judge wanted to bag his own game and did not want any poachers to step in for the kill he himself was preparing so painstakingly.

David Belasco died that May. Allie Walker toured the Middle West. Judge Seabury laid the cornerstone of a new building for the General Theological Seminary. New York had a heat wave, and Clara Bow, the "It Girl," retired from motion pictures. On June 19 Mayor Walker had his fiftieth birthday. He seemed pensive when his associates sang "Happy Birthday" to him at City Hall. "Oh," he said, "it's only another day. I'd like to forget about it and not read about it. It will do no good to remind me how old I am. I refuse to believe it."

Later that day he laid the cornerstone for the new Queens General Hospital with a gold-plated trowel. During the ceremonies the radio microphone set up a screeching noise. "It doesn't sound like a birthday greeting," the Mayor said. "It sounds as if the hospital were already completed, and I was the first patient."

That night the Mayor appeared at three banquets in succession. He spoke first at a Brooklyn dinner given to raise funds for the relief of Jews in Europe. Among his fellow speakers were George Jessel and the French entertainer Maurice Chevalier, who kissed the Mayor on both cheeks. There were two thousand persons of various religious creeds at this dinner in the ballroom of the St. George Hotel.

"I have lived and I have loved," the Mayor frankly admitted to this audience. "The only difference is that I was a little more public about it than most people. After all, maybe it isn't a mistake to be one's self and take one's chances. With all my misgivings, my countless mistakes, with all my multiplicity of shortcomings, I haven't a single regret. I have reached the peak of the hill, and must start the journey downward. I have carried youth right up to the fifty-yard mark. I had mine and made the most of it."

He went on to say, "I am a Catholic by tradition, by choice, and in my sympathies, yet I don't want to see, I don't want to hear of, suffering in any part of the world, because I don't want, or rather I want to believe, that no Jew will want to hear of a Catholic or a Protestant suffering in any part of the world."

After the two other dinners that same night, at almost two o'clock in the morning, Walker remembered that he had promised to call upon his old friend Ernest, the journalist, who had been quite ill these last months with cirrhosis of the liver.

Jim went by cab to Ernest's apartment in the Bronx, where the now-divorced invalid was living with an older sister. She had prepared a meal for Walker and had kept it warm for him in the kitchen oven. Jim sadly explained that, although he had attended three banquets, he had had nothing to eat at any of them. On the way to see Ernest, however, he had stopped at Reuben's for a sandwich and a container of milk, which he had consumed in the cab.

"That's like you, Jim," said Ernest. "Always in the midst of plenty, and having nothing for yourself."

Ernie died toward the end of the year. Whether or not his death was hastened by his having drunk a bottle of hair tonic (when liquor was denied him by his doctor) never was established.

"Come to think of it," Walker said, "the night I called upon Ernest he smelled like Bermuda."

Ernest's sister declined to put upon his headstone an epitaph that his witty friend Herman Mankiewicz composed: "Here Lies A Man Who."

28.

Three Things a Man Must Do Alone

THE STATE legislature had a Republican majority in the Senate as well as in the Assembly in 1931. A joint resolution calling for a city-wide investigation finally was passed, and this time the Governor did not veto it. Senator Samuel Hofstadter became chairman of the legislative committee appointed to survey conditions in the city government.

Early in August of 1931 the Mayor of the City of New York was served with a subpoena. It commanded him to appear in Room 578 of the State Building at No. 80 Centre Street on August 10, and to bring with him all documents and papers having to do with his bank accounts and other personal fiduciary data.

The tempest swirled above the silk hat of the Mayor.

On the date specified for Walker to take his bank papers to the State Building, he was having a glass or two of Rhine wine at the Hotel Adlon in Berlin. He had recovered his land legs now, after two days off the *Bremen.* That German liner had borne him away from one of New York's hottest summers, an especially warm season for Tammany Hall.

When the ship had touched at Southampton, England, the Mayor had assured the correspondents at this port of call that the Hofstadter Committee would discover no embarrassing fictions in the Walker banking diaries. Senator Hofstadter had given his formal consent to Walker's temporary absence from town and country. "The committee," Jim said, "is composed of eight Republicans and five Democrats. There is your answer, a political excursion. Insofar as it concerns me, it is only a tempest in a pot, and not a teapot."

The Mayor's European journey, notwithstanding its ratification by Senator Hofstadter, was assailed by his critics. Newspaper readers drew broad inferences that the Mayor's trip had been undertaken with some dark purpose in mind, such as establishing an asylum abroad after the manner of Bosses Tweed and Croker or hiding the swag.

Judge Seabury, the scalper of the sachems, honed his blade. Numerous Tammany trophies already dangled at his belt as a result of two investigations—that of the Magistrates' Courts and that of District Attorney Crain's office—although neither probe had as yet been concluded. It was quite evident that Judge Seabury coveted most of all the war lock of Mayor Walker. During the Mayor's absence the committee sought to bring Walker's personal accountant, Russell T. Sherwood, to the witness chair. Mr. Sherwood failed to appear in that piece of furniture.

A letter written by Walker in 1935 to Robert Newman contains Jim's retrospective views of that late summer and fall of 1931. Walker wrote this at Vichy, France, three years after his retirement from office.

"Before I left town in 1931 to go abroad," the letter reads in part,

"I saw the chairman of the committee and told him I was considering it but would not go unless I was assured that I would not be needed. The chairman said that he would have to consult counsel, which he did, and then reported that I might leave for eight weeks without interfering with their program. The day before I left, counsel sent me a letter by hand confirming the above, with a request for the names of banks and brokers, which were immediately sent him.

"After I left, and while on the water, Russell T. Sherwood, who knew about the arrangement, was called to appear before the committee, and he informed his legal representative, who said it was a violation of the agreement, and so telephoned the first assistant counsel. In fact Sherwood's lawyer told counsel he could go to hell, and then told Sherwood to take a holiday. The proof that he was located in Atlantic City but not subpoenaed (the process server was ready to testify that the first assistant told him to let it go because Sherwood was more useful absent than present) was offered up-state [at the Roosevelt-Walker hearing in 1932] but not received.

"So, while it is a fact, it did not get into the record. However, after that Sherwood went to Mexico City for a personal reason to await the outcome of a domestic relations case, after which he was married there. While in the Mexican city he was subpoenaed, and he consulted an American lawyer who advised him that he did not have to obey the summons because it was beyond jurisdiction. Whereupon Sherwood issued a statement that if he was wanted in connection with any business matters of mine, I could best answer for them myself, adding that when his honeymoon was over he would return and appear. Then counsel went into court and had an impossible fine imposed, which only had the effect of making it impossible for Sherwood to return without suffering a penalty, though he was not accused of any offense."

Judge Seabury's man hunt for the Mayor's accountant became a matter of much notoriety and speculation. Seabury descended upon his brokerage accounts, and Sheriff Farley seized a bank box held jointly by Walker and Sherwood in the Chase Safe Deposit Company, found it empty, and then attached the Sherwood home at Suffern, New York. Judge Seabury finally had the missing man held in contempt of court and fined fifty thousand dollars.

In commenting upon Sherwood's status, the Walker letter had this to say: "He has had a terrible, almost unbearable time of it, and none of it his own fault. A very fine person, living a decent life, who never was anything but helpful that I know of. And to be dragged from his peaceful, happy life and precipitated into a whirlpool of trouble and notoriety, such as would have driven the average man to distraction. . . . Sherwood never held a public position, and never had a business transaction with the City of New York. He never was a paid employee of mine, but he was employed by the law firm [Walker's former legal associates], and they put the services of all their employees at my disposal to render any reasonable services which I required in my personal matters. The law firm paid Sherwood his salary, but it is true that I made him some presents from time to time. But I never paid him an agreed salary because it was only as matters came up that I called him. And yet, as a result of an investigation of the affairs of a city with which he had nothing to do, he has a fine of fifty grand hanging over his head, after being hounded for four years, his health destroyed, his home wrecked, his position lost and his prestige ruined, five thousand dollars' worth of his property sold at auction to be applied to the fine—and all for what? He followed his lawyer's advice that an American subpoena served in Mexico carried no obligation to obey, a piece of advice that, in my opinion, more than sixty per cent of the practicing American lawyers would have concurred in."

The principal reason Walker went to Europe in 1931, his friends mantain, had nothing to do, so far as Jim was concerned, with the activities of the Hofstadter Committee. He wished to see Betty Compton and to fortify his health at Central European spas. Betty's letters to the Newmans had lately expressed a feeling of uncertainty about Jim's love for her. Her mind still seemed troubled with the suspicion that Walker knew more than he cared to admit about the circumstances which had persuaded her to marry Dowling.

Their transatlantic telephone conversations had not been enough to offset the young woman's imaginings that Jim's ardor had lessened. In her loneliness, as reflected by her letters, she could not shrug off the recollection of such matters as Jim's failure to appear on shipboard the night she had sailed away from him, although they both had agreed, in deference to the advice of mutual friends, that Jim stay away from the pier that evening. As the *Europa* waited for the tide, and the laughter of bon-voyage parties reached Betty's ears, she somehow expected Jim to fling aside all restraints, as he usually had done, and then suddenly appear—late of course. The brim of his

Panama hat would be slanted in jaunty fashion upon his head as he came to the door of the cabin. He would stand framed there for a moment in a relaxed but graceful pose, his shoulders thrust slightly forward, like a dancer waiting in the wings for a cue. Then he would cock his head, smile, and enter with a "Hello, Monk. Going somewhere?"

Then after the whistle blew to warn shipboard visitors to go ashore, Jim would stay until the last possible moment, perhaps saying nothing, and not having to say anything, and looking past her, as he so often did, with a dreamlike expression in his eyes, as though he were expecting tomorrow to arrive ahead of time to overrule the unpleasant verdicts of today. . . . But he had not come.

The Newmans had stayed with Betty in her cabin until gangplank time that night. They noticed that she seemed distressed and preoccupied. She had put on all her rings and bracelets and had dressed herself attractively, as though for some special guest. Newman advised her to put away most of her gems, lest Jim's critics see them and make adverse comments to the reporters about her show of valuables.

Now, after some months abroad with her mother, Betty fretted over Walker's reluctance to reach some firm decision, one way or the other, and thereby remove the cause of her moods. It appeared in her letters that she believed that Jim was practicing what might have seemed to his mind the kindliest of methods, but to a woman of her spirit the cruelest, that of "letting her down gently." No one ever let Miss Compton down gently. She had no disposition toward the long view; patience was not her strong point.

Jim for his own part had begun to worry about Betty's attitude. Whether or not he had received a disquieting letter from her, or had quarreled with her during a telephone conversation, no one can say for a fact. It is known to a few, however, that he was disturbed, uncertain as to what the volatile young woman might do "at the drop of a hat."

Perhaps her unpredictable, wild-willed way with him was one reason he loved her so passionately, for sometimes it would seem that the fun-loving man also had a deep-rooted pull toward martyrdom. Women who flattered or pursued him—and they were numerous—seldom appeared to hold his interest, and never his heart. The ones who turned in the other direction—and Betty above all—enchanted him.

When Betty learned of Jim's plan to visit Europe in the summer of 1931, she wrote to the Newmans that she could not understand why he was crossing the sea to "torment" her. She flatly declared that if he did come she would make it her business not to see him.

But Miss Compton frequently was of one mind today and of quite another one tomorrow. By the time Jim boarded the *Bremen,* he had persuaded her to wait in London for a telephone call from him the moment his ship touched at Southampton. They would discuss matters then, he said, and decide what to do next.

A small group of friends, including Walker's tailor Jeann Friedman, accompanied the Mayor on this voyage. At Southampton Jim at once sought to put in his promised call, but so many correspondents and officials of the town surrounded him that he had no privacy during the next two hours. When at last he did reach a telephone, he was unable to contact Betty. It turned out that his delay in putting through the call had offended her so much that she had ordered her maid to tell Mayor Walker to go fish.

Jim had hoped that Betty would invite him to London for a reunion. When the maid gave him the unfavorable message, Walker decided to stay aboard ship and go on to Germany. Walker himself could be quite petulant and stubborn at times. Besides, he had promised to take his tailor "in style" to Friedman's boyhood home in Hungary, and he wanted to enjoy the baths at various watering places on the Continent.

At Bremen Walker received an official reception, and then a second one next day at Berlin. From there he went on to Carlsbad, and then to Budapest.

There a telephone call came from Betty. It is said that a politician, a visitor to Walker's quarters in a Budapest hotel, answered the telephone while Jim was away from his suite, listening to gypsy music at a sidewalk café. The visitor reported to the long-distance operator that Walker was out, and would not receive any calls whatsoever from Miss Compton.

The fact that Betty finally had decided to telephone Walker, only to be informed that he would not take her call, angered her. Several times during Jim's stay in Europe he endeavored to reach her by telephone. Betty not only refused to speak with him, but left for France as soon as she learned that he was coming to London. They did not meet during the six weeks Jim was abroad.

While in France, Jim was made a Commander of the Legion of

Honor. The Hofstadter Committee immediately announced that it would investigate the background of this award to learn if it had not been bestowed because of the French government's forgiven taxes on land used for the storage of ammunition in New York City during the war. Walker's French friends seemed more interested in a new kind of beret he "modeled" for them at Cannes than by any political reports from America. This beret had a visor, and was said to have been designed by artist James Montgomery Flagg.

Walker was visiting with the King of Iraq on the beach at Cannes when a cablegram arrived with news that Judge Seabury had subpoenaed Sherwood's brokerage accounts and was also studying Walker's accounts.

The Mayor took off his visored beret and held it out to the King of Iraq. "Your Majesty," he said, "if you find it uneasy to wear a crown, I'll trade this for it."

Many things happened in respect to the Seabury probe during the Mayor's six weeks abroad. Tammany tried unsuccessfully to limit the powers of the committee, challenged its constitutional right to proceed with private hearings by subcommittees, and lost a fight against the passage of a bill to relieve witnesses of the safeguard of immunity when testifying before the Hofstadter group. Governor Roosevelt had dismissed charges brought against Borough President George U. Harvey of Queens but had censured that official severely. Judge Seabury's investigation of District Attorney Crain had ended. Upon the Judge's recommendation, the Governor dismissed charges of negligence but soundly criticized the elderly Crain.

"Crain," Judge Seabury long afterward told me in an interview, "was an ineffectual but honest man surrounded by thieves."

The King of Iraq invited Jim to play baccarat at the Cannes Casino. The Mayor lost, although not heavily. To His Majesty's offer to stake his companion to further play, Jim replied, "I'd have to get Judge Seabury's consent as a precaution, sir. I would not like to see *you* investigated."

Jim learned that Betty had returned to London and decided to go there. Dudley Field Malone accompanied him to England, where Walker found, to his pleasant amazement, that Mahatma Gandhi had expressed a desire to meet "the Mayor of New York."

The saintly Gandhi was also endeavoring to see Prime Minister MacDonald; but policy-makers of the Empire frowned upon a visit by the Indian leader to No. 10 Downing Street. Walker and Malone had a dinner engagement at the Prime Minister's residence the evening of the day Walker was supposed to call on Gandhi. Jim, however, stayed at his hotel all afternoon, vainly hoping to receive word from Betty.

"Why in hell don't you go *see* her?" Malone inquired.

"I just couldn't barge in without telephoning," Jim replied. "She'll call."

By the time Jim became convinced that Betty would not call, he had missed his engagement with Gandhi. For this he was severely criticized by the Mahatma's friends.

That night at No. 10 Downing Street Mr. MacDonald revealed to Walker and Malone that he had gone incognito to Gandhi's hotel.

"What did you talk about?" Jim inquired.

"We discussed no affairs of state," replied Mr. MacDonald. "Rather, we exchanged views on how best to enjoy sleep when aboard a ship. I said that I liked to sleep in a deck chair after everyone else had retired for the night. Gandhi said it was best to fall asleep on one's back on the open deck while looking at the stars."

Malone recalls that Walker then observed, "This man called Mahatma Gandhi has found the greatest peace of all—peace within his own clear soul."

Jim and Malone went to Southampton on September 15 to board the *Bremen*, homeward bound. The Mayor of the port city and his wife, a very tall person, greeted them. The wife gazed down upon the bobolink Mayor of New York and said, "You know, when you last arrived here I had one great regret. You did not kiss me."

"My lady," said Jim, looking up at his tall hostess, "that was most negligent on my part; but could we not just let the interest accrue?"

Jim arrived home on September 20. He appeared undismayed by the enormous enterprise of the Seabury forces. The Judge now had twenty-one assistants. He seemed to be examining into more lives than did the Angel Gabriel.

During the magistrates' hearings—a seven-month-long inquiry—Seabury had accumulated more than twenty-three thousand typewritten pages of testimony. Before he was done with his analysis of the city government, he would have compiled more than sixty thousand pages.

"You know," Walker said of this voluminous heap, "the Judge is making a piker of the late Dr. Charlie Eliot and the five-foot shelf."

The cold New Year found thirteen and a half million words already set down from testimony heard by the Hofstadter Committee. Senator Jack Hastings was fighting off a demand that Walker appear before the committee to explain his connection with the now-defunct Equitable Bus Company, a group which had obtained a franchise to operate public vehicles but never had succeeded in getting a single bus upon the city streets.

On March 6 it was confidently predicted that Judge Seabury would at last call Mayor Walker to testify before the Hofstadter Committee. On May 12, J. A. Sisto, a broker who had had a hand in financing the Parmelee Transportation Company, testified that he gave Mayor Walker bonds worth $26,535.51 before passage of the bill that had created the Board of Taxicab Control. It was also testified that John J. McKeon, executor of the estate of Walker's late friend, Jules Mastbaum, had delivered these bonds in a sealed envelope to the Mayor on a winter's day in 1929.

When reporters asked Walker about this matter he replied, "Well, now, don't you think that Judge Seabury has a prior right to the answer to that question?"

With the certainty that he soon would be called upon to fight for his official life, the Mayor sallied out in public for a parade, his last great "show." It was the "Beer Parade" of May 14, 1932. Tens of thousands of marchers participated in this demonstration against Prohibition, which lasted from noon until ten o'clock at night. The Mayor led the marchers for an hour and a half. They moved southward along Fifth Avenue from Seventy-ninth Street to the Plaza Hotel, westward along Fifty-ninth Street to Central Park West, then northward to Seventy-second, and back again across the park.

The Mayor finally sat down on a park bench to review the marchers. Just before he withdrew from the line a man fell from a second-story scaffolding and plunged through the top of a limousine in which a woman sat at the wheel. The horrified Mayor investigated the accident and found that the man was unhurt. In fact he got out of the limousine and was going away from it without a word to the startled but uninjured woman occupant of the car.

"Just a minute, my boy!" the Mayor called out to him. "You forgot to be formally introduced to this charming lady."

The Mayor learned that the man was an elevator operator out of a job. "I'm interested in your technique," Walker said to the man. "Would you mind coming down to the Hall to give me some lessons?"

At last the day arrived for the Mayor to answer his accusers from the witness stand in the County Court House off Foley Square. For the occasion Walker's valet assisted His Honor into a blue ensemble: light blue shirt, dark blue cravat, a one-button double-breasted dark blue suit, and a blue handkerchief.

"Little Boy Blue," the Mayor said, "is about to blow his horn—or his top."

It promised to be a warm day, that May 24, 1932. Reporters clustered around the entrance to the Mayfair, waiting in a sort of death watch.

As the valet carefully inspected the Mayor's garments for signs of imperfection, Jim said, "My learned friend Judge Seabury always wears single-breasted coats. He is a very snappy dresser too, but in a sublime way." Then he asked, "Do you know why professors always wear single-breasted coats?"

"No, sir."

"So that the Phi Beta Kappa key can be plainly seen at all times."

Several of the Mayor's close friends and associates began to drop in at the Mayfair. The first to arrive was His Honor's secretary, George Collins. Reporters asked him to find out for them what Walker had eaten for breakfast.

"That's good," commented Collins. "The condemned man's last meal, eh?"

When Walker appeared outside the Mayfair to be driven downtown, a reporter asked if any of his visitors had advised him in respect to the testimony he was about to give.

"There are three things," Walker said, "a man must do alone. Be born, die, and testify."

He took the blue handkerchief from his breast pocket, dabbed his lips, then restored the handkerchief to its regular place. As he got into the sleek limousine, he said to his chauffeur, "Drive carefully. We don't want to get a ticket."

29.

The Tournament of Champions

ELEVEN o'clock was the hour appointed for the beginning of the Mayor's ordeal. As early as seven o'clock a crowd began to assemble outside the courthouse. At eight-thirty o'clock an attendant, by mistake, opened the doors of the hearing room. The three hundred and forty seats were immediately occupied. Approximately four hundred standees also fought their way inside the relatively small arena.

Belatedly it was announced that only the holders of passes signed by Chairman Hofstadter would be permitted to attend the sessions. The police reserves arrived and began to clear the room—to an accompaniment of catcalls, hoots, cries of injustice to the common man, and here and there a slanderous reference to the chastity of some patrolman's mother. By this time several thousand persons were jamming the corridors and the rotunda or standing outside the courthouse. The bearers of passes had difficulty in getting through the mass of envious citizens.

The crowd obviously favored Walker's cause. When ruddy-faced Judge Seabury appeared among them a slight, grumbling stir of voices rose in the warm May morning. He paid no more attention to the inimical throng than a lighthouse does to a wave. When the Mayor's black limousine drew up at the curb there was a silence, followed by a buzz of excitement, and then a cheer.

The man in blue got out of the car. A squad of policemen quickly surrounded him, in the manner of blocking backs running interference for a ball carrier. One taxpayer managed to slip past the Mayor's police screen long enough to ask him to use his influence to procure a seat inside the courthouse. "I'd be most happy to give you *my* seat," the Mayor said, going up the steps.

Hand-clapping and cheering greeted his entrance into the crowded chamber. He maintained an expression of courtroom gravity as he sat down.

At fifteen minutes to eleven the committeemen filed in to their places on the judicial side of the heavy rail of varnished oak. As if by accident the glances of Judge Seabury and Walker met. Both men smiled slightly, the kind of smiles seen on the marble lips of graveyard angels.

One almost expected to hear the voice of Joe Humphreys, veteran announcer at Madison Square Garden, calling out the names, titles, and respective weights of the principals in a championship boxing bout. Instead, small, bespectacled Senator Hofstadter pounded with his gavel and warned the spectators to maintain order.

"Judge Seabury," he said, "the committee is ready, if you are."

The Grand Inquisitor had been waiting fourteen months to place Tammany's golden boy in the witness chair. The present committee, for which Judge Seabury served as chief counsel, had been gathering evidence during the past seven months. The state had spent seven hundred and fifty thousand dollars on its hunt for corruption in city government.

Calm and confident, the Judge stood with his hips resting against the stout oak bar. "Mr. Mayor," he said courteously, "would you be good enough to take the stand?"

The Mayor stepped briskly to the armchair which stood at Judge Seabury's left. The slim, trim man seemed self-possessed. He held his chin high, as he had in the days of his memorable debates in the Albany Senate.

Judge Seabury asked Mr. Walker to be seated for a few moments before being sworn and then continued, "Mr. Mayor, since the immunity laws were passed, it has been our habit here to tender to witnesses that are called a waiver of immunity. May I, in the light of this statement, tender a waiver of immunity to you?"

The Mayor brought a pair of horn-rimmed spectacles from his inside coat pocket, put them on, signed the paper, and was immediately sworn as a witness.

The Mayor was now asked to identify numerous papers which he had brought with him: bank statements of institutions with which he had had accounts since January 1, 1926; a complete statement of brokerage firms or of other financial institutions with which he had had dealings since 1926; a statement of the corporations in which he had held stock since he had become mayor, and matters of a like nature.

The Mayor sat with one hand gracefully dangling over the oaken rail. At the first direct question put to him, it became apparent that his strategy would be to keep his grim, tireless foe off balance.

"Mr. Mayor, at the time the Equitable Coach Company's application for a franchise was under consideration by the city authorities, there was also, was there not, an application for a franchise from the Service Bus Company?"

"Surface?" asked the Mayor almost sweetly. "Or Service?"

"Service," replied Judge Seabury and began a detailed and documented examination of Mr. Walker in regard to the granting of a franchise to the Equitable Coach Company. He sought to bring out that at no time had that company actually been in a position, financially or physically, to fulfill its contract to put busses on the streets, and that Walker's friend Senator John Hastings had participated as a promoter of the now defunct company.

Judge Seabury also tried to establish that the Service Bus Company, a competitive group, had been ready and able to deliver busses upon better terms than those promised by the Equitable Company. The Mayor replied that the franchise had been voted by the entire Board of Estimate, not by himself alone, and that he had not imposed the granting of the franchise upon his colleagues. Walker testified that his move to ratify the contract had been based on recommendations made by John H. Delaney, Chairman of the Board of Transportation since 1924.

As to the relative merits of competing bidders, the Mayor observed, "Why, the best offer that the city ever had for bus operation came from a company located on Long Island; upon investigation, it turned out that they were in the hay and feed business." When the courtroom laughter subsided, the Mayor went on, "And yet, in their communication, it was the most attractive offer."

Courtroom etiquette soon went by the board. There were frequent demonstrations by the audience, and the minority and majority members of the committee quarreled among themselves, objected, shouted, and made speeches.

Democratic Senator John J. McNaboe, a minority member, aroused the wrath of Chairman Hofstadter by repeatedly objecting to Judge Seabury's questions as put to the witness. He was assisted in this heckling by two fellow Democrats among the four minority members of the committee: Assemblymen Irwin Steingut and Louis A. Cuvillier.

When Steingut wrangled with Judge Seabury over testimony previously given before the committee in respect to the number of years specified by the Service Bus Company in its application for a franchise, the Mayor interrupted with, "You ask me to remember details of a report six years ago, and you can't agree upon what happened last week, can you?"

At one point in the hearing Seabury observed to the Mayor, "You have an appreciative audience."

Senator McNaboe called out to the prosecutor, "You have had *your* appreciative audiences for several months."

Chairman Hofstadter used his gavel so often that he risked the onset of an ailment once known as "gold beater's arm." When he remarked that he did not like to give everyone a headache by rapping so hard with his gavel, Senator McNaboe suggested, "Then why don't you get a rubber one?"

The controversy over the bus contract continued for some time. The Mayor sparred cleverly. When Judge Seabury asked a very long question, Walker replied, "You know I won't answer a question that amounts to a speech."

The arm-weary Chairman now thought it time to take a recess. He suggested that the audience keep seated because of the confusion that might otherwise ensue. "If you want to go out," Judge Seabury said to the spectators, "may the Mayor go out without being rushed?"

To which His Honor replied, "I'm used to traveling in crowds."

"The Mayor will suit himself about that," said Chairman Hofstadter.

"Please don't do me any favors at this time," Mayor Walker retorted. He rose from the witness chair amid great applause and gavel pounding.

After a brief recess Walker informed Judge Seabury that he regarded it as unfair, in the absence of Commissioner Delaney of the Board of Transportation, for the Judge to make statements derogatory to testimony given previously by the Commissioner. "And until someone will look him in the eye," the Mayor said, "and challenge his intelligence or his honesty, I will not believe your statement."

"I don't care whether you believe it or not," said the Judge.

"I expected that," Walker replied. "I know you don't care much about what I think, and that goes double." There was more applause.

In a subsequent free-for-all between the minority members of the committee and Chairman Hofstadter, Judge Seabury observed, "I am perfectly willing to meet one of you at a time, but I would rather not have more than four or five at a time."

"Give me the preference," Walker said, "will you?"

The Judge nodded. "Give the Mayor the preference."

His Honor accused Judge Seabury of unfairly determining the "mental operations" that actuated the Board of Estimate in the years 1926 and 1927 by adducing testimony which did not now appear pertinent to that of a prior time. A general flurry occurred between questioner and witness.

"Well, now," said the Judge with polite irony, "I am trying to prove the facts here, and what I want to know from you, Mr. Mayor, if I can succeed in getting it—"

"Everybody else does," Walker interrupted.

"Is an answer as to facts, not your opinion," the Judge continued.

The Mayor waved his glasses. "Well, on the contrary, don't please then testify for me, and ask me to meet your questions as you frame them."

The Chairman intervened. Seabury then asked if the Mayor remembered what was said on March 4, 1929, at a meeting of the Committee of the Whole, about the General Electric Company supposedly having been behind the Equitable Coach propositions.

"No," said the Mayor, "and I don't remember what I may have said at a meeting two weeks ago."

Seabury: "Doesn't that—"

Walker: "Now, please, let me answer."

S.: "Well, isn't that an answer?"

W.: "No, it is not, and you are not going to make it an answer."

S.: "Well, it is an answer."

W.: "Let's settle that now."

S.: "That's an answer."

W.: "Never mind. I have been through all this. Remember, I am still the Mayor of the City of New York." (Applause, gavel.)

S.: "I recognize that, but you are also a witness here."

W.: "That's correct, thanks to you."

S.: "Now, my question—"

W.: "But you are not going to testify."

S.: "My question is whether you made that statement?"

W.: "My answer is, I don't know; but I will get around to it. You don't need to worry about whether I am going to meet questions or not. I am not going to meet them in your distorted way. Now that was a meeting on what date?"

S.: "March 4, 1929."

W.: "All right. Now you ask me what I said about a matter—one matter on a calendar where there were probably five hundred other matters–"

S.: "Oh–"

W.: "Never mind that. Don't you dismiss it in that way. All you are interested in is one thing. I am interested in the people of this city."

S.: "Oh, I know how philanthropic you are."

W.: "You bet you know, and you have evidence of that."

"Let's get back to the record," said the Chairman.

"Get your counsel back," said the witness, "and I'll be back."

The Mayor said he wanted to refresh his memory by seeing the record and informed his questioner that he didn't remember everything he might have said at weekly meetings over which he had presided during the last six and a half years.

S.: "I refer you to the ultimate fact. You may remember that."

W.: "Do you like interruptions better than answers?"

S.: "No, I like answers, if I can get them."

W.: "Will you give a fellow a chance?"

S.: "You have had every chance. Now read it, if you will."

W.: "I insist for the record–"

"I insist the witness answer the questions," Seabury interrupted, turning to the Chairman.

"What is the matter," asked Walker, "are you afraid of my answers?"

"Not at all," replied the Judge. "Are you afraid to answer?" Then he said in a polite tone, "Mr. Mayor, notwithstanding these statements, I am very pleased to see you here."

"Judge," and Walker became overly polite in manner, "I am pleased to see you. It is a pleasure that has been deferred for fourteen months."

"Now you have it gratified," said the Judge.

Judge Seabury patiently weathered the interruptions. Even the hoots which came from admirers of the little man in blue were received with disdain. He departed but once or twice from his unruffled way of speech, as when he exclaimed "Oh, pshaw!" during one of the Walker accusations that the Judge was playing politics. Then he said to the Mayor, "Apparently you are just making a speech."

"Well," said Walker, shrugging his shoulders, "they're not so bad. Did you ever listen to any of them?"

"There may be no doubt about the excellence of your speeches, Mr. Mayor, but there is doubt about the pertinence of them to the questions I am putting to you."

At the afternoon session Chairman Hofstadter appeared late, and said that he was the first man ever to have kept the Mayor waiting. This he regarded as something of a record.

Judge Seabury now began to examine the joint account of Walker and Paul Block. The Mayor readily admitted that Block had established this account without requiring him to put up any money. Walker had profited thereby to the amount of $246,692 after taxes had been paid.

When asked how he had spent this money, Walker replied indignantly, "Where I got the money I am willing to tell you. But where I spent it, that's going too far, unless there is an implication that I tried to influence another public servant with it."

Walker then volunteered, "I put the money, not in a bank, not in a tin box"—there was laughter and cheers—"but in a safe in my own home for the use of Mrs. Walker and myself."

Block's favors to him were described by Walker as "beneficences." Jim declared that never had he allowed moneys from Block or anyone else to influence his political actions.

Judge Seabury frequently attempted to inquire into the financial affairs of Mrs. Walker. At one time the Democratic minority members of the committee rose simultaneously to protest what they described as Seabury's inquisition into the private life of Mayor Walker and not into the affairs of the city. This view, as expressed by Louis A. Cuvillier, was greeted with cheers for Walker and boos for Judge Seabury.

"Oh," said Mr. Walker airily, "run for mayor, and you will read all about your private life in the newspapers."

"I think," Judge Seabury observed, "I should be permitted to introduce evidence here without hostile demonstrations from Tammany Hall cohorts."

"We demand that you stop referring to Tammany Hall," Senator McNaboe howled above the din, "and stick to the evidence."

When the Mayor was questioned about a ten-thousand-dollar letter of credit issued before his 1927 trip to Europe he put on his glasses and shook his finger at Judge Seabury. "I object to these innuendoes. Let's have it out. If you mean you think it was bribery, say so."

During this phase of the inquiry, in which Seabury obviously was seeking to cast suspicion on the fact that J. Allan Smith, a promoter of Equitable, had bought this letter of credit a day before the bus company's contract was signed, the Mayor said, "If you are trying to write a scenario, why not make it complete and say that I ran off to Europe with a huge treasure stolen from the city and hid it there?"

The timing of this interjection by the Mayor forestalled any possibility that Seabury might suggest a sinister motive for that journey. According to Walker, the letter of credit had been a friendly chore performed for him, he had repaid his share of the debt, and the late Senator Downing, one of his companions on the trip, had underwritten the remainder.

Russell T. Sherwood now came into Seabury's patient examination. The Mayor was asked about the safe deposit box rented jointly by himself and his missing financial agent. Walker testified that the box had been used only temporarily in 1924 to safeguard papers of a client. He added that since 1924 he had never used it, had in fact forgotten all about it. He revealed that he did have a box in his own name not far from City Hall but that little or nothing had been placed in it. He was maintaining it "just in case."

When Seabury asked if Sherwood had been at the pier when Walker sailed for Europe in 1927, the Mayor replied, "About five thousand friends were kind enough to come down to see me off, and I don't know whether or not Sherwood was there."

During this hearing the Mayor scored a point when he compelled Judge Seabury to produce a letter from Max Block of Paul Block & Associates, Inc. It showed that certain traction stock had been assigned to the joint account through an error in a broker's office and afterward was transferred back to Paul Block's personal account.

That night, instead of resting after the battle or "studying" for the morrow, Jim addressed the graduates of the Police Academy.

Tammany and the Mayor's other supporters were of an opinion that Walker had held his own with Judge Seabury during the first day of inquiry. The sachems, however, had great respect for the immense staying powers of the prosecutor. They hoped that their brilliant, resilient Jim would keep fresh during the marathon of questions. If only he would go to bed!

Next morning the Mayor, attired in a suit of powder-blue, gray shirt and tie, and gray spats, entered the second and final round.

He was much grimmer than he had been the day before. He seemed determined to claw and scratch.

A canceled check for seventy-five hundred dollars made out to a person whose name was ruled out of the record became one of the matters of inquiry. Everyone close to Jim guessed, or knew, that the "unnamed person" was Betty Compton.

At a much later day it became known that Betty had received a hot tip during the stock-market boom and had telephoned Jim to buy a block of the stock on margin for her, but he forgot to place the order with a broker. Then, when the stock went up in value, so that Betty would normally have made a profit of seventy-five hundred dollars on its sale, Jim paid her this sum from his own pocket rather than allow her to suffer because of his carelessness.

Robert Newman and others have substantiated Betty's version of this transaction. But Walker, while on the stand, maintained that it was no one's business why or to whom he had given that sum. The seeming gallantry of the committee in withholding the identity of the "unknown person" actually created great mystery and much suspicion in the public mind.

And now there was a development which seemed to work a sudden and severe emotional hardship on the Mayor. It pertained to a side issue which appeared almost trivial. Even now it is difficult to understand why this matter took on such consequential dimensions in the mind of the witness.

Seabury had been questioning the Mayor in respect to bonds obtained by him from J. A. Sisto, a taxicab financier. These securities represented Walker's profits in a stock deal, a transaction in which he had not invested any of his own money. Mr. Walker readily admitted having received the bonds, valued at $26,535.51. He said that while he had not put up any cash or collateral for them, he would have made good any loss, had there been one, and then added that his veto of a bill which would have brought a fortune to the company in which Mr. Sisto was interested should remove any suspicion of bribery. The bonds under consideration were for an oil-company holding, not for a taxicab or transportation venture.

A discrepancy between the Mayor's version and that of a prior witness before the committee as to *where* the bonds were delivered provided the break in Walker's complacency. Walker insisted that the envelope containing the bonds was given to him at his hotel while he was dressing to attend a banquet. His friend John McKeon, however, had testified that he gave Walker the bonds while riding in an automobile. The Mayor obviously felt that some sinister and, to his mind, wholly unjust inference, would be drawn from the transference of a "package" during an automobile ride.

Judge Seabury was quick to seize upon the Mayor's discomfiture and enlarged upon this discrepancy as though it were a most damning circumstance. He had similarly pounced upon other variations in the recorded testimony during the inquiry, but this seemed to be the only one that put the Mayor in a mood of angry defiance.

The hearings, which had lasted for two days, closed with a mighty row. When the gavel fell upon the scene, the minority members of the committee and the spectators cheered and applauded Walker. However, there were also some cheers for Seabury.

Walker emerged from this ordeal angry with McKeon, yet feeling confident that he had met all the issues successfully. "Life," he said, "is just a bowl of Seaburys."

As Walker left the courthouse to enter his automobile some women in the crowd stepped forward to strew roses in his path. He smiled at them and tipped his hat.

The main work of the committee had been accomplished. Paul Block, stung by the insinuations made against his good name, appeared at his own insistence to say that he was devoted to Walker only as a friend. He testified that he had established the joint account after his young son had expressed concern because the Mayor could not live comfortably on his official salary. Block volunteered that this statement might sound "silly," but that it was the fact.

After his last appearance before the Hofstadter Committee Jim spent the evening at the boxing matches in the Garden. The spectators cheered him.

In contrast to this reception, on the afternoon of Memorial Day Walker experienced one of those amazing and almost inexplicable changes in public sentiment which sometimes cause a public official to wonder at the fickleness of mankind.

Jim went that day with sportswriters Garry Schumacher and Dan Daniel to the Yankee Stadium to unveil a memorial tablet to the late Miller Huggins, first great manager of the Yankees. As the Mayor stepped from his box to go across the baseball diamond to the Huggins memorial in centerfield, a boo sounded from the bleachers. This derisive noise was taken up by other spectators.

If the Mayor was shocked to hear the first booing ever accorded him at other than a strictly political scene he gave no outward sign. He walked across the infield grass, then past second base. The boos and groans increased with the Mayor's every stride. He went on to the flagpole in centerfield.

With his hat off, he stood for a long moment at the microphone. "Politics," he said at last, "is like baseball."

His courageous stage presence, a quality that never deserted him, somehow caused the thousands of baseball fans to fall silent.

"In baseball," he went on, "the greatest star may be cheered for a home run today and then, on the very next day, be booed if he strikes out." He paused, then said in a strong, clear voice, "That's the way it is, and that's the way it should be. Freedom of speech"—and he pointed to the flag flying overhead—"is guaranteed by that emblem up there. It also guarantees us the right to criticize, or even to boo. If a politician pops out, fouls out, or strikes out, he must expect adverse criticism. If he cannot withstand the boos—and I mean b-o-o-s, and not b-o-o-z-e"—a roar of laughter swept the stadium—"then he also should not pay attention to praise.

"The great little fellow to whom this memorial tablet has been placed upon the scene of his many triumphs, Miller Huggins, sometimes heard his mighty team booed. Fame is a comet that chases its own tail in the sky. Huggins is now well beyond the reach of criticism or praise, but we still remember him as a wonderful man. It is so important to be a man first, and regard whatever else that comes to you or is denied you in the way of laurels as a secondary consideration. It is much more important, when all else is over, and one has gone through the narrow door from which there is no returning, to have been loved than to have been exalted."

The Mayor stood at attention. The crowd rose. The band played the national anthem. As Jim marched back across the field there was a tremendous ovation, which lasted until he re-entered his box and sat down.

"Play ball," the umpire called.

30.

In the Hall of Governors

WITH the July Democratic convention but three weeks away, Governor Roosevelt found it necessary to interrupt his drive for the presidential nomination and assign his energies to the Walker case. On June 8, 1932, fifteen charges formulated by Samuel Seabury against New York's Mayor reached the Governor's desk at Albany. This broadside accused Walker of malfeasance, misfeasance, and nonfeasance.

Judge Seabury himself has told me that Roosevelt asked him to agree to a postponement of the Walker hearings until national political fires had cooled. The Judge declined to sanction a delay.

No matter which course the Governor decided to steer, he risked losing the support of powerful groups of delegates. Were he to ignore Seabury's demand, Tammany's foes might charge him with condoning the Tiger's sins. Were he to make the opposite decision and bring Walker to trial, an open defiance of Tammany might well cause many resentful delegates to endorse Al Smith's belated move for the nomination.

The Republican party hoped to make the Walker issue a demolition bomb to wreck the Roosevelt bridge. If sufficient dissension could be created, Herbert Hoover, the whipping boy of the century, might stagger back to the White House, which was being besieged by an angry bonus army of war veterans.

Almost everyone concerned with embroiling the Governor apparently underrated Roosevelt's ability to improvise boldly on the field of battle. No one, of course, could foresee his historic tomorrow.

On June 22, the day before Walker left New York to attend the Chicago convention as a delegate, he received notification from Governor Roosevelt that he must answer the Seabury charges.

It was Walker's desire to plead his own case before the Governor. Tammany, however, insisted that he have as his counsel someone agreeable to the Hall. The Mayor yielded to this demand and accepted as his attorney John J. Curtin. Curtin was senior partner in the law office of Curtin & Glynn. John J. Glynn was Al Smith's nephew. Many observers felt that Al Smith was active in the behind-the-scenes direction of the Walker defense. Walker denied this at the time.

A few days after the Seabury charges reached Albany, Governor Roosevelt named attorneys Martin J. Conboy and J. E. Mack as special assistants to advise him on the Walker matter.

Raymond Moley suggested Conboy's appointment. A year before, Conboy and Moley had been fellow members of a commission on the administration of justice. Moley had been named to that commission by Roosevelt and Conboy by the State Bar Association. Conboy for some years previously had been in Tammany Hall's best graces.

At a meeting between Conboy and Moley one day in 1931 in the Buffalo Public Library building, Conboy confided that he had become disgusted with Tammany Hall of late and would like to see the Tiger thoroughly beaten. Moley tucked away this remark for future reference.

In a letter to me Moley wrote in part: "In 1932, a month or less before the Democratic convention, Judge Seabury, as a deliberate means of embarrassing Roosevelt, threw his report on Walker onto the Governor's desk. Roosevelt was confronted with a very serious problem as a candidate for president. He stalled a few days about taking any action. I was pretty close to him in those days, although I was in New York City most of the time. In talking with a judge, who properly should remain nameless, the question came up of a counsel for the forthcoming inquiry by Roosevelt into the Walker administration. This judge and I frankly discussed the religious issue, and at that time I remembered the fundamental attitude of Conboy toward Tammany. So the next morning I called up Roosevelt and recommended two lawyers—one of them was Martin Conboy, a Catholic; the other, Judge Joseph Proskauer, a prominent Jew and a close friend of Al Smith. My suggestion was that, in appointing Proskauer, Mr. Roosevelt would protect himself against the friends of Al Smith—some of whom were, of course, friends of Walker—and that by appointing Conboy he would protect himself against an attack alleging anti-Catholic bias. Roosevelt was much interested in the suggestion. He rejected Proskauer and immediately accepted the Conboy suggestion. There is no question but that the religious point was a predominant one. Conboy was a well-known Catholic. . . . He was also a very able lawyer."

When Conboy was named to assist Governor Roosevelt certain New York newspapers described him as a Tammany man. "This," Moley pointed out, "was excellent for Roosevelt."

In commenting upon Judge Seabury's political estimate of himself, Moley continued: "Seabury was definitely a candidate for the presidency throughout that year. He had no strength, but he deluded himself into thinking he had. A friend of his had lunch with me one day and asked, 'Do you think Uncle Sam has any chance for the nomination?' I said, 'Of course, the lightning might strike anybody; but you have to have a reasonable cause to support it.' "

As a member of the committee on resolutions at the Chicago convention, Walker urged his fellow delegates to disregard the fact that he was facing charges at Albany. The Mayor was ill and sought to keep out of the limelight.

Dudley Field Malone sat beside Walker at the convention. He says that Jim resolved to follow the instructions of Tammany Boss Curry, who not only was supporting Al Smith, but also disliked Roosevelt personally.

When the California delegation, under the leadership of William Gibbs McAdoo, finally threw its support to Governor Roosevelt, Malone went from the convention hall to look for Walker. He managed to locate the Mayor at the apartment of a friend. Jim was alone and fast asleep.

Malone awakened him and explained the urgency of the occasion. Jim did not wait to dress completely. He drew a pair of trousers and a coat over his pajamas and put on his bedroom slippers. The two men then hastened by taxi to the convention hall.

When the New York delegation was polled Walker stood up to announce, "I vote for Alfred E. Smith."

This was regarded as a daring thing for Jim to do. He soon would face as his judge the same man who at this moment seemed assured of the presidential nomination.

Al Smith exclaimed, "Good old Jimsie! Blood is thicker than water."

Malone says that when the Texas delegation climbed aboard the Roosevelt victory wagon, Walker importuned Curry to do likewise. "Now, John!" Walker called out to Curry. "*Now* is the time to join in."

But Curry, Malone says, refused to go along. The Tammany delegation stayed glumly seated during the parade in the aisles.

Walker returned from the convention early in July to compose his answer to the Seabury charges. It was not until July 28, however, that he completed the thirty-thousand-word document. On that same day he received word that his brother George lay dying at a Saranac sanatorium. As soon as Jim had mailed his reply to the Governor he went to Saranac.

"You're looking kind of skinny, Jim," George managed to say. "Go on back to town," he added. "I'll pull out of this as I always have."

Walker's letter to the Governor contained specific denials of the fifteen charges brought by Judge Seabury. As a legal defense, Walker contended that six of the charges should be entirely ruled out and four of them partially overruled, on the ground that they related to matters that had occurred during his first term of office. Walker maintained that his re-election had constituted public approval of his first years of administration and therefore canceled out charges arising from his earlier term.

"Since the day of my birth," a paragraph of Walker's letter read, "I have lived my life in the open. Whatever shortcomings I have are known to everyone—but disloyalty to my native city, official dishonesty, or corruption form no part of those shortcomings."

I now quote from an interview I had with Raymond Moley: "When I talked with Roosevelt at Hyde Park after he was well into the Walker case, he said, in a sort of meditative way to me, 'How would it be if I gave the little mayor hell, and then kept him in office?' Before I had a chance to answer, he did one of those quick turns of mind which were characteristic of him, snapped himself up, and said, 'No, that would be weak.' I then suggested that I did not believe the accusations by Seabury were adequate to sustain a real charge of dishonesty against Walker. I believed Walker was guilty of nonfeasance—not malfeasance. In short, that he was guilty of neglecting his job; that the broad legal aspect of the case was similar to that which arises when a guardian or trustee is neglectful of his obligations. In this instance, Walker bore a heavy responsibility to New York which he had neglected. Consequently, his removal should be on the basis of such neglect rather than for wrong-doing. Since the proceedings before the Governor were not bound by rules of proved wrong-doing, the Governor might remove him on any grounds he might choose."

Moley observed parenthetically: "Incidentally, I had the right to an opinion on this because I had worked with Seabury on his investigation of the Magistrates' Courts and of District Attorney Crain's office."

"I then suggested to Roosevelt," Moley went on to say, "that I look up for him some of the records of the great impeachment trials, such as that of Warren Hastings, President Johnson, and others. And that if it came to a question of removal, he pitch it on the note of neglect of the responsibilities of office. He agreed, and told me to go ahead. In the following days I did some research."

Walker had been advised to make it appear that he and Allie were reconciled. She had just recently left the hospital after undergoing a surgical operation. Jim had posed for the newspaper photographers with his wife the day she left the hospital.

The Mayor, his counsel John J. Curtin, Allie Walker, and several other persons in his confidence arrived by train at the capital city on August 10. It was said that Governor Roosevelt expressed annoyance because Walker had brought Allie to Albany under the pretense that all was well with their domestic life. Allie soon suffered a relapse because of her recent operation and was ordered to return to New York City by her physician.

On August 11 the Governor sat in his high-backed chair at the huge desk in the executive chamber known as the Hall of Governors in the Statehouse. The summer sunlight lanced through windows that reached from the high ceiling almost to floor level. At the left of Governor Roosevelt sat Martin Conboy. The Governor's regular counselor, Maldwin Fertig, sat at his right. Two state troopers stood behind the chair of the man who now was to pass judgment on the long-time idol of the nation's most powerful political machine.

The Governor's desk stood in the center of the east side of the rectangular chamber. To the left of it, and at an angle, the sternly complacent Samuel Seabury and seven young assistants occupied chairs at a table. At another angle, to the Governor's right, and at a similar table, James J. Walker sat with Curtin and his associates.

A brass rail brought from the Assembly chamber served as a bar to separate the participants in the hearing from the sixty newspaper correspondents who were seated at press tables and the sixty or seventy spectators who occupied places against the walls.

"I hope," Jim said of this rail, "that they are not preparing to ride me out of town on it."

Walker cautioned his counselor, as he afterward told me, against being needlessly aggressive at the hearings. Governor Roosevelt's affability and charm, Walker reminded his attorney, could suddenly disappear whenever "Frank's disposition is rubbed the wrong way."

Able as Curtin was, he was perhaps swayed by personal dislike for the man who had just recently defeated Curtin's great friend Alfred E. Smith. Jim's counsel also may have overlooked, or else underestimated, Roosevelt's talents as an examiner, his ability to find needles in documentary haystacks. Conboy stayed at the Mansion during the hearings and each night briefed his apt student on the complex testimony given during the seven months of the Hofstadter inquiry.

There were twelve sessions in all. On the first day, August 11, the Governor questioned Walker on the Sisto transaction. The next day Roosevelt explored the Equitable Coach Company franchise and also looked into the Block gifts. During this second day Curtin argued for Walker's right to summon and cross-examine any and all witnesses who had testified before the Hofstadter Committee. The Governor indicated that he had no disposition to lengthen the hearings unnecessarily by bringing before him the hundreds of witnesses who had testified over a long period of time.

Curtin said, "The earliest recorded–so far as I know–instance of the value of cross-examination is contained in the Bible itself. You may recall one of the Apocryphal books, the story of Susanna and the Elders; Susanna, a beautiful lady, and two of the Elders enamored of her. . . . She repulsed them. Whereupon, to get square, they accused her of impropriety with some other third person. And these Elders were men of good standing in that community, and that is why they were Elders. And they swore definitely before the council that this lady had committed this impropriety; and there was nobody to gainsay that except the lady herself, who met it with tears and denial. There is nothing dramatic about a denial. And she was condemned to death, under the Laws of Moses; and then Daniel arose and said, 'Not so fast!'–I am not quoting accurately–'Not so fast! Let me examine these Elders.' And he put them both out. Then he brought in one of them and said, 'You are sure this thing has happened?' 'Yes.' 'Did you see this thing happen?' He said, 'Yes, and I am sure of it.' 'Where did it happen?' 'Under the mastic tree.'

"He was sent away," Curtin continued, "and the other fellow was brought in. 'You are sure this thing happened?' 'Yes.' 'You saw it with your own eyes?' 'Yes. And I can't be mistaken.' 'Where did it happen?' 'It happened under the yew tree.' Whereupon the council put to death, not Susanna, but the accusers."

The Governor said that he would rely upon the many volumes of testimony taken before the legislative committee and reproved Curtin for having referred to this mass of testimony as "minutes." The Governor added, "I consider them evidence. You have referred also to the interesting case of Susanna and the Elders. I think it is a very apt case. You are in the position of the Prophet Daniel. I will not say that His Honor is in the position of Susanna."

"That isn't so," Curtin retorted hotly.

"I certainly feel like it," the Mayor interposed.

"The Prophet Daniel," the Governor went on to say, "asked the attendance of the two Elders who had previously testified. You are in the same position, and you may ask the attendance of such Elders as have already testified. In other words, the Mayor will be entitled to summon material witnesses."

Roosevelt denied him the request to call or cross-examine all or any witnesses who were not "material" in the Governor's opinion.

Judge Seabury placed several check stubs on the Governor's desk. "These have come to me since the Hofstadter Committee adjourned," he said.

The Mayor turned to the newspaper reporters. "They're pulling checks out of hats now."

At the close of a session Walker was asked by a reporter how he thought he had fared. With complete candor Jim replied, "Papa made me eat my spinach."

On August 15 the Governor questioned the Mayor about the Sherwood "disappearance." Walker said that he himself had long been looking for Sherwood and had originally asked Police Commissioner Mulrooney to institute a thorough search.

"I wish Sherwood were here today," he added.

"So do I," remarked the Governor.

Roosevelt appeared dissatisfied with Walker's explanation as to why he had not made strenuous personal efforts to bring Sherwood back into the jurisdiction of the committee.

"Wasn't it a matter of public notoriety to you that he had slipped out when you got back from Europe?" asked the Governor.

"It was not to me."

"Didn't you know the whole town was looking for him?"

"No, I knew the whole town was not looking for him. The police had been called off."

"You sent him no telegram to come back?"

"No."

"You didn't telephone him?"

"No, I didn't see why I should."

"Isn't it a strange thing you didn't try to locate him by wire or phone when he turned up in Mexico City?"

"It doesn't seem strange to me."

"A man with whom you had been associated for a great many years?"

"Only as an employee in our office."

"A man with whom you held a joint safe deposit box?"

"I didn't consider it a joint box. I used it only once, many years ago. I didn't even know where it was."

"Doesn't it seem a strange thing for you not to have done a thing toward getting Sherwood back into the jurisdiction when he first showed up in Mexico City?"

"Not at all."

Toward the close of the examination on the Sherwood charge Walker cried out, "Whatever his disappearance was, it was not with my connivance!"

"So you just let it ride?"

"You may call it that, if you care to."

Walker was questioned about the purported fee-splitting activities of his brother Dr. William H. Walker. The Mayor said, "I had no knowledge whatsoever of the scope of his business, nor with whom he did business."

The Governor asked if the Mayor had taken any steps to investigate the story, and Walker replied that he had not. This question had to do with moneys supposedly received by a Dr. O'Mara for compensation cases, and the allegation that Dr. O'Mara thereupon had drawn a check for half the amount and given it to Dr. Walker.

The Governor asked, "Do you consider that a proper thing for Dr. O'Mara to do?"

"Well," the Mayor replied, "I don't know the circumstances, if Your Excellency please."

"It is so testified to on the stand by witnesses," the Governor said.

The Mayor replied that he had not read the testimony up to this moment. Then the Governor asked, "But do you consider it a proper practice for a doctor who is receiving pay from the city or any other government to split fees with some other doctor?"

"I do not," the Mayor said, "if it is done along that line. But if he is paying that money for some other purpose, and I hope Your Excellency does not want me to assume that it was for an illegal purpose without any knowledge of it . . ."

After several more questions had been put to him the Mayor said, "I don't know of itself that fee-splitting is wrong. I have done it. I don't know whether Your Excellency has done it in your law practice or not, but most lawyers have."

The Governor said that it had been testified in this present hearing that Dr. O'Mara had received a number of fees for city compensation cases and had given a check for exactly half of these fees to Dr. Walker, whereas Dr. Walker, it was testified, had at no time performed any medical services in connection with these same cases.

To this the Mayor replied that it would be a matter of serious interest if the city had been defrauded. "If, on the other hand," he said, "the city was not defrauded, the service was rendered and the bill was paid, and the doctors, because of some other arrangement between them, were paid off by splitting the check, or as many checks as there were, I don't see anything unethical about that."

The Governor pointed out that he was asking the Mayor to answer a question which was based on events now in evidence before him. Walker wearily answered, "I don't think that anything that is wrong is good for good government."

The Governor charged Walker with being "not responsive." At another point the Governor asked, in respect to the splitting of fees, "Isn't it a bad practice?" To which the Mayor replied, "What is wrong is bad."

The examination turned upon transactions involving an "unnamed person." Roosevelt appeared somewhat astonished when the Mayor revealed "the unnamed person's" sex by referring to her as "she."

The Governor himself, however, continued to speak of her as "this person" and ruled that the name be withheld from the record.

The Governor questioned the Mayor about transactions in which Sherwood allegedly had paid over to the "unknown person" some sixty-eight thousand dollars. Walker denied knowing anything about Sherwood's payments in this instance. The Governor pointed out that it had been testified that Sherwood had given a ten-thousand-dollar letter of credit to "this person" and afterward increased it to sixteen thousand dollars. He then asked the Mayor, "Do you know anything about that?"

"I do not," replied the witness.

After this session a reporter inquired of the Mayor what had been the purpose of his statement that "she" had accounts in several New York banks.

"The purpose," he replied, "is to show that this woman had plenty of money—I understand as much as two hundred thousand dollars—with which she could have purchased letters of credit or made deposits as she saw fit. The Governor has ruled that the name of this person must not be revealed, in or out of the sessions."

Another newsman then asked Walker if the woman referred to was not Betty Compton. He retorted almost angrily, "How long have you been around?" Then he asked, "Who else could it be?"

Thus the name of Betty Compton first appeared in public print in connection with the investigation of the Mayor. Miss Compton was at this time in Paris.

At a conference of attorneys at Governor Roosevelt's desk after the recess Walker said in an aside to the newspapermen, "This fellow Seabury would convict the Twelve Apostles if he could."

During another recess Walker strolled outside the Hall of Governors with his friend Malone. "Dudley," he said, "you know that I am not a crook, and that this is just a political move. If I were a crook, why, during the last year or more, have I been compelled to borrow large sums of money from my friends to support my wife and some twenty-eight dependents and a lot of other people? Had I been a grafter, it must be perfectly plain to everyone that I could have accumulated millions."

While the hearings were on, Curtin applied to Justice Ellis J. Staley of the New York Supreme Court for an order to prohibit the Governor from continuing with the Walker trial. It was counsel's contention, among other things, that the section of the City of New

York's charter under which the Governor was empowered to try the Mayor was unconstitutional.

George Ringler, formerly a reporter for the *New York Daily News*, has informed me that at this point a secret meeting took place at Walker's quarters at the Hotel Ten Eyck. Ringler had known Walker since Jim was a state senator. Upon Walker's election as mayor, Ringler was appointed as an investigator for the Health Department. Walker entrusted to Ringler many confidential matters, such as looking out for the welfare of numerous widows and children of Walker's old friends, all at Jim's own expense. Ringler had accompanied Walker to the Albany hearings.

"One day," Ringler told me, "Edward Ahearn asked me to arrange a meeting with Walker and Curtin. Ahearn was a Tammany District Leader. He was the son of the late John F. Ahearn, who had been removed as Borough President of Manhattan during the administration of Governor Hughes. Walker and young Ahearn had fallen out when Jim supported Curry for the Tammany Hall leadership instead of naming Ahearn for that high post.

"Walker," Ringler went on to say, "did not wish to meet Ahearn, but Curtin prevailed upon him to do so. I then brought Ahearn to the Ten Eyck, where, in my presence, Eddie told Jim that Governor Roosevelt had already made up his mind to remove him. Walker said, 'I don't know why he'd make up his mind to do that. Who told you he would?' Ahearn said that he was bound by confidence not to mention the name of his informant, but he insisted that it was a most reliable source. He then added that if Walker was smart, he would resign, then run for office for vindication."

On August 27 Walker and Seabury returned to New York City on the same train. They avoided one another during the journey.

The Mayor was feeling quite ill when he reached New York. He retired to the Mayfair and stayed in bed. Next day he received the shocking news that his brother George had died at Saranac.

While waiting for George's body to be brought to New York, Jim was too dazed and ill to express much interest, one way or the other, when on August 29 Justice Staley denied the petition for an order of prohibition to take the Walker hearings out of Governor Roosevelt's hands. The Governor had no comment to offer upon the Staley decision until late in December. Then, with political issues dead, and as President-elect of the United States, Roosevelt filed a memorandum with the State Attorney General, strongly criticizing

Justice Staley for having departed from his judicial function to indulge in observations which had been "ill-advised." Justice Staley had upheld the Governor's right to try Walker, but had said, in effect, that the mode of procedure was unfair and that the Mayor should have been permitted to summon certain witnesses for re-examination.

George Walker's funeral was on Thursday, September 1. The ill and grieving Mayor went with his sister Nan to the services. Among the several Walker friends at the church were James A. Farley and Dan McKetrick.

McKetrick told me that Farley said, "Jim looks terrible. In fact he looks worse than George."

Farley was taking a train for Albany that afternoon to confer with the Governor as to when Roosevelt planned to begin his campaign tour of the West. Dan asked Farley if he would plead Walker's case privately with his chief, and Farley replied, "Dan, call me at seven o'clock."

McKetrick then spoke to Walker, who said, "I think Roosevelt is going to remove me. I've got a conference at the Plaza with John McCooey, Curtin, Curry, and the rest. What am I to say to them?"

"Will you wait," McKetrick asked, "until I talk to Jim Farley before you commit yourself to anything?"

"I don't know," Walker replied.

At Calvary Cemetery, after Jim and Nan had seen their brother's casket lowered into the family plot, Walker said, "Sis, take a short stroll with me. I've got something I want to tell you."

Together they went to the near-by grave of Charles F. Murphy. Nan says that her brother stood there for several moments, then said, "Mr. Murphy once told me that most of the troubles of the world could be avoided if men opened their minds instead of their mouths. Sis," he said, "I'm going to resign."

"When, Jim?"

"Now," he said. "Or as soon as I leave the meeting at the Plaza."

Twelve or more Tammany leaders met with Walker at the Plaza. Max D. Steuer was one, Al Smith another. Walker afterward told reporter Nat Ferber that when he asked Al Smith for an opinion, Smith said, "Jim, you're through. You must resign for the good of the party."

"McCooey," Walker added, "stood loyally by me and said that he'd rather meet defeat with me than win without me."

On his return to the Mayfair, Walker was given a message to telephone McKetrick, who had gone to dinner at a nephew's home in Forest Hills. Instead of calling McKetrick or anyone else, Jim silenced his telephone. McKetrick was unable to reach him for some hours. Dan, however, had succeeded in getting Farley on long distance. Farley said he did not wish to speak over the wire but instructed McKetrick to tell Jim not to do anything at all.

When McKetrick did get Walker on the telephone at about eleven o'clock that night, he learned that the Mayor had sent the following message to City Clerk Michael J. Cruise: "I hereby resign as mayor of the City of New York, the same to take effect immediately."

The reporters in Room 9 of City Hall received this news at ten-twenty P.M. That the Mayor had been planning to resign as early as August 14 is strongly indicated by a paper which I came upon in the Walker files. It is a three-page, typed draft, corrected and amended in Walker's own handwriting. It bears the date August 14, is addressed to Governor Roosevelt, and begins with the words: "I am herewith resigning my office of mayor."

The resignation of the tired Mayor brought an air of sadness to thousands. His critics, of course, accepted his action as an admission of guilt. Certain ones among them, however, felt that Walker was cheating them of the spectacle of their victim being beaten to death and disgraced in the open forum.

Whether or not Roosevelt was planning to remove Walker, and on what ground, has been long debated by persons familiar with the political circumstances of the time.

Judge Samuel I. Rosenman, always close to the Roosevelt mind, says that, so far as he knows, Roosevelt never announced publicly what his action was going to be with respect to Mayor Walker. Boss Ed Flynn of the Bronx says that he simply does not know what the Governor intended to do. Raymond Moley believes that Mr. Roosevelt would have removed Walker on the charge of nonfeasance, but not malfeasance. Jim Farley does not have a conclusive opinion as to what might have occurred.

Charlie Hand writes to me: "Conversations I had with Mr. Roosevelt when Jim Walker was answering before him the charges of Samuel Seabury convinced me that, at the beginning, he was decidedly inclined to permit Walker to remain as mayor but subject him to a terrific chastisement. Later he indicated quite clearly that he felt Walker had been careless and neglectful of his job as mayor and indifferent to conditions in his administration with which he should or must have been familiar. He remarked that Walker's personal conduct was 'nothing to brag about. . . .' I can't believe that Roosevelt would have deliberately dismissed Walker to enhance his chances for the presidency. Besides, when the Walker trial was under way, there was every indication of a certain victory for Roosevelt."

Hand was down south with John Nance Garner when he received a telegram announcing Walker's resignation. The vice-presidential candidate said that, in his opinion, Mr. Roosevelt would *not* have removed Walker.

Walter T. Brown, chief of the Albany Bureau of the Associated Press in 1932, writes to me: "When Walker quit, I thought he made a mistake, as by that time Roosevelt had the presidency in the bag and couldn't lose. Walker could have been re-elected on an exoneration platform. In 1941, after I entered the Army, I visited President Roosevelt at the White House. I asked him point-blank if he would have fired Walker. He said he did not believe the Seabury evidence justified it. He agreed with me that the political importance had been lost in the inexorable shift of voters. Roosevelt always liked Walker but wouldn't trust his fluid emotions."

Mrs. Eleanor Roosevelt, in reply to a letter from me, wrote in part: "My husband always liked Mayor Walker, and he was very much troubled over the whole trial. As I remember it, he had made up his mind to remove him from office, but whether it was for nonfeasance or malfeasance I have no idea. I know my husband was vastly relieved when Mayor Walker resigned, because of his personal liking for him."

An hour after he had resigned Jim cabled Betty, who was in Paris. She was delighted that he had quit.

Walker's doctor advised him to take a rest at once, to avoid a complete nervous and physical collapse. The physician suggested that the ex-Mayor go to some quiet place in the country or take an ocean voyage.

On September 10 Walker sailed on the *Conte Grande*, with the announcement that he would visit Paris. He promised to be back in time for the convention of the city's Democratic delegates at Madison Square Garden, and said that he then would present himself as a candidate for renomination for the special mayoral election.

Aldermanic President Joseph V. McKee became mayor pro tem.

A sympathetic reporter said to the ex-Mayor, "Everyone is for you, Jim. All the world loves a lover."

"You are mistaken," Walker replied. "What the world loves is a winner."

Part Three

ACME

Mayor La Guardia, Walker, and Jim Farley at a baseball writers' dinner in 1937

Jim and Betty

PACH BROS.

The Walkers with their daughter Mary Ann

David Dubinsky, Mrs. Eleanor Roosevelt, Harry Hopkins, and Walker at a Garment Workers' Union dinner in 1945

31.

Weep No More, My Lady

WALKER intended to spend his holiday with Betty at some secluded and sunny place in the south of France, and then return home in time for the Tammany convention. But when the *Conte Grande* steamed into the Bay of Naples, Walker's secretary, George Collins, came down with a malady that could not be readily diagnosed, and Walker had to revise his plans. He telegraphed Betty, who had been waiting in Paris for word from the man she had not seen during these past eighteen troubled months, that he must return to New York immediately with the sick man. The next swift ship, the *Rex*, would leave Genoa on a maiden voyage in three days. Would Betty come to Italy for an hour or two with Jim? The tourist season was about at an end at Pompeii, so Jim suggested that locality for a rendezvous. Betty agreed.

Jim was lonely and dejected until Betty's arrival. On the appointed day he went by automobile to the ancient town near the foot of Mount Vesuvius, and for once was early. He waited for Betty in a small museum among the ruins of the old town.

After an affectionate greeting, Betty commented upon Jim's haggard appearance. She importuned him to forget the convention and to remain with her in Europe. He replied that he owed it to his friends to seek renomination and subsequent vindication at the polls.

"All that you owe your so-called friends," Betty retorted, "is payment in kind for the years of unhappiness they have brought to you and me."

Jim argued that he most certainly would be renominated, then re-elected. He would serve out the year which normally would complete his second term and after that retire to private life and marry Betty, even though he might have to obtain a French decree of divorce.

"Jim," Betty predicted, "another year in office will kill you."

They parted on a somewhat melancholy note. Betty found herself unable to smile when they passed the ruins of the forum and Jim said, "The sight of this platform makes me want to climb up and make a speech."

Betty went to Cannes. Jim and his ill secretary took a train to Genoa, where they boarded the *Rex*.

Off Gibraltar the *Rex* developed engine trouble and limped into the roadstead. The passengers went ashore in tenders. For the next three days Jim wandered about the bleak island, detesting the Rock and fretting at the delay.

When Walker learned that several more days would pass before a new turbine part could be installed in the ship, he left Collins, whose health had unexpectedly improved, to continue the voyage home in care of the ship's doctor and sailed on a small vessel bound for a French Channel port. From there he went on to Paris.

His spirits improved. He had reached a political decision. He had decided not to run for office, ever, and so advised Betty. When cables from his political seconds reached him at Paris, he made equivocal answers to their reminders that time was running out and that the convention was almost at hand.

Walker boarded the *Bremen* two days before the delegates were to meet in New York. He could not possibly appear in person at the Garden to receive the fanfare that had been promised him. Jim sent his backers word to withdraw his name from consideration. The delegates nominated the grave-mannered Surrogate J. P. O'Brien, who subsequently was elected.

Several thousand enthusiastic admirers greeted Jim on his arrival in New York harbor. He announced that he would support O'Brien for mayor, Herbert H. Lehman for governor, and Franklin D. Roosevelt for president.

"I'm still a Democrat," he said, "though very still."

Snow fell upon the city. Jim had a sore throat. He went into seclusion at Burkley Crest, the Dobbs Ferry estate leased by A. C. Blumenthal from Billie Burke soon after the death of her husband, Florenz Ziegfeld, in July of that year.

Early in November Betty and her mother returned to New York. Betty's and Jim's close friends, the Newmans, endeavored to shield the homecoming actress from adverse publicity. When reporters asked just why she had come back from Europe, Betty replied, "To eat oysters."

Jim and Betty privately decided to leave for an indefinite stay abroad. Creditors somehow got wind of this and began to harass him on the eve of his self-imposed exile. Stores and shops and hotels presented claims against both Jim and Allie. "They woo you on the way in," Walker observed, "and sue you on the way out."

When creditors sought to attach the Walker properties, it was found that the man who had been so freely accused of graft had but a small equity in the old home on St. Luke's Place. He also possessed no large sums of money. Had it not been for the generosity of friends, themselves trounced by the economic depression, it is conceivable that Jim could not have left the country without great embarrassment. Any gifts which now came to him—and they were necessarily less lavish than in other days—could not be said to have been made for sinister reasons. Jim could grant no political favors as a private citizen.

Newman did what he could to free his idol from lawsuits and other material worries. From some creditors he received promises to postpone litigation, and from others their consent to adjust immediate claims. He sacrificed his own available moneys, and borrowed from Robert Hague and others, to supply Walker with enough cash to pay for his passage to Europe and to defray expenses incidental to a stay abroad.

After Newman had got together a last twelve thousand five hundred dollars, Jim made ready to leave as secretly as possible aboard the *Conte Grande*. A demand for ten thousand by an obdurate creditor left him with only twenty-five hundred in his pocket. On his way to the pier on the day of his departure Walker was asked by a stranger to lend him ten dollars. Jim shrugged his shoulders and handed the man fifty.

As it was late in the travel season, there were only about fifty or sixty people traveling first class. The names of Walker, Betty Compton, and Mrs. Florence Compton were not entered on the printed passenger list, but on the afternoon of November 10, 1932, word reached Park Row city desks that Walker and his beloved were aboard the liner. Reporters and photographers soon arrived on the scene, but no county or district leaders came across town to see the deposed Jimmy off as in the days of hurrah and carnival; not even a clubhouse hanger-on arrived at the pier shed.

It happened that four ship newsmen were sailing on the *Conte Grande* as guests of the Italian line. They had been assigned to return to America on the maiden voyage of the *Conte de Savoia*. These men have provided me with their respective logs of the voyage that carried into exile the man who was still loved by hundreds of thousands of New Yorkers, no matter who had charged him with having done what. He had not whimpered. Ill or well, he held up his head. New Yorkers greatly admire that quality in a beaten man; it is not a city in which a howling loser should give an audition.

Ship news reporter James Edmund Duffy of the *World-Telegram*, one of the waterfront "greats," made this voyage. It had been Duffy's day off duty, and he went aboard late, completely unaware that Walker and Betty were on the ship. Duffy found the passageways in the vicinity of the suites thronged with reporters and photographers.

The pressmen were uncertain as to which suite Walker occupied, so a reporter and a photographer stood on guard at the door of every stateroom aft. When Walker did not put in an appearance the reporters began to grumble among themselves. It was not like Jim, they reasoned, to be aloof or evasive with journalists. They knocked on every door and shouted out angrily for Walker to show himself.

Duffy recalls that someone among the crowd said loudly, "So that's what a dame can do to a good guy like Jimmy Walker!"

The whistle blew. The hawsers were cast off, and the departing liner, her lights shimmering in November's early-coming darkness, backed into the stream and headed down the Hudson.

"For once," Duffy says, "debonair Jimmy Walker, who loved to trade wisecracks with reporters and pose in his natty clothes, quit without even a word of farewell. It may have been that he was being advised by Betty. I know that she was bitterly angry at everything and everybody for having to leave New York. She afterward told me that neither of them really wanted to go away."

Meanwhile Walker stood at the port in his stateroom to take a last look—for what was to be three years—at the city in which he had been born and reared and over which he had presided. "I had little more in the way of money than my father possessed when he arrived from Ireland so long ago," he told me later. "I thought of the thrill he must have felt at seeing a much lower skyline than I now looked upon. I saw the skyscrapers, their many windows glowing, then the tip of Manhattan receding. From my side of the ship

I could not see the torch of Liberty. A sad feeling came over me, but New York still seemed an enchantress, even to the eyes of one who was going away."

Duffy and his colleagues, Frank Jay Markey, Nat J. Ferber, and Carl D. Groat, received wireless messages from their respective journals to keep a close eye on Walker and Betty. Jim was a private citizen now, yet continued to be a public figure.

Duffy says that Walker did not put in an appearance among the passengers that first night. The next night he was seen at late dinner with Betty. He seemed haggard and downcast, nibbled at his food, then retired to his cabin immediately after dinner. He came on deck late the next afternoon.

"I am going to Europe on a confidential business matter of a personal nature," he told the reporters, "the origin of which I cannot discuss at this time."

"That's a good speech," Markey said, "but it means nothing."

When asked if he planned while abroad to take over an American sales agency for a French champagne company, Walker replied, "Perhaps. But I'd rather buy the stuff than sell it."

Other than having wine with his meals, Jim did no drinking. He was ill for several days, not seasick, "but just plain sick as hell." The weather, while not rough, remained gray and foreboding. Rain fell frequently. There were no starlit nights. In the dark hours at sea, a small wind set up a refrain which sounded, Jim said, like a flute solo played by a repentant murderer in a prison orchestra.

Each evening Duffy, at Jim's request, danced with Betty. "Jim was not the happy, carefree wisecracker of old," Duffy says. "I often found him standing by the rail, looking out at the sea, frequently for long periods, as if reviewing in his mind his past life and wondering if he had it to do over again would he have acted differently. He did not seem to have the vitality for wisecracks. He talked to few persons aboard."

At other times Walker would lie back on the steamer chair, his cap over his face, and seldom move. When the ship neared Gibraltar Walker frowned. "I never want to see that Rock or a Prudential Life Insurance Company calendar again."

By the time the ship reached Italian waters Jim seemed more like his former self. He talked of his days in Albany, of his boyhood in New York, and of how the great city had changed.

The *Conte Grande* docked at a long, open pier in Naples harbor on a drizzling afternoon. As the hawsers were being made fast, Walker and Duffy were leaning on the railing. A voice, a loud one, which Duffy says echoed across the Bay of Naples, shrilled the old battle cry of "Jeemy Walker!" Other voices joined in. An amazing change in manner came over Walker, much as when a talented but weary actor responds to a cue for an entrance upon the stage and quite suddenly is transfigured. He lost his dejected, spiritless behavior of the last several days. He seemed suddenly healthy, alert, and once again the Beau James of legend.

"Those yells," he said with a smile, "sound like a Pete McGuinness rally in Greenpoint."

Betty ran over to where Jim stood to ask who the cheering people might be. Walker replied, "Just some of my constituents here on a forced vacation."

The adulatory shouts continued. "Maybe if you made a deal with Mussolini," Duffy remarked, "you could run for mayor here."

Jim raised a brow. "I never make political deals. Anyway, I'd rather be mayor of Greenwich Village than emperor of Rome."

While the gangplank was being secured, a somewhat stout, well-dressed Italian, hoarsely calling out "Jeemy," was spied by Walker among the crowd below on the pier.

"Well!" Jim shouted down to the man, "if it isn't my old pal, Commendatore Graziano! Thanks for coming down from Rome to meet me." The Commendatore bowed and basked in the prominence accorded him by Walker.

The ovation bestowed on Walker made his fellow passengers feel that they had not given him enough attention on the way across, and they too began to cheer. The demonstration seemed a miraculous restorative to Jim's health and spirits, but once or twice Duffy saw a twitch of the lip and what looked like a tear in Walker's eye; but Walker kept on smiling, once again the jaunty cockalorum of his heyday. To see Jim snap out of the doldrums made the newspapermen happy.

"During the time Jim was mayor," Duffy says, "he was the world's celebrity. I learned this at ship news. Seldom did a visitor who never before had been in the country fail to ask, 'And how is Jimmy Walker?' It did not make any difference what part of the world they had come from—they all knew Jimmy, at least by name. They had read of his exploits or had seen him in his happy poses in the newsreels with smiling and cheering crowds of New Yorkers all around him. In my opinion, New York never produced a more celebrated or better-loved public official or citizen."

Led by the officious Commendatore, the crowd at Naples surged up the long gangplank to the deck. With a burst of unintelligible words, the Commendatore embraced Walker. Soon everyone who could manage to do so thronged about Jim in the smoking saloon. Champagne corks popped in salvos. Such welcomers as could not get into the saloon stood out on deck and put their heads through the windows.

After the party was over Jim told the Commendatore that he wished to buy an Italian velour fedora, and he asked Duffy to go along to help select it. The pier was not far from the shopping center of Naples, and the party soon found a hat store. A band of boys, following after Walker, kept repeating his name.

Jim tried on several velour fedoras before making his choice. Then he snapped the brim at the proper angle, sauntered out to the street, and suggested having a drink. The attentive Commendatore recommended the Excelsior, the best hotel in the city, but Jim said he preferred a small place with some atmosphere.

The Commendatore obligingly guided his companions to a quarter that lay below the drive which skirts the Bay of Naples. Here were the restaurants where the Neopolitans met in the evenings to eat, drink, and sing. In the one they entered not a soul appeared to greet the party. The Commendatore proceeded to clap his hands so vigorously that the proprietor ran excitedly out of the kitchen. The café owner recognized Walker at once. Other employees now emerged, buttoning their waiters' coats as they came.

After drinks had been set up Jim said, "How about a little music?"

The Commendatore and the host went into action. A timid little man soon appeared in the doorway and played a tune on a violin. "Too sad," Jim said. "It makes me think about some of the things I'm trying to forget."

There was a volley of Italian from the Commendatore, and a cornet player, as if he had been waiting outside for just such an emergency, blared into the room. Jim shook his head, and another fellow, mustached and sad of eye, entered from the street, strumming a guitar. "I ought to be up on a balcony for this one," Jim remarked. That ended the guitar serenade.

Now the braying of a trombone was heard offstage. Jim announced that the piano was his favorite instrument, and the trombonist was stopped.

Everyone was hilarious by this time. The Commendatore had found a covered piano at the rear of the café and was yelling in Italian for the proprietor to wheel the piano to the Walker table so that the distinguished visitor could play it. The host, however, said that the instrument was in such a state of disrepair that he would be forever disgraced were Jeemy Walker to hear its tone.

A short while later Walker and Duffy and the Commendatore rose from the table and left the place. Outside, they saw their host and two of his men trundling a piano down the sidewalk. They had borrowed it from the owner of a near-by café. "I hope," Jim said, "the neighbors don't think those guys are installment men."

The *Conte Grande* left Naples that night with the Walker party aboard. The next afternoon Jim, Betty, Mrs. Compton, and their Aberdeen pup, went ashore at Villefranche. Duffy and the newspapermen said good-by to Jim on the quay of that quaint town on the French Riviera.

In Nice, Walker stayed at the Villa Variety, which has been described by writer Frank Scully, a fellow guest, as "a Moorish hunk of mortar and cement, a big house with red tile floors that shone like mirrors, a garden, six terraces and porches, and formerly the site where the customs were collected."

When Walker first arrived there he told Scully that he wished to avoid publicity. That same day a copy of *Variety*, three weeks old, reached him. In that theatrical trade journal there appeared a story that a magazine was offering Walker fifty thousand dollars for his memoirs. Jim decided to follow up this opportunity.

On January 10, 1933, a newsreel "clip" released in New York showed Jim "at work" on his "memoirs," with Betty supposedly taking dictation from him and Frank Scully present on the scene as literary adviser. Scully had been chosen by Jim to ghostwrite the proposed Walker autobiography, "Letters I Forgot to Mail." Scully was also commissioned to do magazine articles under Miss Compton's signature, a series to be entitled "Knocking the X out of Madame X."

Eventually Walker abandoned this project, although he needed the money badly. Too many lives would be hurt.

That January Walker fell ill with influenza. His moving from one hotel to another somehow gave rise to a report that he had died. When told of this rumor, he said, "The wish must have been father to the thought."

In March of 1933 Allie Walker sued Jim for divorce. A complaint filed by her attorneys in a Miami, Florida, court charged that Walker had deserted her in 1928. Mrs. Walker just recently disclosed to me her private views of a situation which she has hitherto declined to speak of for publication.

"Jim found himself in too deep at last," Mrs. Walker said in a letter to me. "After he went to Europe Jim wrote that it would be best for me, as well as for him, that I divorce him. This I was most reluctant to do; but he made it clear that if I did not, he would be forced to do so in Paris. He had so many connections there that I knew he could do that without any difficulty; and, furthermore, I had no funds to fight it. I talked to him by transatlantic telephone several times, and we arranged matters. That is, I thought so; but for the first time Jim failed to keep his promises, and I have never received the financial benefits I was promised. I asked for nothing in the divorce action, relying upon his word. . . . I had spent much time in Florida and abroad in the previous years to avoid embarrassment, and lived as happily as was possible away from Jim. . . . He was the light of my life, and still shines in my heart."

Allie Walker never saw Jim again.

On April 19, 1933, Betty Compton and James J. Walker were married at Cannes. The civil ceremony was performed by Mayor Cazagnaire at the City Hall in the presence of Mrs. Compton and Dr. Joseph Fischer. Walker gave his age as fifty-one and that of his new bride as twenty-eight.

Outside the municipal building a large crowd waited. The former Mayor, hatless, held his hands over his face when photographers sought to take his picture. He and Betty got into a limousine and were driven to their hotel.

That same day in New York, Tammany Hall elected Mayor John P. O'Brien as a sachem to succeed Walker.

There were strong rumors, which Jim had read in the newspapers, that his second marriage would cause Church officials at Rome to announce a severe penalty against him. That he felt concerned over this matter is indicated by a letter he wrote at Vichy, ten days before the civil ceremony at Cannes. He did not put this letter in the mail, nor do we know why he didn't do so. The letter, written in Walker's hand and addressed to the rector of the American College in Rome, follows in part:

Dear Monsignor Breslin:

At the risk of imposing upon an old friendship that I value, I am enclosing a newspaper clipping just received from New York. It may just be another newspaper story—but I am keenly interested—may I ask (if it is not a violation) is there anything in it? I wish beyond any expression there is—I don't want to be outside looking in. Should there be nothing to it, I would be very grateful if you could send me a summary of the grounds upon which a petition might be considered. . . ."

Betty's friends have said that the impulsive, strong-willed young woman now became almost meek in her new marital happiness. She sincerely respected Walker, looked up to him, loved him, and declared that their way together would forever be a joyous experience, shared by them away from all public snarls and criticisms.

32.

The Thatch and Other Things

Soon after the wedding Betty fell ill. Her mother crossed over from England, where she had been residing since her daughter's marriage. Mrs. Compton was building a cottage near the village of Dorking in Surrey, at an estimated cost of less than the equivalent of seven thousand American dollars. She showed the Walkers the architect's drawings.

It was one of Betty's keenest pleasures to build, alter, or renovate any place in which she or her friends became interested. She examined the plans, then said with an air of challenge, "If you are building this with the slightest idea that *we* are going to live there, stop. Because we're *not* coming to England to live."

"No?" asked Mrs. Compton. "Well, I read that Mr. Hearst has asked Jim to write a column on the World Economic Conference in London. And I was thinking that—"

"I'm not the least bit interested in that type of house," Betty interrupted. "And I don't want to live in England."

However, the Walkers went to London that summer, and Jim received an assignment from Joseph V. Connolly to write daily pieces for Hearst's International News Service. His articles lacked the professional touch, for his talents lay with the spoken rather than the written word. Westbrook Pegler said of this newspaper column that Jim couldn't wiggle his eyebrows in print.

The new Hearst reporter called upon George Bernard Shaw for advice. Betty went along. She found that the bearded cynic actually was an amiable gallant.

In the Shaw apartment overlooking the Thames, Walker's host said that the forthcoming congress of international experts should be called a "World Idiotic Conference."

"What is the unemployed man going to think of it," Mr. Shaw observed to Jim, "when a statesman says, 'You're going to be all right now; we're going to raise prices'?"

"That reminds me," Walker replied, "of the story of the impecunious Irishman whose landlord visited him to say, 'I'm going to raise your rent.' The Irishman replied, 'Thank God for that! I can't.' "

When Walker inquired about how to procure news on the Economic Conference, his host snorted. "Don't expect to get anything from the so-called statesmen. Do your own lobbying. Leave the statesmen and the banking lunatics alone."

Mr. Shaw asked Betty how she was enjoying London. When he learned that the English-born beauty planned to visit relatives whom she had not seen for twenty-two years, the sage remarked, "Let me warn you, young lady, stay away from relatives. People without relatives ought to thank God for it."

Mr. Shaw's parting comment was that all public speakers should be destroyed or given a dose of cocaine to silence them. To which Walker replied, "Well, I've made a lot of speeches myself, but, speaking as a reporter, maybe you're right."

During the summer months of 1933 a federal grand jury in New York examined Walker's income tax returns for the "boom" years. Russell T. Sherwood appeared before this jury. While under New York State jurisdiction the accountant was given immunity from arrest for the contempt-of-court decree which still obtained there.

Sherwood denied that he had at any time discussed his departure from New York, during the Seabury investigation, with Mayor Walker or with anyone other than Fred Harris of the Bank of Manhattan, of which bank Sherwood had been an employee. The Walker tax inquiry was dropped late in August. The former Mayor was held innocent of tax evasion, in the eyes of this Federal grand jury, which for three months had made an extensive inquiry into the Walker records. A similar probe, however, was to be undertaken in 1935. The threat of repeated exposures to investigation, as well as the pounding by creditors, had much to do with Jim's decision to remain abroad.

Walker made an excursion to Italy late in July of 1933. Betty stayed in London. From Rome, Jim went to Venice.

William Gaxton, on a holiday from Broadway, found the former Mayor on the beach at the Lido. What Gaxton saw was a lone figure, dressed in sports clothes and seated on a piece of driftwood. Gaxton had not notified Jim of his coming. There were no people gathered about Walker as he gazed out at the Adriatic. Gaxton thought that his friend seemed lost, little, forlorn.

"Hello, Jim," said Gaxton.

Walker rose with a start. He embraced his friend. "You'll have to give me a little time to get hold of myself, Billy," he said.

"You're looking fine," Gaxton said in his best white-lie manner.

"I'm not so good, but I feel better with you here. How's Broadway?"

"Fine."

"I read about the closing of *Of Thee I Sing* and that you were coming to Europe. But I didn't think you'd get this far south."

"I came to see you, Jim."

"Not so many people come to see me now, Billy."

"Well," said Gaxton, "that must be your own fault. You never had any trouble making friends."

"Billy," Jim said, "I've been thinking about the old friends. I guess I think about them all the time now. Cohan, Jolson, Cantor, Fanny Brice, Roger Davis, Charlie Silver, Bob Hague, Jessel, and the rest."

"What about this fellow Mussolini?" Gaxton asked.

Walker promptly kicked Billy's shin. "Don't mention his name," he whispered. "The whole place is full of spies. Even if you said something laudatory about him these people might not understand." Walker then said louder, "Why, I haven't seen my pal Mr. Smith for a long time," and veered back to a discussion of Broadway friends. He was thirsty for news of them, homesick for the street on which he had long been a bright and active figure. For the next three hours Walker listened to Gaxton's Broadway report.

Then, with tears in his eyes, he said, "I'd like to be home."

"Why don't you come back, Jim?"

"I don't know." After a long silence Walker went on, as though speaking to himself, "A lot of things have caught up with me. It's not too good. There must be a way somewhere, somehow, for a man to get back. I don't mean politically. I mean with himself."

Gaxton canceled the rest of his tour and remained in Venice with Jim. Billy recalls that Walker was having a great struggle with himself. He was shy, reticent, stayed in his quarters, went alone for gondola rides. Billy, who resembled Jim in appearance, went about town with the Walker swagger and was mistaken for him. Gaxton accepted the adulation of the Venetians and spoke kindly to Jim's admirers.

Billy reported this to Walker, who then decided to go out in public. He seemed to forget some of his woes. When someone whom Billy had met while posing as Walker came up to renew the acquaintanceship, Jim entered into the spirit of the thing. He pretended to "recall" conversations which Gaxton had had with numerous "friends."

By the time Billy Gaxton left Venice his friend had shaken off some of his melancholia; but there were still moments when Jim seemed to be struggling upon what he called "his personal road back."

When Robert Newman visited the Walkers in England in 1934 he was met by Betty and Jim at the boat-train. The Walkers were staying at the Park Lane Hotel and invited him to tea there.

At the hotel Walker suddenly looked up from his teacup. "Monk, let's go home."

"What home?" Newman interposed. "New York?"

"Mother's home," Betty replied sweetly. "She's got a cottage in Surrey. Remember?"

"But," Newman said, "I thought you said you hated the plans for that house and would not live in England?"

"Wait till you see what I've done to it. I've added on a room for Jim and me."

"You know the Monk, Bobby," Jim said. "She takes over whenever there's a house handy. The Duchess has lost the cottage to her.

My good mother-in-law should have played the races instead—she would have had a better run for her money."

Newman motored with the Walkers to their country cottage in a Rolls-Royce limousine lent to them by Sir Louis Sterling. Sir Louis was a Grand Street Boy who years before had gone from the poverty-stricken environment of a New York tenement house to England. There he had established himself in the gramophone and music-publishing business, and had achieved wealth, prominence, and a title. Sir Louis and Lady Sterling were loyal friends of the Walkers and often came to their rescue financially and otherwise.

The Walkers called their cottage "The Thatch." It stood close by the tiny village of Dorking in Surrey, about an hour out of London by train or car. A pub and a few small places of business were within easy walking distance of The Thatch.

It was a neighborhood of pleasant lanes lined with ancient trees. Across from the Walker house was a girls' school. About a quarter of a mile up the lane one of the few hills of the countryside rose gently above the narrow road. Romantic couples would climb Box Hill (and doubtless do so today, unless something has occurred to change young natures) to look out upon the pleasant landscape—or so they said.

When Betty first saw the foundations of native stone being laid for her mother's house she immediately began to supervise everything connected with the construction of the cottage. She drove the contractor, Mr. McCready, an unusually calm man, almost out of his mind.

Betty got into all sorts of altercations with the workmen. She designed herbaceous borders. She had an extra room built on, and then a bathroom. The house originally was small. One walked right into the living-room, and off it was a dining alcove. There was a bedroom, which was Mrs. Compton's, and another small bedroom. Betty and Jim took the side of the house opposite the Duchess's boudoir, occupying a large bedroom in that wing. Betty added a thatch roof to the house. She redesigned the terrace. There was a garret upstairs, which Betty made into a sewing-room. The servants slept there. As Jim had no car, the ten Walker trunks were kept in the garage.

At the rear of the house, which Betty was continually remodeling and redecorating, there was a kitchen garden. Tomato plants grew there, and runner beans, and a squash-like vegetable called marrow, which the English esteem but which Jim said tasted like a bath sponge.

The night Newman arrived at The Thatch a squawk was going on about a draft in the chimney. It was early in the spring of the year, and quite chill and damp. All that first evening was spent by Betty trying to hang a mirror on the wall above the sofa. She couldn't get it placed to her satisfaction. Finally she asked Newman to fix it while she gave directions. The tired Newman at last went to bed—on the sofa. He was just falling asleep when Betty appeared in her negligee and again began discussing the problem. He dropped off to sleep while she was talking. When he awoke next morning, Betty was standing near the couch, telling a strange man, one of the builders, how to "fix the mirror."

It happened that when anyone looked into this mirror he could see plainly reflected in it the bedroom door of the Walker sleeping quarters. If the door was open, one had a view of part of the interior of that private room.

Once when Walker was dressing for a walk to Box Hill, Betty opened the bedroom door to warn him that the plump, middle-aged Vicar was coming toward the house. Jim said to tell the minister that he had gone to London. He liked the Vicar well enough but sometimes grew restless in his company.

Betty neglected to close the bedroom door.

By this time the Vicar had been admitted to the living-room by a servant. "It's so unfortunate," said Betty, greeting the Vicar in her friendliest tone, "that Jim is in London. And I'm worried about him, Vicar, because it's so very cold and damp today. I'll tell him that—"

Betty left off speaking. The Vicar was gazing into the mirror, a look of astonishment on his face. All eyes were drawn to the mirror. Reflected in it was Walker, framed perfectly by the doorway to the bedroom. Completely innocent of the fact that his performance was being witnessed, he was dancing up and down and making faces—clad only in underwear, a long lisle union suit, made to his own specifications, of course, and intended to protect him from the dampness of the English spring.

"Good day then, Mrs. Walker," said the Vicar, recovering himself. "I, too, hope that your good husband has dressed adequately for this cold morning in London."

The mischievous Betty did not tell Jim of his mirror-display. An hour later, strolling along the lane with his dog, Walker encountered the Vicar on the way to Box Hill and bowed respectfully. "Why, Vicar," he said, "we haven't seen you of late at The Thatch."

"I was there this morning," replied the Vicar.

"Oh! You were? Why don't people confide these things in me?"

"You were in London."

"Hmmm!" Jim began to give commands to his dog. "Behave yourself now."

"I trust," said the Vicar, "that you didn't catch a fresh cold?"

"Not at all, sir. Never felt better."

Life at The Thatch seemed to bring Walker a measure of peace. He would go to London on Thursday afternoons to meet friends at the American bar in the Savoy Hotel and to hear at first hand the news from home: what Sime Silverman of *Variety* said just before he died; and how gallant Texas Guinan had been when her colorful life closed in faraway Vancouver. He visited at the Savoy on these Thursdays with Otto H. Kahn, Jack Lait, Bob Hague, Sophie Tucker—friends whom he never forgot and who never forgot him.

Big Jim Farley, now Postmaster General, wrote Jim long and informative letters. In one of them, dated May 15, 1933, Farley said in part:

> I have been busy at times during my lifetime, Jim, but I have never experienced what I have gone through since March 4. It has been a veritable madhouse at Washington from early morning until late at night; the pressure is simply terrible. In addition to my Post Office duties, I have to handle (or direct, if you will) the entire patronage situation. . . . In my opinion, no one would have gone along with me better than the President. . . . He is making a great record, Jim, and right now has a position in this country never before, in my judgment, accorded to a chief executive. He has amazed everyone around him, and everyone with whom he comes in contact. For your information, he himself is directing the show, but, of course, has around him a lot of capable fellows who personally are able to assist him greatly.

Farley also said in this letter:

> Jim, if there is anything in this world that I can do to help you in the slightest degree, it will be my pleasure and privilege to do so, and you may be assured that I will not forget you.

Farley never did forget Walker. While on a long-deferred holiday in Europe the Postmaster General called on Jim in Paris. On his return to New York he was criticized for this by Judge Seabury, who had been on a European vacation at the same time. Of the Farley-Walker reunion Seabury said, "It was not an edifying sight to see the Postmaster General of the United States make a pilgrimage to meet Mr. Walker, and to hear that he eulogized him in Paris. Take this as you like it. I think it was a disgusting spectacle."

In reply Farley observed, "Walker and I have been personal friends, as everyone knows, for twenty years. Perhaps Judge Seabury can't understand what it really means to love a friend."

About this time Walker received a letter from his brother saying that the old home in St. Luke's Place had been sold. There had been a threat to foreclose the mortgage on it. The taxes had not been paid during the year 1934. It took fourteen hundred dollars a year to carry the house. Creditors had agreed to take twenty-five per cent of the eighteen thousand dollars, the purchase price. Nothing was left of this for Jim, but he said it was all right that way. No one could foreclose on the memories of his boyhood in the old home, the bright recollections of Rosie, of the Boss, and of the night when he had written "Will You Love Me in December as You Do in May."

Jim would not stay in London long. After his visits in town, he would take Bus 9 for Waterloo Station and return by train to the country.

When Fanny Holtzman, an American attorney with an immense zest for people who were having a rocky time of it, first saw Jim taking the bus, she said, "That proves to me that Jim Walker has no money, or he'd be riding to the station in a private limousine."

"Fanny," Jim said to her one day, "it's a thrill for me to commute to Dorking. All my life I'd seen commuters, carrying bundles, coming and going to and from New York. I never knew until now what a great pleasure I was missing."

Fanny often invited Jim and Betty to join the informal and intimate parties she gave at her studio apartment located in a wing of the Kinnerton Studio on Wilton Place, back of Lowndes Square, in Knightsbridge. That building originally had been a portion of the manor house of Lord Lumley. It afterward became part of the estate of the Duke of Westminster. Because of its excellent exposure to the north light, it had been a favorite residence of artists. Mrs. Bram Stoker, widow of the author of *Dracula,* also lived there. The cobbled courtyard and gates, the housekeeper in his green baize apron, gave the place a quaint early eighteenth-century flavor.

Fanny Holtzman entertained many persons of importance, among them the Duke of Kent and former King George of Greece. Jim and Betty had not been "taken up" at first by members of royalty, because at that time it was felt that Jim had left America under a cloud. But soon after the members of that "set" talked with Walker at the Holtzman parties, Jim became their favorite.

When Fanny invited Betty and Jim to meet ex-King George of Greece for the first time, the hostess requested the former monarch to leave his monocle at home and wear horn-rimmed glasses instead, so as not to spoil the democratic aspect of the occasion. The onetime King and the ex-Mayor soon became buddies.

Walker told him, "Your Majesty, you and I made one terrible mistake."

"What was it?" asked the exiled ruler.

"We both neglected to take out unemployment insurance."

Fanny often went with Betty and Jim to select antique pieces of furniture for The Thatch. Sir Louis Sterling lent his Rolls-Royce for these expeditions. The eccentric proprietress of one antique shop told Walker that she was the reincarnation of Nell Gwyn. This crone wore a costume patterned after the style of the mistress of Charles II. Her son also clothed himself in seventeenth-century garb. Walker, of course, was enchanted by the old girl's whim, and bought from her a so-called Holbein painting. He even went so far as to kiss her hand.

"My dear Miss Gwyn," he said, "what I am looking for in your charming establishment are some *genuine* reproductions."

One thing that worried Jim most was the fact that he was compelled at times to borrow money from Betty to pay their expenses. She had invested her savings in gold, according to Newman. When the United States raised the price of gold, Betty profited by her investment.

Betty worked for a short time at a motion-picture studio at Teddington on the Thames, in Middlesex, southwest of London. The Warner Brothers producer there was Irving Asher. Jim had been best man at Asher's marriage to film star Laura La Plante in Paris in 1934. Betty became quite nervous while she was working. She had arguments with her director and insisted, against his advice, upon doing a dance routine to the tune of "Shine on Harvest Moon."

When Mrs. Asher was expecting a child, the Walkers turned over

The Thatch to the producer and his wife, so that Mrs. Asher might escape the excitement of London. The Walkers went to the Continent. The Walker servants, as well as their several dogs and cats, remained at The Thatch.

About four and a half months before the Asher baby was expected, Mrs. Asher was in bed with a fever. One night the Walker maid, a quiet-spoken woman, came into the bedroom. "Pardon me, Madam," she said, "but The Thatch is alight."

"Thank you very much," said Mrs. Asher. "Tell the gardener to take care of it."

The obedient servant went outside for a moment or so, then came back. This time her British restraint was shaken. Her eyes were wide. She exclaimed, "Madam!"

This word was followed by a smashing, crashing sound. Part of the roof collapsed in flames. Mrs. Asher barely escaped with her life. The fire department, which consisted of two men, responded with its apparatus. They might have been able to save part of the house but, when they attached their hose to the hydrant, there was hardly any water pressure. Soon all that was left standing of The Thatch were the walls, the chimney, and some twisted plumbing.

An investigation was begun next day. The fire was officially said to have been caused by defective wiring. A report, however, soon spread that Walker had induced Asher to start the fire in order to destroy a mass of incriminating papers locked up in the garret.

The fact was that Jim did have a great many books, letters, and keepsakes stored in the attic. All his official papers, however, had been left in New York, as his executor, Sidney Harris, and I myself can now attest.

In response to a cablegram from Asher, Jim crossed the Channel to view the ruins of the home in which he had enjoyed a brief time of serenity. But his only concern was for Mrs. Asher.

The thatch that had been put on the roof was guaranteed to have been fireproofed. Jim said, "This demonstrates that it was done."

Upon taking up their residence at The Thatch, the Ashers had brought with them from their London house all their wedding presents and many other things of value, but had forgotten to notify the insurance people of their change of address. Technically their policy had been canceled. The insurance firm, however, insisted upon paying Asher the full amount of his loss.

When Asher said, "But I am not insured really," a representative of the company replied, "Oh, we know that, Mr. Asher. But you simply made a mistake, and we do not want you to suffer for it."

When Jim heard of this, he observed, "As much as I love America, if this courtesy had happened in any business there, I know that I would have had apoplexy."

Attorney General Cummings let it be known in Washington, in March of 1934, that Walker's income-tax matters were once again under scrutiny. In January of 1935 United States Attorney Martin Conboy said in New York that the case was still under investigation. Jim and Betty were at this time traveling in Spain.

On February 25, 1935, Walker appeared in Chancery Court, London, to answer suits brought by several American business firms for bills incurred by him and his former wife. On March 5 Jim was served with a bankruptcy notice. He did not, as has been widely reported, take the "Pauper's Oath" in the city in which he once had ridden in the Lord Mayor's coach of state.

When Jim's finances were lowest, and demands were being made that he register as an alien or leave England, he received a heartwarming letter from Jim Farley, who wrote on June 10, 1935:

> The President is standing up well under all the pounding. There are a lot of cross currents, of course, but frankly, Jim, I am not at all disturbed about the ultimate outcome [of the forthcoming national election]. I am going to show your letter to the President, and I know that he will be happy to read it. He frequently asks for you, and no matter what is said to the contrary, Jim, he always has had a friendly feeling toward you.

When a second federal grand jury again found no discrepancy in Walker's income tax reports, one of the highest officers of national government expressed himself to the effect that: If, after two extensive and intensive searches by federal grand juries, and two investigations into Walker's tax affairs, any violation of the law were shown, then let Walker be brought to account. On the other hand, if, as now seemed evident, no evidence of conspiracy or evasion were to be found, then Walker should be treated exactly as any other citizen in like circumstances, and any further dogging of the former mayor should be stopped at once.

On August 27 the income tax charges against Walker were dropped.

Walker received this news during a holiday in Killarney, Ireland. Attorney Nathan Burkan and Robert Newman both cabled their congratulations.

The *New York Times*, in an editorial, said on August 31, 1935:

The decision of the Treasury officials that they have no case which would stand up in court against ex-Mayor Walker for income tax evasions was followed by general expectation that he would soon come back to New York. The government is so stern a creditor that he might well shrink from facing it. If he has other creditors here, they will doubtless be glad to meet him with every form of tolerance and indulgence. It is even predicted that, if and when he comes—and as yet no positive announcement of his purpose has been made by him—he will have a triumphant reception in this city. That may well be believed. . . . It would be a kind of opening of hearts and hands for one who always was a popular favorite here, and very likely still is personally. . . . It is probably true that he retains a firm hold on the affections of the multitude.

James J. Walker hummed the Cohan tune "Give My Regards to Broadway" and turned his eyes toward home.

33.

Home Again

SIR LOUIS STERLING had advised Walker to return to America before the summer was over to take advantage of business or professional offers which had come Jim's way.

From Vichy—where Betty insisted that Jim remain until his health permitted a voyage home—Walker wrote to Newman:

It is not only Sterling's opinion that I go home soon, but the opinion of others, that nothing worth while will ever develop until I remove the thought from some subconscious minds that I don't dare, or can't return to New York.

In this letter Walker wrote of Betty:

You know the Monk has many inhibitions, fears, and some prejudices that do not promise any great joy for her, but if it is the thing to do [to return to America] she will do it. However, I think modesty, dignity, and quiet on our part will be more productive of desired results than ballyhoo. I don't want the impression to develop that I think I am going to show them anything of that kind.

When Walker learned that an organized celebration was being planned for his homecoming, he requested Newman to do everything he could to discourage the enterprise. He wanted no public demonstration. In a second letter to Newman, he wrote:

> Modesty is not only a virtue but an asset. It would take pages to describe my notions of the psychology of the whole thing. I can either get some place in a dignified way that will endure, or I can recklessly wear out a perfect opportunity, and be a mug in thirty days. . . . To exploit my friends and their sympathy and well wishes might very well appear vulgar. Human sentiment and sympathy naturally run to whatever they think savors of martyrdom, but it is dangerous for the martyr to look as if he was bragging about it. . . . In my opinion, it would be a disgusting hunk of presumption for anyone after a long absence to act as if he thought he could walk back into the town and deliver the people and the political organizations for his own personal use. . . . The loyalty of large groups of people I never met, who never lost confidence in my integrity, I shall never forget, but I refuse to exploit them for political office.

Walker's New York friends were casting about for a city job which the former Mayor might take in order to qualify for a pension. Walker had not been consulted as to this ill-advised plan. When he resigned in September of 1932 Walker had the required twenty years of public service behind him, but had not attained the qualifying age of fifty-five years, which would have permitted him to retire on an annual pension of more than fifteen thousand dollars. He would be fifty-five a few months after his proposed return, and would then lack but one other qualification for retirement on a pension: to be in the city service. If he had a job with the city and held it for but thirty days, he would qualify.

This proposal brought immediate adverse criticism. It was mistakenly assumed that Walker himself had devised the plan. The matter was soon dropped.

The Walkers, Mrs. Compton, Sir Louis and Lady Sterling, ten Walker trunks, twenty bags, and two kennels containing Jim's dogs were aboard the *Manhattan* at Southampton, England, on the evening of October 25. The liner lay wrapped in a thick fog. Jim announced to press correspondents that he was through with politics, and that politics also was through with him.

Notwithstanding Walker's request that there be no reception for him in New York, various clubs—the Friars, Lambs, Elks, Grand Street Boys, and others—chartered tugs to go down the Bay. Two broadcasting companies made arrangements to describe the scene. Tammany Hall bowed to Walker's wishes and named no official delegation to go to the pier, but many Tammany members were there. Former Commissioner and Mrs. Mulrooney curtailed their holiday in Bermuda to come home in time to greet Walker.

Toward noon of October 31 the *Manhattan* reached quarantine. There was a gray overcast. Jim said to Betty, "Monk, I'm none too steady. But I'm my old self in one particular—I don't know what I'll do or say."

Boat whistles tooted, and fifteen small craft came alongside the *Manhattan*, all crowded with cheering friends and displaying banners of welcome. Aboard one tug veteran song-writer Joe Howard was playing over a loudspeaker a record of "Will You Love Me in December." Walker stood at the ship's rail, waving his derby.

Robert Hague of Standard Oil of New Jersey, treasurer of the Lambs Club, Mr. and Mrs. Mulrooney, and Robert Newman had passes to go aboard the *Manhattan* when she cleared quarantine. The liner proceeded in tow to its North River pier. The accompanying small craft kept up the whistling, and ferryboats criss-crossing from Staten Island or New Jersey hoarsely saluted the homecomer.

At the pier there were thousands of greeters. The seventy police officers, ten of whom were mounted, assisted by employees of the American Steamship Lines, were unable to hold back the throng.

Mulrooney assisted Mrs. Compton down the third-class gangplank. The Duchess was recovering from a sprained ankle, and Jim feared that she might be injured again.

As Walker himself started down the main gangplank, his characteristic dread of being mauled caused him to lose his poise. He raised a hand and tried to make himself heard, but was carried almost bodily to the pier. He soon was separated from Betty. The Sterlings also fared roughly during this onrush of welcomers. Each fell in turn, and policemen rescued them.

After half an hour apart, the Walkers, breathless and nervous, were reunited and took refuge in the automobile of Dr. Shirley Wynne, former Health Commissioner. They were driven to the Chatham Hotel, where they found another crowd awaiting them.

"I used to think I knew something about receptions," Jim said. "But I find that I could give them better than I can take them."

During the next two years Walker was either unable or unwilling to accept any one of the many positions offered him. Although Betty was quite familiar with Jim's hesitancy to make up his mind, she became displeased with his present slowness. She tried her own hand at various business ventures. She opened a flower store and lost twenty-five thousand dollars on the short-lived enterprise. The Walkers leased a small farm on Long Island, where they bred Irish terriers and raised prize chickens, but they failed to make a profit.

It gradually became apparent to the public that Walker had no intention of re-entering politics. This, together with the fact that Jim never bemoaned his setbacks, helped preserve the popularity which had been his during the gay twenties.

"The reason for his vast popularity," columnist Ed Sullivan said, "was that Jimmy Walker somehow or other seemed to be New York brought to life in one person."

Joel Slonim, of the Jewish newspaper *The Day*, says that certain politicians requested Walker to confer with Al Smith's backers who in 1935 again opposed Roosevelt's nomination. This Jim declined to do.

At a dinner given by Post Office employees for James A. Farley, Walker asked that he and Betty be permitted to sit among the diners instead of on the dais. When it was time for the speeches, however, the three thousand guests in the Grand Ballroom of the Commodore Hotel raised the old cry of "Jimmy Walker."

As Jim rose to speak there was a crashing sound. A waiter bearing a tray of dishes had fallen. "Don't let that bother you a bit," Walker instantly called out to the waiter. "I slipped once myself."

It was during this speech that Walker touched upon the Smith-Roosevelt feud by saying, "I brought my riding habit from Europe, but if I do go to the convention, I'll not ride in on the donkey and then ride out on some other sort of animal." This was correctly interpreted as a gibe at Smith for threatening to bolt his party.

When in 1936 Smith made his "taking a walk" speech at Carnegie Hall, Walker delivered what he called his first and last political speech of the campaign. It was at the dedication of the New Democratic Club in his own Assembly district early in October of 1936. Jim stepped to the microphone and assailed Smith severely, although not by name, and made a political declaration for Roosevelt. There was great applause, although several pro-Smith Tammany leaders were present.

Slonim said that Walker told him, off the record, soon after Jim returned to America in 1935: "I can't imagine how any progressive person can be against President Roosevelt. . . . I feel that I have no right to be against the interests of the entire population of this country just because I once may have had some personal grievance against President Roosevelt. During the years that I lived in Europe, it became clear to me that over the whole world there is now going on a bitter struggle between liberal and reactionary elements, between progress and fascism, and the same struggle has become manifest in our own land. The defeat of liberalism will spell the rise of fascism and Hitlerism in all its ugly forms."

When Slonim questioned Jim in respect to his widely supposed hostility to the President, Walker replied, "Of course I suffered, and suffered very deeply, because of the false charges that were made against me. They were the results of a political maneuver by people who desired to be in the limelight. I have long known that if one goes in for politics, he must be prepared to take it on the chin. I have taken it on the chin many times. I have become used to it. . . . But even if my wounds were now as fresh and painful as they were at that time, I would still regard it as my duty to combat the Liberty League and Al Smith. It is not the personality of Franklin Roosevelt that is the issue in this campaign; the ideas which he represents are important. President Roosevelt has become the symbol of liberalism as opposed to reaction. Reaction goes hand in hand with racial and religious bigotry and with anti-semitism. I shall always be on the side of the masses against their oppressors."

In March of 1936 the Walkers adopted a six-week-old girl from the Evanston "Cradle." They named the child Mary Ann. The next year they adopted a baby boy, and named him "James John Walker, Jr." He was nicknamed "Jim Jim."

During the next four years, the Walkers were looked upon as a happy couple. They spent much time by themselves, or with such close friends as the Mulrooneys, the Newmans, the Hagues, and Dr. S. Sym Newman.

Dr. Newman first met Walker during the homecoming in 1935. He became Betty's physician, then Jim's. From then on he retained

Walker's affectionate esteem. Indeed, Jim said that he felt strangely ill at ease whenever he was more than a few miles away from his physician-friend. They attended boxing bouts together and called each other daily by telephone. Dr. Newman persuaded Walker to take on weight and go to bed earlier than had been the former Mayor's habit of doing.

Betty accompanied Jim to Albany in April of 1935, and they visited the Senate chamber. Jim was invited to address the senators, and was given the privilege—almost unprecedented for a non-member —of speaking from a place in the middle aisle.

In June of that year the Walkers took a brief holiday in London. When they sailed, Jim was asked if his absence from the forthcoming Democratic national convention meant he was "taking a walk."

"I never walk," he replied with a smile. "But I've run for office thirteen times."

When the Walkers returned from abroad, Jim chided Tammany Hall for having rejected the renomination of his friend General Sessions Judge Jonah Goldstein. Walker once again declared that "the brains of Tammany Hall lie in Calvary Cemetery," and suggested that Tammany members make a pilgrimage to the grave of Charles F. Murphy.

By 1937 Walker began to be seen once more as a toastmaster at banquets. The city, it seemed, had missed its foremost master of ceremonies during his exile, as well as during the next two years when he had declined to appear on a dais. Upon his initiation as a member of the Circus Saints and Sinners Club, he said, "There are two places where politicians end up, the farm and the breadline. I am a farmer—at the moment."

Walker accepted his first "regular" job in August of 1937. The State Transit Commission appointed him assistant counsel at a salary of twelve thousand a year. He was to act in behalf of the coordination of the Commission's grade-crossing elimination activities in New York City. Walker, as mayor, had brought about the abolition of "Death Avenue" on the West Side after several other administrations had failed to rid Eleventh Avenue of railway hazards.

This appointment, the Commission spokesman explained, had no bearing upon Walker's right to a pension. Samuel Seabury, however, in a letter to the Commission, attacked the appointment and characterized former Mayor Walker as "Captain of the Tin-Box Brigade."

In May of 1938 Jim Farley informed Walker that President Roosevelt would like to see him for a social hour at the White House. Walker, Betty, and Newman went to Washington. Farley lent them his apartment at the Mayflower Hotel.

Walker telephoned Secretary Marvin McIntyre for an appointment. Soon afterward, McIntyre telephoned Jim and inquired if Betty was with Walker. About half an hour later, McIntyre again called to tell Jim that the "Boss" would like Walker to bring Betty to the White House.

The President and Walker visited alone for ten minutes. Mr. Roosevelt did not mention the hearings of 1932, but spoke warmly of the old days at Albany and of old friends. He was most cordial and asked that Betty be shown in from an anteroom where she had been waiting.

Soon after the Washington trip Walker visited at City Hall for the first time since his resignation. He seemed in better health than in other years. When asked by reporters what he and Mayor La Guardia had talked about, he grinned. "We were trying to find out if Diogenes was on the level."

Several months later, when Walker as master of ceremonies introduced La Guardia at the Carnegie Hall music festival of ASCAP, Jim saluted the Little Flower as "the greatest mayor New York ever had." George M. Cohan, Irving Berlin, Joe Howard, and other members of ASCAP played or sang their old songs, and La Guardia conducted the orchestra.

Almost a year from the night Walker paid this tribute to La Guardia, the Mayor designated Jim to serve as "czar" of industrial and labor relations in the women's coat-and-suit industry at a salary of twenty thousand dollars a year and five thousand for expenses. It was believed by well-informed persons, among them Raymond Moley, that President Roosevelt, at the request of Ed Flynn, endorsed Walker's appointment as impartial chairman.

Samuel Seabury assailed La Guardia during a radio speech delivered in support of Wendell L. Willkie. Mr. Seabury charged that Mayor La Guardia had "stepped down from his position of political leadership among those who are striving for decent municipal government in the United States." He went on to say that the Walker appointment was made to get votes for President Roosevelt and that Mayor La Guardia had "adopted the tactics of his ally in the present campaign, Boss Flynn."

The Judge compared the Mayor to the lost leader of whom the poet Browning wrote: "Just for a handful of silver he left us, Just for a riband to stick in his coat."

Next day Mayor La Guardia said that he was "pained" to learn of this adverse criticism, then added: "Judge Seabury is motivated by an obsessed hatred for President Roosevelt."

Walker applied himself eagerly to his new job of solving problems affecting a two-hundred-fifty-million-dollar industry. About two thousand companies and thirty-five thousand coat-and-suit workers were under his jurisdiction. It was his first important administrative position since his resignation eight years before. All his recent professional activities had been entered upon halfheartedly and had been failures. For a time Jim had been a radio broadcaster, but his forte was speaking extemporaneously, not reciting from any page.

As impartial chairman, Walker decided disputes arising between employers and employees in the industry and ruled upon matters which the parties could not agree upon in their contractual negotiations. He managed this job with conspicuous ability and was liked equally by the company heads and the labor representatives.

As of old, Walker made playful observations about his job. "They are always buttonholing me," he once said. And of the complicated code governing the manufacture of clothes, "If a man makes good suits, he'll go broke. If he makes bad ones, he'll go to jail."

Jim was unaware that his frequent absences from Betty were re-creating in her mind the old-time feeling of loneliness. The Walkers were residing in a comparatively modest apartment in town which they had subleased, furnished, from a retired clergyman. Betty complained that the place was dismal. Walker thereupon wrote to the Irving Ashers, addressing them as his "arson-loving friends," and asked them to move into the Walker apartment to "break the lease by means of the torch."

Betty's loneliness was not the only matter which now plagued her. She became increasingly aware that Jim longed to return to the Church but could not do so while married in violation of Roman Catholic rules. Walker said but little to Betty, or to anyone else, in respect to his desire to regain religious peace. She divined, however, that he had been undergoing a spiritual conflict for considerable time.

One day in the fall of 1940 Betty asked Newman to drive her to the office of a psychoanalyst. Newman at the time paid little attention to this. He knew that she often became interested in various cults, health doctrines, and "isms," and said nothing to Jim. Not until some time later did Newman become concerned, and then only because Betty solemnly asserted that her individuality was being "lost." When Betty eventually confided to Jim that she was being psychoanalyzed, he merely lifted his brows. "Monk, you go right ahead and do anything that makes you happy."

Walker should perhaps have examined more closely into the evidences of his wife's discontent, her sleeplessness, the loneliness which, as at an earlier time, again filled her mind with dread.

One evening in February 1941, while Jim was listening to the radio in the living-room, Betty said abruptly, "Turn that off, Jim. I'm nervous."

Jim obeyed. "Why didn't you say so before, Monk? May I get you something?"

"Yes," she replied.

"What?"

"Listen, Jim," she said hesitantly, "I'm going to get a divorce."

Walker sat wordlessly for several moments and made clicking sounds with his tongue against his teeth.

"Well," Betty said, "say something."

"Monk," he replied, "we have two kids to think about. Have you thought this thing over carefully?"

"I must have a divorce."

"Monk," Jim said, as though continuing with a thought, "I have nothing to give you. That is, nothing but one thing." When she did not ask what that might be, he went on quietly, "I can only give you back to yourself."

Early in March of 1941 Betty Compton sued for divorce in Key West, Florida. Her complaint charged that Walker's return to "public life activities" and the demands made upon her as the wife of a "prominent figure" had caused her intense mental pain and had resulted in illness. The Judge dismissed this suit, ruling that Mrs. Walker had failed to prove a charge of "extreme cruelty." Betty brought suit a second time, in April, also in Florida, and obtained the decree.

Jim had instructed his attorneys, Sylvester and Harris, not to contest either of the divorce actions. The Walkers were to share equally in the custody of their two adopted children. Mary Ann was now five years old, and James, Jr., four.

Soon after the divorce Betty became dissatisfied with her new freedom, and asked Jim "to take her back." He replied, "Monk, I simply never can go back to a personal situation once I have gone away. And this time it is you who have gone away, and I think it best for you not to try to come back."

To the astonishment of Jim's friends, but not of himself, he was seen with Betty at the theatre, the cafés, and elsewhere in public. He seemed most attentive, and obviously still loved the beautiful woman who had divorced him.

"We have kids to look out for," he explained to Robert Newman. "It's important to keep our adult troubles from them."

"That's a lot of nonsense," said Newman, who loved both the Walkers. "Why don't you give the real reason?"

"The kids are the two real reasons."

"No," Newman said. "Betty is the real reason. You love her, and she loves you. If you're going to hang around together, why not remarry?"

"It's better this way, Bobby."

For a time the Walkers resided in separate apartments in the same building. Betty again decided to write a series of articles, this time for a magazine published by an elderly vegetarian. She informed Jim that at a dinner in her apartment she had forgotten the editor's abhorrence of meat and had served a thick steak.

One night when Jim was coming home, he met the publisher and Betty as they got out of the elevator. They were on their way to the theatre. Jim bowed and said, "I hope you *kids* have a good time."

Troubled by loneliness, Betty traveled by motor car from New York to California with a physician and his mother.

About six o'clock one evening the Newmans, who were now living in Los Angeles, received an unexpected telephone call from Betty.

"Where are you?" Bobby inquired.

"At a Santa Monica motel." Betty began to laugh. Always before this, when away from New York, she had stayed at expensive hotels or apartments. "It's funny, isn't it?"

"You sound hysterical," said Newman.

"I am. I'll be over to see you right away."

At the Newmans, Betty said she had made a great mistake in being psychoanalyzed. "I'm fed up on it now," she added. "I'd remarry Jim tomorrow if he would. But he said he'd never go back."

When Mrs. Elizabeth Mulrooney, wife of the former Police Commissioner, died in April of 1942, Jim attended the wake. Two things happened that day to bring peace to Jim's mind.

He met Al Smith at the wake. Then, as though both men were moved by the same impulse to end their estrangement, they clasped hands. They stood for several seconds looking intently at one another.

"Al," Jim said, "we've been apart too long."

"Much too long, Jim," Smith replied.

"It's important to me, Al, that it never happen again."

"It never really happened, Jim."

They shook hands once more.

Now Jim saw a priest whom he knew. The clergyman had just come from the room where Mrs. Mulrooney's body lay. Jim and the Father whispered together for a few moments. The priest then asked Mulrooney if he might use a room privately for a while.

"Of course, Father," was the reply. Mulrooney showed the priest into the bedroom. Mulrooney made no comment when Walker followed after the clergyman.

Walker and the priest stayed behind the closed door for almost two hours. Nothing ever was said by the priest or by Jim as to what they had talked of during that meeting; but when Walker came out his eyes seemed bright, he had an exalted expression, as though he had been freed of some mental burden.

It is believed that Jim now saw the way to return as a communicant to the Church of his fathers. Upon leaving the house, he shook Mulrooney's hand. "Ed," he said, "maybe Elizabeth didn't die in vain."

From that day on Walker seemed more secure spiritually than he had ever been, although he made no public show of piety.

In January of 1942 Betty sailed for South America to try to forget Jim. On her way back aboard a United Fruit ship she met a quiet-mannered, distinguished man, Theodore Knappen, a West Point graduate and a consulting engineer. They sat together at the Captain's table and spent much time in each other's company on deck.

Knappen proposed marriage. Betty replied that she would "have to ask Jim." Knappen's calm deportment as she recited the story of her life with Walker, Knappen's courtesy, his seeming strength of character, deeply impressed Betty.

Knappen said with a smile, "All right, Betty. We'll ask Jim. I think I'm going to like him."

When Betty introduced the men and spoke of Knappen's proposal of marriage, Jim remarked, "Ted, I think you'll be good for Betty."

They were married in Jersey City on May 11, 1942. Jim managed the official details, procured the license, then persuaded the clerk not to notify the newspapers until the ceremony had been concluded and the newlyweds had gone.

The friendship of these three persons caused Jim's Broadway friends to say, "Can you beat it? Walker dining out with his former wife and her new husband! What is he, a chaperon?"

Walker thought it a natural thing for him to do—"for the kids," he said.

The Knappens lived on a beautiful wooded estate at Old Westbury, Long Island. Walker spent his weekends there, played with the children, and seemed most welcome. He occupied a cottage near the main building.

In the late summer of 1943 Betty confided to Jim that she and Ted expected a baby sometime the next January. "Monk," Jim said, "that is simply wonderful! It's what you always wanted most. It's what I always wanted you to have. Now your real happiness will begin."

In the winter of 1943 Betty consulted Dr. S. Sym Newman. He observed that she had a small mammary tumor and recommended that it be removed. Betty insisted that the surgery be performed at once, within the next hours. After the operation a pathologist reported that the growth was malignant. This came as a shock to Dr. Newman, who decided not to inform Betty at once of the full nature of her malady.

The attending physicians recommended that Betty's pregnancy be terminated. They did not wish to alarm her by saying that a malignancy such as hers quite often spreads rapidly during pregnancy.

Asked if she would consent to the taking of her unborn child, Betty replied, "Only if Jim says so." Betty told Walker of the medical advice given her. "What do you say, Jim?"

"Monk," he replied, "it is the dream of every normal woman to give of herself to the future. You have had everything else in life:

beauty, love, applause. But you have wanted a child so much, why not let God decide?"

"That's the way I feel about it, Jim. But I wanted to hear you say it. They'll *not* take my baby from me."

A second and more extensive operation was performed in an effort to arrest the disease. Betty suffered great pain. Jim was constantly at her bedside at Doctors Hospital. Betty's baby boy was born on January 19, 1944. From then on her condition became one of increasing agony. By July she knew that she had not much longer to live.

"No, Monk, no," Jim kept saying as he held her hand. "You must live."

"I never wished to grow old," Betty said.

He kissed her. "Monk, everything's going to be all right."

The dying woman looked at him for some time, then said, "I want you to promise me something."

"Anything, Monk."

"I want all the three children, Mary Ann and Jim Jim and the baby, to be raised together. Understand?"

"Of course."

"I want them all under one roof," she went on, "and never to know the difference between adoption and being born to any special parents. Never. I want you and Ted to live together after I go. Will you do this for the children?"

Walker was unable to speak at once. Betty continued, her voice surprisingly strong, "Ted has agreed."

"I'll agree, Monk. Sure. We'll take care of all three kids together. Sure we will."

"All right then. Now ask the doctor to give me something to sleep."

She slept on until July 12, 1944. She left life, as she had often said she would, at the age of forty.

34.

The Tree and the Gale

THREE weeks before her death Betty made a will in which she assigned a trust-fund income of about five hundred dollars a month to the children she and Walker had adopted and to her own infant son, Theodore Knappen, Jr., with the request that the three children "be kept in a single family group, insofar as may be humanly possible." Knappen was designated as her executor and trustee. In the event of Knappen's death, Walker was to succeed him in this capacity.

Betty dreaded a graveyard burial, and she made Jim and Ted promise that she would be cremated and the ashes strewn on her Old Westbury estate.

Many beautiful trees grew on these thirty acres. One of these, a live oak, stood near the house. We do not know with what memorable event Betty associated this tree. Nor do we know whether or not Jim himself scattered Betty's ashes beneath its boughs. Someone, however, gave her dust to the familiar ground without advertising the ceremony.

Walker would often stand under this tree, in deepest thought, not moving for perhaps half an hour at a time. Then he would turn away slowly, go into the house and up to his room. On such occasions no sounds came from behind the closed door, no playing of the radio as on other days or nights Jim rested in his own quarters.

When, next day, the maid tidied the Walker room, she would find the prayer book open. It had been given to Jim by his pastor at Westbury, the Reverend Father James A. Sullivan. A dark blue tape marked the place of Jim's favorite prayer. *Salve Regina* was a prayer ordered by Pope Leo XIII.

> Hail! holy queen, mother of mercy, our life, our sweetness, and our hope! To thee do we cry, poor banished children of Eve . . .

Walker, Knappen, and the three children lived at Westbury from the time of Betty's death until the following October. Ted and Jim managed for a time to fulfill the conditions of the strange pact Betty had imposed. However well-intentioned she may have been in shaping that request, the design lacked those proportions which suit masculine instincts. While Betty was alive the three principals had regarded any expression of bitterness as an uncivilized show once a divorce and a remarriage had occurred. But for the men to go beyond that modernized code, and for them to be, in a manner of speaking, joint-widowers, co-fathers, placidly living together, facing each other at breakfast almost every morning, may have been "humanly possible" but was not humanly probable.

Jim, sustained by his reverence of her memory, could faithfully adhere to the letter of the plan. He concocted a seraphic version of his and Betty's life together and substituted that dream for the reality. Not only did he say that the physical tie had been cast off when Betty had asked him for a divorce, but he implied that an earthly passion never had existed between them. This, of course, was a mental forgery.

Incongruous as it may appear, Jim spoke of Betty as of some saintly character. Among the friends of the once vital, worldly, impulsive woman, Walker's obsession became a subject of wonderment. What was his motive for enshrining Betty in his own mind? Was he trying to justify to himself the dear price paid years ago when he had surrendered his public position and his private world for love? Or did he now feel morally free to revere her memory—which he insisted was stainless—and to adore her shade without violating religious precepts?

Her fair hand lay even stronger upon him than when she had been alive. Since the divorce Walker had known no other woman, nor would he ever know another in the romantic sense. It may be argued that a man in his sixties is not ordinarily exposed to passionate moods. In Walker's case this rule did not apply. Women still found him attractive, but they also found him politely unwilling to countenance their romantic intentions.

When a friend twitted Jim for his monastic attitude he replied, "When desire left my body, it left my mind." There is medical evidence, however, to show that Jim was chaste during his last years because of his will to be so and not because he lacked masculine vigor.

Knappen found it increasingly difficult to keep a covenant with a ghost. He was in his early forties, a much younger man than Jim, and considerably more of a realist. During his first months as a co-widower Knappen outwardly seemed content with the odd arrangement. But it was natural for him to feel that his own child deserved the care and attention of someone other than a governess. He and Walker seldom exchanged views on this matter during their first year together, but Jim once told me he sensed that Ted was moving against his own center by keeping a bargain described by Paul Gallico as "a kind of sweet, mad, reasoned sanity, in an attempt to save the happiness of the offspring."

The men remained on friendly terms during the fifteen months they lived together: Knappen, the quiet, dignified, scientific realist, and Walker, the polite, generous, daydreaming companion. They played gin rummy on evenings Jim was not making speeches at charitable affairs, or addressing meetings having to do with the war effort, or attending the Friday night boxing matches at the Garden. If, as it sometimes happened, Jim became too moody, he would retire to his room, where he played solitaire, listened to the radio, or read his prayer book.

One night a sudden storm descended. Walker ran out of the house, his eyes fixed, his face twitching. The rain beat down. The wind blew his dressing gown and his hair. He stood beside the live oak tree as though to defend it. Several near-by trees were bowled over during this storm.

After a long vigil Jim went inside. He was wet and cold and tired. He offered no comment other than, "The tree did not blow down! It didn't blow down!"

In September Walker leased a ten-room apartment for the "family" at No. 120 East End Avenue. Together with Knappen, the children, and two servants, he moved into it on October 1, 1944. The apartment house was two squares south of Doctors Hospital, where Betty had died.

These seventh-floor quarters overlooked the East River and the northern tip of Welfare Island. From the front rooms one could see Hell Gate and a soaring segment of the Triborough Bridge. In the foreground lay Carl Schurz Park. From the living-room windows, off to the left, could be seen the roof and chimneys of Gracie Mansion, the official residence of Mayor La Guardia.

Jim brought his "keepsakes" to the apartment. His bedroom furniture was almost bleakly fashioned. A lithograph of the Savior, sent to Walker by a missionary in China, hung over his wide bed. On the opposite wall were two small silhouettes of his adopted children. Other photographs of the children, one of Betty, and a tintype of Jim's mother stood on one of two modernistic chests of drawers arranged end-to-end. A long mirror hung above the chests. On the other chest Jim kept one hundred and sixty cigarette holders of various colors, each equipped with a filtering device. A tobacco company had promised—once the war was over—to manufacture cigarettes which had none of the moisturizing chemicals which Walker believed were injurious to his health.

Suspended on the blue walls between the windows were two sets of shelves. They contained books of a religious nature, with one exception, a biographical work, *The Quest for Corvo.* Beige drapes, silk-lined, could be drawn across the windows.

On the topmost shelf of one wallpiece were three souvenirs prized by Walker: an inflated football autographed by members of the Notre Dame team (for he had been a close friend of Knute Rockne) and signed also by Jim's non-athletic but sports-loving cronies, Toots Shor, Quentin Reynolds, Horace Stoneham, and Harry Cross; a baseball autographed by players of the New York Giants team; and a silk skullcap given him by an elderly, orthodox Jew, of whom Jim once said, "He was one of the finest men I ever knew. He wasn't famous, but he gave this to me for something I had said from my heart about his people, who are my people too; and I like to look at the cap and think and hope and pray for peace among all men."

To the right of Jim's bed was a night table with a radio on it. Beside the radio lay his prayer book and two other religious works, *The Mirror of Christ and St. Francis of Assisi* and *The New Six O'Clock Saints* for children. A clam shell from Rockaway Beach, used as an ash tray, lay on the ledge of the night table. There was a glass-based standing lamp on either side of the bed, and on one of them a green scapular was hung.

In this room, which was reached through a long hallway, Jim spent the hours after dinner with Knappen or playing with the children. Sometimes he would shut himself in for a whole day and night.

The world outside still measured Walker in terms of his legend. For the most part he did not reveal to his audiences (and he spoke at as many as three hundred luncheons, dinners, and meetings in 1944, according to Sidney Harris) that a great change had come to his private life, or that he was searching earnestly for spiritual consolation.

The metamorphosis in Walker's private life may be illustrated by what he did and how he clad himself when he was alone in his bedroom. Clothes had been such an important part of his personal life, a frontispiece, as it were, to his character, that the contrast seems remarkable.

His clothes closet was still well filled with garments fashioned according to his own designs. There were exquisite dressing gowns, hundreds of scarves; and on the old tailor's dummy hung a custom-made heavy silk lounging garment of checkered pattern with braided lapels. But when Jim stayed alone in his room he would put on a somewhat seedy rayon dressing gown and a pair of oft-repaired green scuffs that had been made in Paris.

He would sit in a woman's slipper chair which needed the attention of an upholsterer. He would play solitaire, dealing from a deck of old cards, dog-eared and grimy. For his lone card-playing, and sometimes for the light meals served in his room, he used a battered tea tray. On it was painted a group of elegant ladies strolling in a wood while a flute player and a tambourine player entertained them. A tired-looking dog stood, dimly seen, against a background daub of murky yellow and bilious green.

If anyone removed the slipper chair and installed a better one, or brought Jim a new deck of cards, or substituted a good tray for the monstrosity upon which he played Canfield, or disturbed the tawdry folds of the seedy rayon dressing gown, Walker would become quite angry. Similarly, if anyone in the butler's pantry put out of sight a chipped highball glass which Jim kept in a designated place, or mislaid a tiny mahogany stand upon which he kept a bottle opener and corkscrew, Walker would express his displeasure. He drank but one highball an evening. This chipped glass and other homely things so highly prized by him had been gifts from Betty.

The one, and perhaps only, splendid present he kept on view or wore when attired in formal clothes was a set of shirt studs and cuff-links of star sapphires given him by Betty. Seventeen watches, several of them expensive ones, presented by friends, were kept out of sight and seldom worn.

Jim's library contained two hundred books, none of which he had read. Many of them had his name in the indexes. Here were also the various shovels, picks, and trowels used by Walker as mayor to break ground for public buildings and bridges, or to lay cornerstones. This room might easily have been mistaken for the office of the president of the United Mine Workers.

Jim called the living-room "Betty's room." There were pictures of her here, and an enameled bronze sculpture given Walker by Charles Silver. This work depicted a woman leading a great Dane on a leash. Walker believed that her face was Betty's, and that the way the figure stood was Betty's way.

One April afternoon in 1945, a few days after the death of President Roosevelt, William O'Dwyer called on Walker at the East End Avenue apartment.

O'Dwyer, as district attorney of Kings County, had successfully prosecuted members of the notorious gang known to the public as "Murder Incorporated." He had run for mayor against La Guardia in 1941 and had been defeated. At the beginning of World War II he had become a major in the Army. At the suggestion of President Roosevelt he had been assigned to prosecute sedition cases. O'Dwyer then had become a lieutenant colonel in the Air Corps, and in 1944 had been made a full colonel. He had served in Italy with the Allied Control Commission, and in February 1945 had retired from the Army with the rank of brigadier general.

President Roosevelt had appointed General O'Dwyer executive director of the War Refugees Board. The General served with much distinction in this capacity, and enjoyed the friendship of the President, whom he idolized.

Early in 1945 there was a movement to renominate O'Dwyer for mayor. He hesitated to run, feeling that he had already achieved the greatest honor which he had the right to expect when the President had sent him on a special mission in wartime and had given him his friendship.

"I was an immigrant from Ireland," O'Dwyer said, "and to rise from the job of shoveling coal as a boy aboard ship to being trusted as a grown man by the President seemed enough for any adopted citizen. So I decided to consult Jim Walker, who was more of a philosopher than the public ever could believe or know. Besides, in a poll conducted by the *Daily News*, Walker's name had appeared in first place; my own name was a bad second, and La Guardia's an even worse third."

Johnny O'Connor accompanied O'Dwyer that April afternoon

in 1945. Walker received them clothed in a checked dressing jacket, with pajama trousers to match. He also wore a white silk muffler, for, as he explained, he was suffering from a bad cold.

"I'd like you to see the children," said Walker, "but they also have colds. And I also want you to meet Ted Knappen when he comes home. We are living here together because"—he pointed to one of the several pictures of her—"Betty asked us to."

Walker then suggested going to the library. As they went to that room Walker said, "You have matured a great deal, Bill. And I think you are popular."

The men seated themselves among the shovels and picks. "Jim," O'Dwyer said, "what do you think about my running for mayor again?"

Walker did not reply at once. Then he said, "The facts of life are as follows, my friend: anyone who succeeds La Guardia is bound to have a rough time of it. Just as Mr. Truman who has just succeeded President Roosevelt will have. But that is only one phase of the thankless prospect. The ending of the war will mean, unfortunately, tragically even, the end of united effort by all classes and grades of our people. They can and do pull together as no other people can during a war, but when peace comes they grab and push, call names, squabble and bicker. As mayor you will personally be held accountable for the inevitable rise in taxes, strife among the groups seeking advantages, housing shortages, increased cost of living. The obvious fact that you are honest and capable will cause some of the political leaders to blast at you if you don't bestow patronage on a political basis instead of appointing men you know are capable and efficient. I do not know how strong you are physically. You look tough and sturdy. But even if you were Hercules himself, you face a man-killing job at City Hall. The truth is that your life may be shortened by several years in the performance of mayoral duties. The Little Flower was a sturdy man, but now he is all shot to pieces. Do you want to live long?"

Ted Knappen now arrived home and was introduced to Walker's guests. The men went to the dining-room. No more political questions were discussed.

"Amon Carter has sent us some blue-ribbon steaks from Texas," Walker said. "I'm glad it isn't Friday."

During dinner Jim spoke of the old days in Greenwich Village and of his two visits to Ireland.

While the men were still seated at the table, two dogs, a large one and a small one, entered the room. The larger dog placed its muzzle on Jim's knee and looked up at him. The smaller dog stayed in the background, watching Jim and wagging its tail.

As though addressing a human being, Jim said to the nuzzling pet, "No, I can't take you for a walk tonight. You know very well that I have a cold. Go to Ted and ask him to take you out."

The dog went to Knappen, placed its muzzle on his knee, and looked up at him. Ted also spoke as if to a person. "All right. We'll take a walk. Wait outside."

The larger dog, followed by the tail-wagging smaller one, left the dining-room. Knappen excused himself, then reappeared coated and mufflered, carrying leashes for the dogs.

"Ted," Jim said, as Knappen shook hands with Walker's guests, "don't let those dogs run you."

"I won't," Knappen replied and went on his way.

When Ted had gone Jim explained, "He's not feeling well." Then he said, "I'll have coffee served to you in Betty's room."

After the men entered the living-room O'Dwyer observed that Walker was looking fixedly at one of the photographs of the dead woman and seemed oblivious for a long moment that he had guests. Then he gave a start, smiled, and said, "She was a good kid. But she tore up the papers and told me to go home to my Mother."

This remark was construed by O'Dwyer and O'Connor to mean but one thing: that Betty had told Jim to return to the Church of Rome.

35.

Across the River

WHENEVER we look at the lives of imaginative men, we find more often than not that they came to terms with themselves somewhere along the way. In Walker's case this occurred four years before his dream was done.

Whatever the reasons for Walker's renunciation of worldly ties, he found peace of mind, though touched with trouble and pain. The graciousness which had always been a shining facet of his character made him hold his piety in his heart. He did not pose with head bowed or hands clasped, nor alter his warm, friendly ways.

As he stood in meticulous evening clothes in the halls of the banqueters, he still displayed the magic personality which had brought him his first fame. He turned back the clock and the calendar to remind men of that starry time before a great hush came over the world. For he stayed Beau James, the New Yorker's New Yorker, perhaps the last one of his kind.

He kept his piety, if we may call it that, to himself, practicing it in the seclusion of his apartment across the way from Gracie Mansion or at the small church of St. Stephen of Hungary on East Eighty-fourth Street.

Ted Knappen left the East End Avenue apartment in October of 1945. He married Miss Glorianna Ferguson, a department store executive. Jim was best man at the wedding. The Knappens went with Ted's infant son to reside at the Old Westbury estate.

Nan Burke and her sons, Paul and Luke, moved in with Walker and his adopted children. Walker had a deep affection for his nephews. On alternate evenings he dined alone in his bedroom. After his private dinner he would sometimes stride down the hallway, deliver a short speech on almost any topic to Nan and the young men, and then as suddenly withdraw.

Of these entrances and exits Paul would say, "Uncle Jim has retired to the wings."

Jim called Paul "the reader." Walker's eyes troubled him, and he would ask Paul to sit beside his bed and read aloud from letters or the newspapers.

When alone with Nan, Jim sometimes spoke as though he had a presentiment of death. Their conversations, however, were by no means always of serious import. On one occasion Nan decided that her brother had been alone too long. She knocked at his door and entered the room. Jim was reading his prayer book.

"Jim," she asked, "did you ever pray to St. Jude?"

"Why, no, Nan," he replied, "I can't say that I have. Why do you ask?"

"Because," said Nan, "St. Jude is the saint of impossible things."

"Sis," Jim said gravely, "do you mean to tell me that you pray for material things?"

"Certainly," said Nan. "How do you suppose you got that job with the Garment Workers?"

Walker shrugged. "Well, maybe you're right. But I'd hitherto attributed the miracle to Dave Dubinsky, with an assist from F. D. R. and Fiorello."

Early in 1945 Walker resigned as impartial chairman of the Garment Workers and accepted the presidency of Majestic Records, Inc. His successor as arbiter of the coat-and-suit industry was Harry Hopkins, friend and counselor of Mr. Roosevelt.

Walker was appointed to his new position by Eugene A. Tracey, president of the Majestic Radio and Television Corporation, of which company the record business was a subsidiary. Tracey had been introduced to Walker by attorney Sid Harris at one of the Circus Saints and Sinners luncheons.

Mr. Tracey's rise in the world of business was spectacular. He began his career as a New York subway guard, became a successful salesman, then served as an important official with the Zenith Radio Company. As president of Majestic, he effected the purchase and merger of two companies engaged in making and distributing musical recordings. Tracey saw in Walker a man of ability and personality.

"I used to press suits," Jim waggishly remarked upon accepting the new job, "and now I'm pressing records."

Walker's health was impaired by frequent colds. During one of his visits to California he was taken to the Cedars of Lebanon Hospital in Los Angeles. Penicillin was administered to control a respiratory infection.

During Jim's convalescence he received a long-distance call from Toots Shor. "Jim," said Toots, "the discoverer of penicillin is sitting here in my restaurant. I want you to say something to Sir Alexander Fleming."

"Put him on," said Jim. "I have only one word to say to him."

When Sir Alexander was on the line, Walker said, "Thanks."

In June of 1946 Walker spoke at a communion breakfast of the Catholic Traffic Guild. This speech was not made for publication, and I am indebted to Patrick F. Scanlon, managing editor of the *Tablet*, a religious periodical, for "rescuing" it. It contains Jim's credo in his own words:

"While it is true—too awfully true—that many acts of my life were in direct denial of the faith in which I believed, I can say truthfully that never once did I try to convince myself or others that my acts were anything else than what they were. Never once did I attempt to moralize or rationalize my acts, for I knew that they were denials of the faith in which I believed and to which I was devoted. Never once did I deny my faith to square it with my actions. It is true that I acted against my faith and my Church, but I always believed in and felt with the Faith of my Fathers and the Church of my God. The glamour of other days I have found to be worthless tinsel, and all the allure of the world just so much seduction and deception. I now have found in religion and repentance the happiness and joy that I sought elsewhere in vain."

During the early part of November 1946 Walker kept several engagements of a social, charitable, or religious character. At a dinner of the Boxing Writers' Association he said to heavyweight champion Joe Louis, "You are indeed a credit to your race. By your sportsmanlike actions as an athlete and your behavior as an American gentleman, you have put a rose on the tomb of Abraham Lincoln."

On November 10 Walker was toastmaster at an outing given by Tim Mara of the New York Football Giants at Bear Mountain Inn, their training quarters. Jim had just had several teeth extracted. The temporary bridge in his upper jaw broke in halves on the way to the Inn. The trainer of the Giants mended the denture with a strip of adhesive tape.

During Jim's first remarks, the makeshift repair worked loose. The bridge popped out of Walker's mouth. "I am here only by the courtesy of my dentist," he remarked.

The diners laughed. They felt, as always, that nothing could make their Jimmy back down. When he returned home that night, however, he seemed ill and dispirited.

"What in the world is the matter, Jim?" Nan asked as she helped him take off his topcoat.

"It's all over, Sis."

"What do you mean by that? What's all over?"

"I'm through."

"Talk sense."

"Sis," he said, "I knew it the minute it happened."

Nan looked at him closely. "Jim, let me make you some tea, and then you go on to bed."

"I'll go to bed, Sis. But let me tell you something, when my teeth fell out, it was a symbol of something."

Nan believed that her brother was at last conscious of his years, which were now sixty-five, years which he had carried gracefully, and of which he himself had never seemed aware in any ordinary concept of passing time.

"From then on," Nan told me, "Jim had no will to live."

He had caught cold on the Bear Mountain excursion, but appeared at a New Jersey dinner given by a religious group. On November 12 he went with Dr. Newman to the West Fifty-fifth Street clubhouse of the Grand Street Boys Association, to attend a dinner in honor of Sir Louis Sterling.

Judge Jonah Goldstein, who presided at this affair, observed Jim's weakened condition. After Walker concluded the speech which was his valedictory, Judge Goldstein urged members of the club to let him go on home.

Next day Jim's eyes ached. He sat for many hours in his darkened room. He became lonely and called friends by telephone: Charles H. Silver, Eugene Tracey, Johnny O'Connor, Billy Walsh, and Robert Newman in California.

Finally he could stand the darkness no longer. He turned on one of the lights and sat in the slipper chair to write in pencil his last song lyric:

> There are summer skies in your eyes.
> The bloom in your cheek
> Makes winter retreat.
> There'll be no December
> If you'll just remember,
> Sweetheart, it's always May.

There was a buzzer at Walker's bedside, but he had never used it. Instead, he would bang with his fist upon the wall to summon a servant or to bring his sister to the door. Late in the evening of November 14 he knocked on the wall. His sister presently responded. As she entered the bedroom Jim said, "Sis, I want to talk to you about something."

Nan sat beside his bed. "Yes, Jim?"

"I am halfway across the river."

"Don't say such things."

"I'm halfway across, and I can't swim back. And I want you to look out for the little ones."

When Jim rose from sleep at eight-thirty next morning he suffered an attack of nausea and dizziness and kept his balance with considerable effort. He returned to bed. Nan brought him cereal and warm tea, but Jim could not keep either the food or the liquid on his stomach. Nan put an icebag on her brother's head.

Dr. Newman visited Jim at ten o'clock and advised him to stay in bed. The doctor and Walker had planned to attend the boxing matches that night at the Garden, as was their custom, but Jim was too ill to go. Instead, he and his nephews listened to Bill Corum's radio description of the main event. Paul himself was recovering from an attack of virus pneumonia.

Dr. Newman telephoned Walker after the fights were over at eleven o'clock. Jim reported that the headache persisted. Dr. Newman decided to call at the Walker apartment.

The doctor examined Jim and suspected that something was wrong with Walker's secondary brain area. His temperature was not abnormal, and his blood pressure, which was always low, gave no cause for immediate alarm. However, the headache, the nausea, and Jim's difficulty in maintaining his balance caused Dr. Newman to consult Dr. Arthur Fishberg, noted cardiologist, who in turn suggested that Dr. I. S. Wechsler, a world-famous neurologist, be called.

It was now twelve-thirty Saturday morning. Dr. Wechsler, roused from a deep sleep, listened to Dr. Newman's recital of the Walker symptoms and said he would look in upon the patient next morning. Dr. Newman gave Jim a sedative and remained with him until four o'clock. He placed a nurse in charge and then went home.

At about six-thirty in the morning Jim said to his sister, "I'm pretty sick, Nan, but I don't want anyone to know it." Then he added with a smile, "But a lot of better fellows have been sicker."

"Jim," she said, "there may have been sicker fellows than you, but never a better one."

Walker suffered another attack of nausea. At seven o'clock Dr. Newman arrived with Dr. Wechsler. A brain tracing was made by means of electro-encephalography. It was believed that the nausea was caused by pressure inside the skull, but at this stage the doctors could not attribute Walker's condition to a brain tumor or a blood clot.

"What's happened to me?" Jim asked.

"We will be able to determine that, Mr. Walker, when we get you to a hospital," Dr. Wechsler replied.

"I want to stay here," said Jim. "Hospitals are places for sick persons."

Wechsler and Newman held a two-hour consultation with another celebrated neurologist, Dr. W. Huston Merritt. Since Walker seemed to have improved somewhat, Dr. Newman went to his office to receive patients.

Jim fell asleep while listening to the radio report of a football game. When Dr. Newman returned, Jim awakened to say, "I'm afraid this is curtains, Sym."

"Stop that, Jim," his doctor said. "It's old woman's talk."

Walker turned on his side and said as though to himself, "Well, Monk, I'll be joining you soon."

Dr. Newman saw Jim again at six o'clock Sunday evening. The three other doctors examined the patient and reached the conclusion that there had been no change in Walker's condition, but that some serious thing was occurring to his lower brain.

Dr. Newman stayed on at the apartment until two o'clock Monday morning. He had had little sleep. He decided to go home for an hour or so to bathe, change his clothes, and perhaps take a nap. He advised the nurse to keep close watch and to notify him if any change occurred.

Although the nurse had never before seen Walker until the present time, she knew of his reputation for neatness. Consequently she saw to it that he was shaved, that his hair was carefully brushed back, and that the folds of his silk dressing robe were kept exactly in place.

Early Monday morning Jim moved as though to get out of bed. The nurse admonished him to lie back. Walker disobeyed her. He stood up shakily.

"Am I not the master of my own house?" he asked.

"Yes, Mr. Mayor," she replied. "But you—"

"Oh, you must be a good Democrat," he interrupted.

"Yes, Mr. Mayor, I am."

With a great effort Walker straightened, bowed gallantly, and said, "In that case, nurse, I shall abide by the wishes of a fair constituent."

He lay back on the bed, smiling. Then he suddenly began to

breathe in short starts and stops. The nurse tried to rouse him, but Jim appeared to be unconscious.

The nurse went to a telephone outside the room to call the doctor. On her way she notified Nan Burke that something dreadful had happened.

Dr. Newman arrived at the apartment in a few minutes. Jim was in a coma. The physician telephoned Doctors Hospital for a room and asked that an ambulance be sent at once to the Walker apartment. He then called his colleagues.

Jim never knew that he was taken to the same hospital where his beloved Betty had died. He remained unconscious all Monday. A priest had administered the last rites of the Catholic Church before Jim left home.

At the hospital Dr. Newman permitted Nan Burke, her sons, Eugene Tracey, and Sidney Harris to remain beside the unconscious Walker.

Word reached the newspapers that Walker was dying. Reporters and photographers soon arrived. Hundreds of telephone calls poured in, and additional operators were placed at the switchboard.

Jim's room lay at the end of a corridor on the seventh floor overlooking East Eighty-seventh Street. The blinds were drawn when a press photographer appeared on the roof of a building across the street to take a picture through a telescopic lens.

Mayor O'Dwyer's secretary, William J. Donoghue, arranged for a police officer to stand on guard at the doorway of Jim's room. Walker's friends, Paul Schoenstein, city editor of the *New York Journal-American*, and Richard Buck stayed in a room across the hall from Jim's.

During the afternoon two separate requests were made by clergymen, each asking that he be permitted to come to Jim's room to pray for his recovery. One of these men was a Jewish rabbi, the other a Presbyterian minister.

Tracey, a Christian Scientist, said to Dr. Newman, "They should be permitted in here. It is such a wonderful thing that Jim was loved by men of all faiths."

From Walker's room the prayers of four men, representing as many creeds, went up to one God: the supplications of a Roman Catholic priest, a Jewish rabbi, a Presbyterian minister, and a Christian Scientist.

Late that night Jim's heart grew weaker, the beats further apart.

Then Dr. Newman, bending over Jim, and listening through his stethoscope, heard no beat at all. Yet he stayed there, bent over, a look of great pain in his eyes.

At last Dr. Newman straightened. He folded his stethoscope. He looked for a long moment at the face of his friend and said in a quiet professional tone, "It's over."

The doctor retired to an adjoining room. He stayed there for several minutes alone.

Across the street from the hospital Mayor O'Dwyer and Johnny O'Connor sat in Gracie Mansion. Walker was to have had dinner with the Mayor and Johnny this night.

"Funny thing, Johnny," the Mayor said through his tears, "Jim never has been in Gracie Mansion. It's a pleasant old house, but I guess Heaven is a lot better, and I think there's a special place there for Jim."

"If there isn't," Johnny said, "then I don't want to go there."

Two friends whom Jim especially loved, Arthur Baer and Toots Shor, were sitting in Shor's restaurant the night Walker died. They sat there until everyone but one bartender had gone home. Toots had held in as best he could, but now he began drinking.

At four o'clock in the morning Baer and Shor decided to go to Campbell's "Funeral Church" to look at their friend's body.

"To get Toots there," Baer said, "was like towing a sick whale with no hope of ambergris. We got to the funeral parlor, and as we stood at the casket I thought that Jim looked tiny and unreal, like something cut out of cardboard. I was thinking, and Toots was crying enough tears to float Jim's body out to sea. Then Toots said something spontaneous and unrehearsed, something that he didn't even remember until I told him afterward. He cried out, 'Jimmy! Jimmy! When you walked into the room you brightened up the joint.'

"That's the way it was, I think," Baer continued. "Whenever he walked into a theatre, banquet hall, a fight stadium, or into your life, Jim Walker brightened everything and everyone he touched."

Perhaps thirty thousand persons passed by the Walker coffin at the funeral parlor. A strangely contrasting queue stood outside the apartment house where Jim had lived in recent years. Grieving Nan Burke learned from the doorman that these men and women had gathered on the sidewalk to ask for Jim's clothes. They were informed that his wardrobe could not be distributed among them.

They could not know that Jim had died a comparatively poor man, leaving no life insurance and only fifteen thousand dollars.

There was a service for Walker on Thursday morning at St. Patrick's Cathedral. As the coffin arrived from the funeral parlor, workmen employed on the restoration of the Cathedral's stones stood at various places on the steel scaffolding and bared their heads. A detail of police officers at the doorway raised their white-gloved right hands to their cap brims. A group of elderly women, plainly clad, knelt at the curb, their rosaries in their hands.

There had been several minutes' delay in bringing Jim's hearse through the traffic to the church. A middle-aged police officer, looking in on the choir boys in their robing room, said, "Our little Jimmy is late again."

There were about a thousand wreaths and bouquets sent to Jim's last solemn ceremony in the church which had received the body of her contrite son. After the Requiem Mass the coffin with its blanket of roses was taken to Gate of Heaven Cemetery.

As intimate friends and members of Jim's family stood at the open grave, there was a delay in the interment. A squad of policemen surrounded the coffin, their backs to it, and shielded it from view. No one among the mourners was immediately informed of the reason for the delay.

Sidney Harris, observing the pause in the graveyard procedure, and seeing the police officers standing about the casket, intervened to ask why the coffin was not being lowered into the ground.

A friend of Jim's placed something in the hands of Harris, executor for the Walker estate. He recognized the star sapphire cuff-links given to Jim long ago by Betty. The well-meaning friend, knowing that Walker's estate was small, and believing that these valuable stones should not be buried with Jim, had had the coffin opened beside the grave, while the police officers formed a screen, and retrieved the cuff-links.

The memory of him is green. The love for him is warm. He is a legend now, and when you ride in the taxicabs on the streets of New York, if you ask who best typified the heart of the greatest city in the Western world, you are bound to hear the name "Jimmy Walker." And the smile that goes with the utterance of that name makes you smile, and makes you feel warm and fine and forgiving all day long.

Index